Hither Shore

Interdisciplinary Journal
on Modern Fantasy Literature

Jahrbuch der
Deutschen Tolkien Gesellschaft e. V.

Tolkien and the Middle Ages

Tolkien und das Mittelalter

Interdisziplinäres Seminar der DTG
29. April bis 1. Mai 2011, Potsdam

Herausgegeben von:
Thomas Fornet-Ponse (Gesamtleitung),
Marie-Noëlle Biemer, Marcel Bülles,
Thomas Honegger, Rainer Nagel,
Alexandra Velten, Frank Weinreich

SCRIPTORIUM OXONIAE

Bibliografische Information der Deutschen Bibliothek

Die Deutsche Bibliothek verzeichnet diese Publikation in der Deutschen Nationalbibliografie; detaillierte bibliografische Daten sind im Internet über http://dnb.ddb.de abrufbar.

ISBN 978-3-9810612-6-0

Hither Shore, DTG-Jahrbuch 2011
veröffentlicht im Verlag »Scriptorium Oxoniae«

Deutsche Tolkien Gesellschaft e. V. (DTG)
E-Mail: info@tolkiengesellschaft.de

Scriptorium Oxoniae im Atelier für Textaufgaben e. K.
Brehmstraße 50 · D-40239 Düsseldorf
E-Mail: rayermann@scriptorium-oxoniae.de

Hither Shore, Gesamtleitung: Thomas Fornet-Ponse
E-Mail: hither-shore@tolkiengesellschaft.de

Vorschläge für Beiträge in deutscher oder englischer Sprache (inklusive Exposé von ca. 100 Wörtern) werden erbeten an o.g. Mail-Adresse.

Alle Rechte verbleiben beim Autor des jeweiligen Einzelbeitrags.
Es gilt als vereinbart, dass ein Autor seinen Beitrag innerhalb der nächsten 18 Monate nach Erscheinen dieser *Hither-Shore*-Ausgabe nicht anderweitig veröffentlichen darf.

Abwicklung: Susanne A. Rayermann, Düsseldorf
Layout/Design: Kathrin Bondzio, Solingen
Umschlagillustration: Anke Eißmann, Herborn
Druck und Vertrieb: Books on Demand, Norderstedt
Alle Rechte vorbehalten.

Inhalt

Preface / Vorwort 6

Tolkien Seminar 2011

Quellen mythologischer Vorstellungen in *The Hobbit*
und *The Lord of the Rings* 10
Rudolf Simek (Bonn)

Mundus senescit: Tolkien and
the Allure of Medieval Nostalgia 24
Dirk Wiemann (Potsdam)

Modern Tales in a Medieval Tradition:
Formation of Meaning and Narrative Strategies in
The Children of Húrin 40
Silke Winst (Potsdam)

Mythologie contra Geschichte
oder von der Mythologie zur Geschichte? 56
Thomas Fornet-Ponse (Hildesheim)

Von Mittelerde zum Mittelalter 72
Patrick A. Brückner (Potsdam)

Time and Tide: Medieval Patterns of Interpreting the
Passing of Time in Tolkien's Work 86
Thomas Honegger (Jena)

The Lay of Aotrou and Itroun: Medieval English Literature
and the Early Stages of Sub-creation 100
Rafael J. Pascual & Eduardo Segura (Granada)

Beleg and Túrin in the Light of the Medieval Tradition
of Friendship among Warriors 114
Guglielmo Spirito (Assisi) & Emanuele Rimoli (Roma)

Augustinian and Boethian Insights into Tolkien's Shaping
of Middle-earth: Predestination, Prescience and Free Will 132
Annie Birks (Angers)

Paganism in Middle-earth 148
Cécile Cristofari (Aix-en-Provence)

Is the Table of Elrond's Council Round? 160
Marguerite Mouton (Paris)

Tolkien's Mythopoetic Transformation of Landscape:
Tombs, Mounds and Barrows 170
Judith Klinger (Potsdam)

Old Norse Wolf-Motifs in *Of Beren and Lúthien* 190
Antje vom Lehn (Tübingen)

The Eye and the Tree: the Semantics of the
Middle-earth Heraldry 198
Catalin Hriban (Iaşi)

The Dying Sun: Wagner's *Ring* and Tolkien's *Legend* 212
Renée Vink (Hilversum)

The Middle Ages Tolkien Shunned: Tolkien and Chivalry 228
Martin G.E. Sternberg (Bonn)

Varia

Romantische Sehnsucht im Werk J.R.R. Tolkiens 242
Julian T.M. Eilmann (Aachen)

Simple Pleasures in Tolkien's Poetry:
Eating and Drinking and the Depth of Time 254
Guglielmo Spirito & Emanuele Rimoli (Assisi)

Zusammenfassungen der englischen Beiträge 274
Summaries of the German Essays 281

Reviews / Rezensionen

John Perlich & David Whitt (Eds.): Millenial Mythmaking.
Essays on the Power of Science Fiction and Fantasy Literature,
Films and Games 284

Katherine A. Fowkes: The Fantasy Film 284

Axel Melzener: Weltenbauer. Fantastische Szenarien in
Literatur, Games und Film 284

Fastitocalon. Studies in Fantasticism Ancient to Modern.
Vol I-2 (2010): Immortals and the Undead 288

Tolkien Studies. An Annual Scholarly Review. Vol VII (2010) 289

Liam Campbell: The Ecological Augury in the Works
of J.R.R. Tolkien 293

Paul Kerry (Ed.): The Ring and the Cross.
Christianity and *The Lord of the Rings* 295

Jason Fisher (Ed.): Tolkien and the Study of his Sources 298

Tolkien Studies. An Annual Scholarly Review. Vol VIII (2011) 301

Paul Kerry & Sandra Miesel (Eds.): Light Beyond all Shadow.
Religious Experience in Tolkien's Work 303

Carl Phelpstead: Tolkien and Wales:
Language, Literature and Identity 306

Arne Zettersten: Tolkien and Wales: J.R.R. Tolkien's Double Worlds
and Creative Process. Language and Life 308

Unsere Autorinnen und Autoren 312
Our Authors 316

Siglen-Liste 320
Index 322

Preface

Tolkien and the Middle Ages: a connection that seems self-evident and has frequently been dealt with by Tolkien scholars over the last years. Yet which medieval concept is being referred to in those works has only seldom been discussed. The epochal construction 'Middle Ages' does not only span one thousand years, but also a variety of cultures and contains just as many modern views of the Middle Ages. Which then are the imaginations of the Middle Ages that Tolkien brings into a dialogue with modernity and which are integrated into his conception of the world of Middle-earth?

The 8th Tolkien Seminar, organised by the German Tolkien Society DTG together with the University of Potsdam in April 2011, hinged on this question. The spectrum of lectures ranged from the basics of Tolkien's examination of pre-modernism, to relationships to literary history and the history of ideas, to the analysis of medieval references to single phenomena and motifs. Those references can be identified on different levels: for example in the significance of pre-modern societal and power relationships, behavioural patterns and mindsets, but also in medieval worlds of imagination for the mythology of Middle-earth. The discussion also focused on how Tolkien integrated and transformed these elements into his texts und which poetic strategies he developed in the conception of a historically foreign culture.

Beyond the analysis of medieval influences, the question was raised how to interpret the manifold views and aspects of the Middle Ages in Tolkien's work. Are they, as often alleged, an expression of a nostalgic anti-modernism? Or do the medieval structures serve to elicit a feeling of alienation while reading? Tolkien's conception of the world is in many aspects distinctly different from modern phenomena, for example when he contrasts a modern enlightened 'disenchantment' of reality with a magical world view. Yet this turning towards the Middle Ages also happens in the consciousness of modern world views, which Tolkien does not negate but absorbs as voices and thinking patterns into his epochal dialogue.

As seen in the conference contributions and discussions, Tolkien was inspired by a multitude of medieval sources, texts and environments which, taken together, do not form a completely coherent picture of the Middle Ages. They rather engage in a large scale literary (re-)construction which connects historic foreignness with modern perspectives.

Apart from the numerous contributions to the seminar's topic and extensive reviews of topical secondary literature, that volume contains two further articles: Julian Eilmann adds some theses to his article on Romanticism; Guglielmo Spirito and Emanuele Rimoli turn to the simple pleasures in Tolkien's works.

Finally, we would like to thank the University of Potsdam, *Walking Tree Publishers* and the *Association Modernités médiévales* for their friendly support as well as all the contributors, our co-editors, the publisher Susanne A. Rayermann and the designer Kathrin Bondzio. They contributed to the success of the Seminar and enabled the publication of the 8th edition of the DTG yearbook.

Patrick Brückner, Thomas Fornet-Ponse, Judith Klinger

Vorwort

Tolkien und das Mittelalter: So naheliegend diese Verbindung zu sein scheint und so häufig sie in der Tolkienforschung der letzten Jahre aufgegriffen wurde, so wenig ist bislang gefragt worden, auf welches Mittelalter eigentlich Bezug genommen wird. Denn die Epochenkonstruktion ›Mittelalter‹ umfasst nicht nur tausend Jahre, sondern auch eine Vielfalt der Kulturen und ebenso zahlreiche moderne Bilder vom Mittelalter. Welche Imaginationen des Mittelalters sind es also, die Tolkien in einen Dialog mit der Moderne bringt und in seinen Entwurf der Welt von Mittelerde integriert?

Mit dieser Frage beschäftigte sich das 8. Tolkien-Seminar im April 2011, veranstaltet von der DTG in Zusammenarbeit mit der Universität Potsdam. Die Bandbreite der Vorträge reichte von den Grundlagen für Tolkiens Auseinandersetzung mit der vormodernen Epoche über literatur- und ideengeschichtliche Zusammenhänge bis hin zur Analyse der mittelalterlichen Bezüge einzelner Phänomene und Motive. Solche Bezüge lassen sich auf unterschiedlichen Ebenen ausmachen: so etwa die Bedeutung vormoderner Gesellschafts- und Herrschaftsverhältnisse, Verhaltens- oder Denkweisen, aber auch mittelalterlicher Imaginationswelten für die Mythologie von Mittelerde. Diskutiert wurde ebenso, wie Tolkien solche Elemente in seine Texte integriert und transformiert und welche poetischen Strategien er bei der Konzeption einer historisch fremden Kultur entwickelt.

Über die Analyse mittelalterlicher Einflüsse hinaus stellte sich die Frage, wie die vielfältigen Mittelalterbilder und -aspekte in Tolkiens Werk zu deuten sind. Sind sie, wie oft unterstellt, Ausdruck eines nostalgischen Anti-Modernismus? Oder dient die Fremdartigkeit mittelalterlicher Strukturen dazu, Fremdheitserfahrungen bei der Lektüre auszulösen? Tolkiens Weltentwurf grenzt sich an manchen Punkten entschieden von den Phänomenen der Moderne ab, wenn er beispielsweise der neuzeitlich-aufklärerischen ›Entzauberung‹ der Wirklichkeit eine magische Weltwahrnehmung entgegensetzt. Doch vollzieht sich eine solche Wende ins Mittelalterliche eben auch im Bewusstsein moderner Weltanschauungen, die Tolkien nicht etwa negiert, sondern als Stimmen und Denkmöglichkeiten in seinen Epochendialog aufnimmt.

Wie die Tagungsbeiträge und Diskussionen gezeigt haben, hat sich Tolkien von einer großen Vielfalt mittelalterlicher Quellen, Texte und Lebenswelten inspirieren lassen, die zusammen genommen kein geschlossenes, kohärentes Bild vom Mittelalter ergeben. Vielmehr gehen sie in einen groß angelegten literarischen (Re-)Konstruktionsprozess ein, der historische Fremdheit mit modernen Perspektiven verbindet.

Neben den zahlreichen Seminarbeiträgen und den ausführlichen Rezensionen aktueller Forschungsliteratur enthält dieser Band zwei weitere Artikel: Julian Eilmann ergänzt einige Thesen aus seinem Aufsatz zur Romantik; Guglielmo Spirito und Emanuele Rimoli widmen sich den einfachen Freuden in Tolkiens Werk (Essen und Trinken).

Abschließend danken wir für den Erfolg des Seminars und die Ermöglichung dieser achten Ausgabe des DTG-Jahrbuchs der Universität Potsdam, dem Verlag *Walking Tree Publishers* und der *Association Modernités médiévales* für die freundliche Unterstützung und selbstverständlich allen Beitragenden, den Mitherausgebern und -herausgeberinnen im Board of Editors und schließlich der Verlegerin Susanne A. Rayermann mit ihrer Graphikerin Kathrin Bondzio.

Patrick Brückner, Thomas Fornet-Ponse, Judith Klinger

Tolkiens Verwendung der germanischen Mythologie am Beispiel Odins und der Trolle

Rudolf Simek (Bonn)

Tolkiens Beschäftigung mit der germanischen Mythologie war berufsbedingt: Als Professor für Angelsächsische (und Nordische) Literatur am Pembroke College in Oxford von 1925 bis 1945, als Professor für Englische Literatur und Sprache am Merton College in Oxford von 1945 bis zu seiner Emeritierung 1959 und schon vorher von 1920 bis 1925 als Reader und dann Professor in Leeds (Carter 27ff) hat er neben seiner Tätigkeit als Romanautor zwar nur ein sehr mageres wissenschaftliches Oeuvre produziert[1], seine professionelle Belesenheit in angelsächsischen, altenglischen und altnordischen Texten steht jedoch außer Frage.

So ist es nicht überraschend, dass sich punktuell schon im *Hobbit*, verstärkt dann im *Lord of the Rings* und schließlich auch im *Silmarillion* Einflüsse der germanischen Mythologie finden, die vom Banal-Offensichtlichen wie der Einführung von Zwergen in die Handlung bis zum Kryptischen wie Manwës Einwanderung reichen. Im Vergleich damit treten die Einflüsse des Christentums deutlich zurück, vor allem im Vergleich mit dem Werk seines Freundes C.S. Lewis (1898-1963).

Dabei ist jedoch zu berücksichtigen, dass sich die Quellen- und Forschungslage zur Zeit der universitären Ausbildung Tolkiens, also etwa dem ersten Viertel des 20. Jahrhunderts, anders darstellte als heute. Zwar waren schon damals alle wesentlichen Primärquellen für die skandinavische Mythologie längst ediert, aber nicht durchweg übersetzt, sodass sich zumindest für den Studenten Tolkien ein anderes Lektüre-Corpus an übersetzten altnordischen Werken ergab als für heutige Studenten. Zudem wuchs Tolkien zu einer Zeit auf, als die Rezeption der germanischen Mythologie und Heldensagen durch Richard Wagner die der eigentlichen germanischen Mythologie massiv überlagerte und sogar verdeckte, wobei es aufgrund der Wagner'schen Kreativität im Umgang mit seinen Quellen zu deutlichen konzeptuellen Veränderungen kam, die die Wagner-Rezipienten ebenfalls beeinflussten. Zudem trennte Tolkien nur sehr unscharf zwischen germanisch-heidnischer Mythologie und der (mittelalterlichen) Aufbereitung der älteren Heldendichtung. Dies ist vor allem darauf zurückzuführen, dass einer seiner Lieblingstexte die *Völsunga saga* war, eine um 1250 entstandene

---

[1] Vgl. dazu das nur 18 Titel umfassende Verzeichnis von Tolkiens wissenschaftlichen Veröffentlichungen Simek, *Mittelerde* 189f.

hochmittelalterliche Prosaauflösung der Heldenlieder des Siegfried/Sigurd-Nibelungen/Völsungen-Zyklus der *Lieder-Edda*, die versuchte, eine Anknüpfung des Heldensagenstoffes an die Reste nordischer Mythologie herzustellen. Noch dazu war diese ohnehin schon stark romantisierende Sagafassung der Heldensagen in der noch romantischeren Übersetzung des William Morris von 1888[2] zugänglich, und dieser Erstzugang dürfte Tolkiens Bild von germanischer Mythologie und Heldensage stark geprägt haben.

Keine der erwähnten Quellen ist für die germanische oder auch nur nordische Mythologie im engeren Sinn brauchbar. Aber Tolkien hat dennoch Etliches der altnordischen Primärliteratur entnommen, ohne sich allzu sehr auf die zu seiner Zeit gängigen Darstellungen der nordischen Mythologie zu verlassen, was wohl auch an seinen nicht allzu guten Deutschkenntnissen lag.[3] Die populäreren Darstellungen von Karl Simrock in seinem *Handbuch der deutschen Mythologie* (1853) und Wolfgang Golthers *Handbuch der germanischen Mythologie* von 1895 standen ihm also nicht offen, sondern er musste wohl auf die zu diesem Zeitpunkt schon betagte Übersetzung von Jakob Grimms *Deutsche Mythologie* in drei Bänden von 1843 zurückgreifen, die ab 1882 ein gewisser J.S. Stallybrass in London unter dem Titel *Teutonic Mythology* publiziert hatte.

Es ist hier nicht der Ort, auch nur überblicksartig auf die vielfältigen Einflüsse der germanischen Mythologie auf Tolkiens Werk einzugehen[4]. Im Folgenden sollen vielmehr zwei sehr unterschiedliche Themenkomplexe der Mythenrezeption bei Tolkien exemplarisch behandelt werden: einerseits seine Verarbeitung verschiedenster Elemente des Gottes Odin, andererseits das von ihm nicht sehr deutlich herausgearbeitete Bild der Trolle, also von Wesen der so genannten »niederen Mythologie« im mittelalterlichen Skandinavien, die außerhalb des Nordens allerdings im Mittelalter keine Spuren in den Quellen hinterlassen haben.

Odin bei Tolkien

Der altskandinavische Gott Odin (altnordisch Óðinn), der auch im Südgermanischen als Wodan/Wotan und im Altenglischen als Wōden belegt ist, war nach unseren mittelalterlichen mythographischen Quellen der Hauptgott des nordischen Pantheons, was aber möglicherweise nur die Meinung einer

---

2   Angeblich kaufte sich Tolkien schon 1914 die wesentlichsten Werke des damals in England sehr bekannten William Morris von einem Preisgeld, das er im dritten Studienjahr für besondere Studienleistungen erhalten hatte (vgl. Carpenter 69).

3   Bei Tolkien perfekte Kenntnis des Deutschen zu erwarten, wie es Shippey tut (300), weil er an zwei Stellen seines Oeuvre deutsche Texte zitiert (nämlich das Grimm'sche Märchen *Von dem Machandelboom* in *On Fairy-Stories* und den mittelhochdeutschen *Orendel*), verkennt völlig die Gewohnheiten akademischer Arbeitsweise.

4   Dies habe ich ansatzweise in Simek, *Mittelerde* versucht.

kriegerischen (und literarischen?) Elite darstellt, denn nach Auskunft des Namenmaterials hatte Thor ungleich breitere Verehrung erfahren. Allerdings führt die Dominanz von Odin in den literarischen Quellen zu einer recht ausgeprägten Rezeption dieser Figur bei Tolkien. Dies beruht nicht zuletzt darauf, dass eine ganze Reihe der von Tolkien genutzten Quellen sich mit diesem Gott beschäftigen: Zum einen beschäftigen sich gerade die bekanntesten Götterlieder der *Lieder-Edda* (niedergeschrieben um 1275 im *Codex Regius*), nämlich die *Völuspá* (»Vorhersagung der Seherin«) und die *Hávamál* (»Sprüche des Hohen«) mit dieser Göttergestalt, zum anderen wird er sekundär aufgrund des Vorkommens in Edda- und Skaldengedichten auch von den beiden wichtigsten Mythographen des Hochmittelalters intensiv behandelt: von Snorri Sturluson (ca. 1178/9-1242) in seiner *Prosa-Edda* und von Saxo Grammaticus († 1216) in seinen *Gesta Danorum* (»Geschichte der Dänen«). Zum dritten erwähnen auch einige der Fornaldarsögur (»Vorzeitsagas«, historische Romane über die wikingerzeitliche heidnische Vergangenheit Skandinaviens), die ab dem frühen 13. Jahrhundert entstanden, den Gott Odin, hier meist mit deutlich vermenschlichten Zügen, wie etwa in der *Völsunga saga* (»Saga von den Völsungen«) und der *Hervarar saga ok Heiðreks kunungs* (»Saga von Hervör und König Heiðrek«). Da Odin in den zahlreichen Quellen ein sehr facetten- und funktionsreicher Gott ist, der Rollen als Herrschergott und Göttervater, als Ahnherr von Königsgeschlechtern und Völkern, als Kriegs- und Schlachtengott, als Totengott und Totenführer, als Gott der Runen, der Dichtung und der Magie besetzte, ist das Bild auch in den unterschiedlichen Quellen sehr differenziert.[5]

Nicht alle diese Aspekte hat Tolkien literarisch in seinen Werken umgesetzt (so bleibt Odins Rolle als Kriegsgott oder als Gott der Dichtkunst unerwähnt), im Gegenteil beschränkte sich Tolkien auf nur einige wenige Aspekte, nämlich auf Odin als Wanderer und als Zauberer. Daneben wurden auch noch seine Rolle als Gott der Magie und als Ahnherr von Völkern, vielleicht auch seine Rolle als Anführer eines Totenheers umgesetzt, in diesem Fall aber schon stark mit anderen literarischen Elementen und Quellen vermengt. Gerade die Darstellung Odins als recht menschlicher Wanderer in den letztgenannten beiden Sagas dürfte für Tolkien in seiner Beschreibung der beiden Zauberer Gandalf und Saruman wirksam geworden sein. Abgesehen von der äußeren Erscheinung als Wanderer mit langem Mantel, Schlapphut und Stab (»All that the unsuspecting Bilbo saw that morning was an old man with a staff. He had a tall pointed blue hat, a long grey cloak, a silver scarf over which his long white beard hung down below his waist, and immense black boots«, H 13) hat Gandalf mit Odin vor allem seine Zauberkunst gemeinsam. Diese beschreibt Snorri Sturluson in der mythologischen Einleitung zur *Heimskringla* ausführlich[6]:

---

5 Vgl. dazu Simek, *Lexikon* 310-324.
6 Die beste Zusammenstellung der Quellen zu Odin als Zauberer: siehe Motz 69-101.

Odin konnte seine Gestalt verändern. Sein Körper lag wie schlafend oder tot da, er aber war ein Vogel oder ein Tier, ein Fisch oder eine Schlange und fuhr in Augenblicken in andere Länder, in seinen Angelegenheiten oder denen anderer Leute. Er beherrschte auch das noch, daß er mit Worten allein Feuer schlagen konnte und das Meer beruhigen und den Wind in jede Richtung schralen lassen konnte, wie er wollte. Er hatte auch das Schiff, das Skíðblaðnir hieß, das über die Maßen groß war, aber das man wie ein Tuch zusammenlegen konnte. Er hatte immer Mímirs Haupt bei sich, und dieses sagte ihm viele Nachrichten aus der anderen Welt, aber manchmal weckte er die Toten aus der Erde auf oder setzte sich unter Gehenkte. Deswegen nannte man ihn auch Herr der Wiedergänger oder Herr der Gehenkten. Er besaß zwei Raben, die er mit der Sprache gezähmt hatte. Sie flogen weit übers Land und erzählten ihm viele Neuigkeiten. Deswegen wurde er sehr berühmt. Alle diese Fertigkeiten erreichte er mit Runen und den Liedern, die Zaubersprüche (*galdrar*) heißen. Deswegen heißen die Asen auch Sprücheschmiede. Daneben beherrschte er aber auch noch die Kunst, der er am meisten folgte, und die er selbst betrieb, die Schwarzkunst (*seiðr*) heißt, und damit konnte er das Schicksal der Menschen und zukünftige Dinge erfahren, auch Menschen den Tod oder Unglück oder Krankheit bringen, und Menschen ihren Verstand oder ihre Kraft rauben und sie anderen geben.

(*Heimskringla*, *Ynglinga saga*, Kap. 7; meine Übersetzung)

Es sei hier nicht vergessen, dass auch Gandalf (wie die Zwerge) einen Namen aus dem *Edda*-Lied *Völuspá* trägt, der eigentlich »Zauberalbe« bedeutet. Im Kontext der *Völuspá* wird dieser zwar als metaphorischer Zwergenname verwendet, aber von Tolkien ganz passend dem Zauberer verliehen. Daneben besitzt Gandalf auch noch das schnellste aller Pferde (Shadowfax in LotR I 275f), während Snorri Sturluson in seiner *Edda* (*Gylfaginning* Kap. 14) dem Gott Odin das beste aller Pferde, den ebenfalls grauen, aber achtbeinigen Hengst Sleipnir, zuweist.

Die gerade zitierte ausführliche Beschreibung der magischen Fähigkeiten Odins inkludiert auch die der Tierverwandlung zum Zweck des Wissenserwerbs aus der Anderwelt, wie es in schamanischen Praktiken üblich ist. Aber auch sonst ist Odin auf vielfältige Weise mit Tiergestalten und -begleitern verbunden: Außer seinem schon erwähnten Hengst Sleipnir gehören ihm auch die zwei Raben Hugin und Munin an, die ihn mit Nachrichten aus aller Welt versorgen, sowie zwei Wölfe, die zu seinen Füßen sitzen. Außerdem verwandelt sich Odin auf der Flucht vor dem Riesen Suttungr (im Mythos vom Raub des Skaldenmets, vgl. *Edda*. *Skáldskaparmál* 1) in einen Adler, um dem Riesen, der ebenfalls Vogelgestalt angenommen hat, entkommen zu können. Dieses Detail scheint sich bei Tolkien von der Flucht Odins *als* Adler in eine Flucht Gandalfs *auf* einem Adler verändert zu haben (LotR I 275).

Aber nicht nur Gandalf trägt Züge Odins, auch bei seinem Gegenspieler Saruman hat Tolkien Aspekte des Odinischen eingearbeitet. Ebenso wie Odin als Gott in den altnordischen Quellen als eine sehr wechselhafte, ja geradezu wankelmütige Gestalt gezeichnet wird, so sind auch die beiden Zauberer eigentlich nur unterschiedliche Aspekte ein und derselben Gestalt. Aber während Gandalf durchweg positiv gezeichnet wird, verfällt Saruman bei Tolkien den bösen Einflüsterungen Saurons und wird deswegen fast durchweg negativ konnotiert.

Offenbar waren schon Tolkien die widersprüchlichen Wesenszüge im Charakter Odins aufgefallen und hatten ihn dazu bewogen, diese unterschiedlichen Züge in verschiedenen, aber durchaus zueinander korrelierenden Figuren des *Lord of the Rings* zu realisieren. An Saruman etwa ist es das – mit Gandalf ja gemeinsame – Äußere, das wiederum auf Odin verweist, dazu kommt aber eine Reihe von Eigenschaften Odins, die sich in Saruman gebündelt finden: Zum einen ist es Odins Allwissenheit, die sich in Beratungen mit Mimirs Kopf, mit dem Fernblick von seinem Hochsitz Hliðskjálf und den durch die Raben Hugin und Munin gelieferten Informationen erst entwickelt und manifestiert, zum anderen ist es die ganz eindeutige Unverlässlichkeit und Zweischichtigkeit in Odins Wesen, die sich bei Saruman wiederfindet.

Eine weitere Gestalt, in der sich Odin zu einem gewissen Grad wiederfindet, ist Sauron aufgrund der ihn und Odin verbindenden Einäugigkeit:

> In the black abyss there appeared a single Eye that slowly grew, until it filled nearly all the Mirror... The Eye was rimmed with fire, but was itself glazed, yellow as a cat's, watchful and intent, and the black slit of its pupil opened on a pit, a window into nothing. (LotR I 379)

Dazu kommt, dass Sauron ebenso wie Saruman von Tolkien als *Necromancer* (Schwarzkünstler und Zauberer) bezeichnet wird, und dies geht sicherlich auf die schon oben zitierten magischen Fertigkeiten Odins in Snorris *Heimskringla* zurück.

Dass diese Zuordnung aller drei Figuren (Gandalf, Saruman und Sauron) zu Odin als Quelle keineswegs abwegig ist, beweist Tolkien selbst in seinem Essay *On Fairy-Stories*: Nicht nur ist Odin ein Zauberer »Odin the Goth, the Necromancer« (FS 128), sondern sowohl Gandalf als auch Saruman und Sauron werden von Tolkien mit demselben Wort bezeichnet. Wie Odin, so können auch sie sich in Tiere verwandeln oder werden (wie bei Gandalfs Adlern) mit ihnen assoziiert, was außerhalb des LotR sogar für Sauron von Tolkien bestätigt wird:

> Then Sauron shifted shape, from wolf to serpent, and from monster to his own accustomed form; but he could not elude the grip of Huan without forsaking his body utterly.
> ...
> And immediately he [Sauron] took the form of a vampire, great as a dark cloud across the moon, and he fled, dripping blood from his throat upon the trees, and came to Taur-nu-Fuin, and dwelt there, filling it with horror. (S 175)

Ebenfalls außerhalb des LotR findet sich eine weitere Parallele zu Odin: in der Figur des Manwë im *Silmarillion*. Manwë Súlimo ist der höchste und heiligste der Valar (S 39), der also am ehesten den Asen der nordischen Religion entsprechenden Götterfamilie, wobei Odin häufig als »der höchste und älteste der Asen« bezeichnet wird (*Edda. Gylfaginning* Kap. 19). Manwë ist also schon von seiner Position her mit Odin zu vergleichen, wobei diese Identifikation von Tolkien in *The Book of Lost Tales 2* bestätigt wurde: »Eriol told the fairies of Wôden [Odin], and they identified [him] with Manweg [Manwë]« (LT 2, 295). Daneben haben Odin und Manwë noch die Weisheit gemeinsam, beide besitzen als Attribute zwei Vögel, die ihnen Informationen zutragen, und beide sind auch Götter der Dichtung, wobei Tolkien bei Manwë mehr Gewicht auf die Musik legt, während er die Dichtung fast nur nebenbei erwähnt: »*The Vanyar he loved best of all the Elves, and of him they received song and poetry; for poetry is the delight of Manwë, and the song of words is his music*« (S 40). Auch die Verwendung eines Hochsitzes, der den Blick über die ganze Welt erlaubt, und den Bezug zu den Vögeln als Informationsbeschaffer haben die beiden gemeinsam (»For Manwë to whom all birds are dear, and to whom they bring news upon Taniquetil from Middle-earth, had sent forth the race of Eagles, commanding them to dwell in the crags of the North, and to keep watch upon Morgoth«: S 129).

Saruman dagegen hat mit Odin ganz andere Züge gemein. Der auffälligste außer dem Aussehen ist seine Rolle als Einwanderer:

> Even as the first shadows were felt in Mirkwood there appeared in the west of Middle-earth the Istari, whom Men called the Wizards. None knew at that time whence they were, save Círdan of the Havens, and only to Elrond and to Galadriel did he reveal that they came over the Sea. (S 372)

Das Konzept einer Einwanderung eines Zauberer-Ordens, wenn schon nicht von halb-göttlichen bzw. pseudogöttlichen Ahnherren, hat Tolkien zweifellos aus den beiden Werken Snorris, der *Edda* und der *Heimskringla*, übernommen. Bei Snorri Sturluson im Prolog zu seiner *Edda* weisen nämlich Odin und die anderen aus Asien einwandernden Asen derartige pseudogöttliche Fähigkeiten als Einwanderer nach Schweden auf, die in der Folge dazu führen, dass er wie ein Gott verehrt wird:

> Odin besaß wie seine Frau die Sehergabe, und aus seinen Visionen erfuhr er, daß sein Name oben in der Nordhälfte der Welt bekannt sein würde... Aus diesem Grund wollte er seine Reise von Tyrkland antreten. Er führte eine große Gefolgschaft mit sich, junge und alte Menschen, Männer wie Frauen, die viele wertvolle Dinge bei sich hatten. Und in den Ländern, durch die sie zogen, erzählte man viel Ruhmreiches über sie, so daß sie Göttern ähnlicher als Menschen schienen... Danach zog er weiter nordwärts in das heutige Schweden... Und ihrer Ankunft folgte die Zeit, in der überall dort, wo sie sich aufhielten, reiche Ernten und Friede herrschten. Alle glaubten, daß sie deren Verursacher seien; denn die herrschenden Männer stellten fest, daß sie anders als andere Menschen waren, die sie bisher gesehen hatten, sowohl in ihrer äußeren Schönheit als auch an Verstand. Dort... entschied er sich für eine Stadt, die jetzt Sigtuna heißt. Dort setzte er die Oberhäupter so ein, wie es in Troja gewesen war. Er bestimmte zwölf Anführer in diesem Ort, die Landesgesetze beschließen sollten. So ordnete er alles Recht, wie es früher in Troja gewesen war. (*Edda* 12-14)

Bei Tolkien im *Silmarillion* liest sich die Stelle über die Einwanderung Sarumans nicht unähnlich, wenn auch deutlich knapper:

> Saruman kam als Erster der Istari nach Mittelerde. Seine Haltung und sein Gebaren waren vornehm, er sprach mit kluger und schöner Stimme und hatte großes Geschick in seinen Händen. Wegen seiner weißen Gewänder erhielt er den Beinamen *der Weiße* und wurde von fast allen, auch von den Eldar, als Oberhaupt des Ordens angesehen. (S 373)

Die Gemeinsamkeiten gehen über die bloße Einwanderung weit hinaus: Odin wie Saruman kamen als Ahnherren von Geschlechtern, zeichneten sich durch Vornehmheit und Geschick aus und wurden zu Oberhäuptern eines je von ihnen gegründeten Ordens von Häuptlingen.

Zusammenfassend lässt sich über die Rezeption Odins im Werk Tolkiens sagen, dass er sich der Vielschichtigkeit des nordischen Gottes sehr wohl bewusst war und dass er diese Komplexität auflöste, indem er insgesamt vier Gestalten – Gandalf, Saruman, Sauron und Manwë – mit Eigenschaften dieses Gottes versorgen und diese immer noch zu teilweise recht komplexen und tiefen Figuren ausgestalten konnte.

Trolle bei Tolkien

Ganz anders sieht es mit der Rezeption von Trollen im Werk Tolkiens aus. Trolle sind eine Untergruppe der Riesen in der nordischen Mythologie, zu denen auch Jötnar (mächtige Urriesen wie Ymir), dumme Rísar (die wohl der Volkserzählung oder sogar dem Märchen selbst entlehnt wurden) sowie die mit magischen Fertigkeiten begabte Thursen zählten. Die Trolle sind diejenige Riesengattung, mit der Sterbliche am ehesten in Kontakt treten konnten und die sich zwar durch Kraft und Körpergröße, aber eben sonst nicht allzu sehr von den Menschen unterschied.

Die Trolle (altnordisch Pl. *tröll*, Sg. *troll/tröll n.*) gehören zwar zu den in der altnordischen Sagaliteratur am häufigsten erwähnten Gruppen riesischer Wesen, besonders wohl auch deswegen, weil mit ihnen nur relativ vage Vorstellungen verbunden und alle möglichen Konzepte von der Existenz jenseitiger Wesen unter diesem Begriff zusammengefasst wurden. Jedoch ist auffällig, dass gerade die von Tolkien bevorzugten altnordischen Quellentexte, die beiden *Eddas* sowie die älteren der *Fornaldarsögur*, nur recht wenig über Trolle zu berichten haben, und wenn, dann eher im Sinn eines Kollektivums für diverse jenseitige (wenn auch besonders riesische) Wesen.

In den *Edda*-Liedern findet sich das Wort »Troll« nur ein einziges Mal, in der *Völuspá* Str. 40, aber auch hier ist von keinem Troll die Rede, sondern von einem Wolf *í trollz hami* »in Trollgestalt«. Sonst erwähnt die Lieder-*Edda* nur eine Trollfrau in der jungen Prosa zur *Helgakviða Hjörvarðssonar* 30, hier im Sinn einer Hexe. Da auch die *Völsunga saga*, also die Prosaauflösung der Eddaischen Heldenlieder, einen Troll nur einmal in einer sprichwörtlichen Redensart erwähnt, ist zu vermuten, dass auch dies nicht die Quelle für Tolkiens Trollvorstellungen gewesen sein kann. Die Trolle spielen weder in diesen Werken noch in den meisten anderen Vorzeitsagas als Protagonisten oder überhaupt als Agenten der Handlung eine Rolle. Dagegen sind häufig die Begriffe *trolldómr*, *trollskapr* zu finden, die aber nicht für das Wesen der Trolle verwendet werden, sondern »Zauberei« bedeuten. Darüber hinaus finden sich Trolle vor allem in formelhaften Redewendungen, wie etwa in der Phrase *troll hafi þik* »die Trolle mögen dich holen« in der Bedeutung von »jemanden zum Teufel schicken, jemandem den Tod wünschen« (vgl. Cleasby-Vigfusson, 641).

Trolle im Sinne mythologischer riesenhafter Figuren finden sich erst in den Isländersagas und den jüngeren der *Fornaldarsögur*, von denen Tolkien einige aus der Lektüre der *kolbítar* (»Kohlenbeißer«, ein Figurentypus der Sagaliteratur) kannte, einer losen Vereinigung von an altnordischen Texten interessierten Akademikern in Oxford, die sich regelmäßig zur Lektüre von Sagas im altnordischen Original in Oxford traf. Allerdings ist der ›Lektürekanon‹ der *kolbítar* nicht überliefert, sodass wir nicht wissen, welche der (damals unübersetzten) Sagas Tolkien dabei kennengelernt haben konnte; in Frage kommen dafür nur die *Örvar-Odds saga*, die *Ketils saga hængs*, die *Bósa saga ok Herrauðs* und die *Egils saga einhenda*, wobei in den beiden letzteren sogar ein wenig auf das Äußere der Trolle bzw. Trollfrauen eingegangen wird. Nur in der *Hrólfs saga Gautrekssonar* kommt das Wort wirklich häufig vor, aber ausgerechnet hier fast durchweg für einen menschlichen Charakter, der für einen Troll gehalten wird.[7] Häufiger als Trolle selbst in diesen Sagas sind Trollkonar (»Trollfrauen«, mitunter aber in der Bedeutung »Hexen«) und die Töchter von Trollen, die den Helden durchaus freundlich und hilfreich begegnen konnten.[8] Insgesamt waren Trolle den Menschen häufig feindlich gesinnt, konnten sie oder ihre Tiere im Nebel in die Irre führen und sie anderweitig in Bedrängnis bringen. Trolle lebten in Berghöhlen von rohem Fleisch und waren in der Regel überaus hässlich und ungesittet. Tolkiens Vorstellungen ergeben sich also aus der Summe der Erwähnungen in Isländersagas und Vorzeitsagas, wobei aber seine kreative Ader auch hier zu einer Umdeutung des altnordischen Konzepts führte, denn so humorvoll, wie die Saga-Autoren über die gefährlichen und dennoch ein wenig lächerlichen Trolle berichten, erscheinen sie bei Tolkien keineswegs, vgl. etwa die Schilderung eines Kampfs zwischen einem Riesen und einer Trollfrau in der *Egils saga einhenda* (Kap. 11):

> Da sah er auf einem Hügel einen mächtigen Riesen und ein Trollweib, die beide an einem Goldring zerrten. Sie aber war nicht so stark wie er, und er mißhandelte sie, und man konnte da riesige Geschlechtsteile sehen, weil sie recht kurz geschürzt war.[9]

Tolkiens Vorstellung von Trollen scheint sich im Laufe seines Lebens beträchtlich gewandelt zu haben: Im *Hobbit* stehen die drei als Trolle bezeichneten Kerle William, Tom und Bert (H 37-45), die durch Gandalfs Trick mit der aufgehenden Sonne in Stein verwandelt werden, mehr den *risar*, also den dummen Riesen der Sagas und Volksmärchen nahe als irgendwelchen gefährlichen Wesen. Die Versteinerung von mythologischen Wesen hat Tolkien übrigens dem bekannten *Edda*-Lied *Alvíssmál* entnommen, in dem der Gott Thor den allzu schlauen Zwerg Alviss so lange mit Fragen hinhält, bis dieser von den ersten Sonnenstrahlen getroffen wird und dadurch versteinert – dies sozusagen der *locus classicus* der Versteinerungssagen.

Schon im ersten Band des LotR werden Trolle von Tolkien als wesentlich gefährlicher und unnahbarer gezeichnet, was möglicherweise mit der verän-

---

7 Vgl. dazu den nützlichen Überblick der Erwähnungen von Trollen in den *Fornaldarsögur* bei Schulz 51f.
8 Über die literarische Funktion von sexuellen Begegnungen von Helden und Trolltöchtern vgl. u.a. Simek, Party. Solche Trollfeste sind beschrieben u.a. in der *Egils saga einhenda* und in der *Barðar saga snæfellsáss*, beide auf deutsch zugänglich in: Simek/Hennig.
9 Vgl. Simek/Hennig 547.

derten Intention des LotR, der nun nicht mehr wie *The Hobbit* als Kinderbuch intendiert war, zu tun haben mag:

> Orcs were multiplying again in the mountains. Trolls were abroad, no longer dull-witted, but cunning and armed with dreadful weapons.
> (LotR I 53)

oder:

> Other wanderers were rare, and of evil sort: trolls might stray down at times out of the northern valleys of the Misty Mountains.
> (LotR I 202)

Am wahrscheinlichsten ist es, dass Tolkien diese Art der Trollbeschreibung nicht aus den *Fornaldarsögur*, sondern aus einer eigentümlichen Isländersaga übernommen hat, in der erstaunlich viel von Trollen in Westisland und sogar Grönland die Rede ist: die *Barðar saga Snæfellsáss* (»Saga von Bardr, dem Guten Geist des Snæfell«). Darin heißt es (Kap. 5):

> Im Winter kamen Trolle und Unholde von oben in den Eiriksfjord herunter und bereiteten den Menschen großen Schaden, beschädigten Schiffe und brachen Menschen die Knochen. Das waren insgesamt drei, ein Mann und eine Frau und deren Sohn.
> (Simek/Hennig 488)

Ob Tolkien diese Saga, die zu seiner Zeit zwar schon mehrfach ediert war, aber erst 1984 ins Englische übersetzt wurde, wirklich gelesen hat, wissen wir nicht. Jedenfalls zeigt er im LotR ein Konzept von Trollen, das dem dieser isländischen Saga (und teilweise auch anderer Isländersagas) nahesteht: als den Menschen feindlich gesinnte Unholde, groß, stark und ungeschlacht, wobei Tolkien die Dimensionen der nordischen Saga-Trolle sogar noch steigert. Diese werden etwa in der *Grettis saga* oder der *Barðar saga Snæfellsáss* in einer Größenordnung geschildert, die einen realistischen Ringkampf zwischen menschlichem Helden und Troll noch erlaubte. Tolkien dagegen übersteigert diese Größe im LotR mit der Angabe, dass der Ent Treebeard (LotR II 66) mit 14 Fuß fast so groß wie ein Troll ist; nach gängiger Umrechnung ergibt sich damit eine Trollgröße von gut 4,5 m, was die Angaben mittelalterlicher nordischer Texte wesentlich übersteigt. Der Grund für diese Übersteigerung mag in der von Tolkien erst selbst konstruierten Herkunft der Trolle von den Ents liegen:

> Maybe you have heard of Trolls? They are mighty strong. But Trolls are only counterfeits, made by the Enemy in the Great Darkness, in mockery of Ents, as Orcs were of Elves. We are stronger than Trolls. We are made of the bones of the earth. We can split stone

> like the roots of trees, only quicker, far quicker, if our minds are roused! If we are not hewn down, or destroyed by fire or blast of sorcery, we could split Isengard into splinters and crack its walls into rubble. (LotR II 89)

Diese etwas eigentümliche Herleitung mag auch den frühen Lesern des LotR aufgestoßen sein, die Tolkien offenbar daraufhin ansprachen, denn er fühlte sich in einem Brief genötigt, diese Herleitung der Trolle als Privatmeinung des Ents Treebeard zu bezeichnen (Brief 153 an Peter Hastings, Sept. 1954: L 190). Das macht allerdings diesen Ursprung der Trolle noch unwahrscheinlicher, weil ja damit die Ents, hölzerne Riesen, zu steinernen Riesen werden. Dass die Trolle (wie alle Riesen in der altnordischen Mythographie übrigens) auch von Tolkien mit Bergen und Felsen assoziiert werden, beweist er selbst in einer Erklärung der Olog-hai, die er als Gruppe der Trolle »but harder than stone« bezeichnet. Schon vorher spricht Tolkien selbst dezidiert von der Herkunft der Trolle:

> *Trolls. Troll* has been used to translate the Sindarin *Torog*. In their beginning far back in the twilight of the Elder Days, these were creatures of dull and lumpish nature and had no more language than beasts. But Sauron had made use of them, teaching them what little they could learn, and increasing their wits with wickedness... (LotR III 410).

Hier entgleist Tolkien allerdings wieder in seine eigene Mythologie, mit den nordischen Quellen hat dies nichts zu tun. Es ist aber überlegenswert, ob Tolkien wenigstens im letzten Jahrzehnt seiner Arbeit am LotR nicht schon selbst von Tendenzen der skandinavischen Literatur unwillkürlich beeinflusst worden war, in denen Trolle in Vermengung mit dem skandinavischen Volksglauben an Wichtel, Zwerge und Nissen (allgemein unter hukldrefolk »verstecktes Völkchen« zusammengefasst) zu Konzepten führten, die heute die populären Vorstellungen von Trollen in Skandinavien (und auch außerhalb!) dominieren. Besonders durch den Einfluss der Kinder- und Jugendbuchliteratur (vgl. Simek, *Tolkien*) wurden die Trolle zu niedlichen, kleinen und harmlosen Waldbewohnern, die als Folie kindlicher Ängste fungierten, um damit endgültig demythologisiert zu werden. Ob Tolkiens Trolle als ungehaltene Reaktion auf diese unpassende Verniedlichung immer größer wurden, ist allerdings schwer zu belegen, da Tolkien weder Reisen nach Skandinavien unternahm noch mit skandinavischen Kinderbüchern in Berührung gekommen sein dürfte, bevor der LotR erschien.

Wirksam wurden Tolkiens unorthodoxe, aber immerhin noch der nordischen (literarisierten) Sagenwelt des Mittelalters nahestehenden Trollvorstellungen allemal: Nicht nur Peter Jacksons Filmtrilogie von 2001-2003 verlieh ihnen unglaubliche Popularität,[10] die seine Romane nie in diesem Maße kannten, sondern auch die zahlreichen direkt und noch häufiger indirekt von Tolkiens derivativer Mythologie abgeleiteten Rollenspiele, die die Trolle als gefährliche, meist sogar (und unhistorisch!) bewaffnete Riesen anlegen. Aber immerhin stehen die Trolle bei Tolkien und den von ihm abhängigen Rezeptionslinien der nordischen Mythologie noch deutlich näher als der skandinavischen Kinderliteratur. Somit bildet Tolkiens literarische Welt wenigstens ein Gegengewicht zur vollständigen Verniedlichung der Trollvorstellungen des 20. und 21. Jahrhunderts.

Bibliographie

Aðalbjarnarson, Bjarni, Ed. *Snorri Sturluson: Heimskringla*. Vol. 1, Reykjavík, 1941

Bryce, Lynn. "The Influence of Scandinavian Mythology on the Works of J.R.R. Tolkien". *Edda* 83 (1983): 113-119

Carpenter, Humphrey (Ed. with the assistance of Christopher Tolkien). *The Letters of J.R.R. Tolkien*. London: HarperCollins, 1995

Carter, Lin. *Tolkiens Universum*. München: Ullstein, 2001

Grimm, Jakob. *Deutsche Mythologie*. Göttingen: Dieterich, 1843/1844

---. *Teutonic Mythology*. Transl. by J.S. Stallybrass. London: George Bell, 1882-1888

Golther, Wolfgang. *Handbuch der germanischen Mythologie*. Leipzig: Hirzel, 1895

Krause, Arnulf. *Die Edda des Snorri Sturluson*. Stuttgart: Reclam, 1997

Mitchell, Bruce. "J.R.R. Tolkien and Old English Studies: An Appreciation". *Proceedings of the J.R.R. Tolkien Centenary Conference 1992*. Eds. Patricia Reynolds & Glen GoodKnight. Milton Keynes/Altadena: The Tolkien Society 1995, 206-212

Motz, Lotte. *The King, the Champion and the Sorcerer*. Wien: Fassbaender, 1996

Schulz, Katja. *Riesen. Von Wissenshütern und Wildnisbewohnern in Edda und Saga*. Heidelberg: Winter, 2004

Shippey, Tom. *The Road to Middle-Earth*. London: HarperCollins, 1982

---

10 Peter Jacksons Trolle waren allerdings dann doch kleiner, als die von Tolkien gemachten Angaben es suggeriert hätten, aber noch immer deutlich größer, als die altnordischen Quellen es zulassen würden. Für die Filmversion wurde die Trollgröße mit nur 10 Fuß bzw. 3,048 m festgelegt, also deutlich kleiner als bei Tolkien, der im *Lord of the Rings* von Trollen als »über 12 Fuß groß« spricht; vgl. Sibley 75.

Sibley, Brian. *Der Herr der Ringe. Das offizielle Filmbuch.* Stuttgart: Klett-Cotta, 2001

Simek, Rudolf. *Mittelerde. Tolkien und die germanische Mythologie.* München: Beck, 2005

---. »Tolkien und die germanische Mythologie«. *Die Mumins, Narnia und Der Herr der Ringe: Tove Janssons Beitrag zur kinderliterarischen Mythen-Translation.* Wien 2012 (in Druck)

---. "What a Swell Party This Is...? Giants and Feasting in Old Norse Literature". *De Consolatione Philologiae.* Studies in Honour of Evelyn S. Firchow. Vol. 1. Eds. Anna Grotans, Heinrich Beck & Anton Schwob. Göppingen: Kümmerle 2000, 385-395

---. *Lexikon der germanischen Mythologie.* Stuttgart: Kröner, 2006

---. und Reinhard Hennig (Üb.). *Sagas aus Island: Von Wikingern, Berserkern und Trollen.* Stuttgart: Reclam, 2011

Simrock, Karl. *Handbuch der deutschen Mythologie mit Einschluß der nordischen.* Bonn: Marcus 1853, 6. Aufl. 1887

Tolkien, J.R.R. *The Fellowship of the Ring.* London: Allen & Unwin, 1954

---. *The Two Towers.* London: Allen & Unwin, 1954

---. *The Return of the King.* London: Allen & Unwin, 1955

---. *The Hobbit,* or: There and Back Again. London: Allen & Unwin, 1978

---. *The Silmarillion.* London: Allen & Unwin, 1977

---. *Tree and Leaf.* London: Unwin Hyman, 1988

Völsunga saga: The story of the Völsungs and Niblungs, with certain songs from the elder *Edda.* Edited, with introduction and notes, by H. Halliday Sparling. London: Scott, 1888

Mundus senescit: Is Tolkien's Medievalism Victorian or Modernist?

Dirk Wiemann (Potsdam)

An Ageing World

"The world is grey, the mountains old" (LotR I 308), declaims Gimli in Moria.

The statement is typical of the sentiment that prevails in *The Lord of the Rings*, and so is the place itself: Moria, once the underground capital city of Khazad-dûm, has long been abandoned and has become a gloomy ruin. By the end of the Third Age, almost all regions of north-western Middle-earth appear to share this fate. Much of Eriador is uninhabited terrain only sporadically dotted with the remnants of the Kingdom of Arnor that still overwrite the territory with memories of past grandeur when things were "tall and fair" before the "people dwindled" (LotR III 1019). Also Ithilien, "the garden of Gondor [is] now desolate", and the former Noldor realm of Eregion has been reduced to an altogether empty land that, however, still retains some memory of "happier days" (LotR I 275), as Gandalf observes:

> "There is a wholesome air about Hollin. Much evil must befall a country before it wholly forgets the Elves if once they lived there."
> "That is true," said Legolas. "But the Elves of this land were of a race strange to us sylvan folk, and the trees and the grass do not now remember them. Only I hear the stones lament them: *deep they delved us, fair they wrought us, high they builded us; but they are gone.*" (LotR I 276)

The past, lost as it is, is still vaguely recalled in all this desolation, but the effect is not consoling at all; it rather brings home all the more poignantly that there is a general process of decline that makes the present appear as an age of exhaustion and decrepitude, at best a "rough echo" (LotR I 189) of the greatness that once was "when the world was young" (ibid.). In an ageing world, the future holds no promise for an antidote to such decay. Renewal therefore has to occur as a restoration of the past, which alone can alleviate the malaise of the degraded present. In such a world "which has been 'worn down'... by time" (Shippey 109), it is the mission of Gandalf, bearer of the ring of fire, to "rekindle hearts to the valour of old in a world that grows chill" (S 367).

The notion of a pervasive decay and diminishment is not specific to the final days of the Third Age but an inbuilt matrix of Tolkien's world as such: "the life of Arda, ...though long beyond the reckoning of Men is not endless, and ages also" (MR 212). While this principal mortality of Arda is already part of the creator's master plan, it takes on a sinister quality through the corrupting 'contribution' of Tolkien's Satan, Melkor, who indelibly 'mars' the world. "Arda Marred" is not simply an ageing but a decadent world since "all the matter of Arda was tainted by [Melkor's] malice" (MR 309). All inhabitants of Arda are affected by that corruption. As Finrod asserts in his dialogue with Andreth, this holds true even for the High Elves: "their health and stature is diminished... the change of their bodies is swifter than in the beginning" (MR 309).

The subtext of an ageing world certainly enhances the medieval 'feel' of Tolkien's cosmos. In his classical study on the Latin Middle Ages, Ernst Robert Curtius has identified that subtext as "the senectus-topos" (Curtius 28), and Jacques LeGoff has connected it with "the fundamental pessimism which impregnated all medieval thinking and feeling. The world was restricted, the world was dying. *Mundus senescit*: the present age was the old age of the world" (LeGoff 166f). The medieval concept of *mundus senescit* can be found in the work of another 20th-century populariser of the Middle Ages: Umberto Eco. He however, other than Tolkien, does not at all subscribe to the pessimistic conservatism inherent to the idea of a world that grows old. In *The Name of the Rose*, that ideology is relegated to the dubious defenders of an even more dubious status quo, who predict that "tomorrow men's bodies will be smaller than ours, just as ours are smaller than those of the ancients. Mundus senescit" (Eco 36).

The medieval idea of the world growing old into senility has in most cases been steeped in Augustine's model of the six ages of the world corresponding to the six ages of individual man. But in Augustine and elsewhere, this idea was intimately bound up with the idea of reform: The world, for Augustine, was not facing its incumbent senescence but was reaching its supreme state of full maturity, "ready to welcome the return of Christ in the full splendour of its ripeness" (Eco, *Millennium* 124). In *The Name of the Rose*, that utopia of the Millennium-to-come is given voice by the chiliastic heretics, but more interestingly Eco provides us with a third meta-historical subtext that does away with the *mundus senescit* topos altogether. William of Baskerville appears to represent a genuinely modern optimism that is grounded in a faith in progress:

> "We no longer have the learning of the ancients, the age of giants is past!" — "We are dwarfs," William admitted, "but dwarfs who stand on the shoulders of those giants, and small though we are, we sometimes manage to see farther on the horizon than they."
> (85f)

Such an idea is thoroughly absent in Tolkien for whom the notion of progress is indeed anathema. Learning and knowledge can at best be preserved but never enlarged or improved. From the historical perspective of *The Lord of the Rings*, the lore of the First Age cannot be retrieved. What is worse, most of this grandeur has been forgotten. The archives of Minas Tirith hold "many records that few now can read, even the lore-masters, for their script and tongue have become dark to later men" (LotR I 246) — and 'later men' are by implication lesser men. In fact, all references to the past of Middle-earth are framed with the proviso that they are fragmentary. When Aragorn tells the tale of Lúthien Tinúviel to the hobbits, he starts with the disclaimer that "there are none now, except Elrond that remember it aright as it was told of old" (LotR I 187). This, then, is not only an age of decrepitude but one that has lost its 'organic' tradition, an age without self-knowledge of its own history. This notion points to the discursive arsenal from which Tolkien derives his specific structure of feeling.

In the following, I will argue that much of this pessimistic sentiment is indebted to a specifically late-Victorian approach to the past (not least the Middle Ages). And yet it would be too simple to read Tolkien as a virtual Victorian *only*: As I will suggest in the concluding section of this paper, to read Tolkien's medievalism as a conservative critique of his own time aligns the Oxford inkling, somewhat unexpectedly and no doubt unwittingly, with that literary and artistic movement that he emphatically rejected and detested: modernism.

Tolkien, the Victorian?

Andrew Lynch suggests that one should read *The Lord of the Rings* not simply as a recourse to medieval sources but more precisely as a continuation of a "Victorian medievalist poetics" (Lynch 78), that is, a perspective on the Middle Ages filtered by the conventions of mid-and late-19th-century writers. On that reading, Tolkien's nostalgia is not only for the Middle Ages themselves, but for their mediation through the lens of 19th century sensibilities. Tolkien, according to Lynch, "mourns the sudden modern loss of a sense of continuity with that past. In seeking to reconnect the present to the Middle Ages, he therefore binds himself to intervening ages as well, when it was better remembered" (82). And one of those 'intervening ages' is no doubt the Victorian Age. Accordingly, Tolkien's *legendarium* is to an important degree informed by Victorian conventions of conceiving of the Middle Ages as a happier and more 'authentic' world, "a forlorn golden age" (Biemer 66). In comparison with this lost past, the present appears as decadent as the Third Age appears to its contemporaries. However, while it is true that eminent Victorians like Tennyson, Ruskin or Morris nostalgically turn to the Middle Ages, it is also true that their medievalism is inextricably linked to "their disparate hopes for the future" (Spear 176) consonant with the dominant Victorian faith in steady historical progress. Neither the Pre-Raphaelites nor the Arts and Craft designers, neither Tennyson nor Matthew Arnold actually believed that medieval civilisation were *superior* to modernity. Thus John Ruskin contrasts the "gorgeousness of the middle ages" with the "lowliness" of the present only to reject the former, "which supported itself by violence and robbery", in the name of the latter:

> For us there can be no more the throne of marble… but for us there is the loftier and lovelier privilege of bringing the power and charm of art within the reach of the humble and the poor; and as the magnificence of past ages failed by its narrowness and its pride, ours may prevail and continue, by its universality and lowliness. (Ruskin 157)

The dominant Victorian idea of progress modifies the medieval *senescit* topos and instead enlists the Middle Ages in various projects of improvement: pedagogic in Arnold, liberal in Ruskin, revolutionary in Morris. If these are the giants' shoulders that Tolkien stands on, then he obviously differs from his precursors in one crucial respect: For him, progress is definitely dead. Unlike the Victorians he does not believe in the perfectibility of human society. No claim to present superiority hampers or impedes his nostalgia for the dim and distant past, his "contemplation not of the passing but the past*ness* of beauty and greatness" (Holmes 47). No doubt that has everything to do with the catastrophic experience of the Great War, after which all civilisational optimism is wholly discredited. Tolkien's exposure to the industrialised mass slaughter of WW1 instils in him a life-long horror not only of high-tech warfare (as opposed to chivalric combat) but of "the rawness and ugliness of modern European life" as such (TL 64). Instead of the mainstream of 19th-century thinkers and writers with their ineluctable faith in progress, it is therefore a more pessimistic, escapist and obscure Victorianism that Tolkien adopts: the tradition of late-Victorian romance in whose nostalgic narratives the *senescit* topos hibernates in the age of progress.

In Tolkien, the *senescit* topos is spatially embodied in the abandoned country or city. The probably earliest of all those desolate locations is a town named Kôr, that city that in the later versions of *The Silmarillion* is called Tirion, the Elvish city on the mainland of Valinor. Kôr is mentioned in the 1917 drafts of *The Book of Lost Tales* — notably in the frame narrative about Eriol and his hosts, Lindo and Vaire, who tell him stories about 'Elfinesse'. In those stories, the "time when the Eldar dwelt in Kôr" (LT 1 18) appears as the blissful period before what later became the rebellion of the Noldor. In those earliest sketches, Kôr seems to have been completely abandoned by the 'fairies' and thus becomes a "city lost and dead". Already in 1915, Tolkien had written a sonnet titled 'Kôr'.

> A sable hill, gigantic, rampart-crowned
> Stands gazing out across an azure sea
> Under an azure sky, on whose dark ground
> Impearled as 'gainst a floor of porphyry
> Gleam marble temples white, and dazzling halls;
> And tawny shadows fingered long are made
> In fretted bars upon their ivory walls
> By massy trees rock-rooted in the shade
> Like stony chiselled pillars of the vault
> With shaft and capital of black basalt.
> There slow forgotten days forever reap
> The silent shadows counting out rich hours;
> And no voice stirs; and all the marble towers
> White, hot and soundless, ever burn and sleep.
>
> (LT 1 136)

Reminiscent of Shelley's Ozymandias sonnet, Tolkien's Kôr poem offers not much more than just another variation on the motif of *vanitas* and the passing of empire. Interestingly, however, the sonnet harks back to another pretext too:

> Mysterious Kôr, thy walls forsaken stand
> Thy lonely towers beneath the lonely moon.

Those lines could easily be part of Tolkien's own poem; they are, however, taken from Andrew Lang's 1888 sonnet *She*, dedicated to Henry Rider Haggard, the author of the imperial romance of the same title. In Haggard's *She*, Kôr is an ancient necropolis whose colossal ruins stand as evidence of an extinct 'high' civilisation that had built the city in the as yet unexplored heart of sub-Saharan Africa; at the time of the story, Kôr is the seat of an undying queen, Ayesha, who is exempt from the rule of time and reigns over a debased population of barbarians that conform with the racist stereotypes of Haggard and his late-Victorian British peers. Ayesha is in fact what Galadriel would have become had she accepted the ring from Frodo: a terrible and unbearably beautiful queen "dreadful as the storm and the lightning, stronger than the foundations of the earth" (LotR I 356); a queen whose power is embodied "in a visible majesty, in an imperial grace, in a godlike stamp of softened power" that is "like the lightning: it is lovely but it destroys" (Haggard 160). Like Galadriel, Ayesha lifts information from "a font-like vessel" whose clear water shows scenes from the past or the future (Haggard 155).

More parallels have been identified and enumerated by Tolkien scholars (see Rateliff 6-8; Burns 116-127), so that it appears legitimate to link Tolkien's choice of the name 'Kôr' to some affinity with Haggard's *She*. Those affinities surely exceed those similarities between Haggard's and Tolkien's fictional characters that both Rateliff and Burns make out by way of some archetypal criticism; beyond this level of analysis it seems more rewarding to pursue how the ideological subtexts converge that underpin the works of these two writers. The bottom line of Haggard's yarn is conveniently explicated by Andrew Lang's poem:

> The world is disenchanted, over soon
> Shall Europe send her spies through all the land.

The transformation that 'Europe' imposes on the world is here certainly modernization; but this modernisation leads somewhat paradoxically into sterility, monoculture, and ultimately senescence. This is how Victorians appropriate and modify the topos of *mundus senescit*. Before Max Weber ennobled the phrase of the disenchanted world as a key term of the sociology of modernity, Lang's poem interprets Haggard's imperial romance as a romance of rationalisation whose actors are caught up in an inextricable dilemma: in a world starkly divided into zones of order and disorder, they engage in missions and projects of exploration, charting and mapping, conquest, conversion, and modernisation. They transform disorder into order but without unordered space, it is impossible to stage the wanderings and disorientations, the quests and conquests and conversions, the ordeals and sacrifices and triumphs that are the very stuff of romance, and that meet the deep desires of a readership who are condemned to an existence of bureaucratised routine. Therefore, observes John McClure:

> the ultimate enemies of romance are not the foreign foes confronted on the field of battle in the text itself, but the foes held at bay by these essential antagonists: the banal and quotidian world of calculation from which the heroes of romance are constantly in flight, and the globally routinised world that became only imaginable about one hundred years ago, a world utterly devoid of romantic regions. (McClure 3)

While McClure's diagnosis refers to Haggard, Kipling, Conan Doyle and all those other adventure story writers who, in the late 19th century, attempted to forestall the disenchantment of the world, it could just as well be applied to Tolkien — but with a difference. Clearly the Fourth Age ushers in a world in which men are left alone with no Elves, no dragons, and probably no hobbits either in the long run. As newly installed king, Aragorn will be the driving force of a 'global' modernisation that is at the same time the restoration of bygone Númenórian rule. Gandalf reassures Barliman Butterbur in one of the last chapters of *The Lord of the Rings* that "there will be comings and goings, and the evil things will be driven out of the waste-lands. Indeed, the waste in time will be waste no longer, and there will be people and fields where once there was wilderness" (LotR III 971). This is a modernist dream of imposing order on disorder: Over soon shall Gondor send her spies through all the land and create a wholly disenchanted world — certainly a safer, more peaceful and transparent world that will be knowable throughout. What *The Lord of the Rings* inherits from the imperial romance of the 19th century, then, is this ambivalence about a global modernisation that creates "a world in which there would no longer be any place for monstrosity" (Richards 45) but no place for the marvellous either.

Stemming the Tide of Time

For also the three rings of the Elves have lost their power with the destruction of the One Ring, "for the Firstborn the world grew old and grey" (S 367). The project of Sauron's enemies is therefore a losing battle anyhow: if the quest fails, Sauron's dominion will turn into a global tyranny; if it succeeds, then the "tides of Time" (LotR I 356) will "sweep away" the last remains of "Elvendom of earth" (LotR I 343) and pave the way for an utterly prosaic world ruled by Men alone. What Galadriel calls "the long defeat" is in fact the formula for an essentially pessimistic meta-historical subtext:

> If you [Frodo] fail, then we are laid bare to the Enemy. Yet if you succeed, then our power is diminished, and Lothlórien will fade, and the tide of Time will sweep it away. We must depart into the West, or dwindle to a rustic folk of dell and cave, slowly to forget and to be forgotten. (LotR I 356)

The ideological ramifications of this scenario are obviously very close to the dilemmas of imperial romance: if Tolkien's Fourth Age will be a world without monstrosity, a world fully subsumed under the sway of reason and progress, it will also be a world without pockets of wonder. Therefore it is important to consider what exactly, in this passage, will 'fade' and be 'swept away' by the 'tide of Time'. In other words, what is specific to Lothlórien? Obviously, it is a country temporarily exempt from temporality; to enter it involves a degree of time travel:

> It seemed to him [Frodo] that he had stepped through a high window that looked on a vanished world... Frodo felt that he was in a timeless land that did not fade or change or fall into forgetfulness. When he had gone and passed again into the outer world, still Frodo the wanderer from the Shire would walk there, upon the grass among *elanor* and *niphredil* in fair Lothlórien.
> (LotR I 341; 342)

As so often, it is Sam's job to bring the matter home in a less superior tone: "I feel as if I was *inside* a song, if you take my meaning" (ibid.). And more to the point: "It's wonderfully quite here. Nothing seems to be going on, and nobody seems to want it to" (351).

In Lórien, then, time is suspended. Modelled on the great Elven kingdoms of the First Age (Doriath, Nargothrond, Gondolin), and not least Valinor itself, it is a hidden realm shut off from the disenchanted outer world where time goes on according to the clock. But if being in Lórien equates being *inside* a song (and 'songs' in Tolkien seem to be by definition narrative in nature), then what kind of song would that be if Lórien were actually as static and eventless as it appears to Sam? This question applies to the vast cosmological canvas of Tolkien's world as a whole, since Eä is created by and through song, through the symphonic music of the Ainur. That music, however, gets stirred into dramatic conflict only thanks to Melkor. What soon gets named 'evil' is in fact the necessary prerequisite for things to happen at all, an indispensable ingredient of creation, a "part of the whole and tributary to its glory" (S 18). Melkor brings discord and conflict, in other words, the stuff of drama and narrative. Over-determined by the scheme of Ilúvatar, this innovation turns into a *bonus* through *malum* device: "he that attempteth to alter the music in my despite shall prove but mine instrument in the devising of things more wonderful, which he himself hath not imagined" (S 17f). This line of thought gets reiterated time and again in *The Silmarillion* and *The Lord of the Rings*. When the Valar receive the report of the flight of the Noldor, Manwë confirms Fëanor's defiant assertion "that at the least the Noldor should do deeds to live in song forever":

> So shall it be! Dear-bought those songs shall be accounted, and yet shall be well-bought... Thus even as Eru spoke to us shall beauty not before conceived be brought into Eä, and evil yet be good to have been. (S 115)

There is, therefore, a peculiar circularity: The original, foundational song of creation has to be disturbed so that 'great deeds' may materialise from the discord; these 'great deeds' will post fact be transformed back into song where alone they 'live for ever'. Song comes after the deed is done. Therefore, if walking in Lórien is like being *inside* a song, this is then not only a stepping back into some nook of the Elder Days but also a prolepsis into the future state *that comes after*. This is 'song' but it is also, strange to think given the green and pleasant nature of Lórien, death.

The dilemma that Galadriel captures in the phrase of the 'long defeat' is therefore also a dilemma of narrative itself: in order to stir up a static condition into narrative-ability, some disturbance of an original equilibrium has to occur. Where indeed nothing happens, nothing can be told. But the desire for the restoration of that static equilibrium is, as far as narrative is concerned, the very driving force that turns the process of reading into an "active quest... for those shaping ends that, terminating the dynamic process of reading, promise to bestow meaning and significance on the beginning and the middle" (Brooks 19). Already Walter Benjamin had suggested that, for the storyteller, the ideal point of closure is death itself: the death of the hero whose fictional life therewith gets fully rounded, and which provides "the sanction of everything that the storyteller can tell" (Benjamin 94). For Freudians, narrative is a symbolic discharge of the death drive, the urge in the organism to return to the inanimate. Freud calls the death drive the most conservative instinct built into all life forms: a drive to return to "an *old* state of things, an initial state from which the organism at one time or other departed and to which it is striving to return by the circuitous paths along which its development leads" (Freud 310).

When Freud writes that in 1920, he also responds, however differently from Tolkien, to the shock of the Great War. As a consequence of this shock he revises his prior privileging of the *eros* in favour of the more destructive force of the *thanatos* and proposes a general theoretical model — virtually a universal natural law — according to which "the aim of all life is death" (Freud 311), and the biographical 'progress' of the individual organism in fact only a constant regression back to the point before the beginning: a new, high modernist and scientific recurrence of *mundus senescit*.

Haggard's heroine, Ayesha, finally undergoes this process in a fast-forward mode: within the span of a few moments, "this loveliest, noblest, most splendid woman that the world has ever seen" (Haggard 293) reverts to a "mummy" and a "baboon" and dies as a "hideous little monkey, covered with crinkled yellow parchment" (*ibid.*). What *She* so spectacularly stages is the late Victorian nightmare of Darwinian evolution in reverse, the anxiety of 'reversal to type'. Freud's contribution to this discourse is its universalisation in the death drive that narratologists have applied to the problem of plot resolution and narrative closure. Lórien, however, is not the end point of *The Lord of the Rings*, nor does Galadriel shrivel up like Ayesha. It is true that Galadriel goes 'home' to Tirion at the end of the book — Tirion that was initially called Kôr. It is also true that the fact remains that Lórien is a timeless land. This timelessness, however, is not the Freudian 'inanimate'. Indeed it forms a fully rejuvenating counterpoint to the pervasive sense of *mundus senescit*:

> A light was upon it [Lórien] for which his [Frodo's] language had no name. All that he saw was shapely but the shapes seemed at once clear cut as if they had been first conceived and drawn at the uncovering of his eyes and ancient as if they had endured for ever. He saw no colour but those he knew, gold and white and

blue and green, but they were fresh and poignant, as if he had at that moment first perceived them and made for them names new and wonderful. (LotR I 341)

Tolkien, the Modernist?

Certainly both regression and reversal are prevalent in this passage, not however as reversal to type nor as regression to the inorganic. Tolkien shifts into the reverse gear in order to depart from the alienation of the 'robot age' and to arrive at the recovery of newness. In his lecture *On Fairy-Stories* (1938/1947), he recommends the "re-gaining of a clear view", "so that the things seen clearly may be freed from the drab blur of triteness and familiarity — from possessiveness" (TL 58). This aesthetic imperative is enacted to the letter in Frodo's intense sensation when laying his hand upon a tree in Lórien: "never before had he been so suddenly and so keenly aware of the feel and texture of a tree's skin and the life within it. He felt a delight in wood and the touch of it, neither as forester nor as carpenter; it was the delight of the living tree itself" (LotR I, 342). The necessary de-familiarisation of the everyday in order to re-encounter the quotidian in a 'keen' and non-possessive way involves, however, a certain risk, a letting go of control in the abandonment of the self to the event of the encounter: "We should look at green again and be startled anew (but not blinded) by yellow, blue and red" (TL 57).

With that alertness to the 'startling' intensity of the apparently familiar, Tolkien steps out of the Victorian camp altogether and forms an unforeseen alliance with early 20th-century high modernism which, despite its aggressive imperative to 'make it new', articulates an essentially conservative dissent against modern life as such and 'mass culture' in particular: "Modern art... drew its power and its possibilities from being a backwater and an archaic holdover within a modernizing economy: it glorified, celebrated, and dramatized older forms of individual production" by proclaiming "the aesthetic as sheer autonomy, as handicraft transfigured" (Jameson 307). One central point of that revolt against modern reification is the cult of the epiphanic revelation of the thing-ness of things. Virginia Woolf and the early James Joyce come most readily to mind here: the former for her meticulous recuperations of luminous 'moments of beings', the latter for his systematic poetics of a revelatory significance inherent in trivial things or occurrences.

Like the bark of a tree, even a butcher's basket can occasion an epiphany according to Joyce's protagonist and alter ego, Stephen Dedalus. In his sketch of an aesthetic theory, Stephen interestingly takes recourse to a medieval authority: "Aquinas says: *ad pulcritudinem tria requiruntur, integritas, consonantia, claritas*. I translate it so: *Three things are needed for beauty, wholeness, harmony and radiance*" (Joyce 216). Wholeness and harmony, the first two of the three terms, are adopted more or less wholesale from Aquinas: *Integritas* denotes the demarcation of the object "as self-bounded and self-contained upon the immeasurable background of space or time which is not it" (ibid.), whereas *consonantia* signifies the apprehension "that it is a *thing...*, the result of its part and their sum, harmonious" (Joyce 217). The third entry in the Aquinian catalogue, however, undergoes some modification as Stephen replaces *claritas* ('radiance') by *quidditas* ('what-ness'). This move ensures a strictly anti-metaphysical thrust: Stephen's theory thus discards of all Platonic residues that would assume that "the supreme quality of beauty [is] a light from some other world, the idea of which the matter is but the shadow" (ibid.). Against this obsolete idealism, Joyce's Stephen posits the sheer immanence and contingency of the object in the actuality and absolute singularity of its presence as 'what-ness':

> When you have apprehended the basket as one thing ['wholeness'] and have then analysed it according to its form and apprehended it as a thing [harmony] you make the only synthesis which is logically and aesthetically permissible. You see that it is that thing which it is and no other thing. (ibid.)

In its immanent singularity, the object is released not only from any burden of significance but also from all possible utilitarian purposes: The basket is now no longer perceived as a container or even as a solid peace of craftsmanship but only 'as itself' in its wholeness, harmony and what-ness. Joyce's poetics of the experience of thing-ness as such is surprisingly germane to Tolkien's programme of 'freeing things' from 'possessiveness' as well as to Frodo's rapture with the 'texture and feel' of the Mallorn bark and the non-possessive delight he takes in the tree's 'what-ness', a delight not to be confused with that of the forester or the carpenter. Joyce calls this sensation of pure delight "the luminous silent stasis of aesthetic pleasure", and more poignantly, "the enchantment of the heart" (ibid.). In Tolkien's universe, such immanent enchantment seems to be the prerogative of the Elves, whose way of engaging with the material world is based on the recognition of the immediate presence of things. Men, by contrast, are burdened with metaphysics and hence "look at no thing for itself; ...if they study it, it is to discover something else" (MR 316). That, at least, is Finrod's interpretation of the human condition in his dialogue with Andreth. The early Joyce, on my reading, offers a modernist antidote to that condition: Going back to the Middle Ages, purged of its theological ballast, he projects an immanent re-enchantment derived from 'looking at the thing for itself'.

Virginia Woolf, from her early narrative sketches onward, is engaged in a similar endeavour. In her autobiographical *Sketch of the Past* (1939), roughly contemporary with the first version of Tolkien's *On Fairy-Stories*, Woolf recollects a series of childhood experiences whose overwhelming "ecstasies and raptures" (Woolf, *Sketch* 77) are apparently incongruous with the trifling incidents that caused them. For what Woolf remembers is indeed as simple and inconspicuous as Frodo's touching of a 'tree's skin': the smells and sounds of an apple orchard in summer, the play of sunrays filtered through a nursery blind, the integrity (in Joyce's terms: the wholeness) of a plant in the midst of a flower bed:

> I was looking at the flower bed by the front door. 'That is the whole', I said. I was looking at a plant with a spread of leaves; and it seemed suddenly plain that the flower itself was a part of the earth; that a ring enclosed what was the flower; and that was the real flower; part earth; part flower.　　(Woolf, *Sketch* 80)

In Woolf's account, this apparently simple observation is experienced and remembered as a 'moment of being' because it holds a flash-like insight into the object's real presence (Joyce's what-ness), hence "the revelation of some order... of some real thing" (Woolf, *Sketch* 81). Many of Woolf's narrative texts close with such revelatory moments, such as Lily Briscoe's "vision" in *To the Lighthouse*, or Peter Walsh's sudden apprehension of the actuality of Clarissa's presence at the end of *Mrs Dalloway*.

For Woolf, too, such immediate encounters with the reality of the object world are linked with a peculiar medievalism. Less philosophically inclined than Joyce (and certainly less expert than Tolkien), Woolf constructs 'her' Middle Ages around the idea of an entirely strange life-world. Like Tolkien, Woolf has not only inherited and imbibed much of the idealising medievalism of the Victorians, but also pairs this sanitised image with an acute sense of irretrievable loss: "Nothing happens to us as it did to our [medieval] ancestors; events are seldom important; if we recount them, we do not really believe in them" (Woolf, *Sketch* 59). While contemporary authors have to inhabit a fragmented and damaged world, the medieval writer has a decisive "advantage over the moderns which will never come the way of English poets again. England was still an unspoilt country. His eyes rested on a virgin land, all unbroken grass and wood...; no factory chimneys smoked on the hill-side" (Woolf, *Pastons* 12). By grounding the life-world of the Middle Ages in the definitely unavailable and irreparable environment of an 'unspoilt' England, Woolf constructs a scenario of unbridgeable experiential difference between the medieval and the modern. Unlike the Victorians, she thus envisages a Middle Ages that are in fact an utterly foreign country where people do things very differently. The most significant of these differences is the immediate relation that medieval writers like Chaucer had with an overwhelmingly powerful and decidedly non-idyllic "Nature [that] was herself; sometimes, therefore, disagreeable enough and plain, but always in Chaucer's pages with the hardness and the freshness of an actual presence" (Woolf, *Pastons* 13). For the moderns, by contrast, the world is never a presence in itself but a system of references and correspondences where people, to paraphrase Finrod again, 'look at no thing for itself; ...if they study it, it is to discover something else' (MR 316). Beyond such alienation, the Elvish way of engaging with the material world would be virtually 'medieval' (in Woolf's sense) inasmuch as it is based on the recognition of the immediate presence of the thing.

For the moderns according to Woolf, this medieval (Elvish) experience of the 'hardness and the freshness of an actual presence' of the object world has become the exception and is relegated to those rarer-than-diamonds revelations of the 'moments of being'. Those moments, then, can be perceived as instants that interrupt the continuity of regulated modern life and instantiate an altogether different present that does not pass and thus "challenges the progressive sense of time" (Cutler 86). For "things hat we have felt with great intensity have an existence independent of our minds; are in fact still in existence" (Woolf, *Sketch* 75). Therefore the early memory of a walk to St Ives beach on a hot summer's day "still makes me feel warm...", and "I can reach a state where I seem to be watching [past] things happen as if I were there" (ibid.). To the extent that remembering the past gets temporarily superseded by getting transported back into the past ("At time I can go back to St Ives... completely", ibid.), Woolf's memorable 'moments of being' fall into place with Frodo's anticipation that even "[w]hen he had gone and passed again into the outer world, still Frodo the wanderer from the Shire would walk there, upon the grass among *elanor* and *niphredil* in fair Lothlórien" (LotR I 342).

Such affinities notwithstanding, it would be misjudged to enlist Tolkien fully with the modernists, from whose perspective his style would have appeared as an exhausted idiom handed down from the Victorian age, hopelessly "weighed down and flattened out" by "the techniques of realism" (Brooke-Rose 254). Where modernism claims to immediately *present* the 'hardness and presence of the world' through formal experiments in the "direct treatment of the 'thing'" (Pound 3) in its de-contextualised singularity, Tolkien's tales *represent* in a steady flow of narrative a world that, although wholly imaginary, gains its extraordinary solidity precisely through the "coherence effect" (Pavel 116) that conventional realism creates.

Bibliography

Benjamin, Walter. "The Storyteller: Reflections on the Works of Nikolai Leskov". *Illuminations: Essays and Reflections*. Intro. Hannah Arendt. Transl. Harry Zohn. New York: Schocken, 1968, 83-109

Biemer, Marie-Noëlle. "Disenchanted with their Age: Keats's, Morris's, and Tolkien's Great Escape". *Hither Shore* 7 (2010): 60-75

Brooke-Rose, Christine. *A Rhetoric of the Unreal: Studies in Narrative and Structure, especially of the Fantastic*. Cambridge: Cambridge University Press, 1981

Brooks, Peter. *Reading for the Plot: Design and Intention in Narrative*. Cambridge MA/London: Harvard University Press, 1984

Burns, Marjorie. *Perilous Realms: Celtic and Norse in Tolkien's Middle-earth*. Toronto: University of Toronto Press, 2005

Curtius, Ernst Robert. *European Literature and the Latin Middle Ages*. Transl. Willard R. Trask. New York, 1953

Cutler, Edward S. *Recovering the New: Transatlantic Roots of Modernism*. Hanover/London: University Press of New England, 2003

Eco, Umberto. *The Name of the Rose*. Transl. William Weaver. London: Vintage, 1998

---. "Waiting for the Millennium". *The Apocalyptic Year 1000: Religious Expectation and Social Change, 950-1050*. Eds. Richard Landes et al. Oxford: Oxford University Press, 2003, 121-135

Freud, Sigmund. "Beyond the Pleasure Principle". *On Metapsychology: The Theory of Psychoanalysis*. Ed. Angela Richards. Harmondsworth: Penguin, 1984, 275-338

Haggard, H. Rider. *She*. Harmondsworth: Penguin, 1998

Holmes, John R. "Tolkien, *Dustsceawung*, and the Gnomic Tense: Is Timelessness Medieval or Victorian?" *Tolkien's Modern Middle Ages*. Eds. Jane Chance & Alfred K. Siewers. New York: Palgrave, 2005, 43-58

Jameson, Fredric. *Postmodernism, or The Cultural Logic of Late Capitalism*. London: Verso, 1991

Joyce, James. *A Portrait of the Artist as a Young Man*. London: Paladin, 1988

LeGoff, Jacques. *Medieval Civilization, 400-1500*. Oxford: Blackwell, 1990

Lynch, Andrew. "Archaism, Nostalgia, and Tennysonian War". *Tolkien's Modern Middle Ages*. Eds. Jane Chance & Alfred K. Siewers. New York: Palgrave, 2005, 77-92

McClure, John. *Late Imperial Romance*. London: Verso, 1991

Pavel, Thomas G. *The Spell of Language: Poststructuralism and Speculation*. Chicago: University of Chicago Press, 2001

Pound, Ezra. "A Retrospect". *Literary Essays of Ezra Pound*. Ed. T.S. Eliot. New York: New Directions, 2009, 3-14

Rateliff, John. "*She* and Tolkien". *Mythlore* 8.28 (1981): 6-8

Richards, Thomas. *The Imperial Archive: Knowledge and the Fantasy of Empire*. London: Verso, 1993

Ruskin, John. *The Two Paths*. Ed. John Bryson. London: Dent, 1970

Shippey, Tom. *The Road to Middle-earth: How J.R.R. Tolkien Created a New Mythology.* Boston: Houghton Mifflin, 2003

Spear, Jeffry. "Political Questing: Ruskin, Morris and Romance". *New Approaches to Ruskin.* Ed. Robert Hewison. London: Routledge 1981, 174-193

Tolkien, J.R.R. *The Lord of the Rings.* London: HarperCollins, 1995

---. *Tree and Leaf.* London: HarperCollins, 2001

---. *The Silmarillion.* Ed. Christopher Tolkien. London: Allan & Unwin, 1983

---. *The Book of Lost Tales: Part 1.* Ed. Christopher Tolkien. London: HarperCollins, 1994

---. *Morgoth's Ring: The History of Middle-Earth 10.* Ed. Christopher Tolkien. London: HarperCollins, 2002

Woolf, Virginia. "The Pastons and Chaucer". *The Common Reader: First Series.* Orlando: Harcourt, 1984, 3-22

---. "A Sketch of the Past". *Moments of Being.* Ed. Jeanne Schulkind. London: Grafton, 1989

Modern Tales in a Medieval Tradition: Formation of Meaning and Narrative Strategies in Tolkien's *The Children of Húrin*

Silke Winst (Potsdam)

Gorthol, 'Dread Helm': this is what Túrin calls himself. In battle he wears the dragon helm, the Helm of Hador, as his ancestors did before him. What is more, Túrin kills the dragon Glaurung by thrusting his sword into its belly when the dragon is about to cross the ravine in which Túrin is waiting. This reminiscence of medieval literature could hardly be more marked: the dragon slayer Sigurd is also associated with a dread helm; furthermore, there are parallels to the killings of the dragons by both Sigurd and Beowulf. In terms of medieval genre specifics, *The Children of Húrin* is thus unequivocally placed into the narrative tradition of the heroic epic. Tolkien has emphasised the importance of the act of dragon slaying for heroic identity: "[T]he prince of the heroes of the North, supremely memorable... was a dragon-slayer" (BMC 16). Tolkien classifies the killing of the dragon "as the chief deed of the greatest of heroes" (BMC 16). In addition to that, dragon slaying is "an enhancement" of the "universal significance which is given to the fortunes of [the heroic-elegiac poem's] hero" (BMC 31). That the protagonist in *The Children of Húrin* appropriates this central, identity-enhancing pattern of behaviour from medieval literature corresponds to the significance Tolkien attributes to that text with regard to the historical mythology of Middle-earth. He considered *The Children of Húrin* — as Christopher Tolkien states — not only as "integral to the history of Elves and Men in the Elder Days" (CH 12) but also as "the dominant story of the end of the Elder days" (CH 281).

The text exists in different versions. The fragmentary *Lay of the Children of Húrin* is composed in alliterative verse in two extant manuscripts. The other texts are written in prose, such as *Turambar and the Foalókë* in *The Lost Tales*. *Simarillion* and *Unfinished Tales* contain additional prose redactions of varying length (*Of Túrin Turambar* and *Narn i Hîn Húrin*). After reviewing and re-estimating the material, Christopher Tolkien has recently put forward a new edition presenting the text in a new form with a complete plot and a partly revised narrative structure.[1]

In the following, I mostly refer to this new edition. The alliterative version places itself directly — i.e. metrically — in a medieval (principally Old English) narrative tradition. However, the textual constellation of the story *The Children*

---

1   On the procedure of Christopher Tolkien cf. CT 283-292. Cf. also Fornet-Ponse.

of Húrin — i.e. its existing in several manuscripts versions and in differing redactions — evokes yet another analogy to medieval literature. Diverse modes of existence and plural versions of stories are according to Joachim Bumke "geradezu ein Kennzeichen mittelalterlicher, vor allem volkssprachlicher Textüberlieferung" (Bumke 123).

Nonetheless, Tolkien's texts are no medieval texts. But his knowledge of premodern literature pervades all the tales he tells. Medieval motifs and narrative patterns are taken up, revised, and transformed.[2] In addition, the narrative universe charted by Tolkien — of which *The Children of Húrin* is only a part — is structured by pre-modern orders of knowledge.[3] Medieval models of thinking and patterns of behaviour form the base of the protagonists' identities and actions. Those include the importance of social orders like kinship, lordship and warrior friendship to the formation of identity. Túrin also is bound to those orders. But whereas in the medieval heroic epic the depiction of love between genders is mostly absent, Tolkien introduces it with the topic of incest.

In the following, I show how the social orders of knowledge in *The Children of Húrin* correspond to medieval systems of meaning, but also how modern strategies of narration are used to change pre-modern concepts. Exemplarily, I examine the warrior friendship between Túrin and Beleg and the brother-sister-incest between Túrin and Niënor. Although the different versions of the texts vary with regard to number and scope of the various narrative elements, both the friendship and the incestuous love are found in all complete redactions, even if the depictions may differ considerably. In the fragmentary *Lay,* the relation between genders is missing, probably because the manuscripts were abandoned before the narration reached the point where it begins. This highlights the significance of both bonds in all texts constituting the corpus of *The Children of Húrin*. I compare both episodes with passages from medieval literature to highlight the differences between medieval and modern imagination.

Both relationships ultimately fail, thus making palpable the conception of doom Tolkien employs in *The Children of Húrin*. Morgoth's curse weighing down on Húrin and his descendants, and Túrin's actions which let the threatening disaster become reality are tightly interwoven and explore the connection between predetermined fate and autonomous actions. Thus, the conception of doom also partakes in both medieval and modern ideas. It will be examined conclusively with regard to the conception of the hero and the relations between Middle Ages and modernity in Tolkien's text.

---

2   Cf. for instance Honegger.
3   On medieval orders of knowledge see Friedrich.

Social Orders between the Middle Ages and Modernity

Killing the Friend: Warrior Friendship between Túrin and Beleg

Friendship — predominantly between noble lords — constitutes a central mode of medieval socialisation.[4] That bond based on free will, loyalty and mutual support is described in many pre-modern texts as ideal and powerful. Friendships gain significance both on a personal and a political level. They do not only establish personal identity, but they can also secure acquisition and increase of power (e.g. by military support of the friend). Friendship is often linked to expressive emotionality which makes the bond visible to the outside world. Tolkien takes up that central medieval relationship in his texts.

In *The Children of Húrin*, Túrin's friendship with Beleg constitutes the central tie compensating for Túrin's social isolation. He is forced to leave his family and hereditary territory Dor-lómin early in his life, and although Túrin subsequently lives in several communities, he always remains an outsider. With Beleg, however, he has found a companion to whom he is bound "in love" (CH 112). At the peak of their friendship, Túrin and Beleg are "the Two Captains" (CH 144) of a warrior band dominating a whole region. Túrin calls the area Dor-Cúarthol, "the land of Bow and Helm" (CH 141; cf. 146). The helm refers to Túrin himself, the bow to the Elf Beleg who is called Cúthalion, 'Longbow', because of his favourite weapon. Túrin's "heart was high" (CH 146), it is told, Beleg, however, has dark forebodings: "But to Beleg it seemed now that the Helm had wrought otherwise with Túrin than he had hoped; and looking into the days to come he was troubled in mind" (CH 146). And indeed, the warriors are soon betrayed: many are killed by Morgoth's troops and Túrin is captured by orcs. When Beleg finds his unconscious friend and cuts his bonds, Beleg's sword pierces Túrin's foot. Túrin awakens and kills his friend with the sword that pierced him, mistaking Beleg for one of his enemies. When Túrin realises whom he has killed, he is unable to move or speak. He stands "stonestill and silent" (CH 155), "unmoving and unweeping" (CH 155), even "crazed and unwitting" (CH 156) he sits beside his dead companion.

The military success of the *Two Captains* refers to a political dimension of friendship: lordship is gained and secured by it. After Beleg's death, however, the friendship is transferred onto a solely personal level: Túrin's sanity is defined by his (non-)ability to mourn. Only drinking from the water of Ivrin's lake

---

4   On medieval warrior friendship, especially on that of Amicus and Amelius (one of the favourite pairs of companions in the Middle Ages), see Winst.

enables him to outwardly show his pain: "his tears were unloosed at last, and he was healed of his madness. There he made a song for Beleg, and he named it *Laer Cú Beleg*, the Song of the Great Bow, singing it aloud and heedless of peril" (CH 157). Only now Túrin is able to continue living and communicate, his grief, however, "was graven on the face of Túrin and never faded" (CH 156).[5] The *Lay* contains an additional element: Túrin has a vision in which he strays in a sinister landscape looking for the grave of Beleg. His "longing" (LB 75, v. 1683) call is answered by the voice of his dead friend, telling him to seek no longer since he is "in the halls of the Moon o'er the hills of the sea" (LB 75, v. 1697) and comforting him. When Túrin wakes, "his wit was healed" (LB 75, v. 1699).

Thats concealment of emotions corresponds to Túrin's upbringing and disposition of character attested to him even in his childhood. Thus, Sador assesses Túrin as "a hard mind" (CH 43). Later in Doriath "he became thoughtful, and sparing in speech" (CH 81), "neither did he win friendship easily, for he was not merry, and laughed seldom" (CH 81). Such statements on personal traits are mostly lacking in medieval texts. Furthermore, medieval heroic protagonists do not commonly experience any difficulties in showing emotions.

The German prose epic *Loher und Maller*, originating from the middle of the 15th century, also tells a story in which one friend accidentally kills the other after many years of fellowship.[6] In that text, friendship also occupies a central position: it constitutes the positive counterpart to kinship bonds which are here defined by betrayal and deceit. Only friendship provides loyalty (*truwe*) and help. The circumstances of the killing of the friend differ from those in Tolkien's text, however. Here, Emperor Loher spends many years waiting in vain for his friend Maller. His pain confines him to his bed and he almost dies because of his immense suffering. Whenever Maller is mentioned, Loher falls sick anew. For that reason he decides that henceforth Maller must not be talked about. Any violation of this decree is punished with death. What Loher does not know is that — on command of a heavenly voice — Maller has become a hermit in the woods. When Maller the hermit comes to Rome, years later, Loher does not recognise him although the presumed stranger reminds him of Maller. When the stranger begs for alms for the sake of Maller, the emperor reacts violently: *da gryselt im syn blůt vnd warff mit syme messer zů ime, das es dürch syn leber in syme libe stackt* (*Loher und Maller* fol. 86r) ("then his blood was clotting and shuddering and he threw his knife that it stuck through his

---

5   In the redaction of the text in *Lost Tales* and in the *Lay*, Túrin's delayed tears flow after Flinding has told him about Beleg's rescue quest for Túrin (cf. LT2 81 and LB 74, v. 1641-45).

6   On *Loher und Maller* and the other texts belonging to this tradition, see von Bloh.

liver in his body").[7] The dying Maller reveals his identity and forgives Loher with embraces and kisses. In the following *raufft sich Loher vnd slüg sich mit füsten* (*Loher und Maller* fol. 86v) ("Loher tore [his hair] and beat himself with his fists"), finally he falls seriously ill from grief again. However, Loher has not got time to mourn because Maller's kinsmen begin feuding against him. Loher's assurances that he has killed his friend accidentally, stressing the fact that he has killed the one *denn ich sere recht liep hatte* (*Loher und Maller* fol. 86v) ("whom I have loved very much"), are to no avail. The atonement Loher offers (a naked genuflexion and a war against the 'heathens' without his returning) is refused by Maller's relatives. After that, a long war is waged by the allies of both parties. It does not end until the entirety of Maller's male relatives has fallen in battle.

The grief for the death of his friend is displayed by ritual mourning gestures on Loher's body. His pain is authenticated by the *groß kranckeit* (*Loher und Maller* fol. 86v) ("severe illness") that brings Loher to the verge of death. Sorrow is made visible with and on the body. Unlike Túrin, Loher does not provoke madness by sealing his pain inside himself. Also unlike Túrin's grief, Loher's personal suffering is overshadowed by the social and political consequences his deed entails. The more subjective sorrow seems to be at the same time immobilised and made excessive because harm is put into a broader context and war continually generates new grief. The identity-enhancing force of friendship is accentuated differently in Tolkien's text and in the late medieval epic respectively. Military success and loyal support are constituents of the friendship bond in both texts; in *Loher und Maller*, however, the social context dominates other levels of the relation after Maller's death. By contrast, in *The Children of Húrin* prevails the interest in Túrin's isolation and autism linked to his disposition of character. It is striking that in both texts the killing of the friend is situated at about the middle of the text, thus occupying the central position in the entire plot. But whereas in *Loher und Maller* the subsequent events (war) are closely tied to Maller's death, Beleg's death in Tolkien's text constitutes a disruption: the warrior band is annihilated, Túrin leaves his previous dominion.

One momentous connection between Túrin and his killed friend remains: Beleg's sword Anglachel — the weapon Túrin had used to kill Beleg — remains with Túrin.[8] Beleg had requested it from Thingol because "it was made of iron that fell from heaven as a blazing star; it would cleave all earth-dolven iron" (CH 96). Beleg wants the sword although Melian warns him: "There is malice in this sword. The heart of the smith still dwells in it, and that heart was dark. It

---

[7] Here and in the following, I cite from Ms. Hamburg, Staats- und Universitätsbibliothek, Codex 11 in scrinio (about 1456). An edition of *Loher and Maller*, based on the Hamburg manuscript, is currently prepared at the University of Potsdam.

[8] On swords in Tolkien's texts see Klinger.

will not love the hand that it serves" (CH 97). The text indicates that Anglachel itself is accountable for the circumstances of Beleg's killing: its slipping and pricking Túrin's foot and Túrin's "rage and fear" (CH 154) at his waking seem to be — at least partly — of its making. Although in a way "the dread sword" (CH 156) seems to have provoked Beleg's killing, it grieves like Túrin for the dead Elf: Gwindor interprets the condition of Anglachel ("its blade was black and dull and its edges blunt", CH 157) as a sign of mourning for Beleg. After Beleg's death, the black sword Anglachel is forged anew for Túrin in Nargothrond.[9] "Then Túrin himself became known in Nargothrond as Mormegil, the Black Sword, for the rumour of his deeds with that weapon; but he named the sword Gurthang, Iron of Death" (CH 160). Túrin's weapon as well as his name is closely tied to the sword of his friend. His new identity is thus intertwined with that of his dead companion. At the end of the story Túrin kills himself with the sword Gurthang speaking to him: "I will drink your blood, that I may forget the blood of Beleg my master" (CH 256). Here, at the close of the text, the warrior friendship and its end are evoked once again. Thus, the bleakness of Túrin's death does not only reflect the death of his friend but bitterness and misery are also enhanced by the double death. However, by shedding his own blood, Túrin is re-united with Beleg whose blood had been spilled with the same sword: a strange form of blood-brotherhood in death complements the brotherhood-in-arms in life.

The Incest between Túrin and Niënor

Kinship is the primary form of social order in a pre-modern context.[10] Identity formation of a person is determined by his or her position in a group organised by kinship structures. Both the placement in relation to living relatives — the clan — and to the diachronic entity of the dynasty constitute identity and mark claims to lordship and social status of the individual. Kinship relations in *The Children of Húrin* are aligned to that model of thinking; they are, however, utterly impaired.

In his childhood, Túrin loses his beloved younger sister Urwen, called Lalaith ('laughter'). She dies from a blight sent by Morgoth, 'the Evil Breath'. Túrin is only five years old but already he controls the open display of emotions: "But

---

9 That Anglachel becomes Gurthang is no narrative element of the earlier versions. In *Lost Tales*, for instance, there are two different swords. Túrin gets his, here called Gurtholfin, the 'Wand of Death', from Orodreth. There is, however, still a connection to Beleg's death: "he had not wielded a sword since the slaying of Beleg" (LT 2 84). The story of the reforged sword emerges only in *The Silmarillion*. See on the sword in the different versions of *The Children of Húrin* Klinger 140.

10 On kinship in medieval literature and society see e.g. Kellner.

Túrin wept bitterly at night alone" (CH 40). Soon after that he has to leave his mother and his unborn new sister. Separated from and waiting for his mother and sister, Túrin experiences deep sorrow (cf. CH 75, 78). After Beleg's death, Túrin meets Finduilas, daughter of King Orodreth of Nargothrond. Whereas her interest in Túrin arises from his outstanding warrior deeds and unparalleled valour, Túrin likes to be with her because "she reminded him of his kindred and the women of Dor-lómin in his father's house" (CH 164). He directly formulates that thought: "I would I had a sister so fair" (CH 165). Her later death — for which he partly bears the blame — leaves him so agitated that he lies down on her grave mound like dead. Finduilas' death is not only dreadful in itself. Gwindor forebodes its dire consequences to Túrin: "she alone stands between you and your doom. If you fail her, it shall not fail to find you" (CH 177).

Túrin's ambiguous feelings are made explicit when he finds a strange girl on Finduilas' grave mound a little later. Initially, Túrin — who calls himself Turambar, 'Master of Doom', by now — again seems to be the sole object of desire. Níniel, as he calls the nameless girl, feels comfortable only when he is near: "when her glance fell on Turambar a light came in her face and she put out a hand towards him, for it seemed to her that she had found at last something that she had sought in the darkness" (CH 215). Túrin does not seem to feel any actual attraction[11] and ruminates instead on the symbolism and significance of the place where he has found Níniel: "From the green mound she came. Is that a sign, and how shall I read it?" (CH 218) What nobody knows is that Níniel is his sister Nienor who is subject to a spell of oblivion placed upon her by the Dragon Glaurung. She cannot remember either her identity or her origin. Finally, Túrin and Níniel marry; Níniel becomes pregnant. After the dragon fight, the deadly wounded Glaurung enlightens Nienor on her own and her husband's identity. She kills herself by leaping from a precipice. When Túrin learns about those kinship constellations he kills himself, too.[12]

Túrin's ties to the three women are characterised by loss and failure. The death of his first sister and the absence of his nearest female relatives generate

---

11 Only after a long time he says to Níniel, "it seems to me that what I long sought in vain has come to me" (CH 218).
12 These narrative connections are not developed to the same degree in the other versions of the story. In *The Silmarillion*, for instance, Túrin's grief for the death of his first sister Lalaith is only hinted at; Finduilas is in love with Túrin but he has got no interest in her whatsoever, not even brotherly feelings. The relationship to Níniel, by contrast, is made explicit quite swiftly "His heart turned to Níniel, and he asked her in marriage" (S 265). In the *Lay*, there is no Lalaith at all, whereas the love between Finduilas (here also called Failivrin) and Túrin is not one-sided: "From woe unhealed the wounded heart / of Túrin the tall was turned to her" (LB 89, v. 2213f.). In *Lost Tales*, there is no Lalaith; Nienóri, however, is already born when Túrin is still in Dor-lómin; Túrin thinks of Failivrin first as of a sister, but after the death of her father, "[s]o deep was the ruth of Túrin's heart that in that hour he deemed he loved her very dearly" (LT 2 85). Between Failivrin and Nienóri there is no link in this redaction.

a desire for kinship in Túrin that renders a love between genders not based on kinship impossible. Only after Finduilas is dead, such a possibility becomes recognisable for Túrin. But the renewed displacement of his desire — the time from kinship relations to physical love — is directed at the 'wrong' woman. Those displacements effect a blending of desire absolutely inadmissible in Tolkien's narrative universe. Thus, desire is finally punished with the death of the individuals involved.

Incest prohibition is considered an essential rule constituting and preserving social communities. Exogamy establishes alliances between familial groups. In order to guarantee cultural order, an exchange between groups has to be assured. Specific differences concerning the status of individuals must not be mixed. Any loss of difference, for example between brother and husband, entails the breakdown of sociability and order. At the same time, the social cohesion of families in many societies is so strong that — as Claude Lévi-Strauss puts it — "not... the repugnance towards incestuous relationships, but on the contrary... the pursuit of such relationships" constitutes "a universal phenomenon" (Lévi-Strauss 17).[13] In *The Children of Húrin*, the incestuous relation originates in a force of attraction between Túrin and Niënor based on kinship and thus imagined as 'natural'.[14] After the disclosure of the protagonists' identities, Niënor calls Túrin "twice beloved" (CH 243), thus underlining the special power of their love resulting from the superposition of two concepts: kinship and love between genders.

The story of the prohibited relationship is especially marked — and attenuated — by the fact that Túrin and Niënor do not know their respective identities, thereby committing the violation of the taboo unwittingly. Nevertheless, the breaking of the incest taboo has to be answered with death in the Elder Days of Middle-earth. Medieval renderings of incest between brother and sister present the topic quite differently. Hartmann's von Aue *Gregorius*, for instance, originates from the end of the 12th century and in the first instance describes the close tie between brother and sister as exemplary: *si wâren selten eine, / si wonten zallen zîten / einander bî sîten / (daz gezam vil wol beiden), / si wâren ungescheiden / ze tische und ouch anderswâ. / ir bette stuonden alsô nâ / daz si sich mohten undersehen... er enphlæge ir alsô wol / als ein getriuwer*

---

13 This statement is made with regard to a psychoanalytic view.
14 Kinship is, of course, a social construct which is, however, imagined as a 'natural' correlation of individuals. This notion of the 'natural' operates on a different level than another concept of 'nature' found in *The Children of Húrin*: the incest prohibition is attributed to culture whereas incest is associated with nature. Before Níniel is found in the woods, she is naked and runs "as a beast that is hunted" (CH 213) The loss of her memory and, as a result, her lack of belonging to a family clan, also mark her status as one 'outside culture'. Only under these circumstances, incest becomes possible. Saeros' offending remarks about the women in Dor-lómin — although voiced at a very early stage of the story — belongs to the same sequence of implications (cf. CH 87).

bruoder sol / sîner lieben swester (Hartmann von Aue, *Gregorius*, v. 288-299). ("They were seldom alone, they stayed at all times side by side. [This was a very suitable behaviour for both of them.] At table and anywhere else they were unseparated. Their beds stood as closely to one another that they could see each other. He cared for her very much, like a loyal brother should for his beloved sister.") Finally, the close relation — almost logically — leads to a love relationship. Not only love and the sister's beauty but also devil's advice is blamed for the prohibited bodily union. Both the penance of the siblings and that of their child Gregorius (who himself commits incest with his mother) are integrated into a religious context. Despite this entanglement in sin and guilt, Gregorius pursues a successful religious way of life and finally even becomes pope. Peter Strohschneider has labelled this constellation 'incest sacredness', a sacredness emerging from the destruction of and consequent lack of belonging to cultural order (cf. Strohschneider).

In the *Völsunga saga*, Signy brings about incest with her brother Sigmund in order to produce a strong and valiant heir who alone can avenge the death of their father Völsung: *hefir hann af Þvi mikit kapp. at hann er beði sonar son ok ðottur son volsungs konungs* (*Völsunga saga* 102). ("He gets his matchless prowess from being the offspring of both son and daughter of King Völsung", *Völsunga saga* 103.) The son Sinfjotli accomplishes his task: he kills king Siggeir.[15] As in Hartmann's *Gregorius*, the evaluation of the child's abnormal status receives a positive shift. The child has singular and outstanding powers or abilities arising directly from his embodying the transgression of an absolute taboo. Such a mythical charging of incest is refused in *The Children of Húrin*. Here, incest exclusively marks the destruction not only of cultural but of any order. The individuals involved kill themselves, thus commenting on the irremediable atrociousness of the event. Any saviour's status of the unborn child is blanked out completely in favour of the pure monstrosity of the incest. Niënor shows her revulsion physically: "her whole body shook with horror and anguish" (CH 243).

One element in Tolkien's text linked to this specific constellation is the renewed separation and isolation of the lovers. Niënor assumes that the unconscious Túrin is dead when the Dragon Glaurung discloses her own and Túrin's identity. She is already dead when Túrin for his part obtains the deadly knowledge. This context renders the incestuous union an unbearable burden inevitably leading to death. Personal, subjective forlornness and the irresolvable ambivalence between love and loathing are stressed. After Niënor has plunged into the abyss, Túrin postulates his inner death: "my heart also is slain" (CH 254). When he learns the truth about the identity of his beloved, his inner self is no longer referred to. Instead, nature dying out of season because of

---

15 On further analogies between *The Children of Húrin* and *Völsunga saga* see St. Clair.

Glaurung's fire blast is moved to the centre of attention: "all the trees near and far were withered, and the sere leaves fell mournfully, as though winter had come in the first days of summer" (CH 256). Notions of 'unnaturalness', deep mourning and death are merged in this image. The doom Morgoth has put on the children of Húrin has been fulfilled.

Hero and Doom: Intertwinings of Heroism and Fatality

Doom in *The Children of Húrin* manifests in particular in the killing of the friend and incestuous love. Thus, doom suggests unavoidable grief and inescapable hopelessness. Fate (*wyrd*) also operates in medieval texts. It is described by Kevin Wanner as "a central concept in the religious and metaphysical worldview of Germanic paganism" (Wanner 5). Wanner shows that in different sections of *Beowulf*, the notion of a Christian deity dominates the concept of *wyrd* to different degrees. In other passages, *wyrd* more distinctly emerges as "a pagan conception of causality" (Wanner 5). It is said, for instance, that fate does not grant victory to the protagonist in the dragon fight (*swā him wyrd ne gescrāf / hrēð æt hilde, Beowulf* v. 2574). *Wyrd* is sometimes flanked by the idea that somebody is *fæge* — doomed to die — and that this predestination is irrevocable and cannot even be changed by *wyrd*: *Wyrd oft nereð / unfǣgne eorl, þonne his ellen dēah* (*Beowulf* v. 572). ("Fate often saves a man not doomed to death if his courage is powerful.")[16]

In *The Children of Húrin*, a concept of doom likewise linked to inevitability emerges.[17] Whereas *wyrd* in *Beowulf* is an abstract concept (nonetheless tied to concrete actions), fate in Tolkien's text is to a certain extent entirely factual: the doom lying on the children of Húrin originates in a curse the dark lord Morgoth has pronounced to Húrin:

> But upon all whom you love my thought shall weigh as a cloud of Doom, and it shall bring them down into darkness and despair. Wherever they go, evil shall arise. Whenever they speak, their words shall bring ill counsel. Whatsoever they do shall turn against them. They shall die without hope, cursing both life and death. (CH 64)

---

16 Tolkien uses the word *fey* (CH 200, 204) with regard to Túrin's mother Morwen und to Niënor.
17 Doom has a further meaning in *The Children of Húrin*: it is the judgment King Thingol passes at his court on Túrin (cf. CH 91-95).

In the following, doom determining Túrin's life is referred to everywhere in the text: "but not so light was Túrin's doom" (CH 75), or "his doom delivered him from death" (CH 85), indicating that Túrin's hardships will surpass mere death. Gwindor knows: "A doom lies on him; a dark doom" (CH 168). And both Túrin and Niënor "brought their dark doom's shadow [to Brethil]" (CH 247). As in this last quotation, references to doom are often linked to — or even replaced by — the notion of a shadow or darkness. Thus, Hunthor says: "a shadow lies on this man, and it will lead you to evil" (CH 228), and Gwindor talking to Túrin perceives that "a darkness is on you" (CH 162).

Repeatedly, however, this idea of inevitable doom is modified. When Túrin and Beleg rule the Land of Bow and Helm Morgoth fears "that Túrin would grow to such a power that the curse that he had laid upon him would become void, and he would escape the doom that had been designed for him" (CH 147). The messenger Arminas holds Túrin's pride and his wilful, at times self-important actions responsible for the imminent destruction of Nargothrond: "But you, it seems, will take counsel with your own wisdom, or with your sword only; and you speak haughtily. And I say to you, Agarwaen Mormegil, that if you do so, other shall be your doom than one of the Houses of Hador and Bëor might look for" (CH 175). When Túrin is cross because Gwindor has revealed his right name and, by that, called "down my doom upon me", Gwindor answers: "The doom lies in yourself, not in your name" (CH 170).

The first instance conveys the opinion that Túrin's deeds and decisions influence a predetermined fate: Morgoth himself acknowledges Túrin's power that could efface the curse. In the second example, Arminas does not know about Túrin's doom. He assesses Túrin's conduct solely in terms of adequacy and suspected outcome. The negative results Arminas foresees are — to his mind — due to Túrin alone. Nevertheless, he links them to doom. In the last quote, Gwindor sums it up in a nutshell: no outward force or attribute is to blame for Túrin's fate, it is he alone. Thus, the text varies the concept of an inevitable fate to the effect that individual actions and decisions can influence a predetermined doom both positively and negatively. Any precise estimation of the share of predestination or individual responsibility in the events is, however, impossible since the boundaries between them are blurred.

Túrin's loss of hereditary lordship is also linked to those different facets of doom. As already indicated, Túrin has to leave his home as a child because his father has lost the dominion over Dor-lómin and is held captive by Morgoth. I have already shown that the kinship relations in that text are profoundly disrupted. In addition to that, kinship does not fulfil its function of transmitting and securing hereditary power. Túrin becomes a restless wanderer. He repeatedly occupies military leading positions, thus reinforcing his claim to lordship. In spite of successful battles, however, the communities Túrin is to protect are ultimately destroyed. His extreme opinion on honour and valour occludes rational behaviour like flight or the avoidance of war: "Better to win a time of glory, though it be shortlived; for the end will be no worse" (CH 161), says Túrin just before Nargothrond is defeated and completely destroyed by Morgoth's troops. In the quote above, Arminas comments precisely on that attitude exalting military excess up to the point of one's own destruction. Not in the Arminas passage, but in many others, Túrin's manner is explicitly described as "proud" (cf. e.g. CH 91, 117, 140, 169, 171). Tolkien describes that connection between excess and pride as being the essence of the Old English concept *ofermod*: "Yet this element of pride, in the form of the desire for honour and glory, in life and after death, tends to grow, to become a chief motive, driving a man beyond the bleak heroic necessity to excess" (HB 144).[18]

Judith Klinger argues that in many medieval texts "heroic violence... is played out on the brink between integrative and destructive effects" (Klinger 133), thus creating an ambiguity between safeguarding order and overthrowing it. In her analysis of several Tolkien texts, she shows that "the monstrous aspect of the hero is never more marked than it is in the story of Túrin" (Klinger 134). Klinger stresses the significance of the sword Anglachel-Gurthang in constructing the dark side of heroic aggression: the tale of the sword — like that of Túrin — is "overshadowed by its fated conclusion" (Klinger 141). What is more, the sword "mirrors [Túrin's] shifting identities and contradictory roles: 'treacherous to foes, faithless to friends, and a curse unto his kin', Glaurung calls him" (Klinger 141). Thus, the sword is not only the connection between the companions beyond the grave but also "Túrin's fated counterpart" (Klinger 141).

Walter Haug, too, elaborates on the ambivalence of the heroic in medieval literature. Like Tolkien, he attributes supreme importance to the dragon fight: "Die heroische Urfabel ist... der Drachenkampf. Im Drachen manifestiert sich die Gewalt als dämonisches Ungeheuer" (Haug 79). Haug's definition of the hero concentrates on the effects of his encounter with the monster: the hero himself becomes monstrous: "Der Gegner in seiner übermächtigen Gewalt kann nur dadurch besiegt werden, daß man selbst gewalttätig wird. Man muß zu dem werden, was der Gegner ist, um ihm gewachsen zu sein. So kommt es zu einer erschreckenden Angleichung des Helden an das Dämonische, das zu besiegen er ausgezogen ist" (Haug 80). Haug has proven the validity of his arguments for a number of medieval texts.

The assimilation of the hero to the demonic: this surely coincides with Túrin. One marked difference to Haug's concept, however, consists in the fact that Túrin does not kill the dragon until the end of the story. That is, the adjustment of the hero to the monstrous — which is certainly present — does not linearly follow the story outline but is constructed differently. One of the instances creating

---

18 See West on Túrin's pride.

Túrin's monstrosity is his alignment with the sword Anglachel, as Judith Klinger demonstrates. Another central narrative means is the dragon helm I have mentioned at the beginning. That helm after which Túrin calls himself 'Dread Helm' is not only "heirloom of his fathers" (CH 79), situating Túrin within the dynasty of the House of Hador. And it is not only a symbol for Túrin's warrior identity. In addition, doom materialises in the helm crest which is shaped like a dragon. In the times of Túrin's forebears, the helm had indicated a contrast between the dragon crest and the Dragon of Angband: "Of more worth is the Dragon of Dor-lómin than the gold-worm of Angband" (CH 79). As the story progresses, the dragon helm is, however, increasingly associated with Túrin's doom as Beleg's foreboding quoted above shows. The dragon Glaurung not only executes Morgoth's curse on the children of Húrin, he is also Morgoth's most powerful weapon to conquer and destroy the people of Middle-earth. He thereby becomes a double of Morgoth, at the same time embodying Túrin's doom. "[T]o Beleg it seemed now that the Helm had wrought otherwise with Túrin than he had hoped" (CH 146): this evaluation demonstrates again the bleakness and dreariness of the hero's situation. The heirloom's meaning changes from legitimate violence and claims to power to finally symbolising Morgoth's doom and Túrin's own excessive aggression.

In rapid sequence, the actual slaying of the dragon and Túrin's subsequent suicide bring about the notion that the hero is becoming increasingly similar to the dragon until he is so monstrous that he has to kill himself. This is a modern concept of heroic identity, indeed: although the monstrous hero in medieval texts is sometimes killed by others because society cannot contain his exorbitance, he would never kill himself because of the dark intertwinings of heroism, doom and despair.

Tolkien writes on *Beowulf* that its "deep significance" (BMC 27) of "despair" (BMC 23) derives from "a dark antiquity of sorrow" (BMC 27) that the text evokes. That can be transferred to *The Children of Húrin*: not only the curse weighing down on Húrin's clan lends darkness to the text but also the hopeless situation in the face of Morgoth's increasing power. In addition, there is the darkness of cultural tradition of the Men of Middle-earth: "a darkness lies behind us, and out of it few tales have come" (CH 43). In the light of the old race of the Elves, Men's destiny seems to be oppressive. At the outset of the text Sador says: "In their light we are dimmed, or we burn with too quick a flame, and the weight of our doom lies the heavier on us" (CH 44). Despite the dark story of Túrin and his doom, however, the tale is at the same time constructive, to the extent that its telling establishes a historical tradition which allows the Men of Middle-earth to step out of darkness.

Conclusion: Modern Narrative Strategies in a Medieval Context

In *The Children of Húrin*, Tolkien not only works with medieval motifs and narrative patterns, but also organises Middle-earth along pre-modern orders of knowledge. The social orders are, however, transformed: a modern narrative strategy consists in accentuating the personal and the individual in favour of social significance. This applies to the portrayal of both the warrior friendship and the incest. Túrin's (modern) reserve marks his status as an outsider. Even when he enters relations, he detaches himself from sociability rather than constituting it.

The concept of doom takes up different, even opposing notions regarding the significance of single actions and the exertion of influence: predetermination and personal responsibility interlink, underlining the futility of any effort to escape doom. That does not only concern single protagonists but affects the whole imagined world. In the conception of the hero, again a concept found in medieval texts is taken up and transformed: Túrin's monstrosity — and, connected with that, the impression that he cannot be saved from his doom and from himself — pervades the whole text, thus creating a world full of darkness and despair.

Modern readers are affected primarily by narrative conventions vividly and immediately generating a subjective sense of doom: that Túrin slays his companion, sleeps with his sister and finally kills himself is narrated with an intensity that emotionally includes and touches modern recipients with full force. This sense of doom dominates effects of unfamiliarity sometimes created by the inclusion of medieval narrative strategies. Thus, *The Children of Húrin* is a genuinely modern text gaining its depth and intensity across a dialogue with the Middle Ages

Bibliography

Beowulf. With the Finnesburg Fragment. Eds. C.L. Wrenn & W.F. Bolton. Exeter: University of Exeter Press, 1992

von Bloh, Ute. *Ausgerenkte Ordnung. Vier Prosaepen aus dem Umkreis der Gräfin Elisabeth von Nassau-Saarbrücken: 'Herzog Herpin', 'Loher und Maller', 'Huge Scheppel', 'Königin Sibille'*. Tübingen: Niemeyer, 2002

Bumke, Joachim. »Der unfeste Text. Überlegungen zur Überlieferungsgeschichte und Textkritik der höfischen Epik im 13. Jahrhundert«. ›Aufführung‹ und ›Schrift‹ in Mittelalter und Früher Neuzeit. Hg. Jan-Dirk Müller. Stuttgart/Weimar: Metzler, 1996, 118-129

Fornet-Ponse, Thomas. "*The Children of Húrin* – Its Use for Tolkien Scholarship". *Hither Shore* 2 (2007): 203-206

Friedrich, Udo. »Ordnungen des Wissens. Ältere deutsche Literatur«. *Germanistik als Kulturwissenschaft. Eine Einführung in neue Theoriekonzepte*. Hg. Claudia Benthien & Hans Rudolf Velten. Reinbek bei Hamburg: Rowohlt, 2002, 83-102

Hartmann von Aue. *Gregorius. Mittelhochdeutsch / Neuhochdeutsch*. Mittelhochdeutscher Text nach der Ausgabe von Friedrich Neumann. Übertragung von Burkhard Kippenberg. Nachwort Hugo Kuhn. Stuttgart: Reclam, 1996

Haug, Walter. »Die Grausamkeit der Heldensage. Neue gattungstheoretische Überlegungen zur heroischen Dichtung«. *Brechungen auf dem Weg zur Individualität. Kleine Schriften zur Literatur des Mittelalters.* Studienausgabe. Tübingen: Niemeyer, 1997, 72-90

Honegger, Thomas. »Die interpretatio mediaevalia von Tolkiens Werk«. *Hither Shore* 1 (2004): 37-51

Kellner, Beate. *Ursprung und Kontinuität. Studien zum genealogischen Wissen im Mittelalter*. München: Fink, 2004

Klinger, Judith. "The Legacy of Swords: Animate Weapons and the Ambivalence of heroic Violence". *Hither Shore* 6 (2009): 130-150

Lévi-Strauss, Claude. *The Elementary Structures of Kinship*. Boston: Beacon Press, 1969

Loher und Maller. Ms. Hamburg, Staats- und Universitätsbibliothek, Codex 11 in scrinio (about 1456)

St. Clair, Gloriana. "Völsunga Saga and Naran: Some Analogies". *Proceedings of the J.R.R. Tolkien Centenary Conference 1992*. Eds. Patricia Reynolds & Glen GoodKnight. Milton Keynes/Altadena: The Mythopoetic Press, 1995, 68-72

Strohschneider, Peter. »Inzest-Heiligkeit. Krise und Aufhebung der Unterschiede in Hartmanns Gregorius«. *Geistliches in weltlicher und Weltliches in geistlicher Literatur des Mittelalters*. Hg. Christoph Huber et al. Tübingen: Niemeyer, 2000, 105-133

Tolkien, J.R.R. "Beowulf: The Monsters and the Critics". *The Monsters and the Critics and Other Essays*. Ed. Christopher Tolkien. London: HarperCollins, 1990, 5-48

---. *The Book of Lost Tales II*. (The History of Middle-earth 2). Ed. Christopher Tolkien. New York: Ballantine Books, 1992

---. *The Children of Húrin. Narn i Chîn Húrin*. Ed. Christopher Tolkien. London: HarperCollins, 2008

---. "The Homecoming of Beorhtnoth Beorhthelm's Son". *Tree and Leaf. Including the Poem Mythopoeia*. London: HarperCollins, 2001, 119-150

---. *The Lays of Beleriand*. (The History of Middle-earth 3). Ed. Christopher Tolkien. New York: Ballantine Books, 1994

---. *The Silmarillion*. Ed. Christopher Tolkien. London/Boston/Sydney: Unwin Paperbacks, 1979

Völsunga saga. The Saga of the Völsungs. The Icelandic Text According to MS Nks 1824 b, 4°. With an English Translation, Introduction and Notes by Kareen Grimstad. Saarbrücken: AQ-Verlag, 2000

Wanner, Kevin J. "Warriors, Wyrms, and Wyrd: The Paradoxical Fate of the Germanic Hero/King in Beowulf". *Essays in Medieval Studies* 16 (2000): 1-12

West, Richard C. "Túrin's Ofermod. An Old English Theme in the Development of the Story of Túrin". *Tolkien's Legendarium. Essays on The History of Middle-earth*. Eds. Verlyn Flieger & Carl F. Hostetter. Westport/London: Greenwood Press, 2000, 233-245

Winst, Silke. *Amicus und Amelius. Kriegerfreundschaft und Gewalt in mittelalterlicher Erzähltradition*. Berlin/New York: Walter de Gruyter, 2009

Mythologie contra Geschichte oder von der Mythologie zur Geschichte?

Thomas Fornet-Ponse (Hildesheim)

Hat Tolkien eine Mythologie geschrieben? Auf den ersten Blick kann die Antwort nur Ja lauten – benutzt Tolkien selbst doch mehrfach das Wort ›Mythologie‹ für sein eigenes Werk[1] und hat ein Gedicht namens *Mythopoeia* geschrieben. Auch in der Sekundärliteratur kann nicht von einer heftig geführten Kontroverse zu dieser Frage gesprochen werden – führen doch viele Titel zu Tolkiens *Legendarium* die Wörter ›Mythos‹ oder ›Mythologie‹ wie selbstverständlich im Titel (vgl. beispielhaft Chance; Flieger; Purtill; Shippey). Nun ist es sicherlich nicht unangebracht, in regelmäßigen Abständen solch gefestigte Überzeugungen auf den Prüfstand zu stellen und zu überlegen, welches Potential alternative Erklärungsmöglichkeiten haben – ohne dabei immer das Rad neu erfinden zu wollen. Wenngleich wichtig, ist dies weder das erste Anliegen noch die hauptsächliche Motivation dieser Überlegungen.

Vielmehr geht es mir angesichts der diversen im Seminar 2011 herausgestellten mittelalterlichen Einflüsse und historisierenden Tendenzen in Tolkiens Werk um die Frage: Wie verhalten sich diese zu seinem Anspruch, eine Mythologie für England verfassen zu wollen? Vermag z.B. der ahistorische Charakter einer Mythologie einige der Besonderheiten des Tolkien'schen Rekurses und Bezuges auf das Mittelalter zu erklären? Welche Rolle erlangen die historischen Bezüge in der Entwicklung seines *Legendariums* und durch sein sich veränderndes Selbstverständnis als Autor?

Insofern es grob gesprochen um das Verhältnis von Mythologizität und (behaupteter) Geschichtlichkeit geht, ist es ratsam, zunächst einige grobe begriffsgeschichtliche Linien des Verständnisses von Mythos/Mythologie und Geschichte zu nennen, bevor Tolkiens eigene Position in seinen theoretischen Schriften und der praktischen Durchführung analysiert werden kann.

---

1 Stenström vermerkt dazu, die Phrase »Mythologie für England« werde immer in Anführungszeichen gesetzt und es werde nie eine Quelle angegeben, und sieht ihren Ursprung in der Biographie Carpenters (vgl. 310). In der Tat lässt sich bei Tolkien keine Stelle finden, in der er explizit von seinem Ansinnen spricht, eine Mythologie für England zu verfassen. Am nächsten kommt dem folgende Passage aus einem Briefentwurf von 1956: »Having set myself a task, the arrogance of which I fully recognized and trembled at: being precisely to restore to the English an epic tradition and present them with a mythology of their own« (L 230f). Allerdings bezieht sich dies auf *The Lord of the Rings* und nicht auf sein *Legendarium* (hierfür wird dann auf den Brief an Milton Waldman rekurriert: L 144f).

I. Was ist ein Mythos?

Wenig überraschend, haben beide Begriffe im Lauf der Zeit eine erhebliche Bedeutungsveränderung erfahren (vgl. Brisson; Burkert; Hager; Horstmann; Kobusch; Scholtz).

Beim ›Mythos‹ fängt dies schon in der Antike an, da damit ursprünglich jede Art Erzählung oder Geschichte bezeichnet wurde, unabhängig davon, ob es um eine Alltagserfahrung ging oder eine Begegnung mit Göttern. Nach der Kritik des Xenophanes wurde der Begriff bald negativ verstanden, und es entwickelte sich die zuerst bei Pindar belegte klassische Antithese Mythos-Logos. »Von nun an steht Mythos für das Unwahre, das Erdichtete, die Fabel, das Kindermärchen« (Kobusch 45). In der Philosophie dient der Begriff dazu, literarische Gegner abzuqualifizieren, was sich auch bei Platon zeigt – sowohl hinsichtlich des Mythos im Sinne eines Kindermärchens als auch bezüglich der ›großen‹ Mythen Homers oder Hesiods und sogar für die Tragödie. Platon stellt das Mythologische und das Philosophische als Gegensatz einander gegenüber. Das philosophische Wissen thematisiert die Gesetze und Grundsätze, die dazu dienen, das Wissen der Dichter zu beurteilen. Während die Mythen und Mythologen nicht als solche selbst nach der Wahrheit fragen können, ist dies die Aufgabe des Philosophen. Ganz unversöhnlich stehen sie sich aber doch nicht gegenüber, da auch Platon in seinen Dialogen Mythen erzählt. Die Philosophie erhebt sich zwar in der Mythenkritik als Richterin über den Mythos, aber sie tut dies, indem sie ausdrücklich nach der Wahrheit des Mythos fragt. Vorgegebene Mythen sollen darauf überprüft werden, ob sie philosophische Wahrheiten veranschaulichen können. Insofern die Bilder etwas veranschaulichen, was sonst nur begriffen wäre, bereichert der Mythos den philosophischen Logos, auf den er hinweist und von dem er verständlich wird. Aber er steht immer in dessen Diensten. »Die Wahrheit, die in den Mythen Platons durchscheint, ist deswegen auch immer eine gewissermaßen vom Logos geliehene Wahrheit. Man versteht die bunten Bilder dieser Geschichten nur im Lichte der schon erkannten Philosophie« (Kobusch 50). Diese Einstellung wird anschließend auch von Aristoteles und im Prinzip von den Neuplatonikern vertreten. Dieses Verhältnis von Logos zum Mythos bestimmt das abendländische Bewusstsein, insofern sich die Legitimität des Mythos daran bemisst, wie er die Wahrheit des Logos für das Vermögen der Phantasie ausdrücken kann.

Erst im Denken der Romantik findet so etwas wie eine Rehabilitierung des Mythos statt – Schleiermacher und Friedrich Schlegel prägen beispielsweise den Begriff ›neue Mythologie‹ für eine ästhetische Kategorie, die gegen die aufklärerisch-rationale Philosophie eingeführt wurde. Grundsätzlich bleibt auch hier der Gegensatz zwischen Mythos und Logos bestehen, allerdings mit umgekehrtem Vorzeichen. Denn der Logos gilt als das Überwundene oder zu Überwindende und der Mythos als Produkt schöpferischer Freiheit, wahres

Kunstwerk oder Selbstoffenbarung Gottes. Mythos wird zu »einem Programmwort der Romantik bei der Suche nach der Urweisheit« (Horstmann 295). In der romantischen Tradition steht auch das bekannte Buch *Die Wahrheit des Mythos* von Kurt Hübner: Dieser will den Mythos rehabilitieren, indem er sich darum bemüht, eine dem Mythos eigene Ontologie und Rationalität aufzuzeigen. Hans Blumenberg dagegen entzieht der traditionellen Unterscheidung den Boden, weil die Rolle des Mythos nicht richtig erkannt wurde: »Der Mythos selbst ist ein Stück hochkarätiger Arbeit des Logos« (Blumenberg 18). Ihm geht es aber nicht nur darum, den griechischen Mythos und alle anderen anders einzuschätzen, sondern er preist die Vorzüge einer mythischen Denkform im Unterschied zu Dogmen, da der Mythos heterogene Elemente fast unbegrenzt vereinigen kann. »Er fordert keine Entscheidungen, keine Bekehrungen, kennt keine Apostaten, keine Reue« (Blumenberg 269). Denn er hat eine »eigentümliche Form der Freiheit«, die sich »einem Verzicht auf Wahrheit verdankt« (266). Während der Logos zum kompromisslosen Wahrheitsverkünder wurde, garantierten die vielen Mythen die Freiheit.

Die somit im Lauf der Geschichte sehr unterschiedlich beantwortete Frage nach dem Verhältnis von Mythos und Logos bzw. Wahrheit ist von so großer Bedeutung, weil der Mythos erklärende Bedeutung und moralische Gültigkeit beansprucht.[2] Er tut dies nicht wie die Philosophie in abstrakter Form, sondern indem er »[v]on einem Jenseits, das in einer weit zurückliegenden Vergangenheit und in einem fernen, der Wirklichkeit des Mythenerzählers und seiner Zuhörer entrückten Raum anzusiedeln ist« (Brisson 6) spricht. Dies weist auf den zentralen Unterschied zur Geschichtsschreibung hin.

II. Was ist Geschichte?

Denn dieser besteht in der Schriftlichkeit, da Mythen ursprünglich ausschließlich mündlich überliefert wurden und die Entstehung bzw. Verwendung der Schrift die mentalen Gewohnheiten vieler damaliger Menschen (besonders der Einflussreichen) gravierend veränderte. Luc Brisson nennt sechs Elemente dieser Veränderung: 1) die stärkere Geltung der Prosa, 2) die Ablösung von Erzählungen durch Beschreibungen und Argumentationsketten, 3) die Veränderung des »Wahrheits«-Kriteriums, 4) die Einbürgerung eines begrifflichen Denkens, 5) die Aufbewahrung schriftlicher Zeugnisse, 6) eine größere Freiheit zur Kritik (vgl. Brisson 9f). Zudem sei die Beziehung der meisten Menschen zu den von Homer und Hesiod beschriebenen Mythen erschwert worden, indem

---

2 »The points that should be stressed here are the aura of truth and timelessness that surround myth and, above all, its attempt to explain the world, trying to provide a type of world-formula, a cosmic model in story.« (Hiley 839)

nur noch eine Fassung ihrer Werke als gültig angesehen wurde. »In ihrer nun eingetretenen Erstarrung beschrieben diese Mythen Verhaltensweisen und Einstellungen, die einen in der klassischen oder auch schon am Ende der archaischen Epoche lebenden Griechen anachronistisch, ja schockierend anmuten mußten« (Brisson 10). Der vorher positiv eingeschätzte Dichter gilt nun als Urheber irreführenden und sogar unmoralischen Scheins.

Der Graben zwischen den dichterischen Erzählungen und der Publikumserwartung sowie der Gegensatz zwischen der Leistung des Mythos als Erzeugnis mündlicher Übermittlung und den mentalen Gewohnheiten der Bürger wurden immer größer, weswegen nicht nur zwei neue Umgangsformen mit dem Mythos – die allegorische Deutung und die Tragödie – entstanden, sondern auch zwei neue Diskurstypen: der des ›Historikers‹ und der oben kurz angedeutete des ›Philosophen‹. So grenzt einer der Begründer der griechischen Geschichtsschreibung, Herodot, seinen Diskurs durch zwei Kriterien von dem der Dichter ab, mit denen er zugleich die Gültigkeit seines Diskurses begründet. Er nennt zum einen seine persönlichen Beobachtungen und zum anderen Mitteilungen ausgewählter Informanten – eine methodische Einschränkung, die durch Thukydides noch überboten wird:

> Er hält nur die Ereignisse für gesichert, denen er selbst beigewohnt hat, sowie diejenigen, die durch Zeitgenossen bezeugt werden, sofern ihr Bericht einer Überprüfung standhält; hingegen hält er Begebenheiten, die er nur vom Hörensagen kennt, dann für ungesichert, wenn er den Informanten – mag dieser auch noch so qualifiziert sein – nicht direkt befragen konnte, was ihn freilich nicht hindert, Minos als historische Persönlichkeit gelten zu lassen. (Brisson 13, vgl. Thukydides I 20-22)

Auch wenn Thukydides selbst das Wort *historia* vermeidet, entspricht diese Vorgehensweise dessen Etymologie (der Stamm, von dem es abgeleitet ist, bedeutet *sehen*, wissen), wobei sich anschließend die Bedeutung von der Tätigkeit des Erkundens auf dessen Ergebnis verschiebt, wenn Ephoros als Verfasser der ersten griechischen Universalgeschichte sein Werk vermutlich mit *historiai* betitelt hat (vgl. Hager 344). Seit Aristoteles wird es fest für die literarische Gattung der Geschichtsschreibung verwendet und somit von der Dichtkunst unterschieden.

Die Beziehung der Historia auf das wirklich Geschehene in Abgrenzung von *fabula*, dem Unwahren und Unwahrscheinlichen, und *argumenta*, dem (Denk-)Möglichen, wird in der Folge im Anschluss an Cicero auch bei Isidor von Sevilla und in der mittelalterlichen Rhetorik vertreten.[3] Erst im Humanismus

---

3   Auf im Mittelalter entstehende einflussreiche theologische Geschichtsdeutungen, besonders im Anschluss an Augustinus, kann ich hier nicht eingehen. (Vgl. Scholtz 349-351)

beginnt die Historie in die Universitätsdisziplinen einzurücken, wobei sie nicht Geschichtsforschung oder Universalgeschichte ist, »sondern eine Disziplin, die in enger Nachbarschaft zu Rhetorik und Poesie moralische Belehrung anhand antiker Historiographien zu erteilen hat« (Scholtz 353). Als Wahrheitskriterium gilt in der Folge nicht mehr die Übereinstimmung mit dem christlichen Dogma, weshalb wissenschaftstheoretische und methodische Überlegungen angestellt werden, wozu unter Rekurs auf Aristoteles das Erfahrungswissen betont wird. Deswegen werden bis zum Ende des 18. Jahrhunderts Historie und Philosophie schulmäßig einander gegenübergestellt. Bei aller Kritik gegenüber ihrer Wissenschaftlichkeit wird im 18. Jahrhundert noch immer auch ihr praktisch-moralischer Nutzen gesehen, und zwar allmählich nicht nur für die Staats- und Kirchendiener, sondern auch für den Menschen überhaupt. Im deutschen Geschichtsbegriff setzt sich allmählich das Wort *Geschichte* gegen *Historie* durch, da es »kraft seiner etymologischen Herkunft geeignet ist, den Geschehenszusammenhang selbst und den Bewegungscharakter des Dargestellten zu akzentuieren« (Scholtz 359). Damit wird auch Geschichte als Wissenschaft anders eingeschätzt, indem z.b. mit dem Disziplintitel »Philosophie der Geschichte« die Spannung zwischen Historie und Philosophie aufgehoben wird. Geschichte tritt als Wissenschaft selbstbewusst neben die Naturwissenschaften, wobei auch in ihr sich die Kausalitätskategorie bewähren soll, wie u.a. Herder und Chladenius ausführen.

Die Verpflichtung auf ein wissenschaftliches Vernunftpostulat und eine wissenschaftliche Rationalität zeigt sich sehr deutlich im Historismus, der ersten Epoche moderner Geschichtswissenschaft. Wichtig für unsere Fragestellung ist die »Betonung des Bezugs der Geschichtswissenschaft auf die Wirklichkeit und die Absichtserklärung..., die ›historische Wahrheit‹ abbilden zu wollen« (Jordan 43). Die Historiker des Historismus lösen sich allerdings vom aufklärerisch-philosophischen Ideal einer deduktiv vorgehenden historischen Wahrheitsfindung, wie diese von Geschichtsphilosophen propagiert wurde, und ersetzen sie mit dem Ideal historischer Objektivität. Diese widerspricht nicht dem Bewusstsein der Subjektivität des Historikers, sofern die Methode genau befolgt werde. Droysen und andere Historiker des 19. Jahrhunderts sehen Geschichte daher als Rekonstruktion an: »In einer solchen stehen sich die subjektive Sicht des Erkennenden und der Anspruch auf allgemeine Gültigkeit (Objektivität) der Ergebnisse zwar gegenüber, sind aber durch eine methodisch standardisierte Intersubjektivität vermittelt«[4] (Jordan 50).

---

4   Die Beschränkung des Historikers auf die historische Wahrheit zeigt sich auch im berühmten Zitat Leopold (von) Rankes: »Man hat der Historie das Amt, die Vergangenheit zu richten, die Mitwelt zum Nutzen zukünftiger Jahre zu belehren, beigemessen: so hoher Aemter unterwindet sich gegenwärtiger Versuch nicht: er will blos zeigen, wie es eigentlich gewesen« (Ranke VII). Diese strenge Darstellung der Tatsache sei das oberste Gesetz gewesen; das zweite aber, »die Entwickelung der Einheit und des Fortgangs der Begebenheiten« (VII) aufzuweisen.

Ein solcher Anspruch auf Objektivität bzw. Realismus dürfte zwar auch einem heutigen Alltagsverständnis der Geschichtswissenschaft (und auch der Praxis mancher Historiker) entsprechen, wird in der gegenwärtigen Geschichtstheorie allerdings deutlich kritischer gesehen, zumal diverse Ansätze miteinander konkurrieren (vgl. Jordan 148-213).

III. Tolkien als Historiker?

Schon aus dieser groben Skizze der jeweiligen Begriffsgeschichte wird deutlich, welche Argumente angeführt werden können, um Tolkien eher als Historiker denn als Mythenschaffer anzusehen. An erster Stelle können Aussagen Tolkiens genannt werden, in denen er seinen Schreibvorgang bei *The Hobbit* eher als Entdeckung denn als Erfindung beschreibt, er seiner Fiktion somit eine gewisse Autonomie zugesteht: »But it proved to be the discovery of the completion of the whole, its mode of descent to earth, and merging into ›history‹« (L 145; vgl. Campbell 221-224). Paul Kerry betont in seinem einschlägigen Artikel neben der Bedeutung der Philologie (im weiten Sinne) vor allem die Elemente der Augenzeugenschaft und die Anhänge, auf welcher Grundlage er Tolkiens Werk als symbolische Geschichte verstehen kann.[5] Wenn Tolkien seine Schriften explizit auf die Primärwelt bezieht, entspricht die Unterscheidung zwischen geographischer und historischer Verortung allerdings dem Unterschied zwischen Geschichte und Mythos: »I am historically minded. Middle-earth is not an imaginary world... The theatre of my tale is this earth, the one in which we now live, but the historical period is imaginary« (L 239).

Margaret Hiley deutet nicht nur dies als Zeichen für den modernen Charakter des Werkes, sondern auch die enge Verbindung zwischen Sekundär- und Primärwelt als mythischen Versuch, die konstruierte Natur der Sekundärwelt zu verbergen (vgl. 853f). Dabei sollte auch nicht vergessen werden, dass Tolkien selbst Mythos und Geschichte in enger Beziehung zueinander sieht: »History often resembles ›Myth‹, because they are both ultimately of the same stuff. If indeed Ingeld and Freawaru never lived, or at least never loved, then it is ultimately from nameless man and woman that they get their tale, or rather into whose tale they have entered« (FS 47).

Ein sehr auffälliges formales Argument ist Tolkiens Verwendung der Gattung »Annalen«, die nicht nur im Anhang A des *Lord of the Rings* für die Geschichte der Könige und Herrscher eingesetzt wird, sondern schon viel früher: Anfang der 1930er mit den *Earliest Annals of Valinor* (SM 262-293) und den *Earliest Annals of Beleriand* (SM 294-341), denen im Laufe der Zeit verschie-

---

5 »Tolkien is careful to remain a scholar in the *Appendix* and this reinforces the notion that *The Lord of the Rings* is history, for its tone and presentation mimic the prevailing practices of the historical profession.« (Kerry 74)

dene Versionen nachfolgen sollten, bis zu dem vermutlich auf 1958 datierbaren Typoskript mit den *Annals of Aman* (MR 45-138) sowie den in zeitlicher Nähe dazu entstandenen *Grey Annals* (WJ 1-170).

Bemerkenswert daran ist zum einen die Verwendung einer spezifisch mittelalterlichen Form der Geschichtsschreibung, deren Eigenart darin besteht, »ohne literarische Ambitionen und ohne Berücksichtigung sonstiger Strukturmodelle zu jedem Jahr neben historischen auch naturgeschichtliche Ereignisse und biographische Fakten knapp aneinander« (Ott, *Annalen* 24) zu reihen. Schon ein flüchtiger Blick in Tolkiens *Annalen* reicht aus, um die Übereinstimmung festzustellen, wenngleich naturgeschichtliche Ereignisse eher selten erwähnt werden. Aber sowohl die literarische Anspruchslosigkeit als auch die prinzipielle regionale Begrenzung (die bei Tolkien allerdings wesentlich weniger eng ausfällt als bei typischen mittelalterlichen Annalen) sind deutlich erkennbar. Angesichts der zum Teil recht ausführlichen Einträge in den Annalen bei Tolkien wäre auch die Gattungszuschreibung als Chronik überlegenswert, wofür zwar auch die Erwähnung eines Autoren bei den *Annals of Aman* mit Rúmil (vgl. MR 48) spricht, nicht aber die literarische Form und der Verzicht auf übergreifende Deutungskonzepte. Die Autorenangabe fehlt zudem bei den *Grey Annals*; nur ihr Entstehungsort wird genannt: »These are the Annals of Beleriand as they were made by the Sindar, the Grey Elves of Doriath and the Havens, and enlarged from the records and memories of the remnant of the Noldor of Nargothrond and Gondolin at the Mouths of Sirion, whence they were brought back into the West« (WJ 5).

Der andere bemerkenswerte Aspekt bei den Annalen Tolkiens ist die von ihnen abgedeckte Zeitspanne, da sie schon seit den *Earliest Annals of Valinor* mit der Erschaffung der Welt durch Ilúvatar beginnen (vgl. SM 263) und — wenn man die Anhänge A und B des *Lord of the Rings* hinzunimmt — die Zeitspanne bis ins Vierte Zeitalter der Sonne hinein nahtlos abdecken. Die *Annals of Aman* und die *Grey Annals* überlappen sogar, weil letztere schon weit vor der Ankunft der Noldor in Beleriand einsetzen, nämlich mit der Ankunft Melians aus Valinor und dem Erwachen der Elben in Kuiviénen, wobei dort auf »the Chronicle of Aman« (WJ 5) verwiesen wird.

Nicht nur diese Bezeichnung, sondern die allumfassende Zeitspanne kann als weiteres Argument angeführt werden, Tolkiens Annalen chronikhafte Züge zuzusprechen, da es eine Eigenart der Weltchroniken ist, von der Schöpfung bis in die eigene Gegenwart zu reichen. Dabei dienen als Strukturrahmen oft heilsgeschichtlich bzw. geschichtsphilosophisch organisierte Schemata, z.B. die Aufteilung nach Weltaltern oder Weltreichen (vgl. Ott, *Chronik*) — bei Tolkien entspricht dem die Einordnung nach den verschiedenen Zeitaltern. Diese Zeitspanne impliziert einen bedeutenden Unterschied zwischen antiken Mythologien und Tolkiens Werk: »ancient myth was once believed to be true, and the aura of that truth and universal applicability still clings to it. Within the boundaries of Tolkien's world, however, the myth is not just believed to be true, it *is* true: it is both the mythology and the history of Middle-earth at the same time« (Hiley 844). Ein gutes Beispiel für dieses Überlappen von Mythos und Geschichte ist Elrond. Auch mit Blick auf die großen umwälzenden Ereignisse mit den großen, jeweils Zeitalter beendenden Kriegen sei von einer Konvergenz von Mythologie und Geschichte bei Tolkien zu sprechen. Dies gilt aber auch für (mittelalterliche) Weltchroniken, insofern für die Autoren die dort beschriebene Schöpfung und diverse heilsgeschichtliche Ereignisse als wahr galten.

Indes besteht Tolkiens *Legendarium* nicht nur und nicht einmal primär aus den *Annalen*, sondern umfasst auch die *Quenta Silmarillion* und verschiedene *Lays*, sodass die Existenz der *Annalen* allein nicht ausreiche, um Tolkiens Tätigkeit als die eines Historikers einer fiktiven Welt zu charakterisieren. Aber man könnte zumindest versucht sein, Tolkiens Wirken als ein zweifaches zu verstehen: Einerseits und ursprünglich sah er sich als Mythenschaffer und andererseits – und zwar etwas später – als Historiker. Dem könnte auch die deutliche Veränderung seiner Mythologie vom *Book of Lost Tales* bis hin zum *Later Quenta Silmarillion* entsprechen, die stark geprägt war von seinen theologischen und philosophischen Überzeugungen und von dem Bemühen, eine größere Nähe von Primär- und Sekundärwelt zu erreichen, weswegen z.B. die Valar sukzessive viel weniger nordischen Göttern ähnelten als in den ursprünglichen Versionen (vgl. Fornet-Ponse, *Präsenz*) – obwohl gleich noch eine andere Erklärung für diese Entwicklung der Mythologie angeboten wird.

IV. Tolkiens Sicht und Verwendung von Mythen

Ohne Parallelen zwischen Tolkien und einem romantischen Mythenverständnis sowie den in dieser Tradition stehenden Positionen Blumenbergs oder Marquards näher untersuchen zu wollen, sei zunächst die zentrale Differenz hervorgehoben, da Tolkien im Unterschied zu den beiden genannten Philosophen einem Wahrheitsverzicht nicht das Wort redet: »Myth and fairy-story must, as all art, reflect and contain in solution elements of moral and religious truth (or error), but not explicit, not in the known form of the primary ›real‹ world« (L 144). Dementsprechend kritisiert er auch die wirkmächtige Einschätzung Max Müllers, Mythologie sei eine Krankheit der Sprache; vielmehr ist sie eng mit dem besonderen Vermögen des Menschen verbunden, Zweitschöpfer zu sein. »This aspect of ›mythology‹ – sub-creation, rather than either representation or symbolic interpretation of the beauties and terrors of the world – is, I think, too little considered« (FS 42). Hierin zeigt sich auch der Wahrheitsanspruch eines Mythos.

Die größten Nähen im Mythosverständnis zeigen sich zwischen Platon und Tolkien, wie sich u.a. in seinem Gedicht *Mythopoeia* zeigt, das deutlich von einem christlichen Platonismus geprägt ist (vgl. Fornet-Ponse, *Mythos*). Darin bezieht Tolkien das Mythenschaffen auf die kreative menschliche Schöpferkraft.

Auch verteidigt er die Wahrheit und damit den Wert von Mythen – indem er die menschliche Kreativität als Ausdruck der Gottebenbildlichkeit versteht und seine Theorie der Zweitschöpfung vorstellt. Besonders die dort gegebenen Hinweise auf eine mit Sprache verbundene zweite Existenzebene weisen auf den Platonismus hin, den Frank Weinreich dem gesamten Gedicht zuschreibt, wenn er es als »eine Art poetische Kürzestfassung der Erkenntnistheorie von *Phaidon* und *Politeia*« (48) versteht. Aber nicht nur in der theoretischen Position sind sich Tolkien und Platon sehr ähnlich, insofern sie Mythen ähnlich verstehen und diskursiv anwenden, sondern auch in vielen ihrer gemeinsamen Bilder und Vorstellungen. »The ways the two authors related to tradition and the use of myth give the conceptional frame to their own views and uses, situating these frames themselves in a historical context« (Nagy 82). Insgesamt sieht Gergely Nagy Ähnlichkeiten im Rahmen, in der Methodologie und der Theorie. So benutzen beide Mythen als offensichtliches Zeichen, sich auf eine bestimmte Tradition zu beziehen, die in beiden Fällen primär historisch ist – bei Platon die mythologisch-poetische und die philosophische, bei Tolkien die narrative und linguistische der von ihm untersuchten Texte und Sprachen. Diese Beziehung ist aber zweiseitig: Einerseits bezieht sich Tolkien primär auf Geschichten aus der germanischen Mythologie und somit auch auf den größeren Rahmen eines mehr oder weniger kohärenten Systems von Geschichten und Konzeptionen aus Textkorpora. Andererseits ist das kritische Moment der Philologie zu nennen, insofern Tolkiens Werk und seine Beziehung zu Mythen stark durch seine Annahmen und Methoden geprägt sind (vgl. Shippey 26-50), wie sich besonders an den von ihm betonten Verbindungen von Texten zu bestimmten Autoren zeigt. »His own mythological stories are presented as texts, written accounts, translations, and redactions of other texts« (Nagy 85): beginnend mit dem als Eriols Bericht ausgegebenen *Book of Lost Tales* über diverse Pengolod oder Rúmil zugeschriebene Texte bis hin zum *Silmarillion* als Bilbos Übersetzungen aus dem Elbischen. Gleichwohl betont Tolkien auch den oralen Charakter, wenn er sich auf die Quellen in *The Silmarillion* bezieht, wozu er oft Wendungen wie »it is told«, »it is said«, »said by the wise« verwendet.

Ähnlich wie Platon versteht Tolkien den Mythos als Ausdrucksmittel, der uns etwas über die Welt und ihre Struktur erzählen und somit auch zur Wahrheitsfindung beitragen kann. Hier fügt sich sein (angebliches) Anliegen an, eine Mythologie für England schreiben zu wollen, d.h. »a body of more or less connected legend, ranging from the large and cosmogonic, to the level of romantic fairy-story« (L 144). Dies dient dazu, den nationalen Ursprung und die nationale Identität auszudrücken, übernimmt also diejenige Funktion, die Mythologien für andere Länder wie Griechenland, Italien, Island oder Norwegen erfüllen (vgl. ausführlicher Chance; Honegger; Hostetter/Smith; Stenström).

Dabei kann Tolkien als Philologe nicht umhin, den Mythos zunächst als Rekonstruktion zu verstehen. Die von ihm untersuchten Texte sind viel jünger als der ursprüngliche Gebrauch; als sie verschriftlicht wurden, hatten sie schon ihre ursprüngliche religiöse Funktion verloren. Ähnlich wie er sich als Philologe zur Quelle zurückarbeitet, erschafft er auch seine Mythen zurückgehend. »The mythical background of *The Hobbit* and *The Lord of the Rings* is projected back by the allusions and hints, but *The Silmarillion* itself, as an account going back to sources, is also only a starting point for reconstruction« (Nagy 88). Die mythische Vergangenheit als ursprüngliche Erzählung versteckt sich immer hinter den Berichten, so dass die Wiederherstellung der Vergangenheit die Wiederherstellung einer Mythologie ist, die die Erzählungen in unseren Texten begründet. Die Rekonstruktionstätigkeit führt daher zu einer »Asterisk-Realität«, also einer hypothetischen Ur-Sprache und einer damit verbundenen Weltsicht (vgl. Shippey 17-21).[6]

Indem Tolkien überdies sein Schreiben als Bericht versteht,[7] führt der rekonstruktive Prozess zu Wissen – und zwar der Geschichte und Ursprünge in den Texten sowie der Bedeutungen für den außenstehenden Interpreten. Tolkien schreibt nicht nur die Texte, sondern auch ihre Hintergründe und die Tradition, in der sie stehen. Wie verhält sich nun dieser schriftliche Charakter der Tolkien'schen Mythologie zum definitionsgemäß oralen Charakter eines Mythos? Auch hier sieht Nagy eine Parallele zwischen Platon und Tolkien, insofern beide den Texten einen Hintergrund und eine Kultur schaffen, in der sie stehen. Denn mythisch sind Tolkiens Erzählungen nur innerhalb des Kontextes, den das Gesamtkorpus erzeugt; Mythos ist darin impliziert. »The proliferation of texts is essential, since this implication of tradition (the depth effect) is exactly what leads to the authenticating system of mythology (at least according to Socrates)« (Nagy 93).

Diese Analyse Nagys zeigt sehr deutlich, wie Tolkiens Selbstverständnis als Entdecker oder Rekonstrukteur dem mythologischen Charakter seiner Werke entspricht, da eine andere Vorgehensweise – beispielsweise das direkte Erfinden von Mythen – ihn nicht in die Lage versetzt hätte, ein solches System zu entwerfen (von der definitorischen Unmöglichkeit, einen Mythos schriftlich zu verfassen, ganz zu schweigen). Der von Tolkien über seine Theorie der Zweitschöpfung begründete Wahrheitsanspruch von Fairy-stories und damit auch von Mythologien kann dann auch erklären, wieso er selbst gegen Ende seines Lebens bereit war, einschneidende Veränderungen seiner Mythologie vorzunehmen, um sie beispielsweise an kosmologisches Wissen der Primärwelt

---

6   »Most obviously, the asterisk-mythology view fails in that neither the *Lost Tales* in general nor their mythology in especial can sincerely be regarded as very like anything that might have been told among the ancient English.« (Stenström 311)

7   »The mere stories were the thing. They arose in my mind as ›given‹ things, and as they came, separately, so too the links grew. An absorbing, though continually interrupted labour...: yet always I had the sense of recording what was already ›there‹, somewhere: not of ›inventing‹.« (L 145)

anschlussfähig zu machen. So zeigt gerade sein Hinweis, die Elben könnten aufgrund ihrer engen Beziehung zu den Valar und Maiar nicht eine »astronomically absurd« (MR 370) Vorstellung der Entstehung von Sonne und Mond haben, das Bemühen um Konsistenz und eine stärkere Verzahnung mit unserer Welt. Insofern müssen sie nicht als Absage an das Bemühen um eine Mythologie (für England) verstanden werden.

Tolkiens Betonung der Überlieferungsgeschichte seiner verschiedenen Erzählungen und der historisierende Anschein sind somit nicht als Ausdruck eines Bemühens um Historizität im Sinne der Geschichtsschreibung zu verstehen. Vielmehr stehen sie im Dienste der Mythologie, insofern er auf diese Weise das System erzeugen kann, das mit seinem Tiefeneffekt den authentischen Eindruck einer schriftlichen Überlieferung einer vorliegenden Mythologie erzeugt. Somit widersprechen sich die eindeutig mythologischen Elemente wie etwa die unterschiedlichen Lebewesen in Mittelerde und die historisierenden Elemente wie die mittelalterlichen Anklänge auch nicht, sondern sind Ausdruck ebendieses Systems. »Tolkien wanted his Middle-earth, like any real-world myth community, to have an oral tradition of myths and legends that at one historicized and poeticized his world« (Flieger 55). Aber auch eine schriftliche Tradition muss bestehen, wozu sein *Legendarium* dient. So wie Island, Norwegen und Wales über große Sammlungen verfügen, die von Forschern untersucht werden, verfügt auch Mittelerde über ein fiktives Äquivalent. Ähnlich wie jene wurde es übersetzt, ediert, in der Orthographie angepasst und publiziert, wozu Tolkien auch die Vorgeschichte der existierenden Texte benötigt, eine Genealogie der Übermittlung, beginnend mit Barden und Geschichtenerzählern über »historische« Redaktoren bis hin zu den Manuskripten (vgl. Flieger 61-84).[8]

Zu diesem System gehören ebenso die den Anklang von Geschichtlichkeit erweckenden Annalen, zumal in ihnen auch auf die anderen Texte und Gattungen, besonders auf »songs« verwiesen wird: »There many things afterward came to pass, as is recorded in the *Annals of Beleriand*, and in the *Quenta*, and in other songs and tales« (LR 119). Das Anliegen einer Mythologie für England zeigt sich in den Annalen auch darin, dass in ihnen erstmalig explizit Eriol und Ælfwine identifiziert werden: »These and the *Annals of Beleriand* were written by Pengolod the Wise of Gondolin, before its fall, and after at Sirion's Haven, and at Tavrobel in Toleressëa after his return unto the West, and there seen and translated by Eriol of Leithien, that is Ælfwine of the Angelcynn« (SM 263). Hierin fügen sich auch die altenglischen Versionen der *Annals of Valinor* (SM 281-293) gut ein, zumal in drei der vier gedruckten Texte nur noch Ælfwine genannt wird und nicht mehr Eriol (vgl. 284, 290, 292). Ælfwine erscheint zwar

---

8   In diesem Kontext betont Flieger auch, wie Tolkien sich darum bemühte, Seiten des Buches von Mazarbul als Artefakt, als Buch im Buch mit einigen beschädigten Seiten als Teil des publizierten Bandes zu reproduzieren (vgl. 74-77).

in den späteren Versionen der Annalen nicht mehr, was aber nicht notwendig als Aufgabe der grundsätzlichen Konzeption interpretiert werden muss, da er noch in der wahrscheinlich kurz vor 1951 geschriebenen *Ainulindalë D* und in der *Later Quenta Silmarillion* präsent ist (MR 30, WJ 192f. 206). Auch die *Dwangeth Pengoloð* (PM 395-402) behalten die Konstruktion Pengoloð–Ælfwine bei (vgl. zu Ælfwine Honegger 19-22; Hostetter/Smith 286-288).

Ein anderer Aspekt dieses Systems ist die sorgfältige Autorkonstruktion, die es Tolkien erlaubt, die verschiedenen Geschichten aus unterschiedlichen Perspektiven zu erzählen. Die Differenz zwischen einer elbischen und einer menschlichen Perspektive geht Tolkiens Brief an Waldman zufolge erst mit *The Hobbit* und *The Lord of the Rings* in seine Mythologie ein: »As the high Legends of the beginning are supposed to look at things through Elvish minds, so the middle tale of the Hobbit takes a virtually human point of view – and the last tale blends them« (L 145). Allerdings schreibt Tolkien in dem gleichen Brief etwas später, die Perspektive des gesamten Zyklus sei elbisch (vgl. L 147) und noch später – als Ausgangspunkt der von ihm intendierten gravierenden Änderungen in der Mythologie in den *Myths Transformed*:

> It is now clear to me that in any case the Mythology must actually be a ›Mannish‹ affair. ... What we have in the *Silmarillion* etc. are traditions ... handed on by *Men* Númenor and later in Middle-earth (Arnor and Gondor); but already far back – from the first association of the Dúnedain and Elf-friends with the Eldar in Beleriand – blended and confused with their own Mannish myths and cosmic ideas. (MR 370)

Denn die Hochelben hätten durch ihren Kontakt mit den demiurgischen Valar die »Wahrheit« kennen müssen und daher nicht solche Geschichten über eine flache Erde oder »the astronomically absurd business of the making of the Sun and Moon« (MR 370) verbreitet. Die Frage der Perspektive gewann mithin eine immer größere Bedeutung für Tolkien, wenngleich er offensichtlich bis zuletzt keine ihn absolut überzeugende Lösung dafür fand – denn auch die *Myths Transformed* wurden nicht umgesetzt. Die Frage der Perspektive ist besonders bedeutend beim Verständnis des Todes, den Tolkien aus elbischer Sicht als Geschenk Ilúvatars beschreiben kann, was aber für Menschen zunächst einmal keine befriedigende Erklärung sein dürfte. Um dem Anspruch auf die »inner consistency of reality« (FS 59) einer Zweitschöpfung genüge zu tun, »Tolkien's Men had to do what humans in the real world do – they had to struggle to come to terms with death, and with a purely Tolkienian refinement on that struggle, they had to do it in light of a parallel species that did not die« (Flieger 47). Diese beiden Perspektiven werden in dialogischer Form von Tolkien in der *Athrabeth Finrod ah Andreth* (MR 301-366) vereint, wobei die narrative Stimme lediglich berichtet und nicht interpretiert (allerdings hat Tolkien den Dialog ausführlich kommentiert). Indem Tolkien zwei widerstreitende Interpretationen in einer Geschichte präsentiert, hat er nach Flieger einen Prozess komprimiert, der primären Mythologien eigen ist, »that any and all versions of a story are particular interpretations deriving from particular cultural stances and particular times« (50). Die zentrale Aussage der *Athrabeth* sei es, die notwendige Mehrstimmigkeit eines Mythos zu zeigen.

Ohne die mythologischen Elemente wären seine Erzählungen doch eher historischen Romanen über eine fiktive Welt vergleichbar — und insofern genügten sie sicherlich nicht seinem in *On Fairy-Stories* dargelegten Anspruch an Fantasy. Ohne die historisierenden Elemente aber wäre es der Versuch, eine Mythologie zu verschriftlichen, was definitonsgemäß nur zum Scheitern verurteilt gewesen wäre. Die Kombination beider ist mithin notwendig — und Tolkiens Kunst bestand möglicherweise gerade darin, beide Momente auf eine Weise miteinander zu verbinden, in der keines die Überhand erlangt und das empfindliche Gleichgewicht gestört hätte.

> If we are to take Tolkien's work as he wrote it and as he clearly wanted his audience to read it — as a true mythology, with all the layering and multiple narrators and overlapping texts and variant versions that characterize mythologies in the real world — then we must allow that, like those real-world mythologies, all the parts, even the apparently inconsequential ones, are in the greater service of the whole. To read his work as anything less is to do a disservice, perhaps even a violence, to it.[9]   (Flieger 84)

Die Werke Tolkiens sind somit keine reine Mythologie, sondern eine Sekundärwelt mit einer eigenen Geschichte und einer eigenen Mythologie, die innerhalb der Sekundärwelt genauso als wahr geglaubt wird, wie dies für unsere primärweltlichen Mythologien einmal galt, und genauso gebrochen tradiert wird wie diese. Insofern liegt bei Tolkiens Werk weder ein Widerspruch zwischen Mythologie und Geschichte vor noch entwickelt sich die Mythologie zur Geschichte, sondern beides sind konstitutive Elemente, die zur »inner consistency« der Sekundärwelt beitragen.

---

9   Tolkiens größere Werke »are an attempt to create literary myth that comes as close as is possible in our day to original myth« (Purtill 4). Denn bei einem originalen Mythos verbinden sich Wahrheit und Erzählung, wohingegen bei einem literarischen oder philosophischen Mythos je eines von beiden fehle. Für einen originalen Mythos fehle heutzutage das Publikum. »Tolkien may not have quite succeeded in making a mythology for all of England, but he has created a new mythology that lives in and for some of his readers« (Purtill 58). »Creating an Elvish mythology for the legendary, one which becomes to the reader an awesome and edifying ›mythology once removed‹, was a less problematic enterprise than it would have been to create a mythology for England« (Stenström 314).

Bibliographie

Blumenberg, Hans. *Arbeit am Mythos*. Suhrkamp: Frankfurt am Main, 1979

Brisson, Luc. *Einführung in die Philosophie des Mythos. Bd. 1: Antike, Mittelalter und Renaissance.* Darmstadt: WBG, 1996

Burkert, Walter. »Mythos; Mythologie I«. *Historisches Wörterbuch der Philosophie* 6 (1984): 281-283

Campbell, Liam. *The Ecological Augury in the Works of JRR Tolkien*. Zurich/Berne: Walking Tree Publishers, 2011

Carpenter, Humphrey, with the assistance of Christopher Tolkien. *The Letters of J.R.R. Tolkien*. Boston: Houghton Mifflin, 2002

Chance, Jane (Ed.). *Tolkien and the Invention of Myth. A Reader*. Lexington KT: University of Kentucky Press, 2004

---. "A 'Mythology for England'?" *Tolkien and the Invention of Myth. A Reader*. 1-16

Flieger, Verlyn. *Interrupted Music. The Making of Tolkien's Mythology*. Kent: Kent State University Press, 2005

Fornet-Ponse, Thomas. »Die steigende Präsenz von Philosophie und Theologie«. *Hither Shore* 3 (2006): 37-50

---. »Mythos und Wahrheit. Tolkiens platonisches Lehrgedicht *Mythopoeia*«. *Inklings-Jahrbuch* 26 (2008): 228-238

Hager, Fritz-Peter. »Geschichte; Historie I«. *Historisches Wörterbuch der Philosophie* 3 (1974): 344-345

Hiley, Margaret. "Stolen Language, Cosmic Models: Myth and Mythology in Tolkien". *Modern Fiction Studies* 50 (2004): 838-860

Honegger, Thomas. »A Mythology for England – the Question of National Identity in Tolkien's Legendarium«. *Hither Shore* 3 (2006): 13-26

Horstmann, Axel. »Mythos; Mythologie II-VI«. *Historisches Wörterbuch der Philosophie* 6 (1984): 283-318

Hostetter, Carl F. & Arden R. Smith. "A Mythology for England". *Proceedings of the J.R.R. Tolkien Centenary Conference 1992*. Eds. Patricia Reynolds & Glen GoodKnight. Milton Keynes: The Tolkien Society, 1995, 281-290

Hübner, Kurt. *Die Wahrheit des Mythos*. C.H. Beck: München, 1985

Jordan, Stefan. *Theorien und Methoden der Geschichtswissenschaft*. Paderborn: Schöningh, 2009

Kerry, Paul. "Thoughts on J.R.R. Tolkien's The Lord of the Rings and History". *Reconsidering Tolkien*. Ed. Thomas Honegger. Zurich/Berne: Walking Tree Publishers, 2005

Kobusch, Theo. »Die Wiederkehr des Mythos. Zur Funktion des Mythos in Platons Denken und in der Philosophie der Gegenwart«. *Platon als Mythologe. Neue Interpretationen zu den Mythen in Platons Dialogen*. Hg. Markus Janka & Christian Schäfer. Darmstadt: WBG, 2002, 44-57

Nagy, Gergely. "Saving the Myths: The Re-creation of Mythology in Plato and Tolkien". *Tolkien and the Invention of Myth. A Reader*. Ed. Jane Chance. Lexington KT: The University of Kentucky Press, 2004, 81-100

Ott, Norbert H. »Annalen«. *Lexikon Geschichtswissenschaft. Hundert Grundbegriffe*. Stuttgart: Reclam, 2003, 24-27

---. »Chronik«. *Lexikon Geschichtswissenschaft. Hundert Grundbegriffe*. Stuttgart: Reclam, 2003, 48-51

Purtill, Richard L. *J.R.R. Tolkien. Myth, Morality, and Religion*. San Francisco: Ignatius Press, ²2003

Ranke, Franz Leopold. *Geschichten der romanischen und germanischen Völker von 1494 bis 1514*. Sämtliche Werke Bd. 33/34. Leipzig: Duncker & Humblot 1874

Scholtz, Gunter. »Geschichte, Historie II-VI«. *Historisches Wörterbuch der Philosophie 3* (1974), 345-398

Shippey, Tom. *The Road to Middle-earth. How J.R.R. Tolkien created a new mythology*. London: Grafton, 1992

Stenström, Anders. "A Mythology? For England?" *Proceedings of the J.R.R. Tolkien Centenary Conference 1992*. Eds. Patricia Reynolds & Glen GoodKnight. Milton Keynes: The Tolkien Society, 1995, 310-314

Thukydides. *Der peloponnesische Krieg*. Stuttgart: Reclam, 2000

Tolkien, J.R.R. "Mythopoeia". *Tree and Leaf*. London: HarperCollins, 2001, 85-90

---. *On Fairy-Stories*. Expanded Edition, with commentary and notes. Ed. Verlyn Flieger & Douglas A. Anderson. London: HarperCollins, 2008

---. *The Lord of the Rings*. London: HarperCollins, 1995

---. *The Shaping of Middle-earth*. The History of Middle-earth IV. Ed. Christopher Tolkien. London: HarperCollins, 2002

---. *The Lost Road and other Writings*. The History of Middle-earth V. Ed. Christopher Tolkien. London: HarperCollins, 2002

---. *Morgoth's Ring*. The History of Middle-earth X. Ed. Christopher Tolkien. London: HarperCollins, 1994

---. *The War of the Jewels*. The History of Middle-earth XI. Ed. Christopher Tolkien. London: HarperCollins, 1994

---. *The Peoples of Middle-earth*. The History of Middle-earth XII. Ed. Christopher Tolkien. London: HarperCollins, 1996

Weinreich, Frank. »Die Metaphysik der Zweitschöpfung: Zur Ontologie von Mythopoeia«. *Hither Shore* 4 (2007): 37-50

Von Mittelerde zum Mittelalter – hin und wieder zurück.

Patrick A. Brückner (Potsdam)

Nennt jemand das Mittelalter und Tolkien in einem Atemzug, bedarf es dafür in der Regel keinerlei Rechtfertigung. Die Annahme, dass der Mediävist Tolkien und sein Werk etwas mit dem Mittelalter zu tun haben, wird in der Tolkien-Forschung als selbstverständlicher Fakt postuliert – und dies sicherlich auch nicht zu Unrecht. Selten jedoch wird dabei reflektiert, wovon eigentlich gesprochen wird, wenn von DEM Mittelalter die Rede ist?

Valentin Groebner definiert diese Epoche in seinem Buch *Das Mittelalter hört nicht auf* wie folgt: »Also Mittelalter. Mit dem Begriff bezeichnet man, gewöhnlich etwas unbeholfen, die tausend Jahre zwischen dem Zerfall des Römischen Reiches am Ende des 5. Jahrhunderts und dem Veränderungsschub mit Buchdruck, europäischer Expansion nach Übersee und Reformation um 1500« (Groebner 9). Darüber hinaus sagt er aber auch an gleicher Stelle: »Geschichte [also auch das, was wir meinen, wenn wir vom Mittelalter reden, P.B.] ist eine Wunschmaschine. [Sie] handelt von den Bildern und Inszenierungen einer fernen und manchmal komplett fiktiven Epoche, die fünfhundert, siebenhundert oder tausend Jahre in der Vergangenheit liegt« (Groebner 9).

Nun soll es hier um Tolkiens mittelalterliche Welt gehen und nicht darum, wie sich die tausend Jahre, die gemeinhin als DAS Mittelalter bezeichnet werden, von der vorangehenden Antike und der nachfolgenden Frühen Neuzeit unterscheiden. Wir wollen ergründen, was mit ›mittelalterlich‹ gemeint sein könnte, sollte diese Epoche eine Rolle in J.R.R. Tolkiens Werken spielen.

Einige Thesen diese Frage betreffend lieferte Thomas Honegger bereits auf dem ersten Seminar der Deutschen Tolkien Gesellschaft 2004 in Köln. Obschon sie nicht von einander zu trennen sind, da sie letztlich einander bedingen, lohnt es sich doch, sie hier noch einmal einzeln zu betrachten. Thomas Honegger stellte in seinem Vortrag *Die interpretatio mediaevalia von Tolkiens Werk* die These auf, Mediävisten seien die ›besseren‹ Tolkienleser, was nicht weniger bedeutet, als dass »die Erschließung von Tolkiens Werk aus der Sicht und mithilfe des spezifischen mediävistischen Fachwissens« (Honegger 37) einen wichtigen Beitrag zur Tolkienforschung zu leisten vermag. Im Wesentlichen verweist Thomas Honegger auf die drei mittlerweile geläufigsten mediävistischen Ansätze zu Tolkien und deren heuristischen Nutzen, die hier kurz erwähnt werden sollen:

Erstens: die punktuellen Parallelen und Entlehnungen im Tolkien'schen Werk, die direkt auf andere Texte aus den mittelalterlichen Literaturen hinweisen. Es sei z.B. an die Entlehnung der Zwergennamen aus der *Edda* erinnert.

Als Zweites sind die aus der mittelalterlichen Literatur entlehnten Motive bei Tolkien zu nennen. Thomas Honegger zeigt dies exemplarisch u.a. an der Ankunftsszene Gandalfs und seiner Gefährten in Edoras, die sich stark an die Ankunft Beowulfs und der Scyldinge anlehnt. Es wird hier ein Mehrwert geschaffen, der zum einen darin besteht, dass durch intertextuelle Bezüge ein Verweis auf eine größere Stofftradition gegeben wird. Zum anderen provozieren diese Motive, wenn man in ihnen mehr sieht als Versatzstücke, die Frage nach der Welt, die mit ihrer Hilfe konstruiert wird.

Fast zwangsläufig führt Thomas Honegger als dritte Möglichkeit des mediävistischen Zugangs das Phänomen der alternativen Wahrnehmung von Zeit in Tolkiens *Lord of the Rings* an, wobei er die bekannte Szene von Sams Verwirrung um die Mondphasen beim Verlassen Lóriens beispielhaft zitiert (vgl. Honegger 37ff).

Dieser Aspekt der nicht-linearen Zeit, als etwas der Moderne Fremdes, kann problemlos weiter gefasst und um die Fragestellung erweitert werden, inwieweit neben dieser ideengeschichtlich andersheitlichen Konstruktion weitere Aspekte von alteritärer bzw. möglicherweise mittelalterlicher Kosmologie und Denkmodellen in Tolkiens Werken auffindbar sind. Es ist nicht nur die nicht immer linear verlaufende Zeit, die uns vielleicht irritierend und fremd erscheint. Die Konzeptionen von Raum oder von Geschichte, aber auch die von sozialen Beziehungen, Individualität, Herrschaft usw. zeichnen sich bei Tolkien ebenso durch einen hohen Grad von Fremdheit aus. Wie eng die Benutzung von Motiven und die direkt dadurch entstehende Kosmologie miteinander verknüpft sind, lässt sich an einem von Tolkiens Lieblingsmotiven zeigen: am Drachen. Dieses Motiv taucht bei Tolkien immer im Zusammenhang mit einer uns fremden, von epischem Geschichtsverständnis geprägten Weltkonstruktion auf.[1]

Thomas Honegger zeigt die Zugangsmöglichkeiten zu dieser Fremdheit, die durch die Methoden der Mediävistik eröffnet werden. So weit, so gut – mag man nun meinen. Doch ebenso einfach wie Bezüge zwischen Tolkien und dem Mittelalter lassen sich dem gegenüber gewisse Widerspruchspotentiale in der Tolkienforschung finden.[2]

Während des Tolkien Seminars 2010, ›Tolkien und Romantik‹, wurde in der Diskussion die Honeggers Vortrag widersprechende These aufgestellt, nicht etwa die Mediävisten, sondern die Romantik-Experten besäßen den Schlüssel zum besseren Verständnis Tolkiens. Eine These, die kontrovers, aber letztlich ohne endgültiges Ergebnis diskutiert wurde.

---

1 Dass der Drache in Tolkiens Bild vom Mittelalter eine wesentliche Rolle spielt, lässt sich durch die Lektüre seines Aufsatzes *Beowulf: Die Ungeheuer und ihre Kritiker* unschwer feststellen (vgl. BMC). Zum Drachenmotiv vgl. Brückner 215 ff.
2 Sicherlich ist auch von Widerstand aus Teilen der Mediävistik gegen ein Zusammendenken von Mittelalter und Tolkien auszugehen.

Wiederum besteht Tom Shippey's Interpretation Tolkiens in seinem diskursprägenden Werk *Tolkien — Author of the Century* darauf, Tolkien und seine Texte fest in der Moderne zu verorten (vgl. Shippey 305ff).

Es ist offensichtlich, dass nicht nur die Mediävisten den Anspruch darauf erheben, die besten Tolkienleser zu sein und mit ihren Methoden der Interpretation die besten Zugänge zum Tolkien'schen Werk zu ermöglichen. Die Fremdheit, die in Tolkiens Texten immer wieder aufschimmert und den Mediävisten an Alterität und mittelalterliche Texte denken lässt, scheint nicht ausreichend genug zu sein, um Tolkiens Kosmos zwangsläufig mit den Mitteln der Mediävistik zu interpretieren.

Um herauszufinden, wie berechtigt es ist, Tolkien mit dem Mittelalter (oder mit jeder anderen Epoche) in Verbindung zu bringen, scheint es sinnvoll, sich zunächst dem literaturwissenschaftlichen Epochenmodell zu nähern: Dem Literaturwissenschaftler ist bekannt, dass der Begriff ›Epoche‹ ein theoretisches, positivistisches Konstrukt der Geschichtsschreibung ist. Es ist ein Produkt von Periodisierungsannahmen, durch die ein historischer Zeitraum in Teilzeiträume zerlegt wird. Diese Teilzeiträume entstehen, indem von individuellen Besonderheiten der kategorisierten Objekte abstrahiert wird, wobei bestimmte Merkmale als typisch bzw. spezifisch gesetzt werden. Die Klassifizierung Epoche setzt explizit oder implizit voraus, dass die Objekte (hier also literarische Texte) gemeinsame Merkmale aufweisen, die zumindest in einer Teilmenge ein Alleinstellungsmerkmal für die beschriebene ›Epoche‹ besitzen (vgl. Titzmann 476ff).

Folgt man dem, sind es also die spezifischen mittelalterlichen Merkmale, nach denen gesucht werden muss, will man die Epoche Mittelalter bestimmen. Doch dies ist schwieriger als gedacht. Bemüht man ein Literaturlexikon (hier das *Sachwörterbuch der Mediävistik*), so findet sich dort unter dem Eintrag ›Mittelalter‹ der Hinweis auf die schon erwähnte Abgrenzung zur Antike und zur Frühen Neuzeit bzw. der Renaissance. Die schon erwähnten zeitlichen Epochengrenzen finden sich ebenfalls, und man stößt auf das Problem, einen Zeitraum von ca. tausend Jahren als einheitliche Epoche unter dem Begriff ›Mittelalter‹ zu fassen (vgl. *Sachwörterbuch* 546).

Schon diese Erkenntnis zeigt, wie problematisch es sein könnte, Tolkiens Texte mit einem literaturhistorischen Mittelalter in Verbindung zu bringen. Sie sind in jedem Fall ein literarisches Produkt des 20. Jahrhunderts, wie Tom Shippey in seinem *Author of the Century* es auch beschreibt. Aber sind sie deshalb automatisch modern? Die charakteristischen Konstanten, die für eine Epoche ›Mittelalter‹ anzunehmen sind, liegen, so das *Sachwörterbuch der Mediävistik*, im Bereich Mentalität, Weltbild und Lebensformen. Für das Mittelalter kann ein mehr oder weniger geschlossenes, kohärentes, hierarchisch gegliedertes Bild einer kosmischen Ordnung angenommen werden, in der der Einzelne nicht vorrangig Individuum, sondern Teil dieser Ordo ist (vgl. *Sachwörterbuch* 546; vgl. Brandt). Daraus lässt sich, wie Peter Wapnewski es beschreibt, »die Vorliebe für Formeln... und tradierte Figuren [sowie] die hyperbolische Darstellung von Helden, Damen und Bösewichtern, die immer die besten, schönsten und schlechtesten sind [erklären]« (Wapnewski 48).

Hier kann durchaus mit Thomas Honeggers Thesen eine Verbindung zwischen Tolkien und dem Mittelalter hergestellt werden, die nicht auf ein für den Historiker quellengestütztes Mittelalter abzielt, sondern auf die Frage nach vorhandenen mittelalterlichen Denkformen in Tolkiens Texten. Ein Modell, wie dies zu denken wäre, bietet Peter Prange mit seinen Thesen zum Historischen Roman an. Er stellt fest, dass dessen Autor

> vor allem die sinnbildhafte Bedeutung, die er in einer bestimmten historischen Situation zu erkennen glaubt, [interessiert]. Die historische Realität ist [also] nicht Sinn und Zweck [s]einer Arbeit, sondern ein Steinbruch: Stoff für einen Roman. [Dieser] Roman... indem er von fremden Epochen und Kulturen erzählt, vermittelt... nicht nur einen Begriff von der Gewordenheit unserer Gegenwart, sondern hält uns zugleich einen Spiegel vor, um abgestorbene Wurzeln unseres kollektiven Denkens und Empfindens zu revitalisieren. (Prange 61ff)

Das Mittelalter eignet sich wohl deshalb so gut dafür, weil es, wie Jacques LeGoff in Bezug auf Scotts *Ivanhoe* sagt, »nahezu magische Kraft [besitzt, jemanden] in ein fremdes Territorium zu versetzen, ... aus den Wirrnissen und Unzulänglichkeiten der Gegenwart herauszureißen und sich mir damit gleichzeitig klarer und erregender zu präsentieren« (LeGoff 13).

LeGoffs These und der Versuch, Tolkien mithilfe der Mediävisitk zu lesen, stellt nun das genaue Gegenteil dessen dar, was man gemeinhin von einem modernen Text erwartet, der sich mit der Vergangenheit befasst – einem historischen Roman etwa. Schließlich soll ein jedes fiktionale Werk über Geschichte immer vor allem ein Werk über die Gegenwart sein, die sich im Spiegel der Vergangenheit ihrer selbst zu vergewissern sucht (vgl. Prange 62).

Es soll an dieser Stelle nicht darüber diskutiert werden, ob etwa *The Lord of the Rings* ein historischer Roman ist. Aber es ist anzunehmen, dass hier der Schnittpunkt liegt, an dem sich das Mittelalter zu Tolkiens Werken hinzugesellt. Tolkien selbst verweigert in seinem Vorwort zu *The Lord of the Rings* jede Art von Aktualität: »As for any inner meaning or ›message‹, it has in the intention of the author none. It is neither allegorical nor topical« (LotR xvi).[3]

---

3 Was nicht bedeuten muss, dass eine solche Interpretation nicht möglich ist.

Was bedeutet dieser Satz, gerade für einen Literaturwissenschaftler? Tolkien schreibt nicht über ein historisch verbürgtes Mittelalter, sondern über ein imaginäres. Die Denkweise hinter diesem Vorgehen erläutert Tolkien in seinem Essay *On Fairy-Stories* in einer Metapher, die er bei Dasent entlehnt:

> We must be satisfied with the soup that is set before us, and not desire to see the bones of the ox out of which it has been boiled. Though, oddly enough, Dasent by "the soup" meant a mishmash of bogus pre-history founded on the early surmises of Comparative Philology; and by "desire to see the bones" he meant a demand to see the workings and the proofs that led to these theories. By "the soup" I mean the story as it is served up by its author or teller, and by "the bones" its sources or material — even when (by rare luck) those can be with certainty discovered. (FS 120)

Mit jenen ›Knochen‹ beschäftigt sich Tolkien in seinem akademischen Alltag. Er ist ein Philologe, der mittelalterliche Texte liest, ediert und interpretiert. In seinen eigenen Texten geht es ihm aber nicht darum, diese philologischen Quellen zu zitieren, sie sind vielmehr Ausgangspunkte bzw. Fenster für bzw. zu seinen eigenen Texten. Für Tolkien sind nicht vorrangig die ›Knochen‹ interessant, also die philologischen Quellen bzw. deren Herkunft, sondern das Produkt, d.h. die Texte, die aus diesen hervorgehen. Die Tatsache, dass ihre Quellen nicht verortbar sind, ist für Tolkien kein Indiz, ihre Glaubwürdigkeit oder ihren Wahrheitsgehalt in Frage zu stellen. Es gibt ihm vielmehr eine größere Freiheit, um diese als ›Zutat‹ für seine eigenen Texte zu nutzen:

> Speaking of the history of stories and especially of fairy-stories we may say that the Pot of Soup, the Cauldron of Story, has always been boiling, and to it have continually been added new bits, dainty and undainty. For this reason, to take a casual example, the fact that a story resembling the one known as *The Goosegirl* (*Die Gänsemagd* in Grimm) is told in the thirteenth century of Bertha Broadfoot, mother of Charlemagne, really proves nothing either way: neither that the story was (in the thirteenth century) descending from Olympus or Asgard by way of an already legendary king of old, on its way to become a Hausmärchen; nor that it was on its way up. The story is found to be widespread, unattached to the mother of Charlemagne or to any historical character. From this fact by itself we certainly cannot deduce that it is not true of Charlemagne's mother, though that is the kind of deduction that is most frequently made from that kind of evidence. The opinion that the story is not true of Bertha Broadfoot must be founded on something else: on features in the story which the critic's

> philosophy does not allow to be possible in "real life," so that he would actually disbelieve the tale, even if it were found nowhere else; or on the existence of good historical evidence that Bertha's actual life was quite different, so that he would disbelieve the tale, even if his philosophy allowed that it was perfectly possible in "real life". (FS 125)

Tolkiens literarisches Konzept von (historischer) Geschichte zielt also nicht auf Realität im philologischen bzw. historischen Sinne. Sondern auf etwas Anderes:

> But when we have done all that research — collection and comparison of the tales of many lands — can do; when we have explained many of the elements commonly found embedded in fairy-stories (such as step-mothers, enchanted bears and bulls, cannibal witches, taboos on names, and the like) as relics of ancient customs once practised in daily life, or of beliefs once held as beliefs and not as "fancies" — there remains still a point too often forgotten: that is the effect produced now by these old things in the stories as they are. (FS 128)

Diese Aussagen sind ein erster Ansatz, die Idee eines Mittelalters in Tolkiens literarischen Texten zu verstehen. Hier gibt es kein (literatur-)historisch korrektes Mittelalter, sondern die Imagination eines denkbaren Mittelalters, eines erzählten Mittelalters, dessen Zutaten aus dem ›Suppentopf‹ stammen, in dem sich neben anderen auch Arthur, Beowulf, Froda the King of the Heathobards, aber auch Thórr befinden.

Dass dieses Konzept für Tolkien nicht nur Teil seines literarischen Schaffens, sondern auch seiner wissenschaftlichen Arbeit ist, zeigt die Verteidigung der Monster in seinem Vortrag *Beowulf: The Monsters and the Critics* (vgl. BMC 5ff). Denn,

> man würde gründlich am *Wesen* des [Monsters] vorbeigehen, wollte man dieses auf einen möglichen »Realitätsgehalt« reduzieren. Aus kulturanthropologischer und phänomenologischer Perspektive ist letztlich nicht das Körnchen positivistischer Wahrheit hinter einem Phänomen interessant, sondern das Phänomen selbst. Es gilt zu fragen: Was (und wie) bedeutet das Monster? Was will es uns zeigen und woraus besteht seine Wahrheit? Denn selbstverständlich sind Monster auch ohne leibhaftige Existenz wahr, nämlich dann, wenn sie als Protagonisten eines mythischen Wissens (der Lévi-Strauss'schen *pensée sauvage*) zum Verständnis der Welt beitragen. (Toggweiler 12)

Die mittelalterlichen Figuren, Namen, Motive, die mittelalterlichen Denkmodelle und die Kosmologie funktionieren in Tolkiens Werken ebenso wie die Monster. Sie fungieren als Träger eines mythischen, aber vor allem poetischen Wissens von einer Anderswelt – Tolkien würde sie vielleicht Faërie nennen (vgl. FS 126).[4] Die Folge des Betretens dieser Anderswelt können mit Tolkien gesprochen »Recovery, Escape, Consolation« (vgl. FS 145ff) sein. Es sei an LeGoffs Ausführungen zur Attraktivität des Mittelalters erinnert. Mit diesem Gedanken kann die Frage, ob Tolkiens literarische Werke historische Romane sind, eindeutig verneint werden. Wissenschaftliche Texte jedoch sind sie – natürlich – auch nicht. Tolkientexte sind weder als die Selbstversicherung gedacht, die der historische Roman liefert, noch wollen sie ein historisch korrektes Mittelalter zeigen. Tolkien interessiert der poetische Effekt eines Textes weitaus mehr als seine historische Genauigkeit (im Sinne einer Geschichtswissenschaft). Und so funktioniert das Mittelalter in seinen eigenen Texten als eine Art Brücke, die mit poetischem Sprechen über eine Vergangenheit Fremdheit erzeugt, die wiederum eine Dialogizität mit der Vergangenheit ermöglicht. Diese Möglichkeit des Dialoges mit einer Anderswelt/Fremdheit setzt immer das Bewusstsein eines Dualismus von Eigenem und Fremdem voraus.

Dies hat für die Interpretation zunächst praktische Folgen, die ganz auf der Textebene liegen. Die von Honegger aufgezeigten Phänomene sind zwar Zutaten aus dem ›Suppentopf‹, das kann aber nicht bedeuten, ihre anzunehmenden Alteritäten, d.h. die kulturell-historische Distanz zwischen Mittelalter und Moderne, für Tolkiens Texte zu ignorieren. In einigen Fällen fällt dies leichter als in anderen. Die politische Konzeption des perfekten Königtums, wie es in *The Lord of the Rings* auffindbar ist, wird z.B. augenscheinlich leicht mit dem Modell des feudalen Lehensystems des Mittelalters erklärbar.

Dass mittelalterliche Denkformen in der Interpretation hingegen nicht immer ernst genommen werden, und dies oft gerade dann, wenn der Fremdheitsaspekt möglicherweise besonders hoch erscheint, lässt sich ebenfalls an einigen Beispielen zeigen. Exemplarisch soll hier nur auf eines eingegangen werden: Peter Jackson war nicht der erste, aber vielleicht derjenige mit der größten Diskursmacht, der die Fremdheit, die der Konzeption der Figur Éowyn/Dernhelm innewohnt, missversteht bzw. diese nicht erträgt. Jackson lässt es in seiner Verfilmung nicht einmal zu, dass aus der Frau Éowyn der Mann Dernhelm wird. Das Ausmaß der Fremdheit (und die Möglichkeit des Missverstehens

---

4   Natürlich ist die Wahrnehmung der Fremdheit nicht zwingend für die Lektüre und die Identifikation mit den Texten, jedoch blendet eine solche Lesart zuweilen wesentliche Bestandteile der Texte, deren Disparität und Alterität aus.

dieser Denkfigur) kann stellvertretend an einem Zitat von Fredrick and McBride gezeigt werden.

> For Tolkien, "female warrior" is a conjunction of ... opposites; he can imagine one or the other, but not both simultaneously. ...She is sick in her soul due unwillingness to accept her lot in life: living as female... Tolkien's choice for a would-be female warrior: submit to your alloted role as wife, or die. Éowyns healing is a victory [for] civilization; an unruly impulse to transcend prescribed gender roles has been successfully thwarted.
> (Fredrick/McBride 113)

Dies könnte stimmen, wäre *The Lord of the Rings* ein historischer Roman, der in der Gestalt Éowyns über die Rolle der Frau in der heutigen Gesellschaft reflektieren will[5] — eine Selbstversicherung eben. Dass Konzepte wie »shieldmaiden« (vgl. LotR 679) auf etwas Anderes hindeuten, wird dabei übersehen. Ohne genauer auf die Frage eingehen zu wollen, wie Éowyns Transformation zu Dernhelm und zurück besser zu interpretieren wäre, kann hier gezeigt werden, dass ein Ausblenden der Fremdheit des Textes zu modernen, aber nicht unbedingt tragfähigen Deutungen führt. Folgte man beispielsweise Schiebingers an Laqueurs angelehnter These, dass Geschlechtsunterschiede vor der Moderne im Wesentlichen als soziale Unterschiede gedacht und nicht in biologisierten Dichotomien zu denken sind (»To be a man or a woman was to hold a social rank, a place in society, to assume a cultural role, not to be organically one or the other of two incommensurable sexes«, Schiebinger 124), könnte Éowyns wortwörtliche Vermännlichung durch ihren oder seinen Status als Krieger nicht ohne weiteres als ein störender Impuls, sondern als etwas Fremdes interpretiert werden, das auf das Mittelalter verweist. Diese Liste ließe sich fortführen, wenn man über die Konzepte von Freundschaft, Gewalt, Autorenverständnis, Geschichtsauffassung, dem Verhältnis von Mündlichkeit und Schriftlichkeit usw. in Tolkiens Texten nachdenkt. Letztlich bedeutet dies vorrangig, dass der Fakt der Verwendung mittelalterlicher Stoffe und Motive in ihrer Bedeutung und möglichen Fremdheit zunächst ernst genommen werden muss, um den »effect produced... by these old things in the stories« (FS 128) hervorzubringen. Thomas Honegger ist also zuzustimmen: Es ist nicht von Schaden, eine mediävistische Interpretation der Tolkien'schen Texte immer wieder in Betracht zu ziehen.

---

5 Damit soll nicht gesagt werden, dass die Methoden der Gender Studies o.ä. nicht zur Interpretation des Tolkien'schen Werkes geeignet seien. Vielmehr geht es darum, ein Beispiel von methodisch unhinterfragter moderner Interpretation zu zeigen.

Darüber hinaus scheint es gerade in Bezug auf die Stoffgeschichte lohnenswert, in deren Tradition Tolkien sich begibt, einen weiteren Aspekt des Tolkien'schen Werkes zu beleuchten, bei dem das Mittelalter eine wesentliche Rolle spielt. Shippey arbeitet in seinem *Author of the Century* penibel die Teile des *Hobbit* heraus, die sich direkt auf den *Beowulf*, die *Fáfnismál* und andere mittelalterliche Quellen beziehen. Tolkien selbst sagt in einem Brief:

> *Beowulf* is among my most valued sources; though it was not consciously present to the mind in the process of writing, in which the episode of the theft arose naturally (and almost inevitably) from the circumstances. It is difficult to think of any other way of conducting the story at that point. (L 31)

Tolkien beruft sich hier nicht nur auf eine Quelle, sondern letztlich auf deren Autor als seinen Gewährsmann. Er schöpft — um bei seinem eigenen Bild zu bleiben — aus der Suppe. Es kann also angenommen werden, dass die Quellenberufung zu Recht verdeutlicht, hier wird »nichts Neues dargebracht, sondern, wie auch in der mittelalterlichen Tradition, überliefertes, verbürgtes Wissen« (Pesch 79; vgl. Bauer 169) aufgenommen und weitergegeben.

Dies hat zwei Konsequenzen: Zum einen liegt hier ein Autorenverständnis vor, das dem des Mittelalters sehr nahe kommt. Dort ist der Autor »nicht der Erfinder, sondern der Finder eines Stoffes. Vom Autor wird nicht verlangt, dass er... Originelles präsentiert, sondern er soll sein Publikum mit etwas Altem, per Tradition Bewährtem versehen... Die meisten mittelalterlichen Autoren beteuern also zumindest, dass sie für ihre Werke Quellen benutzt haben, und zwar in den Werken selbst« (Brandt 104).

So definiert auch Tolkien oft seinen Anteil an der Autorenschaft. Im *Hobbit* geschieht dies noch implizit: »Gandalf came by. Gandalf! If you had heard only a quarter of what I have heard about him, and I have only heard very little of all there is to hear, you would be prepared for any sort of remarkable tale« (H 15). Die Isomorphie ›heard‹ kennzeichnet den Erzähler als Vermittler gehörten Wissens (vgl. Bauer 170), wie es ähnlich auch im Nibelungenlied zu finden ist: »Uns ist in alten maeren wunders vil geseit« (Nibelungenlied V.1). Natürlich findet sich dies in dem von Tolkien beanspruchten Referenztext: »Die Gesamtrahmung des *Beowulf* durch das Hwæt, wé Gárdena [in géardagum], die wiederholte Bewusstmachung der erzählerischen Vermittlung durch entsprechende *oral-formulaic devices* wie *ic hyrde*, oder *ic gefrægn*, ...lässt eine selbstreferenzielle Doppelung entstehen, die den *Beowulf* als Stofftradition neben anderen, als Teil einer mündlichen Überlieferungstradition und schließlich als Text an sich bewusst macht« (Eitelmann 97). Dieses wiederum führt dazu, dass die »erzeugte Textbedeutung einem Realitätsbereich zuortbar wird, der außerhalb des kommunikativen Aktes zugeordnet und als ›wahr‹« (Eitelmann

228) angenommen wird. Die Ähnlichkeit zu Tolkiens Konzept des ›true‹ und der Zweitschöpfung, die er in *On Fairy-Stories* entwirft (vgl. FS 132), sind augenscheinlich:

> Children are capable, of course, of literary belief, when the story-maker's art is good enough to produce it. That state of mind has been called "willing suspension of disbelief." But this does not seem to me a good description of what happens. What really happens is that the story-maker proves a successful "sub-creator." He makes a Secondary World which your mind can enter. Inside it, what he relates is "true": it accords with the laws of that world. You therefore believe it, while you are, as it were, inside. (FS 132)

In *The Lord of the Rings* findet sich eine komplexere Quellenangabe, die Zielrichtung bleibt jedoch die gleiche: »This account of the end of the Third Age is drawn mainly from the Red Book of Westmarch« (LotR 15). Es ist anzunehmen, dass dies nämliches Buch ist, das Bilbo am Ende des *Hobbit* begonnen hat (vgl. H 284) und das somit wiederum auf eine mündliche Quelle rückführbar wäre. Neben der Wahrheitsbeteuerung durch die Vorgabe einer Quelle stößt man hier also auch noch auf den Wechsel von Mündlichkeit zu Schriftlichkeit. Nun befinden sich diese Quellen innerhalb des Tolkien'schen Kosmos. Darüber hinaus weisen die Bezüge auf *Beowulf*. Tolkien selbst nimmt für die *Beowulf*-Lektüre des zeitgenössischen Publikums Folgendes an:

> This poem cannot be criticized or comprehended, if its original audience is imagined in like case to ourselves, possessing only *Beowulf* in splendid isolation. For *Beowulf* was not designed to tell the tale of Hygelac's fall, or for that matter to give the whole biography of Beowulf, still less to write the history of the Geatish kingdom and its downfall. But it used knowledge of these things for its own purpose — to give that sense of perspective, of antiquity with a greater and yet darker antiquity behind. (BMC 31)

Der *Beowulf* selbst steht für Tolkien in einer älteren Stofftradition, und in diese Tradition reihen sich nun seine eigenen Texte ein. Die Verbindung zwischen der Mittelerde Tolkiens und middangeard (also der Mittelerde) des *Beowulf*-Poeten ist offensichtlich und beabsichtigt. Spätestens von hier an ist Tolkiens Zugang zum Mittelalter kein philologischer oder literaturwissenschaftlicher, und dies ist ihm sehr wohl bewusst: »Tolkien once said that his typical response upon reading a medieval work was not to want to embark on a critical or philological study of it, but instead to write a modern work in the same tradition« (Anderson 1). Hier wird deutlich, dass der Mediävist Tolkien den Königsweg eines Zugangs zum Mittelalter nicht in einer wissenschaftlichen Herangehensweise, sondern in einem poetischen Sprechen bzw. Schreiben über die Vergangenheit findet. Als Autor stellt er sich auch in dieser Hinsicht in die Tradition des *Beowulf*-Poeten, denn er sagt:

> He cast his time into the long-ago, because already the long-ago had a special poetical attraction. He knew much about old days, and though his knowledge — of such things as sea-burial and the funeral pyre, for instance — was rich and poetical rather than accurate with the accuracy of modern archaeology (such as that is), one thing he knew clearly: those days were heathen — heathen, noble, and hopeless. (BMC 22)

Wie in *Beowulf* findet sich in Tolkiens literarischen Werken die Möglichkeit, historische Distanz zwischen der (vielleicht glorreichen) Vergangenheit und der eigenen Gegenwart im poetischen Sprechen über eben diese Vergangenheit zu überbrücken.

Eben genau darauf zielt das Turmgleichnis in *The Monster an the Critics* mehr als deutlich ab. Das Meer, das von der Spitze des Turmes aus gesehen werden kann, also »the illusion of historical truth and perspective« (BMC 7) ist dem Interesse an dem historischen Dokument *Beowulf* nicht nur vorzuziehen, für Tolkien ist jede Interpretationsweise schlicht ein Irrweg. Denn sonst würden Drachen, Monster und Helden und mit ihnen die poetische Wirkung der erzählten Geschichte zu bloßem (vielleicht gar störendem) Beiwerk. Für Tolkien zählt die Imagination und was diese bewirken kann, wie er es abermals am *Beowulf* beschreibt:

> *Beowulf* is not an actual picture of historic Denmark or Geatland or Sweden about A.D. 500. But it is (if with certain minor defects) on a general view a self-consistent picture, a construction bearing clearly the marks of design and thought. The whole must have succeeded admirably in creating in the minds of the poet's contemporaries the illusion of surveying a past, pagan but noble and fraught with a deep significance — a past that itself had depth and reached backward into a dark antiquity of sorrow. (BMC 27)

Das zeitgenössische Publikum des *Beowulf*-Poeten konnte sich also in einer Imagination dialogisch mit der eigenen (heroischen) Vergangenheit auseinandersetzen, und ein heutiges Publikum, das den poetischen Wert des *Beowulf* ernst nimmt, könnte dies ebenso.

Hierin liegt letztlich auch der besondere Reiz der Monster und des Drachens für Tolkien (und den *Beowulf*-Poeten). Beide scheiden in ihrer absoluten Fremdheit einerseits die Gegenwart von der heroischen Vergangenheit, und andererseits eröffnen sie durch ihre Fremdheit einen Imaginationsraum, der einen Zugang zu diesem Fremden ermöglicht. Der nicht-heidnische Text *Beowulf* bietet die Chance, mit der fremden und doch bekannten heidnischen und heroischen Vorzeit in einen Dialog zu treten. *Beowulf* produziert für den zeitgenössischen Hörer eine historische Realität, die zwar erzählt wird, aber nicht fiktional erscheint.

Tolkien beschreibt in seinem *Beowulf*-Aufsatz zwei Arten der Annäherung an Geschichte. Die eine erscheint als Philologie und Geschichtswissenschaft heute historisch korrekt, doch sein Missfallen gegenüber dieser Methode ist deutlich. Denen, die den Turm einreißen, um versteckte Inschriften auf dessen Steinen zu finden, und die, nachdem der Turm von ihnen eingerissen wurde, beklagen, wie verwahrlost er sei (vgl. BMC 7f), stellt Tolkien den Satz entgegen: »But from the top of that tower the man had been able to look out upon the sea« (BMC 8).

Was bedeutet dies für Tolkiens eigene Texte? Wenn, und davon ist auszugehen, auch er Geschichte als einen Steinbruch betrachtet, der Stoff für einen Roman liefert, der von fremden Epochen und Kulturen erzählt und einen Begriff von der Gewordenheit unserer Gegenwart vermittelt und die abgestorbenen Wurzeln unseres kollektiven Denkens und Empfindens revitalisieren kann (vgl. Gröbner 160ff), dann baut er mit seinen Texten genau wie der *Beowulf*-Poet einen Turm, von dessen Spitze die heroische Vergangenheit sichtbar ist. Die Bausteine dafür findet er eben dort. An dieser Stelle muss darauf hingewiesen werden, dass Tolkiens Profession als Philologe hier eine nicht unerhebliche Rolle spielt. Liefert der Suppenkessel etwas, das mit den alten Steinen des Turmes gleichzusetzen ist, so ist gewissermaßen die Philologie der Schöpflöffel.[6]

Im Zusammenspiel beider erschafft Tolkien das Bild einer fremden Welt, deren Struktur zwar nicht historisch korrekt, aber doch poetisch eine mittelalterliche heroische Vergangenheit imaginiert. Tolkiens Texte sind keine mittelalterlichen Texte, aber sie erlauben einen Blick auf ein poetisches Mittelalter in all seiner Fremdheit und Vertrautheit und eröffnen die Möglichkeit eines Dialogs mit der eigenen Vergangenheit. Tolkiens Mittel-Erde ist wie das Mittelalter selbst eine uns fremde, ferne Welt, doch sie steht in einer direkten Beziehung zu unserer Welt auf der einen und der des *Beowulf*-Poeten auf der anderen Seite.

Man muss hierfür akzeptieren, dass es dabei um poetisches, nicht um ein rekonstruiertes, wissenschaftlich-historisch korrektes Mittelalter geht, womit nicht von vornherein ausgeschlossen werden soll, dass beides ineinander zu fallen vermag. Dass diese Annäherung an DAS Mittelalter durchaus einen

---

6 Natürlich ist die Art des poetischen Sprechens nicht beliebig, die Erschaffung einer Sekundärwelt »inside it, what he relates is ›true‹: it accords with the laws of that world« (FS 132) ist dafür nötig. Dies ist einer der Schnittpunkte zwischen Tolkiens Wirken als Mediävist und seinen fiktionalen Texten.

wissenschaftlichen Wert besitzt, lässt sich durch die Ergebnisse des Versuchs Valentin Gröbners belegen, der u.a. der Frage nach der spezifischen Attraktivität des Mittelalters nachgeht. Eine Befragung von Vertretern der Fachwissenschaften zeigt, dass »das Mittelalter offensichtlich einen idealen Fluchtort vor dem eigenen Alltag darstellt« (Gröbner 12). Hinsichtlich seiner eigenen Motivation beschreibt er seine Erfahrungen als Demonstrant gegen den Bau der Startbahn West in Frankfurt, die ihn an den mittelalterlichen Karneval erinnert habe. »Über diese Mischung aus gespielter und echter Gewalt fing ich an, mich für das Mittelalter zu interessieren« (Gröbner 13). Es ist vielleicht kein Zufall, dass Jacques LeGoff in *Auf der Suche nach dem Mittelalter* Ähnliches von sich selbst beschreibt (vgl. LeGoff 11-13).

Dies ist nun mehr als bloßer Eskapismus (der Tolkien selbst und seinen Texten auch zuweilen vorgeworfen wird). Vielmehr ist hier das von Tolkien beschriebene »echo of an echo [a] call with a profound appeal« (BMC 33f) zu hören; und »to recapture such echoes is the final fruit of scholarship in an old tongue (and it is the most honourable object — rather than the analysis of an historical document) fruit that is good for all to eat if they may, but which can be gathered only in this way« (BC 146). So gesehen könnte Thomas Honeggers These also vielleicht ergänzt werden: Mediävisten sind die ›besseren‹ Tolkien-Leser. Und Tolkien-Leser sind vielleicht auch die ›besseren‹ Mediävisten.

Bibliographie

Anderson, Douglas A. *J.R.R. Tolkien. The Annotated Hobbit.* Revised and Expanded Edition. Boston/New York: Houghton Mifflin, 2002

Bauer, Hanspeter. *Die Verfahren der Textbildung in J.R.R. Tolkiens The Hobbit.* Bern/Frankfurt/New York: Peter Lang, 1983

Beowulf. Das Angelsächsische Heldenepos. Hg. Hans-Jürgen Hube. Prosaübersetzung, Originaltext, versgetreue Stabreimfassung. Wiesbaden: Matrixverlag, 2005

Brandt, Rüdiger. *Grundkurs germanistische Mediävistik/Literaturwissenschaft. Eine Einführung.* München: Wilhelm Fink Verlag, 1999

Brückner, Patrick A. »Der Dichter hält es seltsamerweise für lohnend, Drachen zum Thema zu machen ... der Drache als poetologisches Konzept von Realität bei J.R.R. Tolkien«. *Good Dragons are rare. An Inquiry into Literary Dragons East and West.* Hg. Fanfan Chen & Thomas Honegger. Frankfurt/New York et al.: Peter Lang, 2009, 215-270

Das Nibelungenlied. Mittelhochdeutscher Text und Übersetzung. 2 Bd., Bd. 1. Ed. und Übers. Helmut Brackert. Frankfurt: Fischer Taschenbuch, 2008

Eitelmann, Matthias. *Beowulfes Beorh. Das altenglische Beowulf-Epos als kultureller Gedächtnisspeicher.* Heidelberg: Universitätsverlag Winter, 2010

Frederick, Candice & Sam McBride. *Woman among the Inklings. Gender, C.S. Lewis, J.R.R. Tolkien and Charles Williams*. Westport, London: Greenwood Press, 2001

Dinzelbacher, Peter, Ed. *Sachwörterbuch der Mediävistik*. Stuttgart: Alfred Krömer Verlag, 1992

Groebner, Valentin. *Das Mittelalter hört nicht auf. Über historisches Erzählen*. München: C.H. Beck, 2008

Honegger, Thomas. »Die *interpretatio mediaevalia* von Tolkiens Werk«. *Hither Shore* 1 (2004): 37-51

LeGoff, Jacques. *Auf der Suche nach dem Mittelalter. Ein Gespräch*. München: C.H. Beck, 2004

Pesch, Helmut W. *Fantasy. Theorie und Geschichte einer literarischen Gattung*. 2. Ausgabe. Passau: edfc, 2001

Prange, Peter. »Zehn Thesen zum historischen Roman«. *History goes Pop. Zur Repräsentation von Geschichte in populären Medien und Genres*. Hg. Barbara Korte & Sylvia Paletschek. Bielefeld: transcript, 2009, 61-64

Schiebinger, Londa: *The Mind has no Sex?* Cambridge MA: Harvard University Press, 1991

Shippey, Tom. *J.R.R. Tolkien — Author of the Century*. London: HarperCollins, 2000

Titzmann, Michael. »Epoche«. *Reallexikon der deutschen Literaturwissenschaft. Bd. 1. A-G*. 3. neubearbeitete Auflage. Hg. Weimar, Klaus, Harald Fricke et al. Berlin/New York: de Gryter, 1997

Toggweiler, Michael. *Kleine Phänomenologie der Monster. Arbeitsblätter des Instituts für Sozialanthropologie der Universität Bern. Arbeitsblatt Nr. 42*. Bern: Universität Bern. Institut für Sozialanthropologie, 2008

Tolkien, John Ronald Reuel. *Beowulf and the Critics*. Ed. Michael D. C. Drout. Tempe AZ: Arizona Center for Medieval and Renaissance Studies, 2002

---. "Beowulf: The Monster and the Critics". *The Monster and the Critics and Other Essays*. Ed. Christopher Tolkien. London: HarperCollins, 2006, 5-48

---. *The Hobbit, or, There and back again*. Paperback Edition. London/Sydney: Allen & Unwin, 1983

---. *The Letters of J.R.R. Tolkien*, Paperback Edition. Ed. Humphrey Carpenter with the assistance of Christopher Tolkien. Boston/New York: Houghton Mifflin, 1981

---. "On Fairy-Stories". *The Monster and the Critics and Other Essays*. Ed. Christopher Tolkien. London: HarperCollins, 2006, 109-161

---. *The Lord of the Rings*. One Volume Paperback Edition. London: HarperCollins, 1995

Wapnewski, Peter. *Deutsche Literatur des Mittelalters: Ein Abriß von den Anfängen bis zum Ende der Blütezeit*. Göttingen: Vandenhoeck & Ruprecht, 1990

Time and Tide – Medieval Patterns of Interpreting the Passing of Time in Tolkien's Work

Thomas Honegger (Jena)

The perception and interpretation of time and the passing of things — and the realisation of our own mortality — constitute part of mankind's 'humanity' and distinguish us from most other creatures. The experience of time is thus a human universal, but the interpretation of time is not. Every civilisation and age seems to formulate its own interpretative patterns and it is the aim of this essay to focus on some specifically medieval patterns in Tolkien's narrative fictional works of *The Hobbit* and *The Lord of the Rings*.[1]

Time as an abstract concept is only rarely mentioned. Most readers may remember in this context Gollum's riddle in *The Hobbit*:

> *This thing all things devours:*
> *Birds, beasts, trees, flowers;*
> *Gnaws iron, bites steel;*
> *Grinds hard stones to meal;*
> *Slays king, ruins town,*
> *And beats high mountain down.* (H 82)

The answer to this riddle, as Bilbo found out only by chance and in the nick of time, is, of course, 'Time'. Douglas A. Anderson, in a lengthy note to that riddle, lists two analogues — one from medieval literature and the other from Icelandic folk tradition.[2] Both share the rather grim view of time as a destroyer of life. The fact that Bilbo had such a hard time finding the answer is telling: hobbits do not worry overmuch about the passing of time, about building monuments for eternity ('ruins') or about the continuation of dynasties ('king').[3] They are mortal, of course, but they seem bent on enjoying the time given to them rather than prolonging it — which may be a minor, additional reason why the

---

1 For a more comprehensive discussion of Tolkien's ideas on Time, see Verlyn Flieger's classic study *A Question of Time*.
2 The riddles are from the Old English *Second Dialogue of Solomon and Saturn* ('Old Age') and from Jon Arnason's *Izlenzkar Gatur* respectively (Anderson, *Hobbit* 127f).
3 That observation is in agreement with Shippey's (*Author* 26) classification of the riddles into archaic (asked by Gollum) vs. modern (asked by Bilbo–which I would rephrase as riddles with a 'classical-literary' pedigree (asked by Gollum) and those belonging rather to the folk-tradition (asked by Bilbo).

hobbit-Ring bearers were able to withstand the allure of the One Ring better than members of other races. Since *The Hobbit* and also *The Lord of the Rings* opens the action in the Shire, our discussion of Time begins with observations on 'Rural Time'.

Rural Time

> And so life in the Shire goes on very much as it has this past Age full of its own comings and goings, with change coming slowly–if it comes at all. For things are made to endure in the Shire, passing from one generation to the next.
> (Jackson, *The Fellowship of the Ring*, 11:37-11:54)

Although I usually distinguish very clearly between Peter Jackson's movie-version and Tolkien's book, I for once took recourse to the movie since Jackson captures an essential trait of the Shire and renders explicit what is found only implicitly in Tolkien's text: the apparent timelessness of the Shire. That 'rural timelessness' must not be confused with 'elvish timelessness',[4] as encountered in Lothlórien. For one, hobbits are mortal in the 'human' sense of the word and with a life expectancy of hundred to hundred-twenty years. Second, they know and use clocks. Bilbo has one on his mantelpiece (H 38) and Tolkien's drawing (No. 20 in *Pictures*) depicting the inside of Bag End shows a mounted wall-clock on the right-hand wall. References to the exact time, however, are rare. Thus the dwarves expect Bilbo to meet them at eleven o'clock sharp and the flustered hobbit reaches the inn "just on the stroke of eleven" (H 38). Bilbo then complains that he did not get the note "until after 10.45 to be precise" (H 39), to which Dwalin answers "Don't be precise." This dwarvish piece of advice sets the tone for the rest of the book and its sequel. 'Outdoor Time' and, as we will see, other time-schemes take over, and we never hear about clocks and watches and 'mechanical' time-keeping again. Bilbo pulling out a pocket watch on a chain from one of his waistcoat-pockets would be quite acceptable, but Elrond keeping track of the time at the council with a stylish wristwatch would be quite out of question.

The reader's brush with mechanical time is thus short and fleeting. Hobbit society knows about mechanical time keeping and has therefore the means to structure the passing of time, yet it does not impose a time-schedule on its citizens. Bells toll, but one gets the impression that this is to remind people of taking a break and have their second breakfast rather than to keep track of the working-hours. And adventures are, in Bilbo's mind, "[n]asty disturbing

---

4 See Flieger.

uncomfortable things" not because they disrupt your working day, but because they "[m]ake you late for dinner" (H 16). Life and work proceed at a pace that is not determined by the ticking of the clock, though this does not mean that people are lazy. Sam, for example, may have a lot of work to do on a sunny spring day, but he does not think about it in terms of hours and minutes (LotR 45). He will get up, probably at sunrise, and start work and, eventually, finish it — whether on the same day or not is of no importance. Devices such as time clocks are unknown, even to Saruman, though given time and space he would surely have introduced them.

Tolkien adds some more details that strengthen the impression of the Shire as a rural idyll, which has been forgotten and thus been largely spared by the cataclysms of the larger history of Middle-earth. As a consequence, time in the Shire flows at a more leisurely pace. One such detail is the calendar of the Shire and the Shire Reckoning. In *Appendix D* (LotR 1106-12) Tolkien discusses the nature of the different calendars and their relationship to each other. The technical details need not occupy us here since they play no role in the preceding narrative — with the important exception of the Shire Reckoning itself. As Tolkien explains in *Appendix D*, the hobbits of the Shire took the crossing of the Brandywine in 1601 T.A. as the starting point for their counting of years, and the events described in *The Lord of the Rings* are usually dated according to the Shire Reckoning. The effect of this parallelism of different calendars is a breaking up of the modern (largely Western) concept of a unified time-scheme. Our real-world civilisations know, of course, different calendars, too — thus 1 May 2011 AD corresponds in the Islamic calendar to the 27th day of the fifth month (Jumada I) of the year 1432. Alternatively, we are in the year 2554 of the Buddha Era, or in the year 5771 of the Jewish calendar. Western people usually stick to the Gregorian calendar, which has become the widely accepted standard in the world of international business, commerce and traffic (for obvious reasons). This 'unified perception of time' and the imposition of a universally accepted calendar is a recent achievement and largely due to the needs of a globalised market-economy and large-scale human mobility.

The history of the Western calendar[5] is too complex to sketch within the limits of this paper, yet the most salient facts for time keeping in the Middle Ages may be summarized as follows. The reckoning of the years in the Roman Empire took the foundation of Rome in 753 BC as one possible point of reference. More common was the format of referring to who held the office of consulship or to the year in the reign of an emperor. This latter form of dating, modified by replacing the emperor with the king, was also used by the Germanic tribes

---

5   See Dohrn-van Rossum for a competent account of time keeping in general.

that succeeded to most of the territory of the former Roman Empire.[6] The year itself was subdivided on the one hand by the seasonal changes — with winter and summer as the stable and universal elements,[7] accompanied by the seasonal labours and the astronomical phenomena (sun, moon, stars).[8] On the other hand, the Church calendar with the commemoration of the most important events from the life of Christ provided the spiritual framework. Any finer subdivision of time beyond the units of 'day' and 'night' had to rely on rather crude devices such as water clocks, candles, sun dials or other contraptions and played hardly a role outside the monastery and military. Time was not yet perceived as an abstract unit but as closely related to physical or meteorological phenomena in people's everyday lives. Noon in York was when the sun stood at the highest point and not when a mechanical clock told you that it is now 12 o'clock. Even our modern expression preserves the difference. It is 'twelve of the clock', which may or may not correspond to actual astronomical noon. Needless to say that noon in Holyhead differs from noon in York, and it was only in 1840 that the different (astronomically correct) local times (Local Apparent Solar Time) were supplemented and later replaced by the standard 'Railway Time'.[9] Concerning the Shire Reckoning, it may or may not be of importance that the calendar of the hobbits lags 1600 years behind the standard calendar — the vital point is that it lags behind to a considerable degree.

Tolkien thus alerts the reader to the fact that he or she has entered a world that is not yet 'standardised', that keeps its own identity and its own time-frame(s) — and transports him or her back into a pre-modern and pre-industrialised era with the Shire as an example of a pre-industrialised society not yet under the dictum of profitability. As such it is not specifically 'medieval', though the Middle Ages were often perceived (in hindsight) as an era of 'organic time' similar to the one encountered in the Shire.[10]

---

6 A way of counting years still used in Japan where each new emperor proclaims the beginning of a 'new era'. We are in 2011 in Heisei 23, i.e. the 23rd year of the reign of emperor Akihito.
7 The most common way of counting the years was by counting the winters. See Fischer for an illuminating discussion of the medieval division of the year into a varying number of seasons.
8 Both these elements are united in the (often lavish) illustrations of medieval Books of Hours. See, for example, *Les Très Riches Heures du Duc de Berry*.
9 'Local Solar Time' was sometimes indicated by means of an additional minute hand. See the Exchange Clock at Bristol with two minute hands–one indicating 'London Time', the other 'Bristol Time'.
10 For a discussion of this 'romantic' perception of the Middle Ages, see Honegger, *Past*.

Outdoor Time

> "We have at least a fortnight's journey before us..." (LotR 188)

It is an indication of Tolkien's skill as a narrator that he refrains from swamping the reader with all the confusing technical details of the various calendars and time-schemes. Those who delight in these matters can turn to *Appendix D*,[11] but the average reader need not be burdened with explanations about the differences between the King's Reckoning, the Stewart's Reckoning, and the Shire Reckoning. On the contrary, the narrator, before introducing any other man-made scheme, makes us (and the protagonists) first return to the natural rhythm of things. When Aragorn and the hobbits leave Bree, the last outpost of 'civilisation', and enter the wild country, they also leave behind clocks and the hour[12] as a measurement of time. From now on, time is measured by distances covered and by the astronomical units of 'day' and 'night' (with further subdivisions into 'morning', 'noon', 'afternoon', and 'evening'). It is a return to the basics, a stripping away of the thin layers of bourgeois veneer the hobbits had accumulated. Life follows the natural rhythm of getting up with the sun, of making camp when darkness falls, and of eating when hungry (if possible). The day is no longer structured along meals and snacks to be taken at leisure, but according to the basic 'animal' needs of the travellers.

Imperial Time

ragorn, when they approach Weathertop on their way to Rivendell, explains to his fellow-travellers:

> But long before, in the first days of the North Kingdom, they built a great watch-tower on Weathertop, Amon Sûl they called it. It was burned and broken, and nothing remains of it now but a tumbled ring, like a rough crown on the old hill's head. Yet once it was tall and fair. It is told that Elendil stood there watching for the coming of Gil-galad out of the West, in the days of the Last Alliance. (LotR 185)

So far the lands crossed had not provided any reminder of the past glories of the Númenórean kingdoms, maybe with the exception of the Great East Road

---

11 Real-world time-schemes before the great 'homogenisation' in the 20th century were equally confusing. See Cheney.
12 The narrator's comment "In the end there was more than three hours' delay" (LotR 179) is the last occurrence of 'hour' as a concrete time-unit.

and the (now disused) Greenway. The Shire has been too much of a provincial backwater for most of the time and thus been ignored by imperial building projects. Yet their journey brings the hobbits closer to more important provinces and even the heartlands of the former empire and, as a consequence, the witnesses of imperial glory in forms of ruins or as yet intact structures grow more numerous. This situation is paralleled in the real world in the centuries after the fall of Rome.[13] Ruins were plentiful in the area of the former Roman Empire, and they were a daily reminder of long-past imperial glory and power. The barbarian conquerors would sometimes take over the towns and cities, but the Germanic invaders in Britain preferred to settle in villages that were close to their fields and pastures.[14] The Roman villas and towns were either deserted or suffered a loss in population with an accompanying neglect of public buildings and defensive structures. These soon began to fall into disrepair and finally into ruin. Yet even though the newcomers had little use for the advanced Roman-town infrastructure, they were not completely immune to the melancholy appeal of its ruined grandeur. An unknown Anglo-Saxon poet composed moving lines known under the title *The Ruin*.[15] The poem describes the majestic remains of a Roman town, probably Bath (Aquae Sulis), and Tolkien drew some inspiration from it for Legolas's 'Lament of the Stones' in *The Fellowship of the Ring* (LotR 284; cf. Lee and Solopova 133-38). The reference to glories and empires gone has, of course, more than one dimension. Legolas's lament belongs clearly to the 'ubi sunt' tradition and the ruin of the watchtower on Weathertop, which is the subject of Aragorn's explanations in the quote given above, may also be interpreted in this vein. Yet it is equally — and maybe more so — a specific reminder of the 'imperial tradition'. The explicit reference to the North Kingdom of Arnor and the mention of Gil-galad and Elendil place the ruin within the context of the Númenórean empire and its successors in Middle-earth.

This creates a connection to both the Middle Ages and to classical antiquity. The situation encountered by the hobbits, once they have left their more or less secure homeland, is similar to that in the late 8th and 9th centuries in Europe and the Near East. The Western Roman Empire (read: the North Kingdom of Arnor) has gone while the Eastern Roman Empire (read: the South Kingdom of Gondor) is still in existence, though it also has come increasingly under threat from the newly risen Islamic powers (read: tribes from the East, and later Sauron). I am not arguing for close parallels between real world events and Middle-earth history, but for an overall resemblance of the general situa-

---

13 See Bates for a general discussion of the parallels between Tolkien's Middle-earth and early medieval (mostly north-western) Europe.
14 See, for example, chapter two ('The Lost Centuries: 400-600', pages 20-44) in James Campbell's *The Anglo-Saxons*.
15 Text, translation and commentary at: http://en.wikipedia.org/wiki/The_Ruin

tion[16] and a shared acceptance of what is commonly known as the 'renovatio imperii' and the 'translatio imperii', i.e. the 'restoration and transfer of the empire/power'.[17]

The last Western Roman ruler carrying the title 'emperor' was Romulus Augustulus, who was deposited by Odoacer in AD 476. The incumbent in Byzantium, the Eastern Roman emperor, was thus the only one left and considered himself the rightful heir to the remnants of the Western Roman territories. The Byzantine overlordship was accepted (at least in political theory if not in military practice) by most rulers ('kings') of the remnants of the Western Roman Empire — until the rise of the Franks some centuries later. Charlemagne, by assuming the title 'emperor' upon his coronation by the pope in Rome on Christmas day in the year 800, was challenging this claim. The king of the Franks and new emperor saw himself as *Augustus Imperator Renovatio Imperii Romani*, i.e. as the Emperor of the Renewed Roman Empire and thus as the direct successor of the Western Roman emperors. Later, after the dissolution of the original Frankish empire, the idea of the continuation of the Roman Empire was kept up and found its typically medieval form in the concept of the 'translatio imperii'.

That concept dates from the 12th century (Otto von Freising, Chrétien de Troyes) and tries to place the fall of Rome and the rise of the Carolingian empire (and its successors) within a larger framework of eschatological biblical and Christian history. The point of departure is Daniel's interpretation of Nebuchadnezzar's dream in the second chapter of the *Old Testament* 'Book of Daniel'. Nebuchadnezzar, King of Babylon, had a dream and Daniel volunteers to interpret it. The relevant passage reads as follows: "This image's head was of fine gold, his breast and his arms of silver, his belly and his thighs of brass, his legs of iron, his feet part of iron and part of clay" (*Daniel* 2, 32-33). Daniel interprets the composite elements of the statue as representing Nebuchadnezzar's kingdom (gold) and its inferior successors. The destruction of the statue, then, is explained as follows: "And in the days of these kings shall the God of heaven set up a kingdom, which shall never be destroyed: and the kingdom shall not be left to other people, but it shall break in pieces and consume all these kingdoms, and it shall stand for ever" (*Daniel* 2, 44). Some centuries later Jerome (AD 347-420) identified the four kingdoms as Babylonia, Persia, Greece, and Rome (see illustration) — implying that with the end of the Roman Empire the Kingdom of God and thus the end of the world would be imminent. Little did he guess that the end of the Western Roman Empire would soon arrive (AD 476), yet not the Kingdom of God. In order to save the validity

---

16 See Straubhaar and Honegger, *Rohirrim*.
17 See the entries 'Renovatio' (vol. VII, 732-734) and 'Translatio Imperii' (vol. VIII, 944-946) in *Lexikon des Mittelalters* for concise and competent discussions of the terms.

of the prophecy and Saint Jerome's identification of the four kingdoms, the idea of the 'translatio imperii' was developed. Thus bishop Otto von Freising (AD 1114-1158) argued that the fourth kingdom had not ceased with the last Western Roman emperor, but continued in the form of the Byzantine empire, which was succeeded by the Frankish empire, which in turn passed on the power to the Longobards and they, finally, to the German emperor who established the Holy Roman Empire ('Heilige Römische Reich Deutscher Nation'), which officially lasted till 1806. Other authors and scholars begged to differ from this sequence, but agreed with the general concept of the 'imperial succession'. The linking of biblical history, antiquity, the Middle Ages and the centuries up to the French Revolution into an 'imperial continuum' is an important contribution of the Middle Ages towards the perception of time — a perception that stresses the continuations rather than the breaks and revolutions.

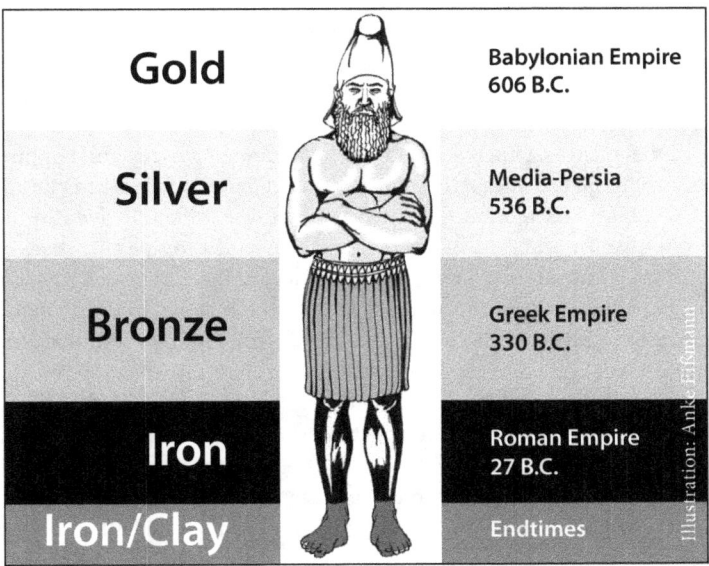

The situation in Middle-earth towards the end of the Third Age is not exactly the same as that of the Roman Empire in any stages of its dissolution, but we have some shared elements that strongly suggest the implied presence of these or similar concepts. Aragorn (Elessar) is undeniably a *renovator imperii* and revealed step by step as the representative of 'imperial time'. He successfully defeats Sauron (with a little help from his friends), is crowned by Gandalf (a *pontifex maximus* figure par excellence), restores the former extent of the

Gondorian lands, and brings to bloom a scion of the White Tree that traces its ancestry back to Númenor and the Undying Lands. However, since the eschatological-biblical framework is not yet available for an interpretation of the events in Middle-earth, they lack the teleological focus that is so characteristic of much of medieval history. All Aragorn can achieve in his time is the re-establishment of law and order, of just rule and peace — an achievement that, however, is not going to last forever. Aragorn's son Eldarion may be expected to continue the good work, yet there is no permanency. Tolkien's drafts for the story 'The New Shadow'[18] set later in the Fourth Age shows that he, too, saw the pattern of decay stopped only temporarily. The king of Gondor is not the messiah himself, at best his 'precursor' and steward.[19] Middle-earth is therefore a world 'in waiting' — we know in hindsight that until the incarnation all victories are "fruitless victories" (LotR 243), merely aimed at warding off evil in order to buy us time.

Yet this is not the place to attempt a discussion of the theological framework of Middle-earth, or to consider such illuminating text as *Athrabeth Finrod ah Andreth*. Instead, we have to stick to the fictional-literary world as presented in *The Lord of the Rings* and, to a lesser degree, *The Hobbit*. Concerning the larger themes and patterns, the pervading tone of much of *The Lord of the Rings* is one of loss, of melancholy, which does not exclude moments of joy and happiness — but these are to be found mostly in places that remain isolated and cut off from the world at large. As soon as we leave the Shire, we come into a world that has grown old and for whom only the incarnation will provide the chance for a new beginning and a permanent reversal of decay. The Fall, it can be argued, is within Christian history the one event that starts 'history' in the human sense of the meaning. Little is said about the 'passing of Time' in Paradise, but it is likely that it was considerably less event-driven than our history. Without the Fall, Adam and Eve would have 'evolved' and 'grown' as much as a tree grows or a caterpillar changes into a butterfly, and they and their progeny would have eventually been taken up into Heaven. Yet the incarnation and redemption of mankind does not automatically mean a return to a pre-Fall state of innocence. The original route towards Heaven has been blocked by the Fall, and mankind had to await the coming of Christ to open up a new route towards the original destination (the Heavenly Kingdom).

Had *The Lord of the Rings* ended with Aragorn's coronation and his marriage to Arwen Undómiel, it would have been more 'medieval' in tone and closer to a fairy-tale ending. Aragorn is, of course, a type of Christ, a messiah, come to deliver his subjects and the world of men from evil — and yet he is not *the*

---

18 The fragment has been published by Christopher Tolkien in *The Peoples of Middle-earth* (409-421).
19 See also Kranz.

messiah, merely a foreshadowing of the real redeemer. The status of Aragorn may be best seen as a pagan equivalent to an *Old Testament* 'type' within the typological framework of the interpretation of the *Bible*, one of the two major approaches developed by Christian interpreters faced with the problem of rendering the stories and histories in the *Bible* relevant for the later teachings of the Church.[20] The *New Testament* poses not that much of a problem and 'the Word of God' could be easily brought in line with Christian dogma. The *Old Testament*, by contrast, proved harder to reconcile with the new creed. Allegorical interpretation was one way of 'preserving' the truth (e.g. Abraham's three wives, Sarah, Hagar, and Keturah, were interpreted as representing three of the cardinal virtues). The other major exegetical approach was the typological interpretation of *Old Testament* events and persons. They were seen as 'types', as real world prophecies foreshadowing events or persons of the *New Testament* ('anti-types', e.g. Abraham sacrificing Isaac was seen as a foreshadowing of the crucifixion of Christ). This way biblical exegesis connected the 'pre-history' of Christianity (i.e. the time before the incarnation) with the time after the birth of Christ and tied it to the larger framework of the history of salvation (see graphic illustration).

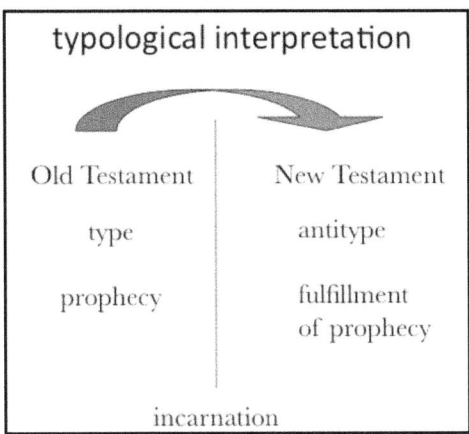

The Middle Ages would have recognised in Aragorn a redeemer figure and a 'type' of Christ (in the 'typological' meaning of the word). To modern readers, this form of interpretation is less familiar than allegory — and yet I believe that Tolkien's skilful implementation of parallels between Aragorn and the messiah and Charlemagne is a conscious attempt at invoking the 'typological'

---

20 See Michel's concise and accessible summary of the various methods used for interpreting the *Bible*.

dimension of time and history. This is even more likely since the typological approach is not as restrictive as full allegory and close to what Tolkien termed 'applicability'. Allegory, without the proper key, remains a 'locked box'. Not so typology, which works even (or especially) well with vague and associative rather than systematic parallels. Thus even without knowing about 'typology' we are able to respond to the figure of Aragorn and all he represents.[21]

The 'medieval' element in all of this is the pervading sense of continuation and coherence. Modern man tends to define himself predominantly in terms of differences and revolutions (the Copernican Revolution, the Enlightenment and as an indirect consequence the French Revolution, the Industrial Revolution, the Digital Revolution etc.) or cataclysmic events (WW I, WW II, 9/11), i.e. events that constitute a break with the preceding traditions and paradigms. Medieval man, by contrast, saw himself very much in a basically unbroken continuum that is only temporarily disrupted by such events as the 'Völkerwanderung' (Barbarian Invasions). Tolkien's depiction of the cultural-historical continuum of Middle-earth, then, is largely based on the implicit application of the medieval 'traditio' idea and thus renders it 'medieval' in the sense of pre-modern and pre-enlightenment with Aragorn as an important 'focus'.

Yet Aragorn is not only the embodiment of 'human Imperial Time' but also the preserver though not restorer of 'Mythic Time', which brings us to our next chapter.

Mythic Time and the Great Narrative

> Already she [Galadriel] seemed to him [Frodo], as by men of later days Elves still at times are seen: present and yet remote, a living vision of that which has already been left far behind by the flowing streams of Time. (LotR 373)

Taking 'myth' as a narrative explaining how the world came to be in its present form, the mythic dimension contributes towards the creation of the continuum that binds the primordial past ('in illo tempore') to the present. For modern man the master narratives of the Big Bang and of evolution have replaced the biblical account of creation, which in turn had superseded and ousted the older aetiological tales featuring deities and heroes. The effect was that with the loss of the biblical framework as the dominant frame of reference we have also lost the teleological orientation.

---

21 The fact that he is also an archetypal figure supports such an interpretation. See Honegger, *Approaches*, and O'Neill (esp. 140-143).

The development of the universe and of our world may be explained and, to some tiny degree even predicted as a highly complex interplay of 'cause-and-effect', but natural science has rightly refused to provide 'meaning' — this is simply not the kind of question natural science has set out to answer. So modern man finds himself caught in a world where the passing of time is accelerated by technological inventions and economic growth, but without an accompanying suitable explanatory narrative that would put things into a human perspective and give us answers to the 'Why?' and 'What for?'. Attempts to replace the former explanations and 'certainties' given by religion and myth by means of ideology have more or less failed (the very pointedly teleological view of history in Marxism comes to mind). Modern man has still the possibility to embrace religion, but it no longer comes 'naturally' and takes a conscious effort to master the art of 'double vision', i.e. to believe in the *Bible* and to accept the scientific point of view as well.

This scenario contrasts with what we know about the Middle Ages. The passing of time back then was perceived as firmly anchored within the framework of Divine Providence and part of the 'Great Narrative' of which human history is only one element. Events may therefore not always make sense immediately (at least from a human perspective), but in the long run they will. And here we have the major parallels to Middle-earth as presented in *The Lord of the Rings*.[22] Even without the information provided in the *Appendices* or in Tolkien's other Middle-earth writings (*The Silmarillion, The History of Middle-earth*), almost all readers will notice or, better, intuit the connectedness of events. Gandalf and other 'wise persons' such as Elrond or Galadriel may hint at what we would call 'Providence', but for the average reader it feels more like elven magic: it exists 'deep down' and is woven into the very structure of the narrative so that it can be perceived clearly only from a vantage point outside and 'above' events.

'Providence' may hide its tracks, but the conflict between the representatives of the forces of good and evil in Middle-earth is clearly discernible. Modern Western European man has been taught to interpret concepts such as 'good' and 'evil' or its representatives ('angels', 'devils') within a psychological framework and the Devil has ceased to be a physical reality. Tolkien's handling of the representation of evil in the Third Age of Middle-earth does not go back to the mythical-biblical bodily presence of the devil (= Morgoth), but it presents an 'intermediary' stage where the reality of evil is out of the question yet it is, at the same time, no longer present in a physically incarnated form — the Lidless Eye can be interpreted as many things, but I see it primarily as Tolkien's perspicuous comment on the continuing 'disembodiment' of evil. The overall effect

---

22 See Dickerson's illuminating study for an in-depth discussion of this aspect.

of this 'presence without a physical presence' recreates very much, as far as we know, the view of medieval man on the reality of evil and thus links the Great Narrative of Middle-earth with the one of Christianity also on this level.

Conclusion

> Yet it is not our part to master all the tides of the world, but to do what is in us for the succour of those years wherein we are set... (LotR 879)

Gandalf's answer to Imrahil sums up the overall scheme of how 'individual time' is linked to 'general time' in Middle-earth — and is equally valid as a description of the overall perception of time in the Middle Ages. This awareness of being part of a larger picture — explicitly so in medieval Christian thought, implicitly in *The Lord of the Rings* — is one of the main characteristics that link Tolkien's work with the Middle Ages. A second feature, which is intimately connected to the one mentioned before, is the pervading sense of continuity.

The form of continuity under discussion does not imply a standstill or presuppose a lack of changes. On the contrary. Both the Third Age and the Middle Ages started with cataclysmic events (the defeat of Sauron by the Last Alliance and the fall of the Western Roman Empire respectively), yet they nevertheless interpreted their own time as a continuation (under somewhat changed circumstances) whereas modern western civilisation often sees breaks (such as the French Revolution or WW I) as points of rupture.

In providing an overall sense of continuity Tolkien is not so much medieval as pre-modern. The specifically medieval flavour is due to the way he structures and alludes to this continuity by means of the typically medieval ideas and concepts — in particular that of the 'translatio imperii' and all it implies. Thus the modern reader may come to realise, like Sam, that in spite of the seemingly cataclysmic events "the great tales never end" (LotR 712).

Bibliography

Anderson, Douglas A., Ed. *The Annotated Hobbit*. Revised and expanded edition. Boston: Houghton Mifflin, 2002

Bates, Brian. *The Real Middle-earth*. New York/Basingstoke: Palgrave Macmillan, 2002

Campbell, James, Ed. *The Anglo-Saxons*. London: Penguin, 1991

Cheney, C.R., Ed. *A Handbook of Dates*. Revised by Michael Jones. Cambridge: Cambridge University Press, 2000

Dickerson, Matthew. *Following Gandalf. Epic Battles and Moral Victory in* The Lord of the Rings. Grand Rapids MI: Brazos Press, 2003

Dohrn-van Rossum, Gerhard. *Die Geschichte der Stunde. Uhren und moderne Zeitordnungen*. München: dtv, 1995

Fischer, Andreas. "'Sumer is icumen in': the Seasons of the Year in Middle English and Early Modern English". *Studies in Early Modern English*. Ed. Dieter Kastovsky. Berlin/New York: Mouton de Gruyter 1994, 79-95

Flieger, Verlyn. *A Question of Time. J.R.R. Tolkien's Road to Faërie*. Kent OH/London: The Kent State University Press, 1997

Honegger, Thomas. »›The Past is another country‹ — Romanticism, Tolkien, and the Middle Ages«. *Hither Shore* 7 (2010): 48-58

---. "More Light Than Shadow? Jungian Approaches to Tolkien and the Archetypal Image of the Shadow". Scholars' Forum at *The Lord of the Rings Plaza*, http://www.lotrplaza.com/forum/forum_posts.asp?TID=240994, 2011

---. "The Rohirrim: "Anglo-Saxons on Horseback"? An Inquiry into Tolkien's Use of Sources". *Tolkien and the Study of His Sources: Critical Essays*. Ed. Jason Fisher. Jefferson NC/London: McFarland, 2011, 116-132

Jackson, Peter (director). *The Lord of the Rings: The Fellowship of the Ring*. Special Extended Edition DVD. New Line Cinema, 2001

Kranz, Gisbert. »Der heilende Aragorn«. *Inklings - Jahrbuch für Literatur und Ästhetik* 2 (1984): 11-24

Lee, Stuart D. & Elizabeth Solopova. *The Keys of Middle-earth*. Houndmills: Palgrave Macmillan, 2005

Lexikon des Mittelalters. Nine volumes. Munich: dtv, 2002

Michel, Paul. »Anhang: Einige Grundbegriffe der mittelalterlichen Bibelauslegung«. *Tiersymbolik. Schriften zur Symbolforschung* 7. Ed. Paul Michel. Bern: Peter Lang, 1991, 205-217

O'Neill, Timothy R. *The Individuated Hobbit: Jung, Tolkien and the Archetypes of Middle-earth*. Boston: Houghton Mifflin Company, 1979

Shippey, Tom. *J.R.R. Tolkien. Author of the Century*. London: HarperCollins, 2000

Straubhaar, Sandra Ballif. "Myth, Late Roman History, and Multiculturalism in Tolkien's Middle-earth". *Tolkien and the Invention of Myth. A Reader*. Ed. Jane Chance. Lexington KT: The University Press of Kentucky, 101-117, 2004

Tolkien, John Ronald Reuel. *Pictures by J.R.R. Tolkien*. Foreword and Notes by Christopher Tolkien. Boston: Houghton Mifflin Company, 1979

---. *The Hobbit*. London: Grafton, 1991

---. *The Peoples of Middle-earth*. Volume 12 of *The History of Middle-earth*. Ed. Christopher Tolkien. London: HarperCollins, 1996

---. *The Lord of the Rings*. One-volume 50th anniversary edition. Boston/New York: Houghton Mifflin Company, 2004

Tolkien's *The Lay of Aotrou and Itroun*:
Medieval English Literature and the Early Stages of Sub-creation

Rafael J. Pascual & Eduardo Segura (Granada)

he Lay of Aotrou and Itroun (henceforth AI) is a fairy-tale[1] by J.R.R. Tolkien cast into the form of a medieval Breton *lai*. The final version that we know is first dated September 1930, and it was published in the *Welsh Review* in 1945. It can be seen as an early example of the coming and going mythopoeic tides that Tolkien was taming by the late 1920s, as the attempt of composing a mythology to dedicate to England progressed.

So far, AI has not attracted much critical attention. In 1972, P.H. Kocher pointed out the influence from Marie de France's Breton *lais*. In his two well-known books on Tolkien, T.A. Shippey suggested that its kernel was in L.C. Wimberly's account of the Breton song "Le Seigneur Nann et la Fée", and remarked on its clear moral content. Jessica Yates carried out an extensive source study in 1991, and concluded that Tolkien's inspiration was not Wimberly but F.J. Child's study of the "Clerk Colvill" story. More recently, C. Phelpstead analyses some important aspects of the poem within the broader context of Tolkien's Breton connections (see Phelpstead 89f).

According to Yates, Tolkien would have felt attracted towards the story, as it answered his obsession with the theme of love between a man and an elf-woman. Further, after reading in Child that there were Scandinavian, Italian, French, and Breton cognates but not an English one, he would have decided to fill in the gap by contributing his own version. Yates's point is, then, that Tolkien's aim was not writing a Breton *lai*, but telling the missing English version of the "Clerk Colvill" story. Adopting the form of a *lai* was a matter of historical consistency: by conforming to that genre, he presented himself as a minstrel who heard the story from a Breton *jongleur* and then gave his own version, just as Marie de France did. In Yates's opinion, Tolkien's interest in the "Clerk Colvill" story is evidenced by the fact that its Scandinavian cognate, the Icelandic folk-song "Ólafur Liljurós", was included in *Songs for the Philologists* (SP). From our point of view, there is more evidence to support this idea. "Ólafur Liljurós", the seventh item in SP, consists only of the first two and the

---

1 The term "fairy-tale" is used throughout to refer to any relatively short story made up of folklore motifs in which the fantastic (though not necessarily fairies) plays an essential narrative role, and in which the characters are developed enough as not to be an allegory and the moral is implicit enough as not to be a fable. Accordingly, "fairy-tale" can be taken as a synonym of myth as a tale, as the result of the telling, i.e., as a narration.

last stanzas of the original. Nevertheless, the last one ends by invoking the Virgin for protection, which is exactly how AI ends. This hints at the possibility that both tales be indeed cognates of the same story. But we may still wonder: is there any clue as for AI being the *English* cognate of the "Clerk Colvill" story? Although Yates does not mention it, it is continuously asserted throughout the poem that the story takes place in Brittany, *beyond the seas*. Besides, Aotrou rides to the forest of Brocéliande without sailing. This necessarily means, as Phelpstead remarks (92), that the story, while set in Brittany, is being told in England. This parallels Marie de France once more, who used the expression *les terres de là* to refer to France. This is given as evidence that she composed in England (see Taylor 54).

Now, it is not our aim to study Tolkien's sources. We rather intend to approach AI in the context of medieval literature, and thereby try to provide an answer to several questions which arise from Yates's article, such as how "Englishness" is conveyed in the poem and what the implications are of casting such a story into the form of a Breton *lai*. Hopefully, the first section of this chapter will make it evident that these two answers are closely related to each other. The second part, then, is primarily concerned with AI as a piece of art in the context of Tolkien's early stages of sub-creation.

The Lay of Aotrou and Itroun and Medieval English Literature

The most evident fact about AI is that it is a Breton *lai*. However, there seems to be some confusion when it comes to talking about Breton *lais*, Celtic mythology, and the Matter of Britain. It will be well to set the stage before proceeding any further by explaining what Breton *lais* are, and how they relate to the Matter of Britain in particular and Celtic folklore in general.

We use the expression "Breton *lai*" to refer to the literary genre as it was practised by Marie de France, a poetess writing most probably at the court of Henry II of England in the second half of the 12th century. These *lais* were short narrative poems in French written in octosyllabic couplets and varying in both length and subject-matter. They enjoyed a widespread popularity all throughout the Middle Ages (see Bédier 840).

The term "Breton" is due to Marie's claim that they have a Breton source. As Hoepffner underlines (112f), there is evidence enough to think this is true. It seems that the proto-*lais* out of which Marie's compositions evolved were Breton lyrics sung to the harp by Breton minstrels. An abridged oral retelling was later done in French for the sake of those who did not know the original language, and these oral renderings turned out to be Marie's source, to which she gave literary form.

As Barron stresses (23), despite their different subject-matters and plots, all of them pivoted around the idea of love as a fatal power. Further, as Taylor points out (54), such an idea was a clear reflection of the courtly mind of 12th-century France. The French influence was such that although some *lais* were written in English in the following centuries for which no French source is known, they were very much like the French in spirit and tone. Taylor also points out that the expression "Breton *lai*" gradually became a way of advertising a poem in the Middle Ages, no matter its relation to Brittany, or its connection to the 'Celtic'.

Sometimes, the plot of a *lai* was very similar to those of the Arthurian stories, or even the protagonists were the same. This was not a precondition, though. In actuality, AI is a *lai* which does not belong to the Matter of Britain. It then follows that the Matter of Britain is the body of legends and tales about King Arthur and his knights, and is therefore a thematic category. Besides, "Breton *lai*" is a formal category used to refer to the literary genre described above. A *lai* may therefore belong to the Matter of Britain as far as its characters, settings or plots are Arthurian. Both the genre of the Breton *lai* and the tales of Arthur and the Round Table (regardless their genre) are characterised by being Celtic in origin.

AI scrupulously conforms to the conventions of the *lai* in terms of form, length, and setting: Tolkien composes a 508-line poem in octosyllabic couplets, sets the story in Brittany, and claims a Breton source for his version (AI, verse 12). If AI was intended by Tolkien to be the lost *English* version of an old tale, how is its "Englishness" conveyed? And what is the point of casting such a tale into the form of a French-originated genre?

In 1925, R.M. Garret claimed that the 14th-century alliterative poem *Sir Gawain and the Green Knight* (*Gawain* hereafter) was the English equivalent of Marie de France's *lais*. His points were that the political circumstances of England at the time favoured, at last, literary instances of English patriotism, and that the *Gawain*-poet refers to his tale as a lay (verse 30). He continues by pointing out that the *lais* of Marie and *Gawain* share the following features: (1) a refined theory of love; (2) scrupulous courtliness embodied by Gawain; (3) an archaic atmosphere; (4) a connection to the Celtic underworld; (5) love of the picturesque; (6) high degree of artistry and polish; and (7) comparative brevity.

Describing a poem as a '*lai*' was a common advertising practice in the late Middle Ages, even if it was not strictly so (see above). Moreover, features 3, 4, and 5 are not exclusively characteristic to the Breton *lai* and *Gawain*, and are rather superficial to be decisive in determining any influence. As for number 7, the longest *lai* by Marie is 1184 lines whereas *Gawain* is made up of 2530 lines grouped into 101 stanzas. This surpasses by far the conventional length of a *lai*. Further, the parallel suggested by Garrett in 6 is even more dubious. The stanzaic grouping of lines and the complex disposition of the plot in *Gawain*, with the structurally-effective interlacement of the hunting- and the castle-scenes, far outreach the simpler structures of the *lais*. This consideration of structure leads us to features 1 and 2. As they refer to thematic rather than formal properties, they are more central to the question of whether *Gawain* is the English equivalent of a *lai*.

Gawain was in Tolkien's mind for most of his life. In the introduction to their edition of the poem, Tolkien and Gordon prais its exceptionally well-accomplished structure and "the strength of its plot" (Davis xiv), which contrasts to the weak plots inherited from Celtic legends in other Arthurian tales, such as Chrétien's *Yvain*. Further, in the introduction to his translation of the poem, Tolkien says that *Gawain* is "the work of a man capable of weaving elements taken from diverse sources into a texture of his own; and a man who would have in that labour a serious purpose. I would myself say that it is precisely that purpose that has with its harness proved the shaping tool which has given form to the material, given it the quality of a good tale on the surface, because it is more than that, if we look closer" (C. Tolkien, *Sir Gawain* 3).

Tolkien states that the structure in which the story of *Gawain* is presented is subservient to, and to a large extent the result of, the purpose the poet had in mind when handling his material. But what is that purpose? What else, besides a good tale, is *Gawain*? The answer to these questions can be found in Tolkien's authoritative *W.P. Ker Lecture* on the poem, published as an essay in *The Monsters and the Critics and Other Essays*.

Tolkien made it clear that the *Gawain*-poet's main motivation was to explore the relationship between courtesy and Christianity. In order to do that, he chose the courteous literary character of Gawain and, by means of combining the ancient folkloric motifs of the beheading game and the temptation of the lady, succeeded in setting up a plot structure effective enough as to be apt for leading its protagonist into a crisis which fundamentally questioned his beliefs, so that he had to opt for either courtesy or Christian religion. When the critical moment comes, Gawain places moral virtue above courteous service to a lady, and this service above mere trifles typical of Christmas pastimes. The last temptation attempt on Gawain is followed by his confession, after which he feels, at last, joyous and light-hearted, even though the menace of the Green Knight's blow is closer than ever. But, although he does not know it yet, he has escaped the real peril by resisting temptation. The lady's sexual insinuations were part of a plot devised by Morgan le Fay in order to make Gawain fall. When the Green Knight inflicts on him a little scar on the neck for having retained the magical girdle and reveals the true nature of the plot, Gawain reacts in a very excessive way, blaming himself of cowardice and covetousness. This characteristic excess of Gawain is, according to Tolkien, a master stroke on behalf of the poet, who avoids succumbing to the temptation of composing an allegory when it comes to giving a moral teaching. Gawain's believable personality is essential for the fairy-story not to become an allegory.

The *Gawain*-author, therefore, skilfully weaves old legendary strings together to produce a new tapestry, that is, a new fairy-story which is more than that. It is also the vehicle to convey the moral that virtue is more important than courteous love-making and knightly games. In actuality, it is the fact of being a fairy-tale, and not an allegory, that makes it the most appropriate channel to carry a moral (see p. 109).

In his article, when expanding on what according to him is the second common feature between the *lais* and *Gawain*, Garrett says that Gawain

> does not fall into the carefully-laid plot which the host's wife has prepared for him, not solely because of his chastity, but even more because his courtesy demands that he do nothing so unknightly as to betray his host's honor. (Garret 128)

Surprisingly, he continues by quoting the lines of the poem which make it evident that Gawain's main concern was virtue, not courtesy:

> *He cared for his cortaysye, lest crapayn he were,*
> *& more for his meschef, ȝif he schulde make synne,*
> *& be traytor to þat tolke, þat þat tolde aȝt.*
> (verses 1773-5)

As Tolkien explains (see MC 87), this is the first and only occasion in which the word "sin" is used in this moral poem. It is at this point that Gawain separates courtesy from Christian virtue, and places the latter above the former. Garrett is then completely missing the point. To be courteous is important, but to commit a sin is more serious stuff. And to be a traitor towards one's host by having an affair with his wife is not merely a matter of being a *crapayn* (a boor), but of being a sinner, as it is explicitly stated. It follows that if Garrett's assumption that *Gawain* is the English equivalent of a Breton *lai* is based on a misconception of courtesy as it is understood in *Gawain*, then such an assumption must with all certainty be wrong.

Garret's first feature in his series of similarities is the refined theory of love. This probably is the most decisive feature to determine direct influence. We have summarised the *Gawain*-poet's conception of love. In that poem, love in a courtly context is presented as something capable of being played "into the hands of the enemy" (MC 86). The whole poem is about the tension between courtesy and morality, its core being Gawain's opting for the latter choice. The following question inevitably follows: how is love conceived of in the *lais*? We have pointed out that they are a clear reflection of the French courtly mind. And if we have a look at Barron's authoritative study, he says that Marie's own attitude in her *lais*

> is amoral: religious issues are ignored, adultery is countenanced, but legal marriage is always the ultimate goal; the power of the institutions and prohibitions of her own society are acknowledged in the tragic outcome of some tales; but blame rests with the cruel fathers and jealous husbands rather than the lovers whose destiny justifies many devious shifts. (Barron 23)

As the reader will notice, it is no easy task to maintain that the late 14th-century poet who sets out to re-shape his old material into an essentially moral tale which severely criticises adultery pertains to the tradition of a 12th-century poetess whose attitude towards her own Celtic-derived material is amoral and whose stories are in fact a vindication of love as it was understood in the established tradition of the *leal amor* of the *Roman d'Eneas* (see Barron 23). Indeed, it may seem that if the *Gawain*-poet was taking Marie's *lais* at all into account, it was with an eye to getting the opposite results.

Now, there is one Breton *lai* to which *Gawain* does bear a number of similarities: Tolkien's AI. In AI we also have a protagonist led by a fay into a trap. And, as in *Gawain*, it is only after the trial has passed that its true nature is revealed. Once Aotrou has rejected the fay's sexual insinuations and thereby resisted the temptation of adultery, he sees in his dreams that the fay is in actuality the crone from which he asked help, and realises that either druery or his own life is the fee claimed for her services. Both Gawain and Aotrou resist the temptation of adultery. But despite that, Aotrou dies because he previously fell into the temptation of despair, which made him pledge that he would give the witch whatever she asked for in return for the fertility potion.

At the very beginning of AI, the Briton lord's fear to die childless is made clear. He also fears his estate to be occupied by strangers and that his lineage should come thus to an end. After much worry, he takes "counsel cold", which makes him finally give up all hope for his wife to become pregnant and to have recourse to the help of a witch. This witch is said to weave webs to snare the heart, and she actually prepares the potion before he ever meets her. In fact, in stanza number 6, when Aotrou gets to the witch's lair, the narrator says that she already knew him. From whom did Aotrou take the "counsel cold" which made him despair so much as to opt for the shortcut of magic? How is it possible that the witch knew what he wanted in advance? It seems that Aotrou was *induced* to fall into temptation. Probably it was part of the witch's plan. As we can see, there is a man who is not happy with his luck, and because of fear and pride tries to change it by means of magic. In doing so, he is putting his wife's life at risk. As the witch herself says before giving him the phial, "such potions oft, men say, have burned | the heart and brain" (verses 82-83). Moreover, Aotrou does not tell his wife that he has asked the witch for help. He secretly pours the potion into a cup of wine and gives it to her, disguising his act of treachery with an air of joyfulness. When his wife gets pregnant, he pretends to be glad that his hope and prayer have at last been answered. By behaving this way, he is betraying his ability to discern good from evil, so that his death at the end of the poem is presented as something he deserves. Itroun's death, which she did not deserve, only makes Aotrou's choice worse, and indeed cruel.

The obvious difference between *Gawain* and AI is that although both protagonists resist the temptation of adultery, Aotrou, unlike Gawain, succumbs to despair. But Gawain and Aotrou are by no means the same kind of character. The former is a young knight who, motivated by humility and altruism (see MC 75), takes his king's place in the perilous test. Aotrou, by contrast, is the sovereign lord of his estate who, out of pride and fear (AI, verse 17), risks his wife's life to have an heir. In this sense, AI is classically Tolkienian. In *The Homecoming of Beorhtnoth* and in his essay *Ofermod*, Tolkien showed his conviction that the 10th-century poet of *Maldon* was criticising the Anglo-Saxon earl who placed his fame and reputation over his subordinates' safety — which resulted in the death of them all. The same motif is appreciated in *Beowulf*. King Beowulf, "most eager for glory" (verse 3172), refuses to summon an army to encounter the dragon. The aftermath is his death and the end of his people. In *Gawain*, too, as Tolkien notes (see MC 75), Arthur himself is criticised, insofar as he allows Gawain to take on the Green Knight's foolish challenge just to safeguard his reputation. By contrast, in Tolkien's works his sympathies are with the humble and self-sacrificing, not with the proud and self-important. Such a preference shows up in AI, but in a negative manner.

It follows that, as is the case with *Gawain*, there is more in AI than meets the eye. The *Gawain*-poet explores the relation between courtesy and morality, and thereby conveys the moral that, when at a crossroads, virtue should be the choice. More concretely, Gawain's test and success conveys the message that, if the courtly love due to a lady leads into adultery, then chastity and loyalty are to be given precedence. In AI, Tolkien explores the relation between a courtly code of conduct and Christianity too, but from a different perspective. Both Aotrou's surrender to despair and magic, and his subsequent death, stress the importance of hope and trust in God. They also stress the danger of pride and fear. Aotrou fears that his lineage may end. The source of his fear is the pride of a lord, and that fear "plays into the hands of the enemy", as it makes him follow the "counsel cold" prepared by the witch as bait to lead him into her trap. To present his death as the result of an immoral action he carried out because of despair unequivocally brings forth the message that virtue lies in hope, prayer and humility.

Tolkien's AI resembles *Gawain* in being a fairy-story which works as the vehicle for a moral. Remarkably, both Tolkien and the *Gawain*-poet do so in a similar manner, i.e., by reshaping their old material anew on the basis of their ultimate moral purpose. In the introduction to their edition of *Gawain*, Gordon and Tolkien (see Davis xiv) stressed the two main adventures that the *Gawain*-poet inherits and re-handles to produce the new plot-structure for his story: the beheading game and the temptation by the lady. Likewise, AI is made up of two adventures inherited from older material: the meeting with the crone and the temptation of the fay. These are skilfully assembled by Tolkien so that they conform to the structure he needs for his purpose as a myth-poet. In *Gawain*, the crone and the deceitfully beautiful lady are also related. Right after Gawain's arrival in Bertilak's castle, he sees his host's wife and the old woman who apparently serves her. At that moment, neither Gawain nor the audience know that the latter is in actuality Morgan le Fay, the deviser of the deceptive plot. However, the poet anticipates it in lines 935-69, where he ironically contrasts the astonishing beauty of the one with the utter ugliness of the other. This opposition is appreciated in AI too, where the image of the crone is superimposed on to that of the fay at the fountain in Aotrou's last dream.

It was made clear above that the idea that *Gawain* is the English equivalent of a Breton *lai*, as Garrett suggested, is difficult to maintain, at least on the basis of Garrett's suggested similarities. But it still seems that Garrett felt there was something really English about *Gawain* beyond its alliterative form.

In an article published in 1997, C. Villar, drawing on previous studies by Jones, Rhys, and others, carried out a general survey of the evolution of three Arthurian characters throughout the history of the Matter of Britain — Gawain being one of them. He points out that in the ancient Welsh legends Gawain was regarded as a knight of very polite manners. That feature made of him a suitable character to fit into the new context where the Matter of Britain was going to occupy a relevant place: the France of courtly love. Thus, Chrétien de Troyes gave him a major role in his romances as the paradigm of courtly conduct. Nevertheless, as time passed by, Chrétien deprived him of his original function and depicted him as a frivolous figure. Such is the Gawain portrayed in some of Chrétien's later works such as his *Yvain*, criticised by Gordon and Tolkien (see Davis xiv). Such an ambivalent character was inherited by the French tradition, and authors had then the possibility to choose which aspect suited them better. Villar makes the interesting point that this duality of the character in the tradition of the French, as well as the predominance in romance of the French-originated character Lancelot du Lac, led English poets to initiate a national vindication of Gawain as a pious and moral character, and it is in this context that *Gawain* belongs. To put it another way, by reshaping his old material into a new story whose protagonist is a virtuous Gawain, the poet is not only conveying a moral by means of a fairy-tale; he is also making the Matter of Britain more English. Its alliterative metre can thus be understood as the upper-level 'Englishing' which naturally results from the deeper 'Englishing' which is the restructuring of the French material.

Both Shippey and Yates point out that in his re-handling of older sources for AI, Tolkien introduces something of his own: the reason for Aotrou's death, that is, his fear and despair, and his dealings with the witch. This is precisely what makes his later death appear not as something fortuitous, as in the stories on which Tolkien drew, but as the consequence of a moral transgression. It is Tolkien's handling and the resulting structure that allows for a moral in the story. In other words, Tolkien's description of the *Gawain*-poet (p. 103) readily applies to himself.

More recently, Honegger has stressed that the author of the Middle English romance *William of Palerne* failed to 'Englishise' it because, despite using the alliterative long line native to England in his translation, preserved intact the spirit and structure of his French source (see Honegger 120). If a comparison is established, *Gawain* clearly appears at the opposite end of a *continuum*. Its anonymous author did not limit himself to tell an old story using a native form. Rather, he completely re-handled his sources and imposed a new moral on them. Additionally, as the resulting new poem stood out against its French counterparts, it meant the English vindication of the Matter of Britain. The following question is then in order: where in the *continuum* does AI fall? It probably does right in the middle. By re-handling his old legendary material, Tolkien is capable of raising the plot-structure he needs for his story to convey the moral that any kind of virtue lies in hope. And by mapping it onto the conventional form of the Breton *lai*, he is contributing to and expanding on the genre. Nevertheless, bearing in mind Barron's overview of Marie's *lais*, Tolkien's contribution should strike us as surprising. His attitude towards his material and his ultimately moral purpose are in stark opposition to Marie's amoral approach. Casting such an utterly moral tale into the form of a Breton *lai* accentuates its morality, which is, in turn, the source of its Englishness. Like the *Gawain*-poet, Tolkien is contributing a peculiarly English work to the literary tradition of his country. But unlike the *Gawain*-poet, whose vindication was thematic, Tolkien is sub-creating the English cognate of a literary genre by conforming to its formal conventions. Consequently, Tolkien's AI is not only the English analogue of the "Clerk Colvill" story, as Yates pointed out. It is also the English version of a Breton *lai* — the version Garrett was looking for in *Gawain*.

The Lay of Aotrou and Itroun and the Early Stages of Sub-creation

A I can also be explored as an example of what a fairy-tale meant to Tolkien from the point of view of mythopoeia, i.e. as a narrative poem to demonstrate his deep conviction, that

> there is indeed no better medium for moral teaching than the good fairy-story (by which I mean a real deeply-rooted tale, told as a tale, and not a thinly disguised moral allegory).
>
> (MC 73)

This standpoint accepted, AI can be read as a purely Tolkienian fairy-story, a piece of the tapestry designed to become part of the vast backcloth of tales and myths intertwined and connected as the composition of the "Book of Lost Tales" was under way. Still, in what sense can AI be described as a 'fairy-story'? To answer this question we should go back to *On Fairy-Stories*, and see what a fairy-story is to Tolkien. It is well-known that in his view no fairies are needed to give a tale the inner consistency of reality.

Indeed, a good fairy-story does not exist to explain, or as an excuse to show, some kind of moral teaching. Instead, believability should rest on its inner structure, as well as on the balance between the beauty of the language and the power of the themes. The different elements must be aligned in order to make the whole understandable as a tale, as a story — as a myth. Its moral should emerge as the obvious reflection of the way things are in the present world, and not as the result of an authorial purpose to instruct — as an allegory. C.S Lewis puts it this way:

> In the sixteenth century when everyone was saying that poets (by which they meant all imaginative writers) ought 'to please and instruct', Tasso made a valuable distinction. He said that the poet, as poet, was concerned solely with pleasing. But then every poet was also a man and a citizen; in that capacity he ought to, and would wish to, make his work edifying as well as pleasing.
>
> (Lewis 45)

It can be assumed that Tolkien the poet shared his friend's opinion. AI can be read as a piece both to please and instruct. Tolkien's aim, we may speculate, was to tell a story in the form of a narrative poem to instruct on the risks of despair[2]. By giving the plot the form of a Breton *lai*, he was adding depth to the story. Now, some questions arise at this point concerning the study of AI. To what extent is Tolkien successful in telling a "good fairy-story" while at the same time teaching a moral? Does the fact that Aotrou means "lord" and Itroun "lady" in Breton influence our view that AI is a "good fairy-story"? If so, what elements in the poem hint at this achievement?

Tolkien underlines two main characteristics that are for a fairy-story to be 'good': it must be told as a tale, and have deep roots. Creating depth for AI is something that Tolkien achieved by giving the narrative voice to a lost Breton minstrel. In doing so, Tolkien was presenting the plot as part of the English tradition, whereas in a mythopoeic perspective his poem can be seen as an effort to remake old Celtic folklore, and then insert the *Book of Lost Tales* into the lost tradition — making it part of the "Matter of Middle-earth", to use Flieger's expression (Flieger 47f). AI is then presented as a myth reconstructed, incorporated into an incomplete tradition, but taken as a "deeply-rooted tale" from the point of view of the bonds between England and 'the Celtic'.

At the same time, AI is told *as a tale*. That means that it is supposed to be understandable as a story in its own right, presenting both the characters and the plot as something believable, and coherent. The very fact that the proper names of the characters are 'lord' and 'lady' can be understood as Tolkien's attempt to provide the poem with a universal meaning. Equal acceptance of happiness and sorrow shows the way to patience, wisdom, and ultimately holiness. The wages for those in despair is sadness, and in the end Aotrou is punished with death. The last stanza again introduces a main Catholic theme: hope beyond merit (as a straight consequence of the grace granted by Redemption), as well as mercy granted by the intercession of the Virgin, as it is stated at the end of the poem.

However, this explanation apparently leads to the conclusion that the poem is an allegory. We can argue that Tolkien was presenting the ballad having the *Gawain*-poet in mind on the basis of the study presented in the first part of this chapter. He would then be grafting a new moral onto his old material — another way to create depth. By the late 1920s, the time when AI was written,

---

2   Some of the most important works by Tolkien are related to hope, and its antonyms. For instance, from the point of view of themes, *The Lord of the Rings* is mainly a tale about hope as the counterbalance between death and immortality, and so it can be described as an epic elegy (see Segura 101f; Simonson 19f and 67f). Similarly, the story of Túrin Turambar provides an interesting approach the relation between hope and destiny. Examples can be easily multiplied.

Tolkien had not yet fully developed his own opinion on fairy-tales, at least with regards to children as the main public for such stories. But by 1945 he had done so, and that could provide an explanation that the end of the poem would be such an obvious moral teaching. After writing *The Hobbit*, Tolkien eventually changed his view on children and tales (see L 215, and FS 33ff), and undoubtedly his vision matured in the course of the composition of *The Lord of the Rings* (1937-1950). It makes sense that all through the years his mind was increasingly convinced that a "good fairy-story" was not related to "fairies" and "allegory" at all, but aimed pleasing its audience and providing links to the experience of the reader. The Preface to the revised edition of *The Lord of the Rings*, written in 1962, is clear and conclusive in this matter, especially concerning the notion of 'free applicability'.

Nevertheless, AI can also be read simply as a lost tale, part of the re-created mythology *of* England, intended to recover the flavour of both English language and belief. In fact, Aotrou's acts are the reflection of his own doubts, pride, and fear. His believable personality would add therefore to the poem's quality as a fairy-tale, in the same manner as Gawain's characteristic excess prevents the story from becoming an allegory. Further, the explicitness of Christian religion in AI might not necessarily be seen as an indication that a didactic purpose prevails over a sense of aesthetics. The story AI tells does not belong in the *legendarium* Tolkien devised *for* his country, but is presented as a lost legend *of* England, of which Christianity and the Virgin are as integral parts as the Valar or Galadriel are of Middle-earth.

In other words, as Yates pointed out, what Tolkien did by writing AI was filling a gap in the mythology *of* England by means of sub-creation. The distinction between a mythology *of* England and a mythology *for* England is the key to understand sub-creation as an artistic mode to intertwine reality and fiction. This distinction is, has been, and surely will be an object of discussion and study (see Drout 229f). In our view, the moment when Tolkien definitely realised that he was making a mythology for England was that of assuming that *The Lord of the Rings* was not the sequel to *The Hobbit*, but the cornerstone to *The Silmarillion*. The 10.000-words letter he sent to Milton Waldman in 1951 is just the reconstruction that Tolkien made of his own 'journey' forty years after he started to work on the *legendarium*[3].

Moreover, his intention can also be described in the outlook of an artist who conceived sub-creation as the precise means to give History the inner consistency of stories. In this way it can be better described how Tolkien came to the belief that his secondary world was 'real', and to what extent the time-

---

3 We take 1911 as the standpoint since we deem the T.C.B.S. as the beginning of the initial inspiration, the start of a task that was seen by Tolkien as a mission, or even better, as a vocation both as an artist and as an Englishman.

travel that his secondary worlds attempted, referred to a precise moment in the past of England. It was not a 'utopia', but more precisely, an experiment in 'ucronia'[4]. AI became a perfect chance to re-discover a tradition that was not purely English, but that *could* have been. This 'could' was a *leit-motif* in the making of Tolkien the inventor of Middle-earth, especially from the publication of *The Hobbit* onwards. And since AI was first composed in the late 1920s, it is easy to conclude that especially from 1916 on — the year when *The Fall of Gondolin* was composed —, Tolkien's main purpose was to sub-create a retold past of England in order to make a gift to his country: a new, or renewed, mythology; a myth that should appeal to the minds of those breathing the air of the North (L 131).

Now, Tolkien knew the attractive elements of AI were rooted in its very flavour, in the beauty of far-away mountains and places one will never explore (L 96 and 247). The elusive Celtic beauty that a consultant of Allen & Unwin perceived in his mythology is itself blurry, and it does not make it easy to define its limits, influences, and final form. From the blurry past of legends, Tolkien sub-created a believable past of his own, an imagined England that once was 'magical', closer to the earth and soil of the image he had of his beloved Lonely Isle. As Shippey has noted, "one extremely unexpected aspect of Tolkien's early writings is his determined identification of England with Elfland" (Shippey 303). Considering the fact that England was, after the Norman Conquest, the most demythologised country in Europe, and provided that Tolkien wanted to create an English-flavoured literary tapestry, he was obliged to make the context where those stories would appear as something believable, and most of all, genuinely English.

---

[4] That Tolkien invented an editor as the introductory figure to some of his major works to underline the 'truth' of the whole shows he was convinced that he was another link in the chain of the history of English 'lit.' by means of a reconstruction of English 'lang.'.

Bibliography

Barron, William Raymond Johnston. *English Medieval Romance*. London/New York: Longman, 1987

Bédier, Joseph. "Les Lais de Marie de France". *Revue de Deux Mondes* CVII (1891): 835-863

Carpenter, Humphrey, Ed. *The Letters of J.R.R. Tolkien*. Boston: Houghton Mifflin, 1981

Child, F.J. *The English and Scottish Popular Ballads*. Volume 1. Dover, 1965 (facsimile reprint of the 1882 edition)

Davis, Norman, Ed. *Sir Gawain and the Green Knight*. (Originally edited by J.R.R. Tolkien & E.V. Gordon). Oxford: Oxford University Press, 1967

Drout, Michael. "A Mythology for Anglo-Saxon England". *Tolkien and the Invention of Myth*. Ed. Jane Chance. Lexington KT: The University of Kentucky Press, 2004, 229-247

Flieger, Verlyn. "J.R.R. Tolkien and the Matter of Britain". *Mythlore* 87, Vol. 23, No. 1 (2000): 47-58

Garrett, R.M. "The Lay of Sir Gawayne and the Green Knight". *The Journal of English and Germanic Philology*, Vol. 24, No. 1 (1925): 125-134

Hoepffner, Ernest. "The Breton Lais". *Arthurian Literature in the Middle Ages*. Ed. R.S. Loomis. Oxford: Clarendon Press, 1959, 112-121

Honegger, Thomas. "Romancing the Form: Alliterative Metre and *William of Palerne*". *Clerks, Wives and Historians*. Eds. W. Rudolf et al. Berne: Peter Lang, 2007, 117-124

Kocher, Paul. *Master of Middle-earth: The Fiction of J.R.R. Tolkien*. New York: Del Rey, 2003

Lewis, Clive Staples. "Sometimes Fairy Stories May Say Best What's to Be Said". *On Stories and Other Essays on Literature*. San Diego: Harcourt Brace & Co., 1982

Phelpstead, Carl. *Tolkien and Wales. Language, Literature and Identity*. Cardiff: Cardiff University Press, 2011

Segura, Eduardo. *El viaje del Anillo*. Barcelona: Minotauro, 2004

Shippey, Tom. *The Road to Middle-earth*, Boston: Houghton Mifflin, 2003

Simonson, Martin. *The Lord of the Rings and the Western Narrative Tradition*. Zurich/Jena: Walking Tree Publishers, 2008

Taylor, Albert Booth. *An Introduction to Medieval Romance*. New York: Barnes and Noble, 1969

Tolkien, John Ronald Reuel. "The Lay of Aotrou and Itroun". *Welsh Review* Vol. IV, No. 4, Cardiff (1945): 254-266

---. *The Tolkien Reader*. New York: Ballantine Books, 1986

---. "On Fairy-Stories". *Tree and Leaf* [1964]. London: Unwin Paperbacks, 9-73

---. *Sir Gawain and the Green Knight; Pearl and Sir Orfeo*. Ed. Christopher Tolkien. London: HarperCollins, 2006a

---. *The Monsters and the Critics and Other Essays*. London: HarperCollins, 2006b

Villar, Carlos. "The British Arthurian Tradition and Its Celtic Origins: Three Characters Transformed". *Papers from the 4th International Conference of the Spanish Society for Medieval English Language and Literature (SELIM)*. Eds. Teresa Fanego et al. Santiago de Compostela: Servicio de Publicaciones Universidad de Santiago de Compostela, 1997, 325-336

Wimberly, L.C. *Folklore in the English Scottish Ballads*. Chicago: University of Chicago Press, 1928

Yates, Jessica. "The Source of *The Lay of Aotrou and Itroun*". *Leaves from the Tree: J.R.R. Tolkien's Short Fiction*. Ed. Alex Lewis. London: The Tolkien Society, 1991, 63-71

Beleg and Túrin in the Light of the Medieval Tradition of Friendship among Warriors

Guglielmo Spirito (Assisi) & Emanuele Rimoli (Roma)

> *It is impossible for me to forget you even for the briefest moment —*
> *I would sooner forget myself*
> St Gregory of Nazianzus

In 1913 Turkish workmen who were restoring the Arap Camii, the Mosque of the Arabs, in Istanbul, broke through its wooden floor and uncovered paving and tombstones. The startled workmen were gazing at what five centuries before had been the Church of the Dominican friars in the bustling neighbourhood of Galata, across the Golden Horn, within sight of the towers and palaces of ancient Byzantium. Galata was an enclave for foreigners, principally the Genoese: a cutting transplanted near the Bosphorus from the West. One of the tombstones they uncovered that day can now be seen in the archaeological museum in modern Istanbul. It commemorates two English knights who died near Galata at the end of the 14th century. Below the inscription are depicted the shields carrying their armorial bearings, together with their helmets. The design on the tombstone is likely to make even the casual visitor pause, for in the engraver's arrangement the helmets of the two men seem as if about to kiss, and the two overlapping shields evoke an embrace.

They were *sworn brothers*, Sir William Neville, who died on 10 October 1391, and Sir John Clanvowe, *miles egregius*, '*a distinguished knight*, who died on 6 October 1391. Sir William, it is said, died of grief for his friend. The *Westminster Chronicle* tells that he was his *comes in itinere*, "companion on the march" — which corresponds to 'freres darmes' —, *quem non minus quam se ipsum diligebat, inconsolabiliter dolens, expiravit*, "for whom his love was no less than for himself, wich such inconsolable sorrow, breathed his last". *Erant isti milites inter Anglicos famosi viri nobile set strenui*, "These two knights were men of high repute among the English, gentlemen of mettle" (cf. Bray 13-19).

> When either Affection or Eros is one's theme, one finds a prepared audience. But very few modern people think Friendship a love of comparable value or even a love at all. Tristan and Isolde, Antony and Cleopatra, Romeo and Juliet, have innumerable counterparts in modern literature: David and Jonathan, Pylades and Orestes, Roland and Oliver, Amis and Amile, have not. To the Ancients,

> Friendship seemed the happiest and most fully human of all loves; the crown of life and the school of virtue. The modern world, in comparison, ignores it. How has this come about? The first and most obvious answer is that few value it because few experience it.
> (Lewis, *Loves* 69f)[1]

Our intention and aim is rather modest: simply to suggest that we may contemplate J.R.R. Tolkien's 'sword friends' *within* the light that shines through the Middle Ages on the matter. We do not intend to explore influences nor argue about forms and styles, but try to *recognise a glimpse of a vision*.

Among the many characters of J.R.R. Tolkien, we have chosen but a few: Legolas & Gimli, Éomer & Aragorn and especially Beleg Cuthalion & Túrin Turambar. They are, we daresay, the most representative.

We might have included perhaps, beside Frodo & Sam and Merry & Pippin, also Elrohir & Elladan, Théoden & Aragorn, and even Merry & Éowyn — in a way *'sword friends'*, at least occasionally... But it seemed to us that these few chosen were good enough to give the *flavour* of the topic (*swordfriendship*, and not friendship as such), in the light of Medieval tradition.

Let us start with the most 'unpairly pair' of friends, doubtless the most agreeable (and humorous) of the combined couples of warriors at stake. Let us start with an Elf and a Dwarf...

Gimli and Legolas: an unlikely Twosome

> 'Two!' said Gimli, patting his axe.
> 'Two?' said Legolas. 'I have done better, though now I must grope for spent arrows; all mine are gone. Yet I make my tale twenty at the least. But that is only a few leaves in a forest.
> ... 'Twenty-one!' cried Gimli. He hewed a two-handed stroke and laid the last Orc before his feet. 'Now my count passes Master Legolas again.'
> ... 'Twenty-one!' said Gimli.
> 'Good!' said Legolas. 'But my count is now two dozen. It has been knife-work up here.'
> (LotR 558f)

---

[1] And then, adding "a bit of demolition: those who cannot conceive Friendship as a substantive love but only as a disguise or elaboration of Eros betray the fact that they never had a Friend. This is not to say that Friendship and abnormal Eros have never been combined in certain cultures at certain periods especially likely in war-like societies. Kisses, tears and embraces are not in themselves evidence of such contamination: Hrothgar embracing Beowulf and all those hairy old toughs of centurions in Tacitus, clinging to one another and begging for last kisses when the legion was broken up...all pansies? If you can believe that, you can believe anything" (Lewis, *Loves* 75).

And later in the story:

> ... 'Where is Gimli?'
> 'I do not know', said Aragorn. 'I last saw him fighting on the ground behind the wall, but the enemy swept us apart.'
> 'Alas! That is evil news,' said Legolas.
> 'He is stout and strong,' said Aragorn. 'Let us hope that he will escape back to the caves. There he would be safe for a while. Safer than we. Such a refuge would be to the liking of a dwarf.'
> 'That must be my hope,' said Legolas. 'But I wish that he had come this way. I desire to tell Master Gimli that my tale is now thirty-nine.'
> 'If he wins back to the caves, he will pass your count again,' laughed Aragorn. 'Never did I see an axe so wielded.' (561)

> ... 'Forty-two, Master Legolas!' he cried. 'Alas! My axe is notched: the forty-second had an iron collar on his neck. How is it with you?'
> 'You have passed my score by one', answered Legolas. 'But I do not grudge you the game, so glad am I to see you on your legs!'
> (566)

> 'Come, you shall sit behind me, friend Gimli,' said Legolas. 'Then all will be well, and you need neither borrow a horse nor be troubled by one.'
> Gimli was lifted up behind his friend, and he clung to him, not much more at ease than Sam Gamgee in a boat. (460)[2]

Gregory, Homer and Medieval Byzantium

It would be quite unfair to believe that the 'Middle Ages' concern only western Europe, though in our *forma mentis* this happens quite spontaneously. What about the eastern half of the old Roman Empire? What about Medieval Byzantium?

Homer's two great epic poems, the *Iliad* and the *Odyssey*, portray the heroes of the late Bronze Age. In those poems warriors could feel intense loyalty to their comrades. Achilles and Patroclus became a paradigmatic pair of warrior friends much admired for centuries. Homer, though mostly lost to the Latin

---

2 Two knights on one horse are represented in the (unofficial) seal of the Templars; in other occasions, Gimli will share horse with Gandalf and with Éomer as well, but always wanting riding nearby his friend Legolas.

(and Barbaric) speaking West, survived in the Greek speaking East for more than a millennium after the fall of (the western half of) Rome. And when the New Rome fell to the Turks in 1453, its exiles brought its scattered heritage to the West.

Less known is the role played by St Gregory of Nazianzus († 390), the closest friend of the great Basil of Caesarea († 379), in the transmission of numerous Homeric and classical *exempla* during the Byzantine Middle Ages. Gregory was regarded as so valuable that his writings remain the most copied of all Byzantine manuscripts after the Bible (cf. McGuckin 399-402).

In a letter to his friend Amazonios, Gregory writes that his weak point is friendship. He begins a letter to another friend, Palladios, with the words: "If anyone were ask to me, 'What is the best thing in life?' I would answer, 'Friends'" (quoted in White 70). "A faithful friend cannot be replaced by anything", he writes to Basil's younger brother Gregory of Nyssa, in the *Oration 11*, "and there is no measure to his kindness. A faithful friend is a strong protection (Ecclesiasticus 6, 14) and a fortress (Proverbs 18, 19)".

Once a friend is chosen, the friendship with him is unconditional. Gregory says in *Oration 6*: "I posit a limit to hate, not to friendship, for hate must be moderated, but friendship should not know any bond" (Florensky 310).

When Basil left Athens — where he and Gregory had shared lodgings and studies: he says "we sharpened upon each other our weapons of virtue" (cf. Daley 7), developing a deep but not easy friendship that was to last all lifelong[3] —, Gregory felt that he had been cut in half; he compares his feelings to those of two oxen that have been brought up together and have drawn the same yoke and are then separated — a comparison similar to that found in the *Iliad* applied to the two Aiaces (cf. White 63). Devastated after Basil's death, Gregory preached a long — piercing — masterpiece panegyric for him (*Oration 43*).

To his friend Eutropius, Gregory wrote exhorting him to imitate the young warriors in the *Iliad* who managed to practise friendship in the midst of war. He twice refers specifically, in the context of close personal friendship, to such warriors, the twin sons of Actor, as a model of intimacy and solidarity in friendship (cf. White 71). In his panegyric about Basil, Gregory mentions the alliance between Orestes and Pylades to avenge the murder of Agamemnon (cf. Van Dam 182-183). He refers also, of course, to Achilles and Patroclus (cf. Demoen 425).

---

[3] William of Malmesbury, in his *Gesta regum anglorum*, vol. IV, col. 356, says that Gregory's relics were at Constantinople at the beginning of the 13th century; taken during the sack of the City in 1204, they were kept with honour in Rome, at St Peter Basilica, until John Paul II gave them back to Bartholmeos I. St Gregory of Nazianzus and his great friend St Basil of Caesarea are celebrated together on January 2: their shared liturgical feast is an unicum, a true paradigmatic celebration of friendship through the ages. Henry Cardinal Newman gives a wonderful portrait of their relationship.

Clearly, the friendship of Achilles and Patroclus is central to the plot of the *Iliad*. Homer uses it to get Achilles back on the battlefield after twenty books on strike. His love for Patroclus explains Achilles' bloody revenge, and his atrocious treatment of Hector's corpse. The *Iliad* concludes with Achilles' grief over Patroclus.

Achilles is *the be(a)st of the Achaians* — as Callen King put it —, especially after being 'wounded' by Patroclus' death:

> in the middle of them godlike Achilles armed.
> There was a grinding of his teeth, his two eyes
> shone like the glare of fire, and into his heart
> there entered unbearable grief
>
> (Callen King 13. 23)

In the Medieval retelling of the siege of Troy, the *Roman de Troie* of Benoit de Sainte-Maure († 1173) — following Dares —, Hector is the real hero, while Achilles, wrapped in lust, pride and wrath (cf. Callen King 162), becomes the anti-hero in western Medieval Europe for a couple of centuries until the retrieval of Homer, whom Byzantium never lost.

A Medieval Russian Inkling

In the furthest reaches of the Byzantine cultural influence we have also Russia. Moscow later claimed to be Constantinople's' heir and so proclaimed itself to be the 'Third Rome'. *Philos* — wrote the Russian thinker and martyr Pavel Florensky († 1937) — derives from the pronominal SFE (which in Russian gives *svoi*, 'own'). Related to it we have *hetairos*, which in Homer signifies ally. A synonym of *hetairos*, the Old Russian *tovar*, i.e., *tovarishch* (comrade) derives, according to S. Mikutsky, from the root *var*, to cover up, to close up, and properly signifies defence, defender. The Old Russian *tovar, tovary*, i.e., camp, military encampment, signifies defence. By the way, the Magyar *var*, fort, fortification, also properly signifies defence.

Thus, if *philos* and *hetairos* are compared, the former signifies a person with whom we are intimately linked by love, while the latter signifies only comrade. In this sense, the following equation is correct: *philos = pistos hetairos*, a friend is a faithful comrade, faithful unto the end and in all (cf. Florensky 289f). This is evident when we look at *friends who are comrades in arms*.

The most important event of the period — for the Russian identity as a nation — was the battle of Kilikovo, fought in 8 September 1380, where the Great Prince Dimitry (Donskoj) from Moscow won over the Tatar Khan Mamaj.

St Sergius of Radonezh († 1392), from his new monastery of the Holy Trinity (where a few decades later, about 1431, Andrej Rublev will paint for the iconostasis of its church his most famous icon), blessed the Prince and gave him two monks to accompany him; they were two former warriors, comrades who from then on engage in combat and help the Russian troops while 'dressed in the angelical habit' (cf. Spidlik 188).

Jonathan and David, and Aelred of Rievaulx

Aelred, the 12th-century saintly Cistercian Abbot of Rievaulx († 1167), drew on Scripture, patristic tradition, and Cicero, in *De spiritali amicitia* his extraordinary literary exploration of 'spiritual friendship' from the early 1160s; we should credit instead St Paulinus of Nola († 431) with the first literary appearance of *'spiritalis amicitia'* (cf. Carmichael 70).

Aelred's *De spiritali amicitia* is not just a vaguely monastic medieval exposition of friendship. It is the distillation of Aelred's life experience into a marvellous book in which he shows his eagerness to spread to others the good news of the worth and necessity of friendship in human life — including spiritual life —, "since the one who abides in friendship, abides in God, and God in him" (1, 69-70).

Throughout his life Aelred looked upon the friendship of Jonathan and David in the *Old Testament* as a model of true friendship (cf. 2 Sam 1ss; *De spiritali amicitia* 3, 92-96). He follows here the footsteps of St Ambrose of Milan († 397; cf. Carmichael 48 and White 113-120) and St John Chrysostom († 407; cf. White 91).

It is the realization of the ideal of friendship in living reality. It is depicted in just a few sentences, but for that reason it is painfully touching: "'Written as if for me,' everyone thinks", says Florensky (299).

In 1 Sam 18, 1 it is said that — after admiring David's victory over Goliath — "the soul of Jonathan was bound to the soul of David and Jonathan loved him as his own soul." There is also a description of the ritual which the two young warriors perform to cement their friendship which is reminiscent of the encounter between Glaucus and Diomedes in the *Iliad* 6. Jonathan and David are described as making a pact, in Latin *foedus*, an expression that may be behind a phrase later popular in medieval times, *foedus amicitiae* (cf. McGuire xvii):

> Jonathan stripped himself of the robe that he was wearing, and gave it to David, and his armour, and even his sword and his bow and his belt. (1 Sam 18, 4)

The scholar and Franciscan friar Gilbert of Tournai († 1284), close friend of St Bonaventure († 1274), was actively involved with the preaching of the cross under St Louis IX: Gilbert quotes Aelred's texts in his writings so that through him Aelred's thoughts on friendship were spread across Franciscan cloisters throughout Europe (cf. Spirito/Rimoli 129-136). David's lament for Saul and Jonathan in 2 Sam 1 was also to haunt medieval literature, an example of which can be seen in Peter Abelard's *Planctus* († 1142; cf. White 47).

> Then David took hold of his clothes and tore them; and all the men who were with him did the same. They mourned and wept, and fasted until evening for Saul and for his son Jonathan, and for the army of the Lord, because they have fallen by the sword.
> ...David intoned this lamentation over Saul and his son Jonathan...:
> Saul and Jonathan, beloved and lovely!
> in life and death they were not divided;
> they were swifter than eagles,
> they were stronger than lions.
> ...How the mighty have fallen
> In the midst of the battle!
>
> Jonathan lies slain upon your High places.
> I am distressed for you, my brother Jonathan;
> greatly beloved were you to me;
> your love to me was wonderful,
> passing the love of women.
>
> How the mighty have fallen,
> and the weapons of war perished!   (2 Sam 1, 11-12. 17-27)

Roland and Oliver:
A Friend is Good because he is Dear

The *Chanson de Roland*, as we have it, is believed to date from shortly after the First Crusade, although the *legend* of Roland must have begun much earlier. The poet, in beginning his story, assumes that his audience knows all about the friendship of Roland and Oliver, their mighty deeds in battle and their heroic deaths. Like Homer, he is telling a tale which is already in men's hearts and memories. But how and when history transformed itself into legend and legend into epic is not yet known.

Roland and Oliver's friendship is *the* friendship in medieval times, we daresay: even St Francis of Assisi († 1226) was so fond of the paradigmatic value of the tale, that he used it for the formation of his friars.[4]

> One cannot utter even the smallest lie in living communion with a friend. 'As in water face answereth to face, so the heart of man to man.' (Proverbs 27, 19)

> 'A friend is I that is not-I. A friend is a contradictio, and an antinomy is interwoven with the very concept of a friend. If the thesis of friendship is identity and similarity, its antithesis is non-identity and non-similarity'. 'According to the Russian proverb, a friend is not dear because he is good but good because he is dear', says Florensky. (315. 319)

These things are to be seen plainly in the tale of Roland and Oliver: Roland is portrayed as brave to the point of rashness, provocative, arrogant and stubborn with the naive egotism of the epic hero, loyal, self-confident, and open as day. Oliver, equally brave, though prudent and blunt, is well aware of his friend's weaknesses (cf. *The Song* 18). "Roland is fierce, and Oliver is wise" (87). Oliver is Roland's "companion", sharing his pursuits and training; but Oliver is a sounder soldier than Roland — more concerned with military necessities than with his own prestige ("You would not sound your Olifant for pride", 87; cf. 129 and 131). He goes grimly and gallantly to a task which he knows to be impossible.

> Fierce is the battle and wondrous grim the fight.
> Both Oliver and Roland boldly smite. (110)

But the battle takes a turn for the worse. Then Roland said: "Here are we doomed to die" (143).

> Oliver feels that he's wounded mortally;
> He calls to Roland his comrade and his peer:

---

4 *Compilatio Assisiensis* or *Legenda Perusina* [103] 23: *Beatus Franciscus tale responsum dedit dicens: "Carolus imperator, Rolandus et Oliverius et omnes paladini et robusti viri, qui potentes fuerunt in prelio, persequentes infideles cum multo sudore et labore usque ad mortem habuerunt de illis gloriosam et memorialem victoriam et ad ultimum ipsi sancti martyres mortui sunt pro fide Christi in certamine; 24 et multi sunt qui sola narratione eorum, que illi fecerunt, volunt recipere honorem et humanam laudem". 25 Et propter hoc scripsit significationem horum verborum in suis Admonitionibus dicens: "Sancti fecerunt opera, et nos, recitando et predicando ea, volumus inde recipere honorem et gloriam". 26 Ac si diceret: scientia inflat, caritas autem hedificat (cfr. 1Cor 8,1).* We used the text edited by Bigaroni.

> 'Sir, my companion, draw nigh and stand with me;
> We must this day be parted to our grief.' (147)
>
> And makes confession aloud, and beats his breast,
> Then clasps his hands and lifts them up to Heav'n;
> In Paradise he prays God give him rest,
> And France the Fair and Carlon prays Him bless,
> And his companion Roland above all men.
> His heart-strings crack, he stops his knightly helm,
> And sinks to earth, and lies there all his length.
> Dead is the Count, his days have reached their end.
> The valiant Roland weeps for him and laments,
> No man on earth felt ever such distress. (150)
>
> Roland is filled with grief and anger sore;
> In the thick press he now renews his war. (153)
>
> The night is clear and the moon shining bright;
> Charles lies awake and weeps for Roland's plight,
> For Oliver he weeps with all his might,
> Weeps his Twelve Peers, his French folk left behind
> In Roncevaux, slain bloodily in fight. (184)

The deep bond between warriors, the dramatic outcome, the grief, and the epic blending of all these elements in the telling, are evocative of other stories: Jonathan's and Saul's death, of course. But may we not — almost spontaneously — recall Boromir's and Théoden's end in deadly battle under the shadow of Tol Brandir and on the Pelennor fields, and the bittersweet songs which put in words the grief and the deeds of the fallen?

Men in the Middle Ages love story telling. C.S. Lewis affirms that

> their favourite stories were about how a holy man went to heaven or how a brave man went to battle… The deepest of worldly emotions in this period is the love of man for man, the mutual love of warriors who die together fighting against odds, and the affection between vassal and lord. These male affections – though wholly free from the taint that somehow hangs about 'friendship' in the ancient (classical) world – themselves lover-like; in their intensity, their wilful exclusion of other values, and their uncertainty, they provided an exercise of the spirit not wholly unlike that which later ages have found in 'love'. The fact is, of course, significant.
> (*Allegory* 9-11)

Ami and Amile: Friendship above all else

The immense popularity of a story like that of Ami and Amile strengthen the impression one has in late Medieval England of hearing, again and again, the same story of sworn friendship tried and tested: among learned courtly knights reading Chaucer, among merchants or their family reading romances, or among peasants in the English countryside listening to a storyteller at a fair or a church courtyard.

Ami and Amile is a medieval work "of hybrid genre, both more than a chanson de geste and less, a hagiographic text devoid of saints, and a romance whose main protagonists are not lovers but friends" (*Ami* vii). But these friends, curiously, are the only ones whose friendship is the very focus of the legend rather than an element, however important, of some larger story — as we have seen in the tales of Jonathan and David, Patroclus and Achilles, Oliver and Roland —, and as we see in Tolkien's tales.

The oldest versions extant are from the 11th century (a Latin verse composition, a résumé by a French monk called Radulfus), then the anonymous Latin *Vita Sanctorum Amicii et Amelii*, from the 12th century, and the Anglo-Norman *Amis e Amilum*, written about 1200. The English version, though the oldest manuscript dates from 1330, seems to be as old as the Latin *Vita* (cf. Ami 3).

Important features are the Carolingian setting — the epic world *par excellence* —, the distinctly marginal role of women, and martial life shared in close friendship.

"Marriage is 'two in one flesh' keeping two distinct souls, while friendship is 'two in one soul', keeping two separate bodies. 'Marriage is unity of flesh, *homosarchia*, while friendship is unity of souls, *homopsuchia*'", says Florensky (325). In few texts is this so evident as here, though even their bodies — strangely enough — resemble each other as if they were twins from a single embryo (we might recall here, perhaps, Elrohir & Elladan, Elrond's sons).

We leave aside the plot itself, interesting as it is — and the miraculous outcome of the tale —, for that is beyond our particular interest here. What is stressed is the unquestionable first place that Friendship had in the author's (and in the public's?) mind, above every other love and commitment. Beleg is, we daresay, the closest to this vision, among all Tolkien's characters: the only one who puts friendship (or better: his friend Túrin) above everything else.

It is not clear where these friends first met: it seems to be on the road from Apulia through Calabria, while Ami rode on towards Sicily (cf. 6)?

> He had never seen him, yet knew him instantly by his fine armour and all else he had heard described. With a kick of his golden spurs, he rushed toward him, and Amile, who had seen him from

> afar, recognized him in turn. He raced forward, and the two met in such a tight embrace, so mighty was their kiss and so tenderly did they clasp each other, that they almost fainted dead away; their stirrups snapped and they fell together to the ground. Only now would they speak. (11)

> The two counts were sitting on the grass. They made a pledge of lasting friendship. Then they saddled their mounts and, hands clasping new-made swords, went riding off through towns and cities. (13)

Hardret said to Amile: "We can be companions, you and I, sir, if you agree." The count said: "That is unthinkable. I already have a companion and lifelong friend, to whom I pledged that, under God's whole heaven, I would never have another." (35) May we not recall Legolas and Gimli?

Ami shows a care and shrewdness lacking — with no fault of his —, in Beleg as we will see later in the example of his freeing Túrin:

> Count Amile lay in the middle of the field. Before him stood his long-manned stallion; his trusted arms were there, his heavy shield and steel sword, new and sharp. His good friend came by and recognized him as soon as he saw him. He moved aside the resting weapons lest Amile, suddenly roused, strike him by mistake. He put his right hand on the other's chest and shook him, the said: 'Vassal, wake up! It's almost evening'.
> Count Amile straightened up. How well he knew his companion Ami! He threw his arms around him and kissed his chin a hundred times. And then they took delight in hearing each other's news.
> (54-55)

We met already a 'kissing scene' at the gravestone in Istanbul. "The very word for 'kiss' in Russian (*potselui*) is close to the Russian word for 'whole' (*tselyi*). The Russian verb for 'to kiss' (*tselovat'sia*) signifies that friends are brought to a state of wholeness (*tselostnost'*) or unity. A kiss is the spiritual unification of the persons kissing", affirms Florensky (316).

We have several examples of '*fratres iurati*' *(sworn brothers)* or '*fedus amicitiae*' *(covenant of friendship)* which reminds us of Tolkien's characters: for instance Robert D'Oilly and Roger D'Ivy, who have come to England with William the Conqueror († 1087). There are also Edmund Ironside († 1016) and the Danish king Cnut, as well as King Edward II and Piers Gaveston in the early 1300s and it can be seen throughout the medieval English Church: sworn brothers figure respectfully in the monastic chronicles compiled near

Worcester, at Durham, and at Malmesbury Abbey; among the Anglo-Saxon canons at Ramsey Abbey or the Franciscan friars in Carlisle, and in Chaucer's *Knights Tale* (cf. Bray 26-35).

The *pledging of brotherhood* or *adelphopoiesis* is well testified also in the Byzantine tradition — both Greek and Slavonic/Russian —, with a gracegiving liturgical office of widespread use, and present in some tales during pre-modern times: a ritual of blessing and thanksgiving for pledged frindship (cf. Florensky 327).

Éomer and Aragorn: Swords which Shine Together

> 'Farewell, and may you find what you seek!' cried Éomer. 'Return with what speed you may, and let our swords hereafter shine together!'
> 'I will come', said Aragorn. (460)

Though perhaps not so intense as the relationship between Ami and Amile, there is between Éomer and Aragorn an eagerness of encounter, a mutual contentment in each other's presence, a shining camaraderie (comradeship) between 'sword friends' or 'sword *brethren*'.

> Éomer and Aragorn stood together on the Deeping Wall. 'Come!' said Aragorn. 'This is the hour when we draw swords together!'
> ...Together Éomer and Aragorn sprang through the door, their men close behind. The swords flashed from the sheath as one.
> (557)

> ...Thus came Aragorn son of Arathorn, Elessar, Isildur's heir, out of the Paths of the Dead, borne upon a wind from the Sea; and the mirth of the Rohirrim was a torrent of laughter and a flashing of swords
> ...And so at length Éomer and Aragorn met in the midst of the battle, and they leaned on their swords and looked on one another and were glad.
> 'Thus we meet again, though all the host of Mordor lay between us,' said Aragorn. 'Did I not say so at the Hornburg?'
> 'So you spoke,' said Éomer, 'and never was a meeting of friends more joyful.' And they clasped hand in hand. 'Nor indeed more timely,' said Éomer. 'You come none too soon, my friend. Much loss and sorrow has befallen us.'

'Then let us avenge it, ere we speak of it!' said Aragorn, and they rode back to battle together. (881-882)

And last of all Aragorn greeted Éomer of Rohan, and they embrace, and Aragorn said: 'Between us there can be no word of living or taking, nor of reward; for we are brethren'...
And Éomer answered: 'Since the day when you rose before me out of the green grass of the downs I have loved you, and that love shall not fail'. (1005)

Beleg Cuthalion and Túrin Turambar

We have chosen to follow the tale as is told in *The Children of Húrin* instead of *The Silmarillion* or *Unfinished Tales*, trusting Christopher Tolkien's words in *Appendix 2*, though for the relationship among Beleg and Túrin the differences do not appear significant. Beleg and Túrin are a quite special pair of friends, somehow a syntesis of the whole tradition, as we have seen it: if Túrin with his vulnerability to pride and stubbornness, reminds us of traits of Achilles and Roland (and Boromir), Beleg recalls Jonathan and Oliver (and Faramir). The depth of Beleg's love for Túrin matches the love of Amile for Ami, though we hardly daresay the same about Túrin.

Certainly this is an unequal relationship, at least at the beginning, which reflects the diversity between Elf and Man, both in wisdom, strength and lifelength. From the initial mentorship (he is undoubtedly the senior), Beleg crosses the gap toward friendship and wins the diffident heart of Túrin, becoming the closest both most faithful and unselfish of all those who Túrin has met in his troubled life. Beleg the Strongbow offered Túrin *attention, affection* and *affirmation*, and bound himself for life and death to the fate — or doom — of his friend. Tragically enough, the sword was the tool and bane of their shared friendship.

Beleg stands on the highest standard of friendship that we already saw in Gregory and Aelred (and Florensky); the same standard shared by C.S Lewis and J.R.R. Tolkien: deep, strong and lasting commitment towards own friend, with whom one shares whatsoever he is and does, through every joyfull or bitter path, until the end.

> Beleg the Strongbow was hunting in that region, for he dwelt ever on the marches of Doriath, and he was the greatest woodsman of those days... And he looked with liking upon Túrin, for he had the beauty of his mother and the eyes of his father, and he was sturdy and strong.

'What boon would you have of King Thingol?' said Beleg to the boy.
'I would be one of his knights, to ride against Morgoth, and avenge my father,' said Túrin.
'That may well be, when the years have increase you,' said Beleg.
'For though you are small you have the makings of a valiant man, worthy to be a son of Húrin the Steadfast, if that were possible.'
(75f)

Their friendship grows through warfare:

Often Beleg Strongbow came to Menegroth to seek him, and led him far afield, teaching him woodcraft and archery and (which he liked more) the handling of swords. (81)
One only was mightier in arms among the marchwardens of Thingol at that time than Túrin, and that was Beleg Strongbow; and Beleg and Túrin were companions in every peril, and walked far and wide in the wild woods together. (86)

Beleg goes after his friend, when Túrin fled from Doriath:

'Give me leave, lord,' said Beleg, 'and on your behalf I will redress this evil, if I can. For such manhood as he promised should not run to nothing in the wild. Doriath has need of him, and the need will grow more. And I love him also.' (96)

Beleg was held captive, and mistreated, after which Túrin expressed — perhaps for the first time — his tender love for him:

Then (Túrin) was struck as with a shaft, and as if at the sudden melting of a frost tears long unused filled his eyes. He sprang out and ran to the tree. 'Beleg! Beleg!' he cried. 'How have you come hither? And why do you stand so?' At once he cut the bonds from his friend, and Beleg fell forward into his arms.
When Túrin heard all that the men would tell, he was angry and grieved; but at first he gave heed only to Beleg. While he tended him with what skill he had, he thought of his life in the woods, and his anger turned upon himself... 'If others will not take this vow with me, I will walk alone,' said Túrin. Then Beleg opened his eyes and raised his head. 'Not alone!' he said. (113-114)

Beleg's love overpowers his wisdom:

> 'If I stayed beside you, love would lead me, not wisdom,' said Beleg.
> 'My heart warns me that we should return to Doriath. Elsewhere a shadow lies before us.'
> 'Nonetheless, I will not go there,' said Túrin.
> 'Alas!' said Beleg. 'But as a fond father who grants his son's desire against his own foresight, I yield to your will. At your asking, I will stay.' (117)

Nevertheless — as Oliver to Roland — he tells Túrin his mind, and as a trustful friend, rebukes him:

> 'A hard man you have called yourself, Túrin. Truly, if by that you meant stubborn (118)
> Túrin's eyes glinted, but as he looked in Beleg's face the fire in them died, and they went grey, and he said in a voice hardly to be heard: 'I wonder, friend, that you deign to come back to such a churl. From you I will take whatever you give, even a rebuke. Henceforward you shall counsel me in all ways, save the road to Doriath only.' (140)

They appear as a typical pair of warriors, in a 'togetherness' similar to Ami and Amile:

> The whisper went, under wood and over stream and through the passes of the hills, saying the Bow and Helm that had fallen in Dimbar (as was thought) had arisen again beyond hope.
> Then many, both Elves and Men, remnants of battle and defeat and lands laid waste, took heart again, and came to seek the Two Captains. (144)

Now is Túrin's turn to be held captive, and by Orcs; and here the care that Ami took not to arouse Amile and be struck by mistake, was of no avail for Beleg, for his doom — tragically — overcame him:

> When all in the camp were sleeping Beleg took up his bow and in the darkness shot four of the wolf-sentinels on the south side, one by one and silently.
> ...Beleg drew his sword Anglachel, and with it he cut the fetters that bound Túrin; but fate was that day more strong, for the blade of Eöl the Dark Elf slipped in his hand, and pricked Túrin's foot. Then Túrin was roused into a sudden wakefulness of rage and fear, and seeing a form bending over him in the gloom with a naked blade in hand he leapt up with a great cry, believing that

> Orcs were come again to torment him; and grappling with him in the darkness he seized Anglachel, and slew Beleg Cuthalion thinking him a foe.
> But as he stood, finding himself free and ready to sell his life dearly against imagined foes, there came a great flash of lightning above them, and in its light he looked down on Beleg's face. Then Túrin stood stonestill and silent, staring on that dreadful death, knowing what he had done. (154-155)

> ...Then Gwindor roused Túrin to aid him in the burial of Beleg, and he rose as one that walked in sleep; and together they laid Beleg in a shallow grave, and placed beside him Belthronding his great bow, that was made of black yew-wood.
> ...Thus ended Beleg Strongbow, truest of friends, greatest in skill of all that harboured in the woods of Beleriand in the Elder Days, at the hand of him whom he most loved; and that grief was graven on the face of Túrin and never faded. (156)

David's piercing lament over Jonathan's death, Achilles' over Patroclus, and Roland's over Oliver have had their worthy match: few pages in contemporary literature can claim such epic and tragic skill! Here Túrin son of Húrin, among the mighty elf-friends of old, stands in all his tragic beauty:

> Then Túrin knelt and drank from that water; and suddenly he cast himself down, and his tears were unloosed at last, and he was healed of his madness.
> There he made a song for Beleg, and he named it Laer Cu Beleg, the Song of the Great Bow, singing it aloud heedless of peril.
> (157)

As King Saul, Jonathan's father, and the heathen kings of old — and Denethor —, Túrin the elf-friend, grasped in his brokenness by dark despair, took his own life (cf. 256).

Conclusion

Pavel Florensky quotes a poem found in a friend's diary and includes his friend's touching comment. Apollon Maikov († 1897) says somewhere:

> If you wish to live without struggle, without storm,
> Without knowing the bitterness of life, to ripe old age,
> Do not seek a friend and do not call yourself anyone's friend.
> You will taste fewer joys, but also fewer sorrows!

What greater testimony to the power of faithful (and suffering) friendship could be conceived? Would this have been Beleg's choice, we wonder? We daresay yes. It is a choice we would make and we wish the same for you.

Deep friendship shows itself to be worth-living for, an everlasting goal, perhaps even extending *beyond the circles of the world*, as in the 'happy ending' described in "one of the last notes in the Red Book" (LotR, *Appendix A*, 1118). There it is written:

> We have heard tell that Legolas took Gimli Gloin's son with him [and sailed over Sea] because of their great friendship, greater than any that has been between Elf and Dwarf. If this is true, then it is strange indeed: that a Dwarf should be willing to leave Middle-earth for any love, or that the Eldar should receive him, or that the Lords of the West should permit it. But it is said that Gimli went also out of desire to see again the beauty of Galadriel; and it may be that she, being mighty among the Eldar, obtained this grace for him. More cannot be said of this matter.

Bibliography

Aelred of Rievaulx. *The Way of Friendship*. Introduced and edited by Basil Pennington. Hyde Park: New City Press, 2001

Bigaroni, M. *Compilatio Assisiensis*. Assisi: Porziuncola, 1975

Bray, Alan. *The Friend*. Chicago/London: The University of Chicago Press, 2003

Callen King, Katherine. *Achilles. Paradigms of the War Hero from Homer to the Middle Ages*. Berkeley et al.: University of California Press, 1991

Carmichael, Liz. *Friendship. Interpretino Christian Love*. London/New York: T & T International, 2004

Cupane, Carolina. »Die Homer-Rezeption in Bysanz«. *Homer. Der Mythos von Troia in Dichtung und Kunst*. Antikenmuseum Basel und Sammlug Ludwig. München: Hirmer Verlag, 2008, 251-258

Daley, Brian E. *Gregory of Nazianzus. The Early Church Fathers*. London/New York: Routledge Taylor & Francis Group, 2006

Demoen, Kristoffel. *Pagan and Biblical Exempla in Gregory Nazianzen. A Study in Rethoric and Hermeneutics*. Corpus Christianorum, Lingua Patrum II. Turnholti: Typographi Brepols, 1996

Florensky, Pavel. *The Pillar and Ground of the Truth. An Essay in Orthodox Theodicy in Twelve Letters*. Princeton, Oxford: Princeton University Press, 1997

Gilbert, Peter. *On God and Man. The Theological Poetry of St Gregory of Nazianzus*. Crestwood/New York: St Vladimit's Seminary Press, 2001

Lewis, C.S. *The Allegory of Love. A Study in Medieval Tradition*. London: Oxford University Press, 1967

---. *The Four Loves*. London: HarperCollins, 2002

McGuckin, John. *Saint Gregory of Nazianzus. An Intellectual Biography*. Crestwood/New York: St Vladimir's Seminary Press, 2001

McGuire, Brian Patrick. *Friendship and Community. The Monastic Experience. 350-1250*. Ithaca/London: Cornell University Press, 2010

Newman, Henry. *Historical Sketches*. Vol. II, part I, edited in 1873

Rosenberg, Samuel & Samuel Danon (translators). *Ami and Amile. A Medieval Tale of Friendship, Translated from the Old French*. Michigan: The University of Michigan Press, 1999

Spidlik, T. "L'immagine della vita monastica secondo la 'vita' di san Sergio". *San Sergio e il suo tempo. Atti del I Convegno ecumenico internazionale di spiritualità russa, Bose, 15-18 settembre 1993*. Magnano: Edizioni Qiqajon, 1996, 175-189

The Song of Roland. Transl. Dorothy Sayers. New York: Penguin Books, 1957

Tolkien, John Ronald Reuel. *The Children of Húrin*. London: HarperCollins, 2007

---. *The Lord of the Rings*. London: HarperCollins, 1991

Van Dam, Raymond. *Families and Friends in Late Roman Cappadocia*. Philadelphia: University of Pennsylvania Press, 2003

White, Carolinne. *Christian Friendship in the Fourth Century*. Cambridge: Cambridge University Press, 2002

Augustinian and Boethian Insights into Tolkien's Shaping of Middle-earth: of Predestination, Prescience and Free Will

Annie Birks (Angers)

Among the thinkers who contributed to the intellectual character of the medieval period are Augustine of Hippo (354-430) and Boethius (ca. 480–524 or 525). Some scholars have already pondered upon possible echoes of their writings in the works of the medievalist and Christian professor J.R.R. Tolkien. Tom Shippey, for example, referred to Augustine and more particularly to Boethius to study the notion of evil in *The Lord of the Rings* (*Road* 128; *Author* 130). John W. Houghton attempted to reconcile Augustine's view of the tale of Creation in the *Book of Genesis* with Tolkien's myth of Creation in the *Ainulindalë*. Bradford L. Eden showed how Tolkien's work on Middle-earth can be linked to the ancient philosophical concept of "The music of the spheres" as standardized by Boethius in his *De Institutione Musica*. Kathleen Dubs examined Boethius' views of Providence, Fate and Chance as a tool of analysis for Middle-earth.

This paper will follow their lead and try to identify further medieval undertones in the history of Middle-earth by placing particular emphasis on the much debated issues of predestination, prescience and free will. In the *Oxford English Dictionary*, predestination, from a general point of view, is defined as "the ordaining or determination of events before they come to pass"; prescience, as "knowledge of events before they happen"; and free will as "the power of directing our own actions without constraint by necessity or fate." These definitions will be kept in mind as benchmarks in our reflections.

The Nun's Priest's Reference to Augustine and Boethius

To put the study in a purely medieval perspective, let us turn to probably the greatest English poet of the Middle Ages, also known as the Father of English literature, Geoffrey Chaucer (ca. 1343-1400). In his most famous work, *The Canterbury Tales*, Chaucer — who had acquired a thorough knowledge of the classics and erudite works such as Boethius' *Consolation of Philosophy* (which he translated) —, referred to both Augustine and Boethius in *The Nun's Priest's Tale* to highlight the complexity of the debate on predestination, prescience and free will which generations of thinkers had been grappling with (and still are).

The Nun's Priest relates the tribulations of the unfortunate cock, Chantecleer, who followed the misleading advice of his wife, Madame Pertelote, the day he flew carelessly into the farmyard in spite of a warning of jeopardy he had experienced in a dream. He had indeed foreseen a russet-coloured, narrow-snouted dog-like beast preying on him in the farmyard with the obvious intention of killing him.

As was "predestined by divine foresight", and as "that which God foresees, must come to pass" (Chaucer 212), the rooster did get caught by a deceitful fox who coaxed him with courtesy and flattery. The narrator laments Chantecleer's fate, blames him for not heeding his dream and naturally comes to tackle the tricky issues of God's prescience and man's predestination and free will. He confesses his inability to solve the puzzling question all the more so since great scholars themselves have failed to do so:

> Any accomplished scholar will bear witness
> That there has been a great altercation
> Upon this in the schools; much disputation
> About the question of predestination;
> It's been debated by a hundred thousand!
> But I cannot sift chaff from the grain
> As can that sainted theologian
> St Augustine, or Bishop Bradwardine,
> Or Boethius, and say whether God's divine
> Foreknowledge constrains me to do a thing
> Of necessity — 'simple' necessity —
> Or whether, if free choice he granted me
> To do that very thing, or not to do it,
> Though before the doing of it, God foreknew it,
> Whether His foreknowledge does not bind me,
> Except by 'conditional' necessity.   (Chaucer 212-213)

This highly serious subject — although embedded in a comic beast fable — could be used as a stepping stone to examine Tolkien's handling of the themes in the light of the Augustinian doctrine and Boethian philosophical reasoning.

Dreams and Visions as Medieval Conventions

Chaucer's narrative poem hinges around a prophetic dream like those encountered in *The Lord of the Rings* possibly regarded by the modern reader as attributes of Faery, which can be expected from the pen of a fantasy writer like Tolkien.

In one of her articles, Amy Amendt-Raduege points out that there are (according to Lindsay) no less than 46 references to dreams in LotR and if one expands the notion of dream to that of vision, the occurrences are close to a hundred (47). Such profusion highlights the author's interest in medieval literature as the dream vision was at the time an important motive and a literary genre *per se*.[1]

Dreams are often regarded as being twofold: in modern psychoanalysis they are considered as manifestations of the unconscious mind and in classical antiquity, they were interpreted as means used by the gods to communicate with men. In the *Old Testament*, dreams and visions were also seen as divine revelations. As is stated in the *Vocabulaire de Théologie Biblique* (p. 1245), these two perspectives are not incompatible: if God acts on man, it is in his deepest recesses.[2]

However, the question raised by the Nun's Priest remains: How can such views fit in with the idea of free will? Had Chantecleer the slightest chance of not being caught by the fox considering that such a mishap had been divinely voiced in his dream? Could Frodo, in Tolkien's mind, have failed to reach the shores of the Blessed Realm in spite of his prophetic dream the second night he stayed at Tom Bombadil's? Could Sam's visions of his journey in Mordor and of his father in the Shire as perceived in the Mirror of Galadriel never materialise?

As an attempt to address these questions, let us first remember one of the laws of Middle-earth clearly expressed in the *Ainulindalë* by the Creator Ilúvatar himself to Melkor: "No theme may be played that hath not its uttermost source in me, nor can any alter the music in my despite. For he that attempteth this shall prove but mine instrument in the devising of things more wonderful, which he himself hath not imagined" (S 17).

Augustinism and Predestination

Such divine prerogative echoes the Christian belief according to which God governs everything, and nothing happens unless He wants it or allows it (Garrigou-Lagrange 217).[3] Ilúvatar later adds: "And thou, Melkor, wilt discover all the secret thoughts of thy mind; and wilt perceive that they are but a part of the whole and tributary to its glory" (S 17).

Augustine went even further by saying that God has chosen some out of the *massa perditionis* as part of the predestination of the saints. His doctrine of predestination thus focuses on the elect, the chosen, the saints, which brings

---

1 Boethius' *Consolation of Philosophy* was shaped around this literary device.
2 A Catholic reference dictionary, edition 7 reprinted in 1991. See Leon-Dufour.
3 Cf. 1 Corinthians 4:7; John 15:5; Philippians 2:13.

us to a second definition. From a theological point of view, predestination can be seen as: "the action of God (held by Christians generally) in foreordaining or appointing from all eternity certain of mankind through grace to salvation and eternal life" (OED).

This paper will focus on that specific point of view, leaving to one side, the notion of reprobation which implies "being rejected [by God] or cast off, and thus ordained to eternal misery" (OED).[4] To be more precise, Augustine even made reference to predestination as being the foreknowledge and preparation of God's benefits, by means of which, whoever is going to be saved will indeed be saved (cf. Garrigou-Lagrange 18). For the modern reader such views might appear somewhat outlandish, however they do not fail to remind us of Gandalf's famous soothing words to Frodo: "Bilbo was *meant* to find the Ring, and *not* by its maker. In which case you also were *meant* to have it. And that may be an encouraging thought" (LotR I 84).

Augustine's motives behind his doctrine emanated from his close study of the Scriptures and developed through his involvement in the Pelagian controversy.[5] The biblical references to the notion of predestination revolve around three parameters (Garrigou-Lagrange 18):

1. God has elected some[6]
2. God has elected them efficiently so that they infallibly reach Heaven[7]
3. God has chosen his elect in a totally free way without previous consideration of their 'works' or their 'merits' (depending on the translation of the Bible)[8]

Gandalf's answer to Frodo's doubts and questions bears such resonances: "I [Frodo] am not made for perilous quests. I wish I had never seen the Ring! Why did it come to me? Why was I chosen?"

"Such questions cannot be answered," said Gandalf. "You may be sure that it was not for any merit that others do not possess: not for power or wisdom at any rate. But you have been chosen, and you must therefore use such strength and heart and wits as you have" (LotR I 91).

---

4 Augustine referred to 'the predestination of the saints' and 'the reprobation of the wicked', a doctrine which the French theologian John Calvin (1509-1564) developed and referred to as 'double predestination'. Such a perspective differentiated Calvin from the other key reformer, the German theologian and priest Martin Luther (1483-1546) who believed in 'single predestination', a doctrine which did not imply the loss and condemnation of the reprobate to eternal hell.
5 Pelagius (ca. AD 354 - ca. AD 420/440) was an ascetic monk probably born in Brittany. He was held to be a heretic by the Catholic Church on account of some of his beliefs. For instance, he considered that grace is not necessary to accomplish good works as man's free will is all powerful. He also denied the existence of original sin.
6 Cf. Matthew 24:31; Romans 8:33; Ephesians 1:4.
7 Cf. Matthew 24:24; John 10:26-28.
8 Cf. Luke 12:32; John 15:16; Romans 11:5; Ephesians 1:4; Romans 8:29.

Augustinism and the Importance of Grace and Free Will

Augustine, who was often called the Doctor of Grace, was convinced that man cannot do anything without divine grace. The history of Middle-earth will not contradict such an assumption given the numerous "eucatastrophes" encountered when situations seem at a dead end. To take but one example, Frodo's salvation at the end of *The Lord of the Rings* did not appear possible without providential intervention.

Augustine insisted that the shift — initially sparked by God — from *homo vetus terrenus* ("old earthly man") to *homo novus caelestis* ("new heavenly man") can only be achieved through permanent support of grace (Neush 213).

Nevertheless, he explained that the divine gift does not deprive man of free will; grace is a fact experienced by man which does not replace man's responsibility. If man cannot achieve anything without God, God cannot achieve anything without man's consent and participation (Neush 214). Let us remember the night when Pippin stealthily retrieves the Palantír from under Gandalf's blanket (as the wizard is sleeping), and looks under the stone only to be terrifyingly confronted by a vision of Sauron. Gandalf lectures the Hobbit with these words: "But mark this! You have been saved, and all your friends, too, mainly by good fortune, as it is called. You cannot count on it a second time" (LotR II 249). It appears that even if Providence seemed to be watching over Pippin and his companions, as Smith wrote: "It is God's good work, but he has called us to participate in it fully, to hope in Providence but not to rely on it to the exclusion of our own participation" (Smith 79).

The Augustinian doctrine excludes any form of passivity in this bi-directional relation between the Creator and his creature (Neush 214): man's destiny is forged over time through the criss-crossed flow between God's call and man's response. It is noteworthy that Frodo's dreams occur once he has accepted his mission as a Ring-bearer.

Visions and Dreams as Possible Pointers to Predestination

Visions and dreams are therefore useful pointers to map out the notion of predestination. Without them the reader, as an external observer, would not be informed about the character's potential trajectory and therefore would not necessarily gain evidence of any type of predestination. Frodo's dreams in Tom's house seem to be concomitant with the emergence of his transformation. It is indeed there that he starts sharing the prerogatives of the great in Middle-earth: his perception of events gains intensity.

The first night, he receives the vision of a scene which has already taken place: Gandalf's imprisonment on top of Orthanc, followed by the latter's liberation by the Eagle Gwaihir. Frodo will not be able to identify the figure of the white-haired man as being the wizard until he is in Rivendell.

The second night, Frodo is offered a vision of what might be awaiting him at the end of his journey. His dream is in fact premonitory since he foresees his arrival on the shores of the Undying Lands, an event which will take place three years later.

Although he is not particularly aware of it, Frodo already bears in himself a ferment of prescience or intuition. Galadriel points it out to him during his stay in Lothlórien: "... as Ring-bearer and as one that has borne it on finger and seen that which is hidden, your sight is grown keener. You have perceived my thought more clearly than many that are accounted wise" (LotR I 475).

Galadriel's address conjures up Romans 8:30: "And those whom he predestined, he also called; and those whom he called, he also justified; and those whom he justified, he also glorified."

When Sam is given the chance to look into Galadriel's Mirror, he sees "devilry at work in the Shire" and when he catches sight of "the poor old gaffer going down the Hill with his bits of things on a barrow", he is determined to rush back home. But Galadriel dissuades him from doing so and explains to him that "the Mirror shows many things, and not all have yet come to pass. Some never come to be, unless those that behold the visions turn aside from their path to prevent them" (LotR I 471).

She also warns him that "seeing is both good and perilous", for as Amendt-Raduege remarks: "she knows, perhaps even better than Gandalf, that if benevolent forces can use dreams to guide an individual, the Enemy is equally capable of using visions to deceive" (50). Indeed Frodo's visions become even more deceitful as he draws closer to Mount Doom.

Predestination and Determinism

The hypothetical aspect of these projections tends to exclude rigid determinism. It might be more appropriate to speak about a character's possible trajectories depending on his choices, whether he stays on the path (Frodo's second dream) or goes astray (Sam's potential attitude in front of the mirror), not to mention the number of intangible factors which can come into the picture, like other characters' choices for instance.

This is confirmed by Tolkien's own comments about Gandalf's trajectory in Middle-earth. As an incarnate 'angelic' power, Gandalf, and more generally the five Istari, were sent to Middle-earth by the Valar in order to encourage "the enemies of evil, to cause them to use their own wits and valour, to unite and endure" (L 159), "not just to do the job for them" (L 202). In spite of their angelic nature, none of the Istari was exempt from straying or erring. When Saruman, the greatest of the Order, passed into the enemy's camp, forces were unbalanced and Gandalf was too weak to face both Sauron and his former Master.

Gandalf's mission was most likely to fail. The situation was so critical that the 'good character', as is often the case, had to make "greater effort and sacrifice" (L 237). Tolkien himself explains that Gandalf's power had to be enhanced, hence the change of plans of the "Authority" transcending Middle-earth: Gandalf had been "sent by a mere prudent plan of the angelic Valar or governors; but Authority had taken up this plan and enlarged it, at the moment of its failure" (L 203).

As Ruth Noel points out, the change of plans corroborates the idea that the fate of Middle-earth is not entirely predestined for it appears that the outcome of certain events depends on particular individuals' choices (26).

In Tolkien's myth of creation it appears that the history of Middle-earth has been devised, composed, played and even revealed as a vision; it has been in a way "pre-determined". But it also appears, as we go along, that the unfolding is in no way "frozen" in an ineluctable determinism. The preliminary data, as depicted in the *Ainulindalë*, rather constitute outlines whose details the Creator can modify at any time. The Composer can decide, if need be, to introduce new themes and enrich the Music with varied harmonies and unexpected elements.

Boethius's View of Providence, Fate and Chance

As explained in great detail by Dubs, Tolkien's *Ainulindalë* echoes Boethius's views of Providence, Fate and Chance as expressed by Lady Philosophy in *The Consolation of Philosophy*.

We are presented with a universe created and governed by a benevolent Providence (the divine logos), where everything has a purpose which goes beyond human understanding. Hence our inability to grasp the often unexpected turns of events and to reconcile the apparent disorders of our world with the perfect attributes of God: "Although the general picture may seem to you mortals one of confusion and turmoil because you are totally unable to visualize this order of things, all of them none the less have their own pattern which orders them and directs them towards the good" (Boethius 89).

In Tolkien's *Ainulindalë*, the Creator could be perceived as going along these lines when he rejoices to hear the beauty flowing from the music of the Ainur and is said to foresee the end of days as an even greater Concert. "It has been said that a greater still shall be made before Ilúvatar by the choirs of the Ainur and the Children of Ilúvatar after the end of days... And Ilúvatar shall give to their thoughts the secret fire, being well pleased" (S 15).

Boethius establishes a distinction between Providence who, like a craftsman "envisages in his mind the shape of the object which he is to create" and

Fate which is the earthly and temporal manifestation of the divine project in all its complexity.

As for chance, Boethius regards it as the unexpected turns of Fate as perceived by men: "Thus we can define chance as the unexpected outcome of a conjunction of causes in actions carried out for some purpose. What causes the conjunction and the coincidence of these causes is that order which unfolds in an irresistible chain, descending from its source in Providence, and allocating all things to their due place and time" (Boethius 98).

Tom Bombadil's comments after rescuing Merry and Pippin trapped by Old Man Willow tend to support such a standpoint. When Frodo asked him if it was "just chance" that had brought him there at that moment, Tom answered: "Did I hear you calling? Nay, I did not hear: I was just busy singing. Just chance brought me then, if chance you call it. It was no plan of mine, though I was waiting for you. We heard news of you, and learned that you were wandering" (LotR I 174).

Prescience and Free Will

Boethius's view of chance also corroborates Gandalf's soothing words to Frodo and sheds light on a number of anecdotes in the story. However the question of God's prescience and man's free will is once more at stake. Boethius himself expresses his doubts to Lady Philosophy: "So if God has prior knowledge from eternity not only of men's actions but also of their plans and wishes, there will be no freedom of will" (Boethius 100). She explains that God's foreknowledge of things does not necessarily imply that these things are going to happen. Indeed, God sees as being present all future events which result from free will: "Since God's status is abidingly eternal and in the present, his knowledge, too, transcends all movement in time. It abides in the simplicity of its present, embraces the boundless extent of past and future, and by virtue of its simple comprehension, it ponders all things as if they were being enacted in the present" (Boethius 111-112).

In his letters, Tolkien tackles the notion of free will, namely when he explains that in *Leaf by Niggle*, he attempted (allegorically, and among other things) "to make visible the effect of Sin or misused Free Will by men" (L 195). He insists on the necessity for a writer to guarantee free will to his characters in the story.[9]

---

9   See the entry on "Free will and Fate" in Scull/Hammond's *Reader's Guide* together with the references they made to Kocher and Purtill. Concerning Théoden and Denethor, Frodo and Gollum, Gandalf and Saruman, Boromir and Faramir..., Richard Purtill says: "Tolkien often gives us pairs of characters faced with basically the same problem and shows one handling the problem in the right way, the other in the wrong way... The fact that one character fails and the other does not, in what is essentially the same situation, is one way of dramatizing in fiction the idea of genuine free will ..." (158).

Free will is put to the test at the very beginning of the history of Middle-earth with Melkor's refusal to compose in harmony with Ilúvatar's themes. Augustine speaks of a "dark parody" of God's omnipotence and of "false freedom" (Neush 21) which leads to chaining instead of growing (the chaining of Melkor by the Valar is in many ways most symbolical). The case of Miriel, Fëanor's mother, whose decision to live or die is left to her in spite of the Valar's disapproval provides another fitting illustration.

Another dream could at first sight raise controversial comments about free will, prescience and predestination: the dream shared by the two brothers Faramir and Boromir (LotR I 322). If we check the chronology of the events, this dream took place, for the first time, on the eve of the Battle of Osgiliath (June 20th 3018). It clearly announces the Council of Elrond (Imladris) with the presence of Aragorn (the broken sword), a Hobbit (the Halfling) and the Ring (Isildur's bane). Interestingly, the moment Faramir has this dream Frodo has not yet left the Shire, since he leaves on September 23rd. At first sight, this observation could back up any suspicion of rigid determinism since a gathering is in the offing and, as we all know, it will indeed take place and some of the participants are not yet on their way. However closer scrutiny shows that the dream occurs after Frodo decides to leave Bag End with the Ring, that is to say in April.

Again it appears that in Tolkien's Middle-earth the moment a character makes a decision, a possible path unfolds in front of him (Birks 342). For example, Frodo agrees to leave the Shire with the Ring and his choice is explicitly announced in Faramir's dream. Nevertheless, given, on the one hand, the extent of the task and, on the other hand, the potential hazards involved, providential help is reserved to him, without which nothing is possible.

The path to follow, which can quickly be identified as an endless internal struggle, requires strength which this particular character might not necessarily be endowed with at the outset. This strength cannot be granted to him by magic. He has to participate in his way and according to his capacities; otherwise he would be transformed into some sort of puppet, which would make a mockery of his free will and of the laws underlying the functioning of Middle-earth. It is therefore fair that Frodo is offered the opportunity to grow to be able to carry out the mission he has been entrusted with, in a credible manner (like Gandalf's ordeals because of Saruman's choices).

Universal Fate and Individual Choices under the Prism of Etymology

Carl Hostetter (by courtesy of Christopher Tolkien) presents to us some of Tolkien' notes on fate and free will which tend to corroborate the previous observations. The data originally stem from linguistic discussions on the Eldarin base MBAR, as found in the two Quenya words, *ambar* (world) and *umbar* (fate) and refer to "Eldarin views and ideas"[10] (Tolkien's notes italicized in the text are my own emphasis):

> §1. MBAR 'settle, establish' (hence also, settle a place, settle in a place, establish one's home) also to erect (permanent buildings, dwellings, etc.); extended form mbarat- with greater intensity ... > Common Eldarin mbar'tā 'permanent establishment' > *fate of the world in general as, or as far as, established and pre-ordained from creation; and that part of this 'fate' which affected an individual person, and not open to modification by his free will.*

> §2. *E.g. one of the Eldar would have said that for all Elves and Men the shape, condition, and therefore *the past and future physical development and destiny of this 'earth' was determined and beyond their power to change, indeed beyond the power even of the Valar to alter in any large and permanent way.* ([Marginal note:] *They distinguished between "change" and redirection. Thus any 'rational [?will-user]'could in a small way move, re-direct, stop, or destroy objects in the world; but he could not "change" into something else. They did not confuse analysis with change, e.g. water / steam, oxygen hydrogen.*) *The Downfall of Númenor was 'a miracle' as we might say, or as they a direct action of Eru within time that altered the previous scheme for all remaining time. They would probably also have said that Bilbo was 'fated' to find the Ring, but not necessarily to surrender it; and then if Bilbo surrendered it Frodo was fated to go on his mission, but not necessarily to destroy the Ring — which in fact he did not do. They would have added that if the downfall of Sauron and the destruction of the Ring was part of Fate (or Eru's Plan) then if Bilbo had retained the Ring and refused to surrender it, some other means would have arisen by which Sauron was frustrated.*[11] *Just as when Frodo's will prove in the end inadequate, a means for the Ring's destruction immediately appeared–being kept in reserve by Eru as it were.* (185)

---

10 As Hostetter points out, these data complete earlier notes published in *Parma Eldalamberon* XVII which "likewise range beyond strictly linguistic discussion into the nature and relations of fate and the created world." As some words were difficult to interpret, Hostetter gives "all uncertain readings in square brackets with a query mark" (187). Cf. Flieger and Fornet-Ponse.

11 This view is also expressed by Scull and Hammond (326).

Tolkien also explains how, from an Eldarin point of view, a person's "will" may trigger (providential) turns of fate, such as "chance-meetings" for example. However even if opportunities are indeed provided, the person remains responsible for his/her behaviour:

> §4. They [the Elves] would not have denied that (say) a man was (may have been) "fated" to meet an enemy of his at a certain time and place, but they would have denied that he was "fated" then to speak to him in terms of hatred, or to slay him. *"Will" at a certain grade must enter into many of the complex motions leading to a meeting of persons; but the Eldar held that only those efforts of "will" were "free" which were directed to a fully aware purpose.* On a journey a man may turn aside, choosing this or that way — e.g. to avoid a marsh, or a steep hill — but this decision is mostly intuitive or half-conscious (as that of an irrational animal) and has only an immediate object of easing his journey. His setting-out may have been a free decision, to achieve some object,* but his actual course was largely under physical direction — and it might have led to/or missed a meeting of importance. It was this aspect of "chance" that was included in umbar. See L.R. III p. 360: "a chance-meeting as we say in Middle-earth." *That was said by Gandalf of his meeting with Thorin in Bree, which led to the visit to Bilbo. For this "chance," not purposed or even thought of by either Thorin or Gandalf, made contact with Gandalf's "will," and his fixed purpose and designs for the protection of the NW frontiers against the power of Sauron. If Gandalf had been different in character, or if he had not seized the opportunity, the "chance" would, as it were, have failed to "go off" (misfired). Gandalf was not "fated" to act as he did then. (Indeed his actions were most odd, idiosyncratic, and unexpectable: Gandalf was a powerful "free will" let loose, as it were, among the physical "chances" of the world).*
> §5. *Thus if a man set out on a journey with the purpose of finding his enemy, and the purpose then of doing this or that (pardoning him /asking his pardon / cursing him / seeking to slay him): *That purpose governs the whole process. It may be frustrated by "chance" (in fact he never met him) or it may be helped by chance (in fact against likelihood he did meet him), but in the latter case if he did evil he could not [?throw] the blame on "chance".* (185f)

From what appears in another note (in spite of laborious deciphering), one might assume that the Creator of Middle-earth had a detailed pre-knowledge of the multitudinous possible choices (and related outcomes) of his creatures (also taking into account the intermingling web of events and interaction with other creatures' choices) but perhaps could not foretell what each creature was going to choose for sure (as the case of Saruman and Gandalf seems to testify):

> §10. [??] Music of Ainur ancient legend from Valinorean days. Firs[t] stage the music or 'concert' of voices and instruments — Eru takes up alterations by [?the] created wills ('good' or bad) and adds of His own. Second stage the theme now [?transformed is provided with] a Tale and presented as visible drama to the Ainur [?bounded but great.] *Eru had not [?complete] foreknowledge, but [?after it His] foreknowledge was [?complete] to the smallest detail* — but [?He] did not reveal it all. He veiled the latter part from the eyes of the Valar who were to be actors.
> (*Tolkien Studies* VI, p. 187)

Thomas Fornet-Ponse skilfully demonstrates this "conception of freedom in Arda" with regards to Elves and Men, while keeping in mind that characters' choices can only redirect but not change the ultimate plan of the Creator.[12] He makes the following statement:

> That means that under given circumstances, they [Elves and Men] have real alternatives and may produce really different worlds without thereby frustrating Eru's plan since he has—like an author who integrated actions of his characters he did not foresee—integrated their action in his plan for the fulfilling of Arda. (84)

Prophecies

There also appear a number of prophecies in the story with sometimes such a long time span between the moment they are voiced and the moment they indeed materialize that the whole history of Middle-earth seems to be geared towards them.[13] Such is the case of the prophecy of Malbeth the Seer

---

12 Fornet-Ponse focuses on free will for both Elves and Men alike differing from the interpretation of Flieger who argues that only Men enjoy free will in Middle-earth; all the other creatures, including the Elves being ruled by fate. Flieger's argumentation is partly and surprisingly based on her interpretation of the "gift" given to Men by Ilúvatar as being "free will". Fornet-Ponse argues that the gift Tolkien referred to was "death" whose "positive function" Melkor (and later Sauron) "tainted" (75).

13 "Another technique Tolkien finds handy is to couple every incident anyone calls foreordained with some notable exercise of free will by one of the characters involved in it... Yet another device is to let most of the major characters voice premonitions or prophecies,

which points to Aragorn's releasing of the oathbreakers and retaking of the throne of Gondor (LotR III 59):

> Over the land there lies a long shadow,
> Westward reaching wings of darkness.
> The Tower trembles; to the tombs of kings
> Doom approaches. The Dead awaken;
> For the hour is come for the oath breakers;
> At the Stone of Erech they shall stand again
> And hear there a horn in the hills ringing.
> Whose shall the horn be? Who shall call them
> From the grey twilight, the forgotten people?
> The heir of him to whom the oath they swore.
> From the North shall he come, need shall drive him:
> He shall pass the Door to the Paths of the Dead.

One could easily argue, if the time had been deemed ripe by the "Authority" behind the prophecy, recorded at the time of King Arvedui (1864-1975 TA) that the wording is sufficiently vague to enable it to apply to one of Aragorn's ancestors — an argument which would discourage any assumption of rigid determinism. Moreover, these prophetic words would have been (in those days) regarded as a promise of future "divine" intervention, especially when voiced by a wise man expected to know and understand divine laws.

It is interesting to note that the prophecy does not indicate that its accomplishment will prove positive or otherwise, it only suggests that, at a specific moment in time, when the situation appears dire, that other, unseen or unlooked for forces will be at work and that this fact should be taken into consideration. In any event, it is noteworthy that, in this particular case, the knowledge of the prophecy helped the future king in his decision to act. Aragorn chose what seemed at the time to be a most bizarre and difficult route, i.e. the Paths of the Dead. His decision should be compared to that of King Arvedui (and/or that of the Council of Gondor *cf.* Eärnil) when faced with Malbeth's prophecy made to Arvedui's father: "*Arvedui* you shall call him, for he will be the last in Arthedain. Though a choice will come to the Dúnedain, and if they take the one that seems less hopeful, then your son will change his name and become king of a great realm. If not, then much sorrow and many lives of men shall pass, until the Dúnedain arise and are united again" (LotR III 405). Arvedui (and/or the Council of Gondor *cf.* Eärnil), unlike Aragorn, did not see the need to act

---

seeming to entail a definite foreseeable future, yet to keep these either misty in content or tentative in tone, so loosening their fixity and hinting that the routes are various by which they may come true." (Kocher 40)

according to the prophecy's prompting and the North Kingdom together with the kingship of Gondor failed. Once more it seems that even with prophecies, the outcome is not a foregone conclusion and that a character's choices can influence future events.

Conclusion

There is no doubt that the history of Middle-earth abounds with issues related to predestination, prescience and free will. Turning to Augustine and Boethius (as would also be the case with the medieval theologian Thomas Aquinas who built his doctrine on Augustinian bases) only helps the reader to shed some speculative light on these awkward matters, which, apparently at least, puzzled the Nun's Priest to such an extent that he ended up reminding us that, after all, it was just a story about a cock.

Augustine's doctrine according to which man alone cannot reach salvation without divine grace pervades the history of Middle-earth, if one considers all the cases of divine intervention clearly underlying eucatastrophes for example. Augustine believed that free will is a gift of God, making evil possible, but that evil was not created by God. It can only be allowed in so far as human will can be deficient by turning away from good. One of Tolkien's letters supports this point of view in relation with the history of Middle-earth: "In my story I do not deal in Absolute Evil. I do not think there is such a thing, since that is Zero. I do not think that at any rate any 'rational being' is wholly evil" (L 243). During the Council in Rivendell Elrond said: "Nothing is evil in the beginning. Even Sauron was not so" (LotR I 350).

Saint Paul's well-known assertion — "God wants all men to be saved and to come to the knowledge of the truth" (1 Timothy 2:4) — finds resonances in a number of situations in Middle-earth: e.g. Melkor, after his unchaining in Valinor; Sauron, when he is summoned by Eönwë after Morgoth's expulsion into the void; Saruman, when he meets Galadriel on his way to the Shire; Gollum, considering Frodo's attitude towards him… and such is the case of other darker characters who are given the chance to reconsider their behaviour and to compose in harmony with the Music; but their necks are so "stiff" that they are hermetic to divine grace.[14]

Hence maybe Matthew's statement in the *New Testament*: "Many are called, but few are chosen" (22:14), which would tend to point to an observation more than to a divine decree.

The fate of the characters that are willing to compose in harmony with the Music appears to echo Augustine's belief that God will infallibly guide them to the end of their journey. Given the hardships encountered by those who could

---

14 Cf. Exodus 32:9; 33:3; Deuteronomy 9:13; Jeremiah 7:26; 48:4; Baruch 2:30.

be considered as the "elect", it appears clearly, still according to Augustine, that grace is not given to them for them to fall asleep in negligence but for them to fully participate in their salvation (Garrigou-Lagrange 216).

But as some scholars will argue "if you are not one of the saints — one of those looked after by God — you are certainly lost; your lot in life is to remain part of a ruined race, squandered in sin (*massa perditionis*)" (Wetzel 49). Hence the controversies revolving around pure Augustinian predestinarianism throughout the centuries. As Pelikan once wrote about Augustine: "What was embarrassing about him on predestination was his clarity" (81). There does not seem to be any evidence of such a disheartening theology of election in Tolkien's history of Middle-earth.

However when Augustine says that the elect are not chosen because of their works/merits but because God wills it so, it may be wise to remember that mortal judgment might be totally misled by appearances: "Only God knows the hearts of Men" (1 Kings 8:39).

Let us recall on the one hand the noble and splendid impressions left by Saruman when he set foot on the shores of Middle-earth, and on the other hand, the suspicion raised by Strider in Bree. "Men of good will" might not be easily identified by mortal eyes, or might not be characterized by their status, strength, reputation, intelligence... Gandalf knew that. Didn't he say to Frodo in Khaza-dûm: "You take after Bilbo... There is more about you than meets the eye, as I said of him long ago" (LotR I 426)?

Boethius's views of Providence, Fate and Chance, appear to fit the myth of creation. Nevertheless, the notion of God's prescience as presented by Lady Philosophy might need further consideration in the context of Middle-earth.

Regarding the matter of free will, one may nevertheless wonder whether the characters of Middle-earth are actually free from Ilúvatar's will in the long term. Or as Rutledge wrote, should we consider that "there is no real freedom outside the will of God: the paradox is that 'slavery' to the will of God is the only true freedom" (180)?

Tolkien might not have approved of the word "slavery". When addressing relations between the sexes in a letter to his son Christopher, he used the word 'fidelity': "... the essence of a *fallen* world is that the *best* cannot be attained by free enjoyment... In this fallen world we have as our only guides, prudence, wisdom..., a clean heart, and fidelity of *will*..." (L 51/52).

Bibliography

Amendt-Raduage, Amy M. "Dream Visions in J.R.R. Tolkien's *The Lord of the Rings*". *Tolkien Studies* 3 (2006): 45-55

Birks, Annie. *La Rétribution dans l'œuvre de J.R.R. Tolkien*. Doctoral thesis, 2007, Paris IV – Sorbonne

Boethius. *The Consolation of Philosophy*. Transl. P.G. Walsh. Oxford: Oxford University Press, 1999

Carpenter, Humphrey, Ed. *The Letters of J.R.R. Tolkien*. London: George Allen & Unwin, 1981

Chaucer, Geoffrey. *The Canterbury Tales*. Transl. David Wright. Oxford: Oxford University Press, 1985

Dubs, Kathleen E. "Providence, Fate, and Chance: Boethian Philosophy in *The Lord of the Rings*". *Tolkien and the Invention of Myth*. Ed. Jane Chance. Kentucky: The University of Kentucky Press, 2004, 133-142

Eden, Bradford Lee. "The 'Music of the Spheres': Relationships between Tolkien's *The Silmarillion* and Medieval Cosmological and Religious Theory". *Tolkien The Medievalist*. Ed. Jane Chance. London: Routledge, 2003, 183-193

Flieger, Verlyn. "The Music and the Task: Fate and Free Will in Middle-earth". *Tolkien Studies* 6 (2009): 151-181

Fornet-Ponse, Thomas. "'Strange and free'—On Some Aspects of the Nature of Elves". *Tolkien Studies* 7 (2010): 67-89

Garrigou-Lagrange, Réginald. *La Prédestination des Saints et la Grâce*. Paris: Desclée de Brouwer Et Cie, 1935

Gilson, Christopher, Ed. *Parma Eldlamberon* XVII: J.R.R. Tolkien, Words, Phrases and Passages in *The Lord of the Rings* by J.R.R. Tolkien. California: Mountain View, 2007

Hammond, Wayne G. & Christina Scull. *The J.R.R. Tolkien Companion & Guide*. New York: Houghton Mifflin Company, 2006

Hostetter, Carl F., Ed. "Fate and Free Will". *Tolkien Studies* 6 (2009): 183-188

Houghton, John William. "Augustine in the Cottage of Lost Play: The *Ainulindalë* as Asterisk Cosmogony". *Tolkien the Medievalist*. Ed. Jane Chance. London: Routledge, 2003, 171-182

Kocher, Paul. *The Fiction of J.R.R. Tolkien*. New York: The Random House, 1972

Leon-Dufour, Xavier, Ed. *Vocabulaire de Théologie Biblique*. Paris: Le Cerf, 1991

Neush, Marcel. *Initiation à Saint Augustin*. Paris, Editions du Cerf, 1996

Noel, Ruth S. *The Mythology of Tolkien's Middle-earth*. London: Granada Publishing, 1979

Pelikan, Jaroslav. *The Growth of Medieval Theology (600-1300)*. Chicago: The University of Chicago Press, 1978

Purtill, Richard L. *Myth, Morality and Religion*. San Francisco: Harper and Row, 1984

Rutlege, Fleming. *The Battle for Middle-earth*. Grand Rapids: Eerdmans, 2004

Shippey, Tom. *The Road to Middle-earth*. London: HarperCollins, 1992

---. *Tolkien: Author of the Century*. London: HarperCollins, 2001

Smith, Mark Eddy. *Tolkien's Ordinary Virtues: Discovering the Spiritual Themes of The Lord of the Rings*. Downers Grove: Inter-Varsity Press, 2002

Tolkien, J.R.R. *The Fellowship of the Ring* [1954]. London: HarperCollins, 1993

---.*The Two Towers* [1954]. London: HarperCollins, 1993

---. *The Return of the King* [1955]. London: HarperCollins, 1993

---. *The Silmarillion*. Ed. Christopher Tolkien. London: HarperCollins, 1999

Wetzel, James. "Predestination, Pelagianism, and Foreknowledge". *The Cambridge Companion to Augustine*. Eds. Eleonore Stump & Norman Kretzmann. Cambridge: Cambridge University Press, 2001, pp. 49-58

The Holy Bible. Catholic Edition Revised. Victoria: Nelson, 1966

The Oxford English Dictionary. Oxford: Clarendon Press, 1989

Paganism in Middle-earth
Cécile Cristofari (Aix-en-Provence)

Much has been written of Tolkien's works as fundamentally Christian, and Tolkien himself stated as much (L 172). However, his works are not an elaborate retelling of the Bible. Tolkien deliberately avoided simplistic religious allegories, and as Tom Shippey pointed out, his inspiration was very diverse and included texts that did not focus exclusively on religion. Anglo-saxon literature thus played a pre-eminent role in the genesis of Tolkien's works, including such texts as the *Beowulf*, which, according to Tolkien himself, staged the continuity between paganism and Christianity, and revived the old worldview of paganism in a world where the new God had already wiped out the old.

Indeed, in both *The Lord of the Rings* and *The Silmarillion*, one can glimpse something of this dualism. Arguably, Tolkien's works are in fact neither entirely Christian nor pagan, but focus on transition and change between a pagan world, mythical and heroic, and a Christian one, where the heroes have lost their place and a new world is built on the remnants of the ancient order.

But the question of religion in Tolkien's works is a complicated one, in particular because no religious order is explicitly mentioned. It is the way the world itself is arranged that expresses a religious worldview or another. And the transition between two religions is expressed by the changes in the world itself; but what we have here hardly is a carefully constructed metaphor, where all possible contradictions have been smoothed out. Instead, we have a multi-layered world, where some characters represent religious figures and others represent lay ones, some characters are mythical heroes while others are believers.

If *The Lord of the Rings* is a Christian work, it certainly cannot be compared to works such as C.S. Lewis's *Space Trilogy*, where the religious message is explicit, and it cannot be interpreted in a similarly univocal way. Not all of it is explicitly Christian: Frodo or Aragorn, for instance, have been described as Christ-like figures by many commentators (among others, Shippey 208), yet none of them is truly God incarnate, and their destiny differs widely from that of the biblical Jesus. And while it is always possible to find similarities in details, with Christianity or with Norse mythology (Boromir as Judas could be one, or the Valier Vairë as one of the Norns, weaving fate in her tapestry), the meaning of the whole architecture is less clear-cut.

This is why I have chosen to emphasise the fluidity of the theme of religion in Tolkien's works, and to link it to a time of transition between two religions. I will attempt to show how, beyond the expression of a set of moral values, the very structure of Tolkien's world pictures it as pagan, slowly turning towards Christianity, and how *The Lord of the Rings* represents the culmination of this change.[1]

It has been stated often enough that Middle-earth is a pre-Christian world in terms of cult. What could be remarked, moreover, is that the first ages of Middle-earth according to *The Silmarillion* correspond to what is described by many mythologies as an age of heroes, men with superhuman capacities that battle demons and gods, capable of physical prowess beyond the power of modern humans. Examples of this age of heroes can be found in both Northern and Southern myths (the *Eddas*, the *Iliad*…). In *The Silmarillion*, however, the heroes are most of the time not powerful humans, but Elves, in particular the Noldor, after their exile from the sacred land of Valinor.

A word should be said first concerning the physical appearance of the Elves. Popular culture has been influenced both by Elizabethan and Victorian representations, and by post-Tolkienian fantasy, that usually portrays the Elves as small, slender beings, more furtive than strong, who prefer to hide in forests rather than directly confront their adversaries. This popular representation, however, is quite remote from the description of the Elves that is given in *The Silmarillion*. More details are given that indicate the superior strength and physical resilience of the Elves, and a few scenes show them actually battling against demons, which the humans never do. It is an Elf, Fingolfin, who manages to maim the first Dark Lord Melkor in a duel (S 179), in a fight that could remind one of some scenes from the Iliad, when the hero Diomedes wounds Apollo in a fight, for instance. Another Elf, Finrod, more renowned for his wisdom and singing abilities than for his physical prowess, kills a werewolf bare-handed in the jails of Sauron to protect Beren, a human who had nonetheless won fame as a fierce killer of Orcs (S 204). Moreover, the emblematic weapon of Elves is the bow; while some modern critics (Isabelle Smadja, among others) have interpreted this as a hint at their frailty and relative etherealness (they do not engage in close combat), this may actually be a dramatic misunderstanding of the sheer strength that was required to shoot an arrow from a long bow, a fact that Tolkien, as a devoted medievalist, was doubtlessly aware of. One may remember the end of the *Odyssey*, when Penelope's pretenders have to prove their worth by drawing Ulysses's bow, and where Ulysses himself proves his superiority by shooting an

---

1   For the sake of concision, I have chosen to discuss general structures rather than focus on the detailed similarities between Tolkien's world and pagan myths; however, an enlightening discussion of correspondances between Tolkien's invented myth and the myths of pagan religions can be found in Shippey and Hutton.

arrow through the hole of several axes (*Odyssey*, canto 21), demonstrating that dexterity was as essential a heroic trait as strength. In *The Lord of the Rings*, Legolas kills the mount of a Nazgûl that flies so high in the sky it is barely visible; this feat should be linked to Ulysses's, indicating once more how closely the Elves may be related to the heroes of ancient mythologies.

Thus the Elves do not only have a more advanced civilisation that humans; they are also shown as frequently interacting with gods (in Valinor and in Middle-earth), and as physically superior. Some humans, of course, do attain the status of heroes as well: Turin, slaying the dragon Glaurung, for instance, or Beren who retrieves a Silmaril from Morgoth's crown. Nevertheless, the domination of an entire race that could be described as heroic shows the particular nature of the First and the Second Age in *The Silmarillion*: an age when heroes and gods walked the earth together, and when divine powers took an active part in earthly conflicts.

The Silmarillion, moreover, contrasts with Tolkien's view of the eucatastrophic ending of fairy tales, where the happy ending is supposed to mirror the joy of the good news of the Gospel (MC 155). Indeed, while the ending of *The Silmarillion* is not entirely pessimistic, there is little in it that can be described as truly joyous. The initial conflict with Morgoth has been solved, but the price was the loss of the light of Valinor, the death of most of the heroes that came to Middle-earth, and finally, the return of the remaining Elves to Valinor, marking the end of a civilisation of Middle-earth that remains unsurpassed by humans. The sense of hope that the world exists to be mended, that there will be a happy resolution to the conflicts created by the theft of the Silmarils, is extremely hesitant. The light cannot be recovered; Fëanor's pride kills him, but also causes the death of many of his companions who were not directly concerned by the Silmarils, or did not take part in the slaughter of the Teleri in Aqualondë (Fëanor's sin, that caused the Doom of Mandos: S 93-5). The Silmarils are lost forever and though Morgoth is imprisoned, Sauron soon takes his place. Evil is so resilient that even the intervention of Ilúvatar that seals the doom of Númenor does not erase it, only forestalls it, as Sauron takes Morgoth's place during the following age. At the end of the *Akallabeth*, when Númenor sinks under the sea, there is a last mention of the queen Miriel, who was ravished by Ar-Pharazôn and married against her will (S 322), as she tries to reach the sanctuary and save herself, but drowns with the rest of the island (S 335). There seems to be very little justice or divine mercy in this death, as Miriel was taken against her will and it is never said that she contributed in any way to the evil deeds of her husband. It takes place nonetheless; what is at work here does not seem to be a merciful wrath, but the doom of a people engulfing the guilty and the innocent alike. There seems to be as little hope at the end of the Second Age: evil has been kept at bay, but the heroes of the war are dead, the Ring has corrupted and killed Isildur, and the Elves and Men are estranged. The first three ages follow a steady descent, where the heroes can keep evil in check but never vanquish it, and where the divine powers, the only ones who would have true power to end evil, withdraw more and more from Middle-earth.

Tolkien stressed in *The Monsters and the Critics* that the idea of 'eucatastrophe' was generally absent from Germanic narratives (MC 21), and also remarked that there was no idea of salvation in Germanic religions, where death and obliteration were the only outcome (MC 30). The idea, however, is that it is more important for heroes to fight bravely than to win, and that the ultimate destiny of the world will be sealed in a battle where gods and heroes will fight the forces of evil, and be destroyed, before, according to the *Eddas*, the world is made again as new and purified. While it is not clear whether the remaking of the world after the Ragnarök was originally present in Norse myths, or springs from Snorri Sturlusson's Christian interpretation, it is probably the version from the *Eddas* Tolkien was more familiar with. This prophetic end of the world, moreover, provides a good opportunity to operate a transition between pagan and Christian myths, as we will see later on. Let us simply stress for now that the dramatic endings of the first two ages, where the forces of evil are kept in check but not destroyed, where the heroes die in nearly-apocalyptic battles, fighting evil on their own or with divine help, owes a lot to the Germanic conception of desperate courage. Even in *The Lord of the Rings*, it is not trust in God and in the righteousness of their fight that drives the heroes, but the idea that they are meant to battle evil, and have no honourable choice in the matter, whatever the outcome: the members of the Council of Elrond stress how little hope there is for the Fellowship, and at the same time emphasise that any other choice would be irresponsible (LotR I 351).

Hope, however, is not completely absent. While the battles against evil in *The Silmarillion* end with loss and gradually destroy the civilisation of the Elves, it must be remarked that none of them ends in complete disaster. After the fall of Gondolin, Tuor does save a few inhabitants of the city, to continue the fight against Morgoth. At the end of the First Age, while a vast part of Middle-earth is destroyed, Eärendil still manages to travel to Valinor and obtain forgiveness for the exiled Elves, who earn the permission to go back to the lands they left after they have lost everything in the new lands they founded. The end of the battle against Sauron, where Isildur conquers the Ring, is probably the darkest of all, yet while the Ring kills Isildur and is lost, hope remains that the Ring may be found first not by Sauron himself but by someone who will be able to resist its power. While the structure of Tolkien's *legendarium* is at first glance more reminiscent of pagan myths (an age of heroes starting with the birth of an unparalleled civilisation, whose realisations remain fabled in later times, that is gradually devoured by the forces of evil, in a downwards dynamics that could be compared to the fall from a golden age to an iron age in some conceptions of the world), some elements also hint at a Christian conception, where the driving force in the world is hope and the knowledge that God will mend what went wrong, behind the prominently pessimistic view of a world where evil must be fought at the cost of the heroes' lives and civilisation.

The real transition between paganism and Christianity happens during *The Lord of the Rings*. While that novel only represents a chapter in Tolkien's *legendarium*, it is the most detailed of the whole continuity, and arguably the most important too, as it is meant to represent the transition from a legendary and alien world (represented in *The Silmarillion*) to a world dominated by humans, where the ancient races are only remembered in dim legends — the world as we know it, in short.

From the start of the novel, it is obvious that the heroic age is over. First, the writing at the beginning of *The Lord of the Rings* is widely different from the style of *The Silmarillion*: less archaic, with more dialogue, words and grammatical structures that are reminiscent of everyday speech. Then the story starts with an event that, while not being exactly common (Bilbo's birthday), is nonetheless neither out of the ordinary nor heroic. The characters' everyday life is described in great detail, down to the most trite (the description of Bilbo's gifts of spoons and umbrellas to his cousins, for instance: LotR I 49). We have stepped into a different world, a world where characters have at first sight less archetypal importance and more individuality. While Fëanor could be understood as an archetype, the genius who trespasses the limits of what is normally allowed to humans and falls victim to his own hubris (like Prometheus or Icarus), but has little individuality, Frodo, on the other hand, is presented as an ordinary individual living in an ordinary world. These ordinary characters, the hobbits, will nonetheless be the ones thanks to whom the world will be changed.

This change in focus may bring to mind the emphasis that the Gospels put on humble, ordinary people, who will inherit the Kingdom of Heaven (Matthew 5:3). We are no longer in a pagan worldview, where important changes are wrought by heroes, but in one where humble believers are the ones who transform the world.[2] However, the hobbits are never described as believers. What, then, do hobbits represent? I will have a brief look at the definitions of the words 'pagan' and 'heathen' first.

'Paganism' is a word of Latin origin. *Pagus* originally meant 'country' (as opposed to the city); however, the word soon took pejorative connotations as the city was associated with *civilisation* (from *civis*, meaning 'citizen, inhabitant of a city'), and came to indicate the parts of the Roman Empire that were

---

2   Hutton argues that this emphasis on humble people is in fact quite theoretical in Medieval narratives, where the heroes are generally noble-born, and that humble heroes are much more common in fairytales of lay origin (67). While this point is absolutely valid, I believe that the biblical narrative may still be viewed as one facet of Tolkien's rather complex hobbits.

perceived as uncivilised. However, another suggested etymology of 'pagan' is the word *paganus*, which some scholars understand as 'civilian' (*Wikipedia*). Both possible meanings may well have existed, since soldiers in ancient Rome were most often mobilised citizens, rather than the inhabitants of remote, newly-conquered parts of the empire (Grimal 10). In any case, *pagani* initially referred to a whole that was opposed to the community of Christians: either the 'civilians', as opposed to the army of Christ, or those who were not 'citizens of God'. Three notions then coexist in the word 'pagan': country people, civilians and people who live outside the community that is favoured by God. The etymology of 'heathen' is unclear, although it is usually linked to a Gothic word for 'heath-dweller' (which suggests an imitation of the word *paganus*, formed in Germanic roots); it was also possibly derived from the Greek word *ethnikos*, 'gentile', from *ethnos*, 'people' (from which the modern word 'ethnic' is derived), or favoured because of its similarity to that word (*Etymonline*).

If we take the etymology into account, the notion of paganism is a complex one that speaks of a peaceful, agrarian, sedentary community, with strong ties to the earth it inhabits, and little advancement in terms of civilisation (which, in turns, can be taken to mean no large cities). It is striking how this is a precise description of the hobbits: a community whose members hardly ever leave their land, in a remote part of Middle-earth, far from the centres of civilisation, Human or Elven, and where, moreover, war is virtually unknown, thanks to the Rangers that keep it safe (LotR I 7). The pejorative connotations of the word 'pagan' are the only ones that jar with that almost perfect correspondence; but in a work where explicit mentions of Christianity are deliberately omitted, and where a Christian community would have been anachronistic and out of place, this is in fine no reason to include them. In fact, if we understand 'pagan' as referring to a rural, telluric worldview and community, then we are definitely referring to the world the hobbits life in. To them, the Elves are legendary beings, and the Gaffer recalls Sam's wonder at listening to tales about them, and how Bilbo's adventures seemed all the more fabulous because he had met Elves on the way (LotR I 31). Legends about the Elves are, for them, not much more immediately real than the tales of gods and heroes must have been for the Norse pagans of the 10th century. The hobbits' life is grounded in the land they inhabit, their ties are the ties of the clan and of their particular ethnicity (the prologue to *The Lord of the Rings* implies that the hobbits are men of diminutive size: LotR I 2). They could easily represent the believers (albeit not particularly devout ones) in a religion represented by the Elves from their folk-tales.

Yet there is more than that to the hobbits' world. Just like the world of the Elves embodies a mythical worldview, reminiscent of the *Eddas* and possibly the *Iliad* as well, the world of the hobbits embodies a particular type of religion. This one is centered around the earth itself, and that is believed to have preceded not only monotheism, but also the cult of celestial gods (such as the Ases or the Olympians), that is believed to have been brought by Indo-European peoples.

Again, the Hobbits are not literally believers in chthonian divinities. But their world is resolutely centred around chthonian concepts. Even though they make buildings that stand above ground, they are said to favour the traditional housing in luxurious burrows when they can afford it (LotR I 8). In the Prologue to *The Lord of the Rings*, Tolkien insists on their "close friendship with the earth" (LotR I 2), and on the antiquity of their presence in Middle-earth, despite the fact that Men and Elves hardly ever noticed them (LotR I 3). Their way of life revolves around agriculture, and faces destruction when industry is introduced (LotR III chapter 8). Frodo and Sam feel an instinctive sympathy for Elbereth, the Vala that the exiled Elves are said to prefer, even though they have only a very dim idea of who, or what, she is; although that probably comes from their fascination with all things Elven, one could remark that earth goddesses are common in chthonian cults — which is why the cult of Hera predates the cult of Zeus, for instance, or some scholars believe the cult of the agrarian Vane divinities probably preceded that of the warlike Ases in Scandinavia (Guelpa 28f). Finally, the menacing creatures they happen to meet as they leave the Shire are all strongly linked to nature, or underground milieus: the Old Man Willow, for instance (LotR I 170), or the Barrow-wights, that dwell underground and are not said to be Sauron's followers; or even the mountain Caradhras, which Aragorn says is "not in league with Sauron, but ha[s] purpose of [its] own" (LotR 376). One last figure must be noticed: Tom Bombadil, a mysterious character that may almost seem out of place in the epic *Lord of the Rings*.

Tom Bombadil is the protagonist of a series of independent poems, set in a universe that has, at first glance, little to do with epic Middle-earth. When he appears in *The Lord of the Rings*, he proves able to dispel monsters with his songs, is unaffected by the Ring, and appears to be married to a spirit of the forest (LotR I 161). Gandalf describes him as extremely old (LotR I 345), and he appears to have no links to either Elves, or Men, or the Valar. Yet his unknown origin does not seem to be a puzzle for anyone: Tom Bombadil simply 'is' (LotR I 163). Should this be taken to mean that he is a veiled representation of God walking the earth? Too many of his characteristics, in particular the facts that he does not care about evil one way or the other, and is married to a spirit, run against that conclusion. Yet we may remember that in medieval folklore, beings that had nothing to do with either God or the devil were by no means unknown, in spite of the efforts of the Church to assimilate all supernatural to religion, and preferably to the devil. Fairies, like *Mélusine*, are one of the best examples: some narratives define them as neither good nor bad, coexisting with the world that was created by God, and they can easily be interpreted as remnants of an ancient religion, whose gods were replaced by the Christian one, but whose supernatural creatures remained in popular tales and beliefs

(Lecouteux 165). Tom Bombadil, and also other creatures such as the spider Ungoliant (S 76), are said to be of uncertain origin, and to have no tie with the Valar or Ilúvatar. The parallel is easily drawn.

The world of the Hobbits and of the creatures that surround the Shire, plus Ungoliant and her descendant Shelob, thus add another layer to the complex worldview exemplified in *The Lord of the Rings*. While *The Silmarillion* focused on the myths of a heroic age, *The Lord of the Rings* brings into focus another dimension of what has been called paganism: the ancestral, chthonian religion of agrarian populations. The world of the Hobbits shows a natural environment that is alive with primal forces, and a people living in harmony with nature, as close to the earth as can be imagined, since they live inside it. They represent the peasant world that Unamuno described as unchanging, transmitting traditions of ancestral origin from one generation to another, impervious to the revolutions that happen outside their community (Unamuno 63). Is it a paradox, then, that the Hobbits find themselves in the first ranks of the War of the Ring that transforms the face of Middle-earth?

Actually, if we read *The Lord of the Rings* as a metaphor (not an allegory, as the correspondences are too vague for that) of the transition between paganism and Christianity, where at least two and possibly three worldviews collide and influence each other (the monotheist, the polytheist and the chthonian religions), it is appropriate that all three worlds should be represented, and that Hobbits should be actors in the change as well. What Tolkien stages is not the disappearance of one world and the arrival, out of nowhere, of another, but mutual influence and continuity in change.

The Christian elements in *The Lord of the Rings* have been emphasised often enough: the importance of the notion of self-sacrifice (of Frodo and Gandalf), of hope, in the most desperate situations (Aragorn's Elvish name, Estel, means 'hope'), as well as the numerous allusions to the Apocalypse: the very name of the place where Frodo must cast the Ring (the Crack of Doom), the symbolism of the volcano (a mountain that rises towards heaven but also plunges into a fire pit, making it the place where Heaven and Hell come together: Jourde 74) and of the 'wheel of fire' Frodo mentions seeing several time during the ascension of Mount Doom (perhaps reminiscent of the wheel of fire from Ezekiel 1:4, that represents God's wrath)… Christian principles are much more present in *The Lord of the Rings* than in *The Silmarillion*; and in the end, it turns out that the protagonists were right to keep faith and hope, and that the self-sacrifice of Frodo and Gandalf has not been in vain. On the other hand, while some of the heroes of the ancient times (particularly Elrond and Galadriel) are still present the world they represent plays a very passive part in the war against Sauron. The Elves do not fight, and only welcome the heroes in temporary havens: first Gildor and his companions, whom the Hobbits meet on their way to Rivendell, and who protect them for an evening against the Nazgûls; then Elrond in Rivendell, and finally Galadriel in Lothlórien, shelter the heroes for a while before they can carry on their quest. It must be noticed that the only Elf who does fight alongside the Fellowship, Legolas, is not a Noldo but a 'dark elf', one of the Elves who never went to Valinor, and who played no part in the events of *The Silmarillion*. Even though the heroes of ancient times are still present, they make it abundantly clear that their time, and the world they represent, is over.

The opposition of values represented by Elves and Men is interesting. Men have a direct interest in fighting Sauron, as his victory would mean destruction of their own world, and they need to save their own kin from the domination of evil. They insist on alliances that will ultimately allow them to form an army strong enough to keep evil at bay while Frodo goes to the Crack of Doom. There is a certain similarity with early Christians, who insisted on forming a united and strong community, and called themselves the 'soldiers of Christ' (*Wikipedia*). The Elves, on the other hand, have no direct interest in the destruction of Mordor. Even the Dark Elves have their place in Valinor, and they could simply choose to leave Middle-earth for the safety of their homelands. As Elrond puts it during his Council, Elves and men are 'estranged' (LotR I 318), and what concerns Men does not concern the Elves. They nonetheless choose to side against Mordor, not to defend their brethren, but because evil must be fought, and the question of benefit or loss is irrelevant. There might be a possible comparison between the Elves, who fight evil one last time at the dusk of their days before returning to their homelands, and Beowulf, who returns to fight the dragon in his old age. And while the Elves do not truly die at the end of the novel, their departure is described ambiguously as their 'passing', and there is strong symbolic presence of death in the fact that they leave on a ship to an unknown, blessed lands (burial in ships was common for Norse royalty, and Beowulf's father himself receives a sea burial). An old world dies, and the birth of a new one is further underlined by the last paragraphs of the novel, where Sam returns home to his new-born daughter.

Nevertheless, there is continuity in change, and traces of the old world remain in the new. The new king of Arnor and Gondor, Aragorn, is descended from the old Númenórean nobility, and his wife Arwen is the descendant of some of the most important heroes of *The Silmarillion* (Beren and Lúthien, Eärendil and Elwing, Galadriel, and of course Elrond). The blood of the Elves and of the Númenóreans is in fact fundamental for the new nobility: the prince Imrahil, who joins Aragorn, is said to be descended from Elves (LotR III 1141), and the Rangers, who become vassals to the new king, are of Númenórean blood. In fact, much of the old order is restored with Aragorn's accession to the throne: the divided kingdoms of Arnor and Gondor are reunited, the white tree in Minath Tirith, that grew from a seed of one of the Valinorean trees, blossoms again, and Sam even plants a mirroring tree in the Shire, from a seed from Lothlórien. The war was not a revolution: its aim was not so much to end an unbearable order than to restore the old one where there was no order in place (as symbolised by the empty throne in Gondor, or Théoden's temporary senility and dependence on Wormtongue). But the restoration cannot prevent the old world from ending. There are deep changes indeed (what symbolic apocalypse would not bring them?): the moment when Frodo casts the Ring in the fire is the moment when Tolkien achieves his goal to write a Christian narrative.

While the heroic world of the Elves ends, the world of the Hobbits knows a different fate. Merry and Pippin become knights of Rohan and Gondor, and their travels have transformed them physically as well as morally (they appear taller to the other Hobbits: LotR III 1336). Sam brings back a tree from Lothlórien. The Shire is no longer as isolated as it was; as Aragorn restores the kingdom of Arnor, the Hobbits become his vassals, and are integrated in a vaster realm. Vincent Ferré supposed that the Hobbits would eventually be completely assimilated to Men and would lose their physical and cultural specificities (Ferré 267), which sounds like a reasonable supposition. As for the woodlands around the Shire, it may be supposed that they will lose their dangers, as civilisation progresses in Arnor. Tom Bombadil, who was immune to the power of the Ring and ignored all that happened in the outside world, will probably stay in his forest, unseen except on rare occasions. Evils older than Mordor may not be completely eradicated, but will be more efficiently kept in check by the power of Arnor than by the solitary Rangers.

As *The Lord of the Rings* ends, we can suppose that more traces of the chthonian world will remain than of the heroic pagan one. Moreover, the chthonian world is likely to survive not as memories and legends, but as an integrated part of the new world, albeit more discreet than it used to be. It can be supposed that the Hobbits will leave the bowels of the earth, or (as Tolkien wrote in *The Hobbit*) that they will hide deeper and will not be seen anymore, but they do not depart like the Elves. There is indeed an element in nature that resists change. The Hobbits do try, under Saruman's influence, to change their way of life and try to use nature as a tool instead of living in harmony with it, but it soon appears that this attempt brings only misery. As the order is restored, the Shire enters an era of mixed continuity and change, comparable to what happens at the same moment in Gondor. It is fair to say that the similarities between the world of Men and the Shire are numerous enough to state that the two worlds are becoming one.

At the beginning of the Fourth Age, the world is unified again. The dominant values are Christian, yet the legitimacy of the new order comes directly from the ancient order of the Elves, and an important factor of continuity in change is a close relationship to nature in some parts of the world, embodied by the newly-integrated Hobbits.

If Christian ethics are present in *The Lord of the Rings*, it is still very far from being a proselyte novel. A reader of *The Silmarillion* will know that there is a God in Middle-earth that is very close to the Christian God, and will recognise Christian values in both texts. But Tolkien's works are multi-layered, and the Christian view should be studied against the background of the other narratives that are present as well in the text.

I have tried to prove that *The Lord of the Rings* could be interpreted as the story of a transition between two (or three) religions, and that this story is narrated in a mythical, rather than a historical fashion: in other words, *The Lord of the Rings* is not a pseudo-historical work showing believers of different faiths interacting with each other, abandoning their old religion to adopt a new one. The characters and events represent the religions themselves. The departure of the Elves from Middle-earth can be read as the end of a pagan religion that emphasised belief in heroes fighting the forces of evil. Their passing does not show a failure of the pagan worldview, either, as Germanic religions did not believe in the ultimate victory of good against evil; gods and heroes were bound to be destroyed in the ultimate fight, and it could be said that this is, metaphorically, what happens to the Elves. They are not physically destroyed, but they leave Middle-earth in a scene where the symbolism of death is rather obvious. What Tolkien shows is thus not a victory of Christianity over paganism, but the gradual replacement of the latter by the former. The replacement is not total either: many elements of the ancient order survive into the new, and the new world is built on the foundations of the old one.

Paganism also survives in its chthonian avatar, embodied by the world of the Hobbits, that joined Aragorn's new kingdom while retaining their ties to their lands: this can be read as a metaphor of the many non-Christian customs and legends that survived well into the Middle Ages, and occasionally into the 21st century: celebrations of nature and fertility, that survived in the Christian celebrations of Christmas, Easter or Midsummer celebrations; or tales of fairies and other magical creatures, that do not belong to God or the devil. In fact, the shift that happened in the Middle Ages between paganism and Christianity is pictured quite accurately.

This does not mean that we should understand *The Lord of the Rings* as a rewriting of *Beowulf*, or an allegory of the religious changes in the Middle Ages, any more than we should understand it as an allegory of global wars. It is simply one of the many layers that lend its depth to Tolkien's work.

Bibliography

Anonymous. *Beowulf. Poèmes héroïques vieil-anglais.* Ed./transl. André Crépin. Paris: 10/18, Bibliothèque Médiévale, 1981

Anonymous. *La Bible: Ancien Testament.* Ed. Edouard Dhorme, transls. Edouard Dhorme, Antoine Guillaumont, Jean Hadot, Jean Koening, Franck Michaéli. Paris: Gallimard, Bibliothèque de la Pléiade, 1959

Etymonline. 'Heathen'. (2001-2011), www.etymonline.com/index.php?search=heathen&searchmode=none (8-27-2011)

Ferré, Vincent. *Tolkien: sur les rivages de la Terre du Milieu.* Paris: Christian Bourgois, 2001

Grimal, Pierre. *L'empire romain.* Editions de Fallois, 1993. Paris: Le Livre de Poche, 1993

Guelpa, Patrick. *Dieux et mythes nordiques.* Paris: Presses Universitaires du Septentrion, 1998

Jourde, Pierre. *Géographies imaginaires de quelques inventeurs de mondes au XXe siècle.* Paris: José Corti, 1991

Homer. *L'Odyssée.* Transl. Philippe Jaccottet. Paris: La Découverte, 2004

Hutton, Ronald. "The Pagan Tolkien". *The Ring and the Cross: Christianity and the Writings of J.R.R. Tolkien.* Ed. Paul E. Kerry. Lanham: Fairleigh Dickinson University Press, 2011, 57-70

Lecouteux, Claude. *Au-delà du merveilleux: essai sur les mentalités du Moyen Âge.* Paris: Presse de l'Université de Paris-Sorbonne, 1998

Matthew, Saint. *Gospel. La Bible: Nouveau Testament.* Eds. Paul Gros, Jean Grosjean, Michel Léturmy. Paris: Gallimard, Bibliothèque de la Pléiade, 1971

Shippey, Tom. *Tolkien, Author of the Century.* London: HarperCollins, 2001

Smadja, Isabelle. *Le Seigneur des anneaux ou la tentation du mal.* Paris: PUF, 2002

Tolkien, J.R.R. *The Letters of J.R.R. Tolkien.* Ed. Humphrey Carpenter with the assistance of Christopher Tolkien. London: Allen & Unwin, 1981

---. "On Fairy-Stories". *The Monsters and the Critics and Other Essays.* Ed. Christopher Tolkien. London: HarperCollins, 1983

---. *The Silmarillon.* London: HarperCollins, 1999

---. *The Lord of the Rings.* London: HarperCollins, 2005

Unamuno, Miguel de. *En torno al casticismo.* Madrid: Biblioteca Nueva, 1996

Wikipedia. 'Paganisme'. http://fr.wikipedia.org/wiki/Paganism (8-27-2011)

Is the Table of Elrond's Council Round?
Marguerite Mouton (Paris)

There is no evidence that there really is a table at the Council of Elrond. The author mentions only seats, and they may even be set irregularly: Aragorn sits "in a corner" (233), Sam is in a "corner... on the floor" (264) and Boromir is "seated a little apart" (234). But the lack of precision in the overall description sets the reader's imagination at work as may be seen from the dramatisations of this scene in films. Ralph Bakshi's cartoon in 1978 offered the picture of a long wooden rectangular table, whereas Peter Jackson's film showed a small, stony, octagonal table, in the middle of a circle of regularly arranged seats with a special throne for Elrond.[1]

Readers are free to imagine the council's arrangement as they wish. Yet there is a great medieval tradition of councils held around a round table, and we know of Tolkien's professional interest — but not only professional — in the literature of the period. Why then has the council not been represented around a round table? And should it be? In order to determine whether it would be right to represent the table of the council of Elrond as a round table or not from a symbolical point of view, it is interesting to study how Tolkien's work stands with regards to this tradition, how the author's imagination takes up, sometimes splits up, aspects of it and fits them into an original pattern.

I will distinguish two types of communities within the chapters of *The Lord of the Rings* devoted to "The Council of Elrond" and "The Ring goes South": the gathering of the Council itself and the Fellowship of the Ring it founds. I will study successively the aspects of the Round Table that can be identified in the meeting of the Council on the one hand and the election of the members of the Fellowship on the other hand.

I. Aspects of the Round Table in the Meeting of the Council

The Round Table appears in various threads of medieval tradition. It was first mentioned in 1155 by Wace, in his *Brut*, an adaptation of the *Historia regnum Britanniae* published (by Geoffroy de Monmouth) in 1138.[2] Chrétien de Troyes took it up in his romances, and later Robert de Boron in his prose novels at the beginning of the thirteenth century.[3] Different bits and pieces of

---

1   The scene is set outdoors, as Tolkien's text indicates (the meeting place is under a "porch"). Yet Hammond/Scull have stressed the author's hesitations as to location in which the Council should take place (222).
2   Wace acknowledges that the Round Table was inspired by a Breton memory preserved in "many tales".
3   I translated the quotations from these works.

these various traditions about the Round Table emerge in Tolkien's description of Elrond's Council and first of all in the functions it grants to it.

1. Traditional functions of the Round Table

Chrétien de Troyes takes as granted the reader's familiarity with the Arthurian universe and he never troubles to present King Arthur, Guinevere, nor the Round Table, its customs and its knights.[4] The poet only lists them as something well-known when their mention gives brilliance to a ceremony, a feast or a tournament.[5] If the Round Table was a mere ornament to the festivities of the court, it would be very far from the gravity of the Council of Elrond, but we are here interested in the features it shows when it is mentioned.

a. A harbour where famous wanderers exchange news

It is presented as a kind of harbour where famous wanderers exchange news. In Chrétien's books, the Round Table is an institution rather than a piece of furniture. It is associated with fame. Belonging to the Round Table is a token of renown. Indeed, when Guinevere enters the great hall with Enide, the narrator declares: "there were so many knights there who rose before them that I cannot call by name the tenth part of them... But I can tell you the names of some of the best of the knights who belonged to the Round Table and who were the best in the world" (v. 1687-1690). And he goes on to name them over the next sixty lines. Similarly, we are introduced to the Council by Elrond who presents the great people that are gathered there to "Frodo, son of Drogo" (LotR 233f).

Paradoxically, the same Chrétien sometimes reduces the Round Table to its bare material aspects. Thus, at the beginning of *Yvain*, the Knight of the Lion does not mention the institution itself but only its concrete conditions: the scene takes place on Pentecost when the Knights of the Round Table are supposed to gather at court according to the tradition, and the knights meet around a table. While the name of "the Round Table" added to the fame and majesty of its members, simple tables tend to be associated with the reunion of wandering knights between their adventures (v. 1-12). Thus, at the beginning of *Yvain*, Calogrenant tells of what happened to him while he was "making [his] way in search of adventures", treading "very bad [roads], full of briars and thorns" (v. 173-183). The theme of wandering knights introduced here is broadly explored in the chapter dedicated to the Council of Elrond. Some of the

---

4 See Zink 144.
5 The White Council and all the past alliances between peoples of Middle-earth are presented analogously in Tolkien's work where a coherent and continuous story is built up through allusions. The foundation of the White Council is never told in any detail, its existence being taken for granted. We know very little of the manner and the time of its gathering, save that at some stage Gandalf refused its leadership and it was given to Saruman instead. In that sense, the White Council is similar to the Round Table according to Chrétien de Troyes.

wanderings that are discussed look like those of Arthurian knights when they are away, for instance those of Radagast.[6] Yet if the Round Table is the place from which the knights leave on their wanderings and where they come back from time to time, the wanderings of the members of Elrond's Council are of a peculiar kind since, like Boromir for example, they are aiming at Rivendell all along.[7] When the knights eventually reach the King's Court, they exchange news and tell their adventures as Calogrenant does at the beginning of Yvain. Similarly, everybody has a "tale" of his own to share at the Council of Elrond, like Glóin (LotR 234), or a "true story" to unravel like Bilbo (243).

b. The feudal pattern
The meeting of the knights can also acquire the status of a feudal council where all can talk and be heard equally and decisions are taken collectively. For instance in Erec and Enide, the king asks for the consent of all before settling something. The matter at stake is not of the gravest kind: the council is to decide who is the most beautiful woman at the court. But Chrétien transposes to the field of love a practice originally developed to prevent war. And Arthur's speech could be the same in both cases: "And you, my lords, what do you think about it? Can you make any objection? If any one wishes to protest, let him straightway speak his mind... It is the business of a loyal king to support the law, truth, faith, and justice. I would not in any wise commit a disloyal deed or wrong to either weak or strong." (v. 1789-1803) And such practice is directly associated to the Round Table as it was founded by his father: "I am bound to keep and maintain the institution of my father Pendragon, who was a just king and emperor. Now tell me fully what you think!" (v. 1808-1813) As a result of the king's speech, "they all cry with one accord" (v. 1821) and "all agree in sanctioning" his choice (v. 1829).

Thus the Round Table appears to be the symbol of the feudal practice of giving counsel where each lord takes part in the common decisions. Tolkien takes up this tradition but he explores in greater detail how such a council could work. The Council of Elrond has something to decide, namely what to do with the Ring.[8] Various solutions to the problem are considered: entrusting it to Tom Bombadil, throwing it into the sea, sending it beyond the sea, hiding it in Rivendell, or even giving it to the Men of Minas Tirith to be used rather than destroyed. Everybody's arguments are listened to, discussed, and the strengths

---

6   Radagast is thus presented as a "traveller", "stranger" in the Shire when he arrives (250).
7   Boromir is exemplary: he appears as a wanderer with "his [rich] garments... stained with long travel" (234); but he comes upon "an errand over many dangerous leagues to Elrond" (239). Throughout his long and lonely journey, he has made for Rivendell all the time.
8   The difficulty the Council has in reaching a decision comes back as a leitmotiv throughout the chapter, particularly in Bilbo's remarks but also Erestor's and Gandalf's: "we have not yet come any nearer to our purpose. What shall we do with it?" (258).

and possibilities available conscientiously measured. No authority prevails in the discussion: the wisdom of the Wise[9] and of Elrond himself are questioned and debated. In keeping with the feudal conception, the outcome of such an exchange between all participants moderated by a central character explicitly surpasses in the end what one man on his own, or a council of the Wise only could have devised. Elrond notes that "none could lay [the Ring] on another" (LotR 264). Each one must make up his own mind with the advice of the whole Council. And Elrond adds: "Who of all the Wise could have foreseen it?" (264) The Council collectively surpasses the Wise and makes clear the decision to be taken by each and everyone.

2. Traditional members of the Round Table

But who, then, are the members of the Round Table who take part in such a collective assembly? Some traditions develop the idea of the knights' having a special calling. Similarly, Elrond insists on the fact that all people present at the Council have been called to him though not by him.[10] In Robert de Boron's book, it is Merlin who chooses the members of the Round Table, but through him, a "mysterious voice" speaks; according to Paul Zumthor, "we don't know whether it is God's or Merlin's" (161). There is a similar ambiguity as to the origin of the call that gathered all the members of the Council of Elrond. The characters are called to Elrond in such a way that some critics like Paul Kocher (36-37) or Irène Fernandez (91-101) have interpreted it as a manifestation of Providence in the text.

Between the chosen people of Elrond's Council as well as between the Knights of the Round Table, there is a "strange" bond of friendship. The knights of the prose *Merlin* by Robert de Boron declare that "None of [them] knew one another, but when [they] sat together, each of them became dear to the others, as a father or a son" (106). There is no such mutual recognition of the members of Elrond's Council, but the characters insist on the need for solidarity in their common distress. Glóin the Dwarf himself, who nearly starts a quarrel between elves and dwarves at the Council, expresses the desire that the "strengths [be] joined, and the powers of each [be] used in league" (LotR 261).

---

9   Each one must account for his own behaviour and opinions and submit them to the judgement of the Council notwithstanding his wisdom or degree of nobility. Thus, Gandalf gives a lengthy account of his actions and thus justifies both his delay and the absence of Saruman. This concern to account for himself is made explicit when he says: "such a thing has not happened before, that Gandalf broke tryst and did not come when he promised. An account to the Ring-bearer of so strange an event was required, I think." (258).

10 You are called hither. Called, I say, though I have not called you to me, strangers from distant lands. You have come and are here met, in this very nick of time, by chance as it may seem. Yet it is not so. Believe rather that it is so ordered that we, who sit here, and none others, must now find counsel for the peril of the world. (236)

To produce such solidarity, the equality of the members has been an essential aspect of the Round Table since it was first mentioned by Wace, according to whom the Table was a symbol of peace and equality for there could be no precedence among its members. Yet the seats do not seem to be settled equally or uniformly in Rivendell, as we saw earlier. Moreover, there are places of honour in the order of speaking: for example, Gandalf speaks "last, for it is the place of honour" (243).

The Council rather possesses a universal dimension. Thus, Beroul, in *Tristan et Iseut*, associates the Round Table with the shape of the world itself, noting that "the Round Table turn[s] like the World" (v. 3361-3362). Indeed, Elrond's Council is not reserved to the Wise but is open to all free Peoples of Middle-earth, without regard for their nobility, might or seniority. Thus the Hobbits, the smallest of peoples, sit "by [the] side" of Elrond. Yet, such openness is presented as new and exceptional: "This is the hour of the Shire-folk, when they arise from their quiet fields to shake the towers and counsels of the Great" (LotR 264).

II. Aspects of the Round Table in the Election of the Fellowship of the Ring

The meeting of the Council of Elrond is indeed the occasion for the election of a new community, the Fellowship of the Ring. Yet only two of them are chosen during the Council itself, and their election appears to be exceptional. To analyse this choice, we will follow two prose novels of the beginning of the thirteenth century, *Merlin* and *Perceval*[11]. Unlike his predecessors, Robert de Boron feels the need to narrate the foundation of the Round Table and the election of its members, a moment comparable to the foundation of the Fellowship and the election of its members at the end of the Council of Elrond. Two passages of the prose novels can be compared to the choice of Frodo and Sam as the core of the future Fellowship of the Ring during Elrond's Council: the scene of Arthur's election as head of the kingdom of Logres and heir of the Round Table in the prose *Merlin*; and Perceval's arrival at the court and his election to the Grail Quest in the prose *Perceval*. Even though both Robert de Boron and Tolkien tell of two elections (Arthur and Perceval; Frodo and Sam), there is no one-to-one equivalence between the two sets of characters.

---

11 Merlin is inspired both by the Historia regnum Britanniae published by Geoffroy de Monmouth in 1136 and its adaptation by Wace in his Brut in which the Round Table is first mentioned. The prose *Perceval*, called either Didot-Perceval or Modena Perceval, is focussed on the quest of Perceval, the chosen knight who would find the Grail and thus perfect the previously imperfect Round Table.

It is not a case of finding direct equivalents of elements of one narrative or hero in the other but of analysing the way Arthurian features and memories are transformed in Tolkien's imagination.

1. Arthur

In the prose *Merlin* as edited by Nathalie Desgrugillers, when the young Arthur, whose lineage is still unknown to the knights, draws the sword from the stone and thus wins the leadership of the Round Table founded by King Uther, the archbishop who presides over the ceremony declares that "anybody could attempt it, wherever he comes from" (144). Elrond's words are similar when he says that "This quest may be attempted by the weak with as much hope as the strong." (LotR 262) The words apply directly to Frodo but can also be understood as referring to Sam, the smallest of the Company. And Elrond adds: "Yet such is oft the course of deeds that move the wheels of the world: small hands do them because they must, while the eyes of the great are elsewhere." It would be tempting to see in this sentence a reminiscence of Arthur's election. The boy, squire of his foster brother, is sent to fetch Kay's gear. Whereas all the "great" look to the tournament about to take place, the young Arthur has to find a sword and thus goes on to draw the one which is set in the stone, without knowing its fate.[12]

This may be going too far in the interpretation of Tolkien's words. Anyway, Frodo and Sam are thus joined in this praise of the industrious small through the memory of the young Arthur; on the contrary, their comparison with Perceval allows a distinction between both characters and their respective places at the council and in the quest.

2. Perceval

At the starting point of Perceval's story lies a seat that has been left vacant at the Round Table in memory of the one Judah left at the Christ's table on the day he betrayed him; and Merlin made a prophecy that this vacant seat was prepared for the chosen one who would find the Grail and thus complete and perfect the Round Table. He therefore strictly forbade that anybody should sit there. When Perceval comes to the Court, he wants to sit in the vacant

---

12 On the occasion of this deed by which the young Arthur of unknown birth becomes the lawful king, the same question of wisdom and folly is raised as when the Council of Elrond speaks of sending Frodo to destroy the Ring. The barons are reluctant to acknowledge such a youth as their sovereign. Therefore the archbishop tells them that "it is great folly to go against God's will." And the knights reply: "We don't want to go against it, but we can't be ruled by a child!" (147). Similarly, the enterprise to destroy the Ring without relying on "strength" appears sheer folly to Galdor: "What strength have we for the finding of the Fire in which it was made? That is the path of despair. Of folly I would say" (LotR 262).

seat and Arthur fails to prevent him. As soon as Perceval is seated, there is a noise like an earthquake, smoke arises, and a darkness falls. Everyone hears a mysterious voice that both rebukes Perceval for breaking the ban and appoints him as the chosen one for the Quest of the Holy Grail. Perceval then swears never to sleep two nights under the same roof until he has found the castle of the Fisher King.

About this passage, Paul Zumthor notes that there is "an apparent contradiction contained in Merlin's own words (the order to leave the seat vacant and the promise that Perceval would sit on it): contradiction from a human point of view, but not from that of Providence… Before the test, the knight could not know that he was the chosen one. So there would be a moment when, forcing somehow, by an audacious folly, the hand of Providence, he would commit the sin of disobedience and would be immediately glorified as a consequence. Such an idea is less heterodox than it may seem: God has no responsibility in the sin, Perceval is perfectly free, but the Eternal Wisdom knew beforehand of his redemption" (162).

The story of Perceval's election to the seat of the one who is called to accomplish the Quest of the Grail offers a number of common points with the scene of the Council of Elrond where Frodo and Sam are chosen to be sent to Mordor and accomplish their anti-Quest, that is to destroy the Ring rather than to find a Holy Cup.

Frodo's place, like Perceval's, is prepared among the great: Elrond's words depict a circle of chosen Men among whom a seat is set for Frodo when he says: "though all the mighty elf-friends of old, Hador, and Húrin, and Túrin, and Beren himself were assembled together your seat should be among them" (LotR 264). On taking this seat, Frodo has an experience close to Perceval's. It is not Elrond who chooses him as the Ring-bearer, and yet not himself alone either. He is chosen in a mysterious way both by himself and perhaps by "some other will… using his small voice" (263). His freedom is respected, as Elrond notes afterwards, but we don't know to whom the actual words by which he takes up the mission should be attributed. This strange fact may remind us of the "mysterious voice" speaking when Perceval sits on the forbidden seat, a voice that could, according to Zumthor, be attributed either to God or to Merlin. Yet such a voice comes from Frodo himself in Tolkien's text and is said to be "small" rather than thunderous. And if there is a dramatisation of the choice, it does not consist in an earthquake and lightning, but in Elrond's look at Frodo which makes him feel like "his heart [had been] pierced by the sudden keenness of the glance" (263).

But it is Sam who commits an act that is the equivalent of Perceval's disobedience by sitting where he is not allowed to. In his case, as in the Grail story, this forbidden action paradoxically designates him for the Quest and eventually the bearing of the Ring. Elrond confirms the choice of Sam with a sentence uniting his disobedience and his election: "You at least shall go with him. It is hardly possible to separate you from him, even when he is summoned to a secret council and you are not." (264) And Pippin will remark in the next chapter on the strangeness of Sam's having been chosen (that is, to his mind, "rewarded"), as a consequence of his disobedience (265).

Thus, Frodo and Sam share the features of Perceval's election: Frodo because he sits among the great elf-friends and takes freely the burden that is laid on him; Sam because he disobeyed and sat on the floor uninvited. Paradoxically, these two opposite features (sitting among the great or on the floor) designate them both for the quest, which shows the way Tolkien's writing can break up cultural memories and piece them together anew into an original scene.

3. The Other Knights

The other members of the Fellowship of the Ring as well as their number are chosen after the Council of Elrond. Their mission seems like a sort of wandering: Elrond "can foresee very little of [their] road", but they "will meet many foes, some open, and some disguised; and [they] may find friends upon your way when you least look for it" (268). Frodo is the only one to be sworn to accomplish his quest. The others are but support and help on his road and are free to change their course. The members of the Fellowship are called (they are "summoned" by Elrond) (268f) and they answer the call freely; like the knights of the Round Table, they are equals (Hobbits are as serious candidates to the Fellowship as "an elf-lord, such as Glorfindel"), they come from throughout the world (since it is said that they "represent the other Free Peoples of the World: Elves, Dwarves, and Men") and they are brothers (Gandalf declares that "it would be well to trust rather to their friendship than to great wisdom").

The question of the number of the Company is intriguing: in the tradition of the Round Table, the number and the names of the knights who belong to the Table varies: Chrétien talks of thirty, Robert de Boron of fifty, and Layamon, in his *Brut*, of one thousand six hundred. The number nine is explicitly symbolical in reference to the number of the Black Riders. Such symbolism parallels the symbolic dimension of the Round Table itself as a sign of equality and universal companionship. And this limited number produces a constraint which makes being chosen a desirable honour. Hobbits fear that they might not be admitted, that Elrond's choice should "leave no place for [them]" (269). Setting a maximum number is a way of realising the paradoxical union between universality and election that is central to the Round Table: like Arthurian knights, the Nine Walkers of the Fellowship represent the whole world, but are also the few glorious ones elected to participate in the quest.

Two different treatments of the Round Table appear through this study: Chrétien mentions it occasionally and sometimes ornamentally, and its function in his work is social rather than political and deliberative, though there are traces of feudalism in its symbolism; whereas, Robert de Boron, in contrast, develops the theme of the election of the members, within the Christian scope in which he is interested. I have tried to show how the Council of Elrond and the foundation of the Fellowship of the Ring inherit from both traditions, and how Tolkien's imagination works on the medieval literary material of councils held among knights and how he gives them a new shape, sometimes going beyond it, or changing its meaning, selecting between the possibilities, rejecting or mixing elements. Hence it is doubtful that Tolkien imagined that the Council of Elrond was held around a Round Table like the one hanging in the Great Hall in Winchester. Yet there are parallels and links with the tradition of the Round Table, which we can make out in spite of the transformations effected in Tolkien's imagination. Therefore I would say that Peter Jackson's solution of an octagonal table is not inappropriate since it situates the Council around a table, even a globally round table — but a small one, a mere memory of the great one, and with some new angles.

Bibliography

Boron, Robert de. *L'Intégrale du cycle du Graal*. Translated by Nathalie Desgrugillers. Clermont-Ferrand: Paleo, 2003

Fernandez, Irène. *Et si on parlait du Seigneur des Anneaux*. Paris: Presses de la Renaissance, 2002

Hammond, Wayne G. & Christina Scull. *The Lord of the Rings: A Reader's Companion*. London: HarperCollins, 2005

Kocher, Paul. *Master of Middle-earth. The Fiction of J.J.R. Tolkien*. Boston: Houghton Mifflin Company, 1972

Tolkien, John Ronald Reuel. *The Lord of the Rings* [1954-1955]. London: HarperCollins, 2002

Zink, Michel. *Littérature française du Moyen Âge*. Paris: PUF, 2004

Zumthor, Paul. *Merlin le prophète*. Un thème de la littérature polémique, de l'historiographie et des romans [1943]. Genève: Slatkine Reprints, 1973

Tolkien's Mythopoetic Transformation of Landscape: Tombs, Mounds and Barrows
Judith Klinger (Potsdam)

> The Golden Hall was arrayed with fair hangings and it was filled with light, and there was held the highest feast that it had known since the days of its building. For after three days the Men of the Mark prepared the funeral of Théoden; and he was laid in a house of stone with his arms and many other fair things that he had possessed, and over him was raised a great mound, covered with green turves of grass and of white evermind. And now there were eight mounds on the east-side of the Barrowfield. (LotR 954)

This description of the burial of Théoden, King of Rohan, resounds with echoes from the early Middle Ages. The chambered tomb that serves as a house for the dead, the rich grave goods that proclaim the dead man's social status and extend it into an afterlife of equal pre-eminence: these elements are paralleled by archaeological findings from princely burials such as Sutton Hoo, Vendel or Old Uppsala.

Throughout north-western Europe, kings, nobles and chieftains were buried in carefully constructed graves that contained halls or ships as their final dwellings, furnished with weapons, treasures, musical instruments, insignia and household items (cf. Pollington 49-53). Sometimes the dead leaders were buried or cremated in the company of their horses, dogs, hunting birds, or even human attendants (cf. Ellis Davidson, *Road* 14f, 50-58; Fern; Pollington 59-61). Even as the bodies disappeared from view, the burial mound remained as an enduring visible mark of distinction. The same notion emerges when the dying Beowulf in the 10th-century poem envisions the barrow to be raised over his grave:

> Hatað heaðomære   hlæw gewyrcean
> beorhtne æfter bæle   æt brimes nosan;
> se scel to gemyndum   minum leodum
> heah hlifian   on Hronesnæsse,
> þæt hit sæliðend   syððan hatan
> Biowulfes biorh,   ða ðe brentingas
> ofer floda genipu   feorran drifað.

> Bid battle-famed men raise a mound,
> bright after the fire, on the foreland by the sea,
> that shall remind my people,

> towering high on Hrones Headland,
> so that seafarers will afterwards name it
> Beowulf's barrow, as their ships
> from afar they drive over the sea's mists.
>
> (*Beowulf* ll. 2803-08)

Archaeological evidence corroborates this literary evocation of the barrow as a memorial and a territorial beacon. Throughout the Middle Ages, the barrows of kings and leaders occupied significant sites in the landscape: situated on territorial boundaries or at the very centre of a domain, near crossroads and major routes, burial mounds served to sustain and legitimise claims to power, land, and privilege of travel.[1]

Burial sites thus map out the political landscape, proclaiming traditions of ownership and dominion, and by the same token connect the spheres of the dead and the living. Among the royal mounds of Old Uppsala, fairs and assemblies were held, and Scandinavian literature suggests that access to a founding ancestor's barrow served as concrete proof for one's lineage and territorial claims (cf. Ellis Davidson, *Road* 107; Siewers 22; Thäte, *Question* 189).

This feature, too, is paralleled by Tolkien. Below Edoras, Rohan's royal court, extends the ancient range of the Barrowfield, so that travellers encounter the departed rulers before they approach the present king:

> At the foot of the walled hill the way ran under the shadow of many mounds, high and green. Upon their western sides the grass was white as with a drifted snow: small flowers sprang there like countless stars amid the turf.
> 'Look!' said Gandalf. 'How fair are the bright eyes in the grass! Evermind they are called, *simbelmynë* in this land of Men, for they blossom in all the seasons of the year, and grow where dead men rest. Behold! we are come to the great barrows where the sires of Théoden sleep.'
> 'Seven mounds upon the left, and nine upon the right,' said Aragorn. 'Many long lives of men it is since the golden hall was built.' (LotR 496)

---

1 Cf. Brookes 143-145 on the close connections between travel routes and burial sites; on mounds as boundary markers see Ellis Davidson, Hill 173f; Shephard; van de Noort. The territorial significance of burial mounds often operates in conjunction with genealogical implications (cf. Holtorf; Petts 168; van de Noort).

The Barrowfield serves to sustain dynastic memory and asserts the unbroken authority of a long-established rule.[2]

While these supremely political functions of the royal barrow resonate with medieval practice, two aspects that seem fundamental to mortuary rites in premodern cultures receive little or no emphasis in Tolkien's description of Théoden's obsequies: the invocation or enactment of religious beliefs on the one hand and collective expressions of grief on the other. Aside from Merry, a hobbit and an outsider who sheds tears at Théoden's grave, only an anonymous group of weeping women receives passing mention. References to an afterlife are equally absent from the text, though possibly implied by the "arms and many other fair things" placed in Théoden's grave — intended, it may be assumed, to maintain his ancestral identity and ensure his royal status beyond death.

While mourning and religious conceptions thus remain on the margins of the scene, the focus is placed on vivid, collective remembrance achieved by the conjunction of ritual movement, poetry and song:

> Then the Riders of the King's House upon white horses rode round about the barrow and sang together a song of Théoden Thengel's son that Gléowine his minstrel made, and he made no other song after. The slow voices of the Riders stirred the hearts even of those who did not know the speech of that people; but the words of the song brought a light to the eyes of the folk of the Mark as they heard again afar the thunder of the hooves of the North and the voice of Eorl crying above the battle upon the Field of Celebrant; and the tale of the kings rolled on, and the horn of Helm was loud in the mountains, until the Darkness came and King Théoden arose and rode through the Shadow to the fire, and died in splendour, even as the Sun, returning beyond hope, gleamed upon Mindolluin in the morning. (LotR 954)

The riders' circling of the barrow is again paralleled by the burial rites described in *Beowulf* (ll. 3156-72), which may in turn hark back to Jordanes' account of Attila's funeral in the 6th-century *Getica*.[3] Although the symbolic implications

---

2 Cf. Ellis Davidson, Graves 27 on the political significance of royal graves in Scandinavian tradition: "The great burial mound of a king was not only a fine memorial and a new landmark, but a pledge of the continuation of the established order and of prosperity for the new king, who would now have the support of his predecessor as well as that of the gods. Thus the mound itself was an important symbol."

3 *Getica* XLIX.256-258: *Cujus manes quibus modis a sua gente honorati sint, pauca de multis dicere non omittamus. In mediis si quidem campis et intra tentoria serica cadavere collocato, spectaculum admirandum et sollemniter exhibetur. Nam de tota gente Hunnorum lectissimi equites in eo loco, quo erat positus, in modum circensium cursibus ambientes, facta ejus cantu funereo... Postquam talibus lamentis est defletus, 'strawam'*

of this peculiar ritual remain a matter of debate, an implicit connection with the sun's cycle (cf. Puhvel 109) is suggested by Tolkien's concluding emphasis on the returning sun as well. At the same time, the riders' circling contributes to an entrancing effect that transforms the mere recollection of heroic achievements into an acutely experienced present. This effect stands out all the more in comparison with the earlier scene introducing the Barrowfield below Edoras. The poem Aragorn recites there highlights absence and a past that seems irretrievably lost: "Where now the horse and the rider? Where is the horn that was blowing?" (LotR 497). Yet Théoden's funeral, a future event at this point, will bring this glorious past back to life. The riders' circling and singing does not merely invoke an unbroken tradition of rulership and a shared heroic identity, it merges past, present and future into a single moment of exaltation.[4]

With this altered experience of time and history, Tolkien's description certainly illuminates the imaginative power of premodern oral traditions beyond mere factual remembrance. But at least as noteworthy is the conjunction of burial, poetry and landscape. From the echoes of hooves, battle-cries and horn-calls to the light on Mindolluin, Gléowine's song conjures the space measured out by heroic deeds and renders the landscape vibrant with meaning. What the distribution of barrows across the countryside suggests to archaeologists is turned into actual experience by poetic invocation, both Gléowine's and Tolkien's.

Although Théoden's burial stands out, the connection of burial sites with a specific perception and experience of space that transforms the landscape can be traced throughout *The Lord of the Rings*. Not only rulers are honoured with barrows to commemorate their achievements after all. As Gandalf and the Rohirrim approach Isengard, they come upon a fresh burial mound:

---

super tumulum ejus, quam appellant, ipsi ingenti comissatione concelebrant; et contraria invicem sibi copulantes, luctu funereo mixta gaudia explicabant, noctuque secreto cadaver terra reconditum. We shall not omit to say a few words about the many ways in which his shade was honoured by his race. His body was placed in the midst of a plain and lay in state in a silken tent as a sight for men's admiration. The best horsemen of the entire tribe of the Huns rode around in circles, after the manner of circus games, in the place to which he had been brought and told of his deeds in a funeral dirge... When they had mourned him with such lamentations, a strava, as they call it, was celebrated over his tomb with great revelling. They gave way in turn to the extremes of feeling and displayed funereal grief alternating with joy. Then in the secrecy of night they buried his body in the earth (transl. Mierow). On the implications of the 'barrow-circling' in this text and *Beowulf* cf. Puhvel 109.

4 Tolkien's description effectively reproduces the premodern interconnections of burial practice, collective memory and social identity: "At the funeral, there is an interaction between the past, present and future through the process of social memory" (Devlin 43).

> And they saw that in the midst of the eyot a mound was piled, ringed with stones, and set about with many spears. 'Here lie all the Men of the Mark that fell near this place,' said Gandalf.
> 'Here let them rest!' said Éomer. 'And when their spears have rotted and rusted, long still may their mound stand and guard the Fords of Isen!' (LotR 538)

While the fallen warriors remain nameless, their heroic distinction is nonetheless written into the landscape. The same basic principle emerges from the Welsh *Stanzas of the Graves* (9th-10th cent.). This catalogue of burial sites celebrates legendary heroes and warriors and at the same time serves to mythologize the Welsh landscape (cf. Petts 164):

> Piev y bet in yr allt trav?
> Gelin y lauer y lav,
> tarv trin, trugaret itav.

> Whose is the grave on the slope yonder?
> A foe to many was his hand,
> bull of battle, mercy to him!
> (*Englynion y Beddau* 69, transl. Jones 131)

The poetic recital of names and burial sites lends spatial dimension to memory; in turn, the landscape reflects a history of heroic achievements and conflicts. Yet the interconnections extend further than this. Some of the warriors' names in the *Stanzas of the Graves* appear to be eponyms derived from the names of landscape features (cf. Jones 109; Petts 164), so that their identity effectively merges with the landscape. Jointly, actual monuments and poetic invocation create "a story about the tombs of heroes as guardians against foreign incursions" (Petts 166). The same notion is articulated in *The Lord of the Rings*, albeit in a different manner. If the mound 'guards' the Fords of the river Isen, a landscape feature becomes imbued with the fallen warriors' animate presence.

Evidently, Tolkien did not merely adopt the surface appearance of medieval burial practices but sought to re-imagine the mindset and conceptions that shape their historical significance. While modernity conceptualises space as a unified, empirical and neutral continuum set apart from human activity and experience, the medieval perception of space is based on an intrinsic conjunction. The specific meanings attached to a diversity of sites and regions are shaped by their external qualities as much as the events and experiences they accommodate. In a heroic context, the landscape is therefore not just inscribed with the memory of momentous events, it actively resounds with their significance. However, Tolkien also moves beyond adapting medieval concepts when he explores and develops the transformation of space.

Both descriptions of the Barrowfield below Edoras contain another remarkable element. The presence of *simbelmynë*, the white flower that blossoms through all seasons and grows "where dead men rest," suggests an intimate correlation between burial, remembrance and natural surroundings. When Théoden's horse Snowmane has been buried, this underlying idea recurs: "Green and long grew the grass on Snowmane's Howe, but ever black and bare was the ground where the beast [i.e. the Witchking's mount] was burned" (LotR 827). Nature responds to the cultural valuations implied in the respective burials. The condition of burial sites, then, is not a result of cultural activities alone but pertains to a greater system of meaning, articulated by nature itself.

From this particular configuration of culture and nature emerges a fundamental pattern that shapes the significance of graves in Tolkien's text. The consistent semantic distinction between 'tombs' and 'mounds' draws attention to the discrepant connotations of these two burial types. Tombs (such as Balin's tomb in Moria or the 'houses of the dead' in Minas Tirith) are associated with severe risks and disastrous events. Balin's tomb commemorates his failed efforts to reclaim Moria, which, in the course of events, once more summons the terror of the Balrog. The tombs of Minas Tirith are the site of Denethor's attempt to burn his living son and his subsequent suicide. Tolkien introduces these burial grounds as a bleak range of "pale domes and empty halls and images of men long dead" (LotR 808), thus preparing the stage for a drama of "pride and despair" that unfolds in the "deadly house" (LotR 835).

In the larger context, it seems clear that the fundamental opposition of tombs and mounds arises from the discrepant constellations of nature and culture. As mansions (or cities) of the dead, carefully constructed tombs impose man-made structures on the surrounding space and constitute segregated spheres with restricted access and visibility. Inscriptions on the tombs and sculpted images of the dead seek to perpetuate their presence in a sterile state of "endless life unchanging," as Faramir describes the Númenórean cult of the dead (LotR 662; cf. L 155). Burial mounds, on the other hand, generally point to an integrative approach. As landmarks and visible parts of the landscape,[5] they represent a successful transition from a limited cultural to a deeper and more permanent natural order. It is therefore no coincidence that tombs are frequently associated with dangerous hybris, whereas burial mounds possess an animate presence that blends cultural and natural forces. Tolkien's use of the term 'mound' itself

---

5   Access and visibility are crucial to the various socio-political purposes burial mounds served in premodern culture. Frequently located at "key points to dominate the visual experience of travellers", "funerary monuments were used to visibly differentiate community territories", "naturalising and legitimising some link between past and social present" (Brookes 149, 150). Christopher Tilley points out that the "tombs presenced and marked out the bones of the ancestral dead in the landscape... Their settings were deliberately chosen to fix a certain vantage point in relation to perception of the world beyond" (202f).

reflects this integrative principle by adhering to the semantics of medieval languages that propose no decisive distinction between natural hills and burial mounds (e.g. Old English *beorh* or *hlæw*, Cymric *gorsedd*).[6]

No immediate analogy for this dichotomy of mound and tomb seems to exist in medieval culture, yet it is interesting to note that the contrasting burial types correspond to the coexistence of pagan and Christian burials during the period of conversion. Charlemagne's *Capitulatio de partibus Saxoniae* (782/785 A.D.) specifically forbids burial in a 'pagan mound' (*tumulus paganorum*) in favour of churchyard burial.[7] From the early Middle Ages onward, Christian kings and leaders increasingly preferred the burial *ad sanctos*, near a holy place, the tomb or relics of a saint — in consequence, either within a church or by its walls.[8] Against this historical backdrop, it seems striking that the tombs of Minas Tirith are also known as 'the Hallows' and thus constitute the most conspicuous site explicitly identified as 'sacred' (or consecrated) in the entirety of *The Lord of the Rings*.

The matter of sacred sites ties in directly with the medieval perception of 'natural space' which also embraces what modernity labels the 'supernatural', a transcendent reality that may be conceptualised in terms of an afterlife, as the abode of gods, demons, elves or spirits. This wider concept adjoins ordinary space to Otherspace and includes sacred sites: bounded zones with limited access, where the laws governing ordinary space are suspended and superseded by different rules and principles, enabling exchange between the diverse spheres. In that context, the grave, the barrow, the mound occupy a special place. Medieval tradition frequently invokes 'hollow hills' that provide access to the realm of the dead as well as Otherworlds inhabited by supernatural beings.[9] As liminal

---

6 Cf. Hall, Sanctity 216; Robinson 195f; Semple 115 for the Old English nomenclature, Ó Cathasaigh 149f; Sims-Williams 64 on the Celtic counterparts. The Barrow-downs episode (see below) seems at variance with this clear-cut opposition, yet the sinister and secluded nature of these particular burial sites also constitutes a travesty of their original purpose. The Barrow-wight's intrusion effectively turns the barrow into an inaccessible tomb where past political conflicts and claims to power are reiterated with deadly consequence.

7 *Capitulatio de partibus Saxoniae* 22: *Iubemus ut corpora christianorum Saxanorum ad cimiteria ecclesiae deferantur et non ad tumulus paganorum.* We decree that the bodies of Christian Saxons are to be buried in churchyards, not in pagan mounds. Similarly in the 10th-century *Decreta Synodorum Bavaricarum*; cf. Thäte, *Denkmäler* 111.

8 Cf. Hoggett; Petts 168f. However, as Jo Buckberry points out, "burial continued to be used as a medium for social display" even in a Christian context (125), and the great variety of burial rites — including barrows within Christian cemeteries — warns against a simplified juxtaposition of pagan and post-conversion practices.

9 A. Siewers summarises: "Judging by early medieval Irish and Welsh literature, mounds were entry points to the indigenous Otherworld" (16). This applies not only to the *síd* and 'fairy mounds' of Irish tradition (cf. Sims-Williams 61) but also to the social and religious practices surrounding barrows during the early Middle Ages. S. Semple concludes: "The prehistoric barrow may... have been perceived in the early Anglo-Saxon period as

spaces between life and death, burial mounds are sites of transition from one world to the other and may be accessed from both sides.

The opposition of 'haunted' and 'hallowed' spaces surrounding graves in Tolkien's works give evidence of this basic principle. In *The Lord of the Rings* entering the Paths of the Dead summons the shadow army of the Oathbreakers ("the ghosts of Men"; LotR 769), and the Barrow-downs are haunted by dreadful wights, reminiscent of the *draugr* and *haugbui* from the Icelandic sagas (cf. Chadwick; Ellis Davidson, *Road* 35-38, 94-96; Simek 176f). Yet no concept of an afterlife is ever put into words, and there seems to be no temple, shrine or place of worship in all of Middle-earth. The transcendent reality of Valinor, the Undying Lands, emerges only from Galadriel's song, Frodo's dream in the house of Tom Bombadil and a glimpse of his final journey at the very end of the book.

The Hallows of Minas Tirith, according to Tolkien's own commentary in two letters, represent a problematic state of impoverishment, however. The Men of Gondor, Tolkien writes, are "a withering people whose only 'hallows' were their tombs" (L 197; cf. L 206). Yet the only other 'hallow' so named in *The Lord of the Rings* is the site on the slopes of Mindolluin where Aragorn, in the company of Gandalf, discovers a sapling of the White Tree — a place reached by "a path made in ages past that few now dared to tread" (LotR 949). Very little about the nature and history of this 'ancient hallow' can be gleaned from the description. Two examples from Tolkien's works outside *The Lord of the Rings* may then serve to illuminate how burial sites allow for a transition towards the sacred and the otherworldly, and here I will focus specifically on the poetic means by which ordinary space is transcended and extended towards Otherspace.

The most fascinating and complex example comes from *Cirion and Eorl*, a late text (written no earlier than 1969), which introduces a 'Holy Mountain', the Halifirien, and the hidden grave of Elendil. Like the hallow on Mindolluin, the path to this site is known only to a privileged few, and the 'Whispering Wood' on the mountain's slopes discourages any attempt to enter (cf. UT 389). *The Lord of the Rings* merely introduces the Halifirien as the seventh of Gondor's beacons, where fires are lit in order to call allies to aid in a military emergency. The later text then reveals that the beacon's name — "a modernized spelling for Anglo-Saxon *hálig-firgen*" (UT 407), 'holy mountain' — is to be taken literally. As a sacred site, it is recognised by the Men of Gondor and Rohan as well as

---

the home of spirits, ancestors or gods and was a focus of pagan spiritual activity" (118). Similarly, C. Holtorf suggests that the locations of ancient burial mounds were seen as the "natural realm of the dead"; they "may also have been regarded as liminal and timeless places that existed in both the past and present, the world of the living and the world of the supernatural" (Williams 25).

the Elves who call it *Amon Anwar*, Hill of Awe (UT 389). In *Cirion and Eorl*, an event of great political import takes place on the Halifirien. On its summit, the Steward of Gondor and Eorl, Rohan's founding ancestor, swear solemn oaths of allegiance, and Cirion grants land (which is to become the kingdom of Rohan) to Eorl's people. Yet it is the mountain's sanctity that must be of interest here.

Rather strikingly, articulations of, and explanations for, the sacredness of this site abound in the text. The oath of allegiance and Cirion's unparalleled invocation of Eru, the All-father, alone may suffice to explain why the Halifirien is holy to the Rohirrim. However, the mountain was 'hallowed' prior to this event, due to the presence of an "ancient monument" that Tolkien discussed at length in an earlier draft, concluding with: "It may however have been a tomb" (VT42: 21). In *Cirion and Eorl*, the puzzling monument emerges as the tomb of Elendil, the Númenórean forefather of Gondor's kings:

> Then Cirion went up the stair with Eorl and the others followed; and when they came to the summit they saw there a wide oval place of level turf, unfenced, but at its eastern end there stood a low mound on which grew the white flowers of *alfirin* [i.e. *simbelmynë*], and the westering sun touched them with gold. (UT 393)

To Eorl's great surprise, Cirion confirms that this is indeed the grave of Elendil: "and from it comes the awe that dwells on this hill and in the woods below" (UT 393). His explanation that the site was chosen by Isildur, Elendil's son, as "the mid-point of the Kingdom of the South," and that Isildur committed this "memorial of Elendil the Faithful" to "the keeping of the Valar" (UT 393f) is elaborated in the next chapter, which details how the site was kept secret and access to it restricted, permitted only to the king who visited the hallow especially "in days of danger or distress; and thither also he should bring his heir..., and tell him of the making of the hallow, and reveal to him the secrets of the realm" (UT 399).

Clearly, the Halifirien's exceptional significance is inextricably linked to the kingdom of Gondor both in territorial and dynastic terms (as the 'midpoint' of the realm and the burial site of a founding ancestor), thus corresponding to the traditional function of royal barrows in the early Middle Ages. However, the secrecy surrounding Elendil's grave directly contradict this recognisably political dimension of the sacred site. The hidden grave cannot operate as a visible memorial to a renowned ancestor and a site of origin that sustains territorial and social identity. The grave itself thus combines aspects of the tomb and the mound, and Tolkien's description in fact collapses the semantic distinction so consistently maintained in *The Lord of the Rings*.

As a site where gods and supernatural powers may be invoked, the Halifirien rather resembles a place of worship or a shrine. Indeed, the figure of the king on the mountain who summons blessings or seeks counsel from the gods is evocative of a concept of sacred kingship. Irish and Welsh literature suggests that a — sometimes perilous — exchange with the Otherworld of the *áes sídhe* founds and legitimises the ruler's power.[10] Such a context would certainly account for secrecy and segregation of the sacred site, but Tolkien's commentary (in the draft as well as the final description) emphatically avoids this conclusion. Since the complex textual history and the possible reasons why the mountain's sanctity may have been difficult to construe[11] cannot be discussed here, it seems more profitable to examine how the tale itself articulates and displays sacred space.

Quite surprisingly, there is no recognisable connection to any of the explicit reasons given for the mountain's holiness. Not so surprisingly, its otherworldly aspects manifest primarily in natural features: an altered state of nature lends a 'supernatural' quality to the site. Once again, the presence of *simbelmynë* acts as a distinguishing feature, and the flower's ability to defy the passage of seasons is complemented by the "ever-green" grass of the Hill's crown, which remains "unweathered and unprofaned" at all times (UT 400, cf. 392).

In its altered state, nature shapes an ideal space, elevated above the passage of time (and in this regard reminiscent of Cerin Amroth in Lothlórien), just as the mountain's summit is elevated above the land and the sphere of ordinary activities. This uppermost level also constitutes the hallow's inner core, surrounded by a belt of birches and guarded by the 'Whispering Wood', whose daunting presence alone inspires recognition of the mountain's sacredness among travellers (cf. UT 389). The Beacon-wardens and guardians of the Halifirien, too, respond with considerable unease, yet for entirely different reasons:

> beneath the sounds of the winds, the cries of birds and beasts, ... there lay a silence, and a man would find himself speaking to his comrades in a whisper, as if he expected to hear the echo of a great voice that called from far away and long ago. (UT 389)

---

10 Cf. Carey 5, 13; Ó Cathasaigh 144; Sims-Williams 63. Pagan Scandinavian beliefs appear to have encompassed a deification of dead ancestors, worshipped at their burial mounds (cf. Ellis Davidson, *Road* 100-105). F. Robinson argues that Beowulf's twofold burial may be interpreted as the hero's apotheosis (184), retaining traces of a traditional (pagan) deification of the deceased (194-196).
11 Tolkien's highly involved considerations regarding the historical origins of the mountain's sacredness at least suggest certain difficulties (cf. Tolkien, *Rivers* 21). The complicated process of envisioning sacred and haunted spaces could be further pursued by examining the Halifirien vis-à-vis Dunharrow, its ominous counterpart. Christopher Tolkien comments: "The original 'Firien' was the 'black hill' in which were the caverns of Dunharrow (WR 251); it was also called 'the Halifirien' (WR 257, 262), and Dunharrow was 'said to be a *haliern*' (Old English *hálig-ern* 'holy place, sanctuary') 'and to contain some ancient relic of old days before the Dark'" (Tolkien, *Rivers* 22).

This description of a disconcerting silence directly contradicts the 'whispers' of the forest. At the same time, the opposition of sound and silence is bridged by the anticipated "echo of a great voice". Much remains undisclosed here: What is it that the wood whispers? Where in space and time does the 'great voice' originate and what does it communicate? The text offers no answers to these questions, leaving readers to wonder whether the voice belongs to Elendil or Isildur — if there is any connection at all between the unheard echo and the hidden grave.

The mountain's sacredness thus remains poised between factual historical explanations on the one hand and the experience of a transformed, mystifying state of nature on the other. While Cirion and Isildur have access to a secluded space of communion beyond the mortal sphere and the secret knowledge that pertains to it, it is the subjective perception of travellers and wardens (ordinary people on the lower tiers of the mountain as well as social hierarchies) that translates the site's 'sacred' quality into actual experience. This experience in turn is defined by unknowing — awareness of a clearly perceptible yet unidentified potential — articulated here across a correlation of resonant space and silence. The "echo of a great voice that called from far away and long ago" extends space beyond the bounds of ordinary experience, yet it does so only in the conditional mode, as it is never actually heard. In this it transcends the limitations of sensual perception to the same degree that natural space expands towards a mythical 'elsewhere'.[12]

Several significant factors are at work here that recall the description of Théoden's burial: a specific combination of voice/sound and resonant space that permits the transcendence of linear time and the framing of this event by subjective experience. These features recur in a second (much earlier) text.

In the earliest version of the alliterative *Lay of the Children of Húrin*, composed during the first half of the 1920s, Tolkien dwells at great length on the major tragedy of Túrin's early years. By unfortunate accident, Túrin kills Beleg, his closest friend and brother-in-arms, and is afterwards driven almost mad with grief. A dream finally ends his excessive sorrow. Within this dream or "vision", Túrin's desperate search for Beleg's grave leads him to a forbidding landscape. Among bleak hills, he discovers a "cruel hollow" surrounded by torn and lightning-struck "thorn-trees":

> There called he longing:
> 'O Beleg, my brother, O Beleg, tell me
> where is buried thy body in these bitter regions?' —

---

12 I borrow this term from *Beowulf*, where an indeterminable *ellor* (elsewhere) refers to spaces beyond mortal access and knowledge, encompassing both the spheres of spirits and demons, and the afterlife — as it does in the composite *ellorsíð*, the 'journey elsewhere'.

> and the echoes always him answered 'Beleg';
> yet a veiled voice vague and distant
> he caught that called like a cry at night
> o'er the sea's silence: 'Seek no longer.
> My bow is rotten in the barrow ruinous;
> my grove is burned by grim lightning;
> here dread dwelleth, none dare profane
> this angry earth, Orc nor goblin;
> none gain the gate of the gloomy forest
> by this perilous path; pass they may not,
> yet my life has winged to the long waiting
> in the halls of the Moon o'er the hills of the sea.
> Courage be thy comfort, comrade lonely!'
> Then he [Túrin] woke in wonder; his wit was healed,
> courage him comforted... (LB 64f)

Doubtless, this text portrays a highly unusual constellation. Beleg the Elf has died in the world of Middle-earth, but as an immortal, he has also passed on to another place.[13] His "bow" remains in the barrow, while his "life" has travelled elsewhere to re-assume corporeal form after a period of waiting.

At the same time, the description challenges the notion of an irrevocable severance. Beleg's barrow is still protected against intrusion after all (albeit in a grislier manner than the hallow of Halifirien), and Beleg's voice crosses the boundary of death to reassure his friend. "Gloomy forest", "angry earth", and "perilous path" act as (super-)natural guardians of the hidden grave in rather the same way that the Whispering Wood protects Elendil's tomb. In addition, the peculiar quality of Beleg's voice in relation to an unknown space presents a close parallel to the 'echo of a great voice' that haunts the Halifirien. "Veiled, vague and distant," Beleg's voice resounds "like a cry at night | o'er the sea's silence". Instead of locating the voice in space and time, this portrayal evokes a dream-perception of immense distance, of a sound traversing the vast expanse of the nocturnal sea, poised against its (unnatural) silence, so that Beleg's voice seems adrift in an unfathomable 'elsewhere'.

In this case, medieval literature provides a fascinating parallel. In a puzzling section of the Old English poem *The Wife's Lament* (ll. 27-32), the female speaker deplores her exile in an equally hostile wilderness. She dwells in a grove (*wuda bearwe*) in an earth-cave that may represent a barrow, surrounded by hills and *burgtunas* ('mound-enclosures', in Alaric Hall's translation), overgrown with thorns. Those lines reveal the same close correspondence of loss and ruin with a

---

13 It should be noted that Tolkien had not yet produced any definite account of an immortal's passage to the Undying Lands after death at this time.

grim and marred landscape that marks Tolkien's description as well. Two points made in the ongoing debate about the many ambiguities of *The Wife's Lament* are of particular relevance here. It has been suggested that the grove may be an ancient (pagan) sanctuary (cf. Doane 87f; Hall, *Images* 9f; Hall, *Sanctity* 229; Wentersdorf, *Situation* 508), and that the speaker may be dead and talking from her grave (cf. Jensen 450f; Semple 111). Both readings are based on the peculiar topography and imagery that may connote the underworld and (now dismal) pagan sites of worship.

However, I have introduced this parallel to highlight Tolkien's specific strategies of transforming the landscape, so that it extends towards Otherspace. Instead of identifying his otherworldly dwelling, Beleg's words allude to it in the diction of myth ("the halls of the Moon o'er the hills of the sea"), which collapses apparent opposites (such as 'sea' and 'hills') and invokes a cosmic order beyond measurable space. On the hither side, the ruinous landscape mirrors the hideous tragedy of Beleg's death and, by means of evocative contrast, suggests the peaceful nature of that other place. As in *Cirion and Eorl*, a resounding voice bridges and reconciles discrepant regions of the larger world.[14] At the same time, voice and sound are inseparable from the spaces they traverse and fill with echoes. In their altered state, nature and landscape articulate and project a 'sacredness' that mediates between seclusion and visibility, the very tension that creates the impression of a perceptible yet unknowable 'elsewhere'.

This configuration then characterises Tolkien's literary technique of conjuring Otherspace, which, though based on medieval conceptions, aims to convey a specific experience of a transformed landscape. Against a medieval backdrop, the emphasis placed on subjective experience indeed stands out all the more. In both texts, this experience is framed and conditioned by a dream-state or vague anticipations, shaped by slippery impressions, half-grasped through metaphors. Couched in poetic speech, Otherspace thus emerges as a site within the imagination (which makes it no less real).

This basic conception also informs a particularly complex episode in *The Lord of the Rings*. The hobbits' dangerous adventure on the Barrow-downs surely presents one of the most intriguing configurations of burial mounds, transformed landscape, and experiences of the 'supernatural', not least because it combines the tomb's sinister aspects with the peaceful accord of barrows and landscape.

The closest medieval parallels for this episode can be found in the Icelandic sagas where the haunting *draugar*, the unquiet barrow-dwellers and revenants,

---

14 Tolkien's poetical construction thus precisely captures "the paradoxical opposition of separation and immediacy" that characterises many depictions of Celtic Otherworlds (Carey 6).

make frequent appearances (cf. Chadwick). Saga heroes, such as Grettir the Strong, battle with *draugar* who jealously guard their treasured possessions. Much could be said about the layering of diverse contexts surrounding barrows in both medieval texts and the Barrow-downs episode — such as the vivid connections to past political conflicts and territorial boundaries, the liminal state of passing through the realm of the dead, or the transmission and recovery of ancestral memories — here, however, I will focus on the issue of transforming space.

As a segregated, deserted area, the Barrow-downs are entirely dominated by burial mounds, stone circles and pillars: a landscape of the past and a domain of the dead. Unlike the Barrowfield of Edoras, the Downs are disconnected from the living memory, the histories and social order of the adjacent regions (Breeland and the Shire); they've become a place of 'sinister reputation' in 'hobbit-legend' and are thus marked by uncanny Otherness (cf. LotR 111).

Nevertheless, Frodo, Sam, Merry and Pippin intend to traverse the Downs in order to reach Bree, but — after sleeping too long by a standing stone on a hilltop — find themselves astray in an altered landscape veiled by a strange mist. Separated from his companions, Frodo passes the "pillars of a headless door, two huge standing stones" that he mistakes for a "gap in the hills, the north-gate of the Barrow-downs" (LotR 135), and after his hopeless attempt to reunite with his friends finds himself trapped inside a barrow.

The origin of the sudden, omnipresent fog that leads up to this entrapment is left unexplained. In the Icelandic sagas, the *draugar* occasionally command such a mist to cloak their activities (cf. Chadwick 54). Significantly, the mist seems to possess an independent agency in Tolkien's text and thus contributes to the impression of an animate landscape. Arising from the Downs themselves, the disorienting mist shapes a space of its own:

> The fog rolled up to the walls and rose above them, and as it mounted it bent over their heads until it became a roof: they were shut in a hall of mist whose central pillar was the standing stone. (LotR 135)

At the same time, the fog that distorts shapes, proportions and distances, reduces space to (Frodo's) subjective experience in the following account. The limitations and uncertainties of subjective perception are stressed with regard to the 'headless door'. Frodo cannot remember having noticed these pillars earlier, and even though he watches out for them the next day, when the hobbits have been rescued by Tom Bombadil, there is no more "sign of the great stones standing like a gate" (LotR 143). The suspicion remains, however, that Frodo entered a fundamentally altered space when he passed that threshold.

Ambiguities characterise the topography of the Barrow-downs and recall equally uncanny sites in medieval texts, such as the dragon's lair — itself an ancient barrow — in *Beowulf*, which "occupies a shifting and ambiguous place", "near at hand and yet invisible" (Michelet 82).

Overall, the description is marked by a gradual transition from ordinary, detached appraisal of the landscape to subjective disorientation and exposure to the uncanny and unfamiliar, culminating in an unsettling experience of Otherspace.[15] The mist that combines natural with 'supernatural' properties acts as a medium of crossing the boundary between the realm of the living and that of the (living) dead. In addition, an otherworldly light manifests the altered conditions of space. Inside the barrow, Frodo notices that

> the darkness was slowly giving way: a pale greenish light was growing round him. It did not at first show him what kind of a place he was in, for the light seemed to be coming out of himself, and from the floor beside him, and had not yet reached the roof or wall. (LotR 137)

This sourceless radiance is paralleled by the 'shadowless light' that surrounds barrows or shines within them in Icelandic literature, for instance in an episode from *Njáls saga*.[16] In *The Lord of the Rings*, the pale greenish hue suggests emanations of death and decay, a 'corpse-light', reminiscent of Minas Morgul (cf. LotR 688), superseded and obliterated by "real light, the plain light of day" (LotR 139) when the hobbits are rescued. In the familiar, seemingly objective medium of plain daylight, space assumes its ordinary appearance once again.

However, the clear dichotomy of real/natural and 'unreal'/supernatural light is drawn into question soon afterwards. When Tom Bombadil removes a great load of gold, silver and jewellery from the barrow and places it on the mound's top, light itself responds vividly. As the hobbits look back one last time, "the sunlight on the gold" leaps from it "like a yellow flame" (LotR 143). While the 'yellow flame' may allude to the fire which, in the Icelandic sagas, burns above barrows and indicates hidden treasure, as it does in *Grettis saga*,[17]

---

15 The hobbits' experience renders the geography of the Barrow-downs similar to the *hvammr* of Scandinavian tradition, "a short valley or dell, surrounded by mountains, but open on one side in one direction", itself associated with a borderland between the living and the dead (Christiansen 87-89).

16 *Brennu-Njáls saga*, k. 78: *Þeir þóttust sjá fjögur ljós í hauginum brenna og bar hvergi skugga á.* They thought they saw four lights burning in the mound, and none of them threw a shadow. (transl. DaSent)

17 Cf. *Grettis saga*, k. 18: *Það var eitt kveld harðla síð er Grettir bjóst heim að ganga að hann sá eld mikinn gjósa upp á nesi því er niður var frá bæ Auðunar...'Það mundi mælt,' sagði Grettir, 'ef slíkt sæist á voru landi að þar brynni af fé.'* Now one night very late, as Grettir made ready to go home, he saw a great fire burst out on a ness to the north of

the description leaves it hovering between subjective impression, metaphor and a momentary merging of natural with 'supernatural' light that possesses an agency and a significance of its own. At the same time, this moment signals restored visibility not only of the hidden treasure, which presumably attracted the Barrow-wight, but of the burial mound as part of the landscape: an interesting parallel to the Halifirien, since the holy mountain with its hidden grave eventually becomes a beacon hill.

The transformation of space, conveyed chiefly through Frodo's subjective experience as an alternation of mist and light(s), foregrounds visibility. Yet Frodo's experience of altered space is itself framed by another mode of relating to the landscape. Even before the hobbits enter the Barrow-downs, Tom Bombadil introduces them to their temporal rather than their spatial dimensions:

> Suddenly Tom's talk left the woods and went leaping up the young stream, over bubbling waterfalls, over pebbles and worn rocks, and among small flowers in close grass and wet crannies, wandering at last up on to the Downs. They heard of the Great Barrows, and the green mounds, and the stone-rings upon the hills and in the hollows among the hills. Sheep were bleating in flocks. Green walls and white walls rose. There were fortresses on the heights. Kings of little kingdoms fought together, and the young Sun shone like fire on the red metal of their new and greedy swords. There was victory and defeat; and towers fell, fortresses were burned, and flames went up into the sky. Gold was piled on the biers of dead kings and queens; and mounds covered them, and the stone doors were shut; and the grass grew over all. Sheep walked for a while biting the grass, but soon the hills were empty again. A shadow came out of dark places far away, and the bones were stirred in the mounds. Barrow-wights walked in the hollow places with a clink of rings on cold fingers, and gold chains in the wind. Stone rings grinned out of the ground like broken teeth in the moonlight.
> (LotR 128)

A history of kingdoms and conflicts unfolds, as it were, in fast-forward, viewed by an external observer who remains unaware of (or indifferent to) names, territories and heroic feats, and who offers nothing like the tale of origins and ancestry that shapes, for instance, cultural memory in Rohan. Instead this

---

Audun's farm... 'It would be said,' quoth Grettir, 'if that were seen in our land, that the flame burned above hid treasure.' (transl. Morris/Magnusson) – In the sagas, a barrow's presence is frequently indicated by a fiery light surrounding the mound or emanating from it. That mysterious fire seems to form "a barrier between the worlds of the living and the dead" (Ellis Davidson, *Road* 161).

account records, from a bird's-eye view, the signs of change in the landscape at breathtaking speed. In Tom's tale, the deserted, forbidding Barrow-downs come alive with past transformations, conveyed in highly visual terms (at least until the arrival of the shadow, at which point acoustic impressions emerging from forcefully barred sites take over). The narration's pace furthermore suggests an altered perception of time, one that approaches the memory of the land itself, yet the narrated landscape is inseparable from this extraordinarily condensed account and the voice that achieves it.

It is Tom's voice as well that literally breaks into the confinements of the barrow, liberates the hobbits, and restores a sunlit landscape.[18] Yet besides chanting spells, this voice once again shifts space in time when Tom reveals the origins of the swords taken from the barrow:

> The hobbits did not understand his words, but as he spoke they had a vision as it were of a great expanse of years behind them, like a vast shadowy plain over which there strode shapes of Men, tall and grim with bright swords, and last came one with a star on his brow. Then the vision faded, and they were back in the sunlit world. (LotR 142f)

While readers may recognise the arrival of the exiled Númenóreans in Middle-earth, the description itself does not portray an historical event but conjures time as a landscape in the mythical mode. Within this visionary space, the sights and details flash with condensed significance of their own but cannot be deciphered or translated. In fact, words as signifyers are bypassed in favour of immediate vision, and Tom's voice, more than any other, highlights the poetic quality of language that stirs the imagination even when meaning is lost to the passage of time:

> Tom sang most of the time, but it was chiefly nonsense, or else perhaps a strange language unknown to the hobbits, an ancient language whose words were mainly those of wonder and delight.
> (LotR 143)

---

18 In addition to Scandinavian analogues, a close Christian parallel for the barrow's liberation and subsequent re-integration into ordinary space may be found in the Anglo-Saxon *Guthlac* legend, especially the Old English B version, which dwells at great length on the saint's struggle with the spirits or demons haunting the *beorg* Guthlac successfully appropriates as his hermitage (cf. Hall, *Sanctity*; Siewers; Wentersdorf, *Guthlac*). Like the barrows in *The Lord of the Rings*, Guthlac's *beorg* is located in a (spiritually and politically) "disputed borderland" (Wentersdorf, *Guthlac* 140).

Once again, as with the 'echo of a great voice' on the Halifirien, a specific resonance — the combined qualities of sound and site — takes precedence over historical recollection with its attached meanings, and reveals its capacity of extending space beyond the limitations of ordinary perception. As narrated space, the Barrow-downs emerge within the imagination prior to actual experience. Yet this landscape is also transformed by Tom's evocative, resonant speech and its poetic qualities, which ultimately allows for a mythical perception of time within space.

In conclusion, a few important points deserve to be emphasised. As sites of intersection and transition, mounds and barrows specifically lend themselves to an exploration of diverging orders of space, ranging from historical and political to the interplay of culture and nature and, finally, their extensions towards Otherspace. This last feature also presents an extreme of otherness and thus the greatest challenge to modern perception. In medieval literature, certain sites — like the hollow hills of Irish tradition — operate as gateways to Otherworlds as a matter of course. No explanations, justifications or attempts to mediate strangeness by poetic means are required. The modern conception of space, by contrast, no longer allows for such a potential: a development that may be viewed as a process of 'disenchantment'. Although even within industrial cultures, insular sacred sites persist, they are firmly attached to institutionalised religions (of which there is no trace in Middle-earth).

Tolkien's texts, as I've argued, repeatedly seek to reveal the 'supernatural' as nature's innermost potential rather than conceptualising a difference or even an opposition between the two. In this regard, Tolkien certainly incorporates a medieval figure of thought, and a fundamental one at that, but his texts do not reproduce or repeat it. To the contrary: the various textual strategies and shifts in perspective outlined above all point to an acute awareness of difference and historical distance and amount to a concentrated literary effort of 're-enchanting' space from a modern point of perception. Clearly, these strategies are developed in order to re-create a premodern mode of experiencing the landscape as animate and replete with meaning.

Resonant space with its extensions into a perceptible, yet unknowable 'elsewhere,' is one of the unique configurations that result from these efforts. The framing of subjective experience as much as the evocative power of voice and sound (with their poetic potential that picks up where cognition ends), stand out as techniques employed to mediate between the modern and the premodern mindscape. And instead of taking us back to a simulated Middle Ages, they seek to unlock a new space of imagination.

Bibliography

Brookes, Stuart. "Walking with Anglo-Saxons: Landscapes of the Dead in Early Anglo-Saxon Kent." *Anglo-Saxon Studies in Archaeology & History* 14 (2007): 143-153

Buckberry, Jo. "On Sacred Ground: Social Identity and Churchyard Burial in Lincolnshire and Yorkshire, c. 700-1100." *Anglo-Saxon Studies in Archaeology & History* 14 (2007): 120-132

Carey, John. "Time, Space, and the Otherworld." *Proceedings of the Harvard Celtic Colloquium* 7 (1987): 1-27

Carpenter, Humphrey (Ed. with the assistance of Christopher Tolkien). *The Letters of J.R.R. Tolkien*. London: Houghton Mifflin, 1995

Chadwick, Nora K. "Norse Ghosts: A Study in the *draugr* and the *haugbui*." *Folklore* 57.2 (1946): 50-65

Christiansen, Reidar T. "The Dead and the Living." *Studia Norvegica* 2 (Oslo 1946): 3-96

Devlin, Zoë. "Social Memory, Material Culture and Community Identity in Early Medieval Mortuary Practices." *Anglo-Saxon Studies in Archaeology & History* 14 (2007): 38-46

Doane, A. N. "Heathen Form and Christian Function in *The Wife's Lament*." *Mediaeval Studies* 28 (1966): 71-91

Ellis [Davidson], Hilda R. *The Road to Hel. A Study of the Conception of the Dead in Old Norse Literature*. Westport CT: Greenwood Press, 1943

Ellis Davidson, Hilda R. "The Hill of the Dragon. Anglo-Saxon Burial Mounds in Literature and Archaeology." *Folklore* 64.4 (1950): 169-185

---. "Royal Graves as Religious Symbols." *Anglo-Saxon Studies in Archaeology and History* 5 (1992): 25-31

Fern, Chris. "Early Anglo-Saxon Horse Burial of the Fifth to Seventh Centuries AD." *Anglo-Saxon Studies in Archaeology & History* 14 (2007): 92-107

Hall, Alaric. "The Images and Structure of *The Wife's Lament*." *Leeds Studies in English, New Series* 33 (2002): 1-29

---. "Constructing Anglo-Saxon Sanctity: Tradition, Innovation and Saint Guthlac." *Images of Sanctity: Essays in Honour of Gary Dickson*. Ed. Debra Higgs Strickland. Leiden: Brill, 2007, 207-235

Hoggett, Rik. "Charting Conversion: Burial as a Barometer of Belief?" *Anglo-Saxon Studies in Archaeology & History* 14 (2007): 28-37

Holtorf, Cornelius. "Secondary Burials in the Mounds of Megaliths." 10 July, 2002: https://tspace.library.utoronto.ca/citd/holtorf/5.1.1.html (3-25-2011)

Jensen, Emily. "The *Wife's Lament's Eorðscræf*: Literal or Figural Sign?" *Neuphilologische Mitteilungen* 91 (1990): 449-457

Jones, Thomas: "The Black Book of Carmarthen 'Stanzas of the Graves'. The John Rhys Memorial Lecture." *Proceedings of the British Academy* 53 (1967): 97-137

Michelet, Fabienne L. "The Centres of Beowulf. A Complex Spatial Organisation." *Creation, Migration, and Conquest: Imaginary Geography and Sense of Space in Old English Literature*. Oxford: OUP, 2006, 74-114

Ó Cathasaigh, Tomás. "The Semantics of *síd*." *Éigse* 17 (1977/78): 137-155

Petts, David: "*De Situ Brecheniauc* and *Englynion y Beddau*: Writing About Burial in Early Medieval Wales." *Anglo-Saxon Studies in Archaeology & History* 14 (2007): 163-172

Pollington, Stephen. *Anglo-Saxon Burial Mounds. Princely Burials in the 6th and 7th Centuries*. Swaffham: Anglo-Saxon Books, 2008

Puhvel, Martin. "The Ride around Beowulf's Barrow." *Folklore* 94.1 (1983): 108-112

Robinson, Fred. "The Tomb of Beowulf." *Beowulf: A Verse Translation.* Transl. Seamus Heaney. Ed. Daniel Donoghue. New York: W.W. Norton, 2002, 181-197

Semple, Sarah. "A Fear of the Past: The Place of the Prehistoric Burial Mound in the Ideology of Middle and Later Anglo-Saxon England." *World Archaeology* 30 (1998/99): 109-126

Shephard, John F. "The Social Identity of the Individual in Isolated Barrows and Barrow Cemeteries in Anglo-Saxon England." *Space, Hierarchy and Society. Interdisciplinary Studies in Social Area Analysis.* Eds. Barry C. Burnham & John Kingsbury. (BAR International Series 59) Oxford 1979, 47-79

Siewers, Alfred K. "Landscapes of Conversion: Guthlac's Mound and Grendel's Mere as Expressions of Anglo-Saxon Nation-Building." *Viator* 34 (2003): 21-25

Simek, Rudolf. *Mittelerde. Tolkien und die germanische Mythologie.* München: C.H. Beck, 2005

Sims-Williams, Patrick. "Some Celtic otherworld terms." *Celtic Language, Celtic Culture: A Festschrift for Eric P. Hamp.* Eds. Ann T. E. Matonis & Daniel F. Mela. Van Nuys, Ca.: Ford & Bailie, 1990, 57-84

Thäte, Eva S. »Alte Denkmäler und frühgeschichtliche Bestattungen: Ein sächsisch-angelsächsischer Totenbrauch und seine Kontinuität. Eine vergleichende Studie.« *Archäologische Informationen* 19 (1996): 105-116

---. "A Question of Priority: The Re-use of Houses and Barrows for Burials in Scandinavia in the Late Iron Age (AD 600-1000)." *Anglo-Saxon Studies in Archaeology & History* 14 (2007): 183-193

Tilley, Christopher. *A Phenomenology of Landscape.* Oxford: Berg Publishers, 1994

Tolkien, J.R.R. *The Lord of the Rings.* London: HarperCollins, 1995

---. "Cirion and Eorl." *Unfinished Tales of Númenor and Middle-earth.* Ed. Christopher Tolkien. London: HarperCollins, 1998, 373-414

---. "The Rivers and Beacon-hills of Gondor." *Vinyar Tengwar* 42 (2001): 5-31

---. *The Lays of Beleriand.* (*The History of Middle-earth* 3). Ed. Christopher Tolkien. London: HarperCollins, 2002

van de Noort, Robert. "The Context of the Early Medieval Barrow in Western Europe." *Antiquity* 67 (1993): 66-73

Wentersdorf, Karl P. "*Guthlac A*: The Battle for the *Beorg*." *Neophilologus* 62 (1978): 135-142

---. "The Situation of the Narrator in the Old English *Wife's Lament*." *Speculum* 56 (1981): 492-516

Williams, Howard. "Ancient Landscapes and the Dead: The Reuse of Prehistoric and Roman Monuments as Early Anglo-Saxon Burial Sites." *Medieval Archaeology* 41 (1997): 1-32

Old Norse Wolf-Motifs in *Of Beren and Lúthien*

Antje vom Lehn (Tübingen)

Tolkien's knowledge of not only Old English, but also Old Norse sources has been shown a number of times. So far, however, only few motifs have been looked at in detail. In order to help amend this situation, in this paper I will compare the wolf-motifs in the story about Beren and Lúthien with their sources in *Völsunga saga*,[1] *Gylfaginning*[2] and *Völuspá*.[3]

In his famous lecture and essay *Beowulf: The Monsters and the Critics*, Tolkien recommends taking a step back from the view that the monsters in the Old English heroic epos *Beowulf* are only nice, but somehow not quite fitting accessories to the heroic plot. To him, the monsters are as important as the human protagonists and well worth taking a closer look at for their own sake (BMC 19).

I have taken the liberty to use this, Tolkien's own approach, on his story of Beren and Lúthien. Even though the story is usually reduced to its human and elvish protagonists, as exemplified in *The Lord of the Rings* (LotR 187-189), its main sources in *The Silmarillion* and *The History of Middle-earth* are full of wolves, wolfhounds and werewolves of all kinds.[4] If all of those were to be edited out, the plot would collapse.

I start out with a few general thoughts on the different kinds of wolves and the varied sources. The Old Norse literature is especially rich in stories about werewolves (Roberts 580). Here, as was generally the case in the Middle Ages, the werewolf is not seen as an evil being per se, but as the victim of a curse. This stands in contrast to both the ancient perception of the werewolf

---

[1] The *Völsunga saga* from the 13th century is counted as an Icelandic Legendary saga (de Vries 470). Its contents are the rise and fall of the family of the Völsungs — the subject matter that is also known as the *Nibelungenlied* or, in Tolkien's version, as *The Legend of Sigurd and Gudrún*.
[2] *Gylfaginning*, which is part of the *Snorra-Edda* from about 1220 (Simek/Pálsson 352f), is a dialogue about Old Norse mythology. With the help of strophes from different poems, an overview over the world history is given, from its creation to its destruction.
[3] *Völuspá* is part of the *Poetic Edda* which has the *Codex Regius* from the later half of the 13th century as its main manuscript (Simek/Pálsson 56). The poem also gives an overview over the world history, yet in a shorter version than in *Gylfaginning*.
[4] Unless stated otherwise, I am referring to the *Silmarillion*-version of the story ("Of Beren and Lúthien", S 189-221). In those cases where differences in the other versions have an impact on my thesis, I will make note of this.

as a malefactor and the view on the real wolf of the Middle Ages (Roberts 568) who was seen purely negatively in Scandinavia (Davidson 103f).

The view of the wolf as a negative loner can be seen in the Old Norse term *vargr* which means both literally "wolf" and figuratively "outlaw" (Davidson 136). A *vargr* thus is positioned somewhere between animals and humans, while at the same time being on the border of human society, sometimes even crossing it — a perfect case for the modern study of monsters and monstrosity.

Wolves of one kind or the other are to be found in all of Tolkien's bigger works. Their depiction is always adapted to fit the text. The Wargs in *The Hobbit* are in allegiance with the singing goblins, which is in accordance to the sometimes fairy-tale like character of the novel. In *The Lord of the Rings*, however, they are more serious and demonic — the morning after the fight near Moria, their dead bodies cannot be found anywhere (LotR 291). Yet they still remain an anonymous mass in the service of the enemy and are usually reduced to their animal aspects. The focus thus remains on the Elves, Men, Dwarves and Hobbits whose fate is at the centre of the story.

The beings that are called werewolves in *The Silmarillion* are not beings that change their shape from human to wolf as is usually the case. They are never-theless composite beings — "fell beasts inhabitated by dreadful spirits that [Sauron] had imprisoned in their bodies" (S 192). These incarnated evil spirits serve Sauron and make him the "Lord of the Werewolves". Most of the werewolves still remain an anonymous mass, but we also meet wolves with a name and a history for the first time: Draugluin is the ancestor of the werewolves, Carcharoth his biggest, strongest and most terrible descendant. These two, and especially Carcharoth, are of vital importance for the plot concerning Beren and Lúthien.

There are, however, also beings in Tolkien's writing that conform at least for some time to our modern image of the werewolf as a human in the shape of a wolf.

I would like to begin my analysis with *Völsunga saga*. Two text passages concerning wolves are to be found in the beginning.
King Völsung is killed in a fight by King Siggeir, the husband of Völsung's daughter Signy. All his men die, while only his ten sons survive. Signy pleads for their lives and Siggeir agrees not to kill them right away. He has them brought into the woods and has a large tree felled over their legs, so that they are trapped. For nine nights a wolf comes and devours one of the brothers each night. This wolf is Siggeir's mother who is capable of changing into a wolf by witchcraft. On the tenth evening, Signy has a servant smear honey onto the face and into the mouth of the last surviving brother, Sigmund. When the wolf appears and starts to lick the honey from his face and finally out of his mouth,

Sigmund bites into her tongue. The wolf is caught and in her fight to get free destroys the tree which Sigmund had been caught under. The wolf's tongue is ripped out and she dies. Sigmund, however, is free and can now, together with Signy, turn his mind to avenging their father (Ebel 65f).

Heroes from the legendary past live, naturally, by different rules than those of modern society, so that Sigmund and Signy finally beget a child together, a son who will help in avenging their father. Sigmund and his son Sinfjötli live in the woods where they rob and kill men to prepare Sinfjötli for the revenge. One day they find two king's sons who had been wandering around as werewolves. Sigmund and Sinfjötli steal the wolfskins hanging above them and as they put on these skins they transform into wolves. They then continue roaming the woods alone. Sinfjötli, however, does not adhere to the rule that neither of them is to fight against more than seven men without calling the other one to help and is wounded in this fight. When he tells Sigmund about this, his father attacks him and bites his throat. Cursing the wolfskins he brings his son back to their earthen house. He heals him with a special leaf and they stay in the house until the ten days they have to remain in the wolfshape are up and they can turn back into their human shape. They take this opportunity to burn the skins, conjuring them to do no more harm (Ebel 68f).

That passage contains several motifs that can also be found with Beren and Lúthien. Perhaps the most important one is that of the shape change which can happen either, on the side of the enemies, through witchcraft and supernatural powers, or, on the side of the heroes, through enchanted objects. This division is also to be found in Tolkien.

The shape changer par excellence in Tolkien's *legendarium* is Sauron. He does not need external aids for this, as his own powers are enough to enable him to change into any desired physical shape — be it the form of the wolf at the beginning of the fight against Huan or the subsequent quick succession of several shapes as he tries to escape and finally flies away as a vampire (S 205f).

Beren, Lúthien and in some versions of the story also Huan need their enemies' skins as well as Lúthien's powers to take on the shape of their enemies. In doing this they also possess the abilities of these beings — Lúthien for example can fly due to Thuringwethil's skin — yet keep their own abilities and can remove the skins at any time (S 210f).

That shows that Tolkien uses both approaches to the shape changing — through magic and through aids. Those aids are, as in the Old Norse, the skins which also have to be enchanted. In the *Völsunga saga* this is a curse on the skins, with Tolkien it is Lúthien whose powers makes the camouflage convincing. But even if the enchantment is needed for the shape change, it would not be possible without the skins. Tolkien thus confers the connotations of both approaches — the heroes need the aids, the enemies do not.

A further look at the conditions of the shape change reveals some interesting details. In the *Völsunga saga*, the wolfskins have the power over the heroes — Sigmund and Sinfjötli can only return to their human shape after ten days and, during this time, are even more impulsive and violent than usual. It is for this reason that Sigmund in his wolf shape inflicts a mortal wound on his son. Beren and Lúthien, on the other hand, are not under any negative influence from the skins — they change their shape and can possess the positive abilities of their enemies, such as the ability to fly, while keeping a level head and can freely dictate the duration of their shape change.

In my opinion the reason for that difference lies in the differing contexts of the episodes. For Beren and Lúthien, the shape change is just a means to the end of getting to Morgoth unhindered and unrecognised. The shape change serves that purpose; it does not have to show anything else. The shape change and life as a wolf in the *Völsunga saga*, on the other hand, are the purpose in and of itself. It is a time of initiation for the young Sinfjötli, a time that has to prepare him for his life as a warrior and avenger of his grandfather.

The double meaning of the Old Norse word for wolf plays an important part in this: Sigmund and Sinfjötli are *vargr* in both meanings of the word. They have literally changed into wolves, but on top of that they are also outlaws in the land of their enemy. Tolkien introduces this double meaning during a different episode of his story. In the *Lay of Leithian*, he describes Beren during his time of being an outlaw as "Beren like a wolf alone" (LB 166) — one of many small hints where the mediaevalist Tolkien can be seen.

Another point where his scholarly background becomes apparent is his choice of words. The wolfskin that Beren puts on to change his shape is called "hame". That word is related to the Old Norse *hamr* which is used for the skins employed for changing one's shape (Gilliver et al. 140f). Thus even the choice of words reveals that Tolkien refers back to the mediaeval tradition for the manner of his shape change, not to the modern one which happens as a transfer through a bite than through putting on skins.

Another motif out of the *Völsunga saga* is that of the wolf that kills the captives one by one. I will return to that at a later point, because this in itself relatively simple motif can be used well to illustrate my conclusion.

But let us turn first to the Fenriswolf and the motifs connected to him. The motif that is perhaps most obviously taken from a source is that of the hand bitten off by a wolf. The source for this is to be found in *Gylfaginning* from the *Snorra-Edda* which, among other stories, describes the youth of the Fenriswolf. A prophecy exists about Fenrir and his siblings Hel and the Midgard Serpent that these three will bring great harm to the Æsir. The Æsir therefore try to either bring them as far away as possible or, in Fenrir's case, to render them harmless. Masked as a test of his strength they make the wolf agree to being enchained by them. However, he does become suspicious and demands that one of them put their hand in his mouth as a security. Týr agrees to this, but when Fenrir realises that he cannot break the fetters, despite the Æsir's promise, and that the Æsir of course will not take the fetters off him, he bites off Týr's hand, as he had said he would do, and thus leaves a visible sign of the Æsir's broken promise (Pálsson 43-46).

With Tolkien, it is Beren who loses his hand to a wolf — but here it is a sign for the oath he kept, stealing a Silmaril from Morgoth's crown. Tolkien thus simplifies a motif that is more complex in its original context. With Tolkien, the hero keeps his promise, the enemy of the hero is "the evil one" who mutilates the enemy and proves himself to be an obstacle.[5] It is not this easy in the Old Norse sources. The sympathy in the stories usually lies with the Æsir, but these are also shown to have weaknesses and faults and are not strictly "good". The chaining of Fenrir is one example where the audience's sympathy might lie with the wolf — he has not yet proven himself to be evil, whereas the Æsir have not been honest and sworn a false oath. (Of course the prophecy about Fenrir as bringer of harm does turn out to be true during Ragnarök, but at this point of the story it is the Æsir who swear the false oath and it is Týr who has to pay for this with his hand. The enemy Fenrir, however, has acted morally correct during this episode.) This changing of sympathy in the big fight of good versus evil is something that Tolkien has no place for in his mythology. It is unthinkable that any being on Morgoth's side might show more moral integrity than the hero, as Fenrir does when he is true to his word, contrary to the Æsir and Týr. This has made it necessary for Tolkien to invert the motif of the hand as the symbol of the oath and thus to simplify it.

Perhaps it is to make up for this that Tolkien uses the motif of the severed hand a second time: After having killed Beren's father Barahir, Morgoth's Orcs cut off his hand bearing the ring of Felagund and want to bring it to Morgoth as proof that Barahir really is dead. This time it is the enemies for whom the severed hand is the sign of the deed done.[6]

We thus find a sort of double echo in Tolkien's text: The motif of Beren's hand is an echo of Barahir's hand, yet both are also an echo of the Eddaic story about the Fenriswolf. The result of this accumulation is that all the occurrences of a

---

5 At least Tolkien simplifies the motif if it is seen only with its three components "wolf–owner of the hand–oath". A further analysis of the motif could include a possible hubris on Beren's part — which I here will not look at because it moves beyond the wolf-motif itself.

6 In this case the hand is not bitten off by the wolf; it is simply cut off by one of the enemies. There are many possible sources for this version of the motif, for example Beowulf cutting off Grendel's arm as a symbol of his victory. Nevertheless, I see Barahir's hand as an echo of the wolf-motif: Tolkien introduces the fact that Barahir's hand is cut off by the Orcs quite late (WJ 59), in all the other versions the Orcs simply take his ring (cf. among others LB 165f, LR 134). That suggests to me that he, having discovered and extended all the other repetitions of motifs in the story about Beren and Lúthien, now wants to repeat the motif of the hand as well.

motif resonate in every one of them and that they thus intensify one another. I will return to this phenomenon of the double echo later on.

During all those oaths and severed hands in Tolkien's story, the wolf remains a minor — at this point there is no connection between Carcharoth and Beren's oath concerning the Silmaril. Yet when he bites off the hand holding the Silmaril, the wolf is turned from this minor character into a character which is of vital importance to the larger fates. The Silmaril in his belly drives Carcharoth mad and in his wrath he helps prophecies come true. The story of the Silmaril is the thread that runs through all of Tolkien's First Age and Carcharoth is now involved in exactly this story.

This is parallel to the Fenriswolf. A prophecy exists of him and his siblings bringing great harm to the Æsir. It finally comes true in Ragnarök where they play important parts and where Fenrir kills, among others, Odin (Pálsson 77-80). Ragnarök is on the whole a time that is marked by wolves,[7] a time of chaos and violence. An echo of this in Tolkien can be found in the madness to which Carcharoth is driven by the Silmaril and during which he finally gets to Doriath. There he has a memorable fight with Huan: "in the baying of Huan was heard the voice of the horns of Oromë and the wrath of the Valar, but in the howls of Carcharoth was the hate of Morgoth and malice crueller than teeth of steel" (S 219). The description of the battle is reminiscent of a doomsday battle with both sides facing each other — and thus reminiscent of Ragnarök. This, among other parallels, makes Carcharoth a parallel figure to Fenrir, which makes him gain the gigantic size and terror of the Ragnarök-wolf.

Tolkien creates another parallel to the Fenriswolf in the wolfhound Huan and the prophecy that only the greatest of all wolves will defeat him. Huan's enemies know about this prophecy and this knowledge drives their actions. Sauron changes himself into a wolf, but loses the ensuing battle so that Huan and Lúthien can take power over his island. Morgoth rears Carcharoth and sets him as a guard on his gate to be ready for Huan. It is because he guards the door that Carcharoth steps into Beren's way on his way out, bites off his hand, falls into madness, wreaks destruction on Doriath, wounds Beren mortally, finally kills Huan and is in turn killed by him.

The Æsir in *Gylfaginning* also know about the prophecy concerning Fenrir and his siblings. It is that knowledge that makes them try to chain Fenrir (Pálsson 43f).

The knowledge about the prophecy is in all three cases (Carcharoth, Huan, Fenrir) a prerequisite to the following chain of events which make the prophecy come true. The prophecies also show that, both in the Old Norse sources and in Tolkien, the fate of the world is not only concerned with Men, Elves, Ainur and Æsir, but those monsters and animals play their part in it as well.

---

7   Compare *vargöld* (Neckel 11) = "wolf-time".

As I mentioned before, I would like to come back to the motif of the wolf devouring the captives one by one.

Tolkien takes this motif from the *Völsunga saga* without any major alterations — the captivated heroes are Beren, Felagund and their fellowship, the wolf comes in the dark, the heroes cannot defend themselves against it, only one of them survives and is finally freed by a female figure, in this case Lúthien. Yet Tolkien does not leave it be with this simple adoption of the motif. As with the severed hand, he brings it up a second time, adapted to the context. When Lúthien and Huan arrive at Sauron's isle, Sauron sends out his wolves, one after the other to fight against Huan. But Huan kills them and only Draugluin makes it back to Sauron to tell him about Huan. Contrary to the earlier occurrence of the motif, the fights in that scene are fair — both opponents know that the fight will happen and are in full possession of their power.

Tolkien plays with the motif. On its first occurrence, it serves as a symbol of the malignity of the enemy and of the nearly hopeless situation the hero finds himself in. On its second occurrence, it is a symbol of the fairness and strength of the hero's helper who meets his enemies in a fair fight and wins every time. The episodes follow each other rather quickly and thus stand in a direct contrast to one another, which strengthens their respective effect and evaluation — compared to each other in this way, the enemies seem more negative, the hero's side more positive.

The repetition of this motif seems especially important to me because we have not only a repetition "Tolkien from Tolkien" but also "Tolkien from the *Völsunga saga*" — this is another case of the double echo. And that double echo in Tolkien gives a special depth to the episode.

Using the history of the *Völsunga saga* and the texts related to it, Tom Shippey describes in *The Road to Middle-earth* how literary depth can be created — through a web of texts, their predecessors and successors that all influence each other, are similar, differ, use the same motifs and yet treat them differently. He then looks at the story of Beren and Lúthien in all its versions as an analogue — here we find a similar web of texts that introduce motifs, drop them, take them up again and change them (Shippey 310-317). This creates the feeling of depth in a text, so that each single text is more than just itself and resonates the other texts, either visibly, as with the references to the *Lay of Leithian* in the prose versions, or invisibly.

I would go a step further than Shippey. In my opinion it is not only the web of texts about Beren and Lúthien that resonates in all its varieties. Tolkien uses motifs from many different sources in that particular story, and those texts resonate as well, so that a complex network of Tolkien's own and his source texts is offered to the reader. And in my experience and observation this can be felt, even if the reader does not know about the existence of Tolkien's other versions or his sources — one can still feel that the text one is reading is not all there is to it, that there is something else underneath which gives a depth to the text that a reader of modern literature may not encounter quite so often.

Maybe, that network reaches its highest density in the story of Beren and Lúthien. Hardly any of his other stories exists in as many versions as this one, and hardly any of his other stories uses so many motifs from different sources as this one.

The Fenriswolf is the most important source for the wolf-motifs — which is fitting, seeing that Fenrir as a mythological being is very suitable for *The Silmarillion*. But the heroic tradition can be found as well: for example, through the motifs from the *Völsunga saga*, just as references to other literary and cultural traditions.

As a conclusion one can say that Tolkien manages to integrate a range of motifs from different sources into his texts. In doing this he does not merely copy the motifs, but always adapts them to the specific context. Through this they will probably not be obvious as borrowed motifs to a reader without previous knowledge in these areas, but they will nevertheless give a depth to the texts that most readers will discern. And perhaps it is exactly this depth which makes Tolkien's work so fascinating for so many people.

Bibliography

Davidson, H.R. Ellis. "Shape-changing in Old Norse Sagas". *Animals in Folklore*. Eds. J.R. Porter & W.M.S. Russel. Cambridge: D.S. Brewer, 1978, 126-142

de Vries, Jan. *Altnordische Literaturgeschichte*. Berlin: de Gruyter, 1999

Ebel, Uwe. *Völsunga saga*. Frankfurt am Main: Haag und Herchen, 1983

Gilliver, Peter, Jeremy Marshall & Edmund Weiner. *The Ring of Words: Tolkien and the Oxford English Dictionary*. Oxford: Oxford University Press, 2006

Neckel, Gustav. *Edda. Die Lieder des Codex Regius nebst verwandten Denkmälern*. Heidelberg: Universitätsverlag, 1983

Pálsson, Heimir. *Snorra-Edda*. Reykjavík: Mál og menning, 2003

Roberts, Keith. »Eine Werwolf-Formel: Eine kleine Kulturgeschichte des Werwolfs«. *Dämonen, Monster, Fabelwesen. Mittelalter-Mythen 2*. Hg. Ulrich Müller & Werner Wunderlich. St. Gallen: UVK, 1999, 565-581

Simek, Rudolf & Hermann Pálsson. *Lexikon der altnordischen Literatur*. Stuttgart: Kröner, 2007

Tolkien, John Ronald Reuel. "Beowulf: The Monsters and the Critics". *The Monsters and the Critics and Other Essays*. Ed. Christopher Tolkien. London: Allen & Unwin, 1983, 5-48

---. *The Lays of Beleriand*. Ed. Christopher Tolkien. London: HarperCollins, 2002

---. *The Lord of the Rings*. London: HarperCollins, 1995

---. *The Lost Road and other Writings*. Ed. Christopher Tolkien. London: Unwin Hyman, 1989

---. *The Silmarillion*. London: HarperCollins, 1999

---. *The War of the Jewels*. Ed. Christopher Tolkien. London: HarperCollins, 2002

The Eye and the Tree.
The Semantics of Middle-earth Heraldry

Catalin Hriban (Iaşi)

Since the raising of the Tolkienian *cosmos* to the status of High-fantasy paradigm, through the innumerable fantasy texts of different value and derivativeness (from *Shannara* to *Eragon*), the *interpretatio mediævalia* (Honegger 45) became somehow the canon for the popular appreciation of *The Lord of the Rings* and its foundational *legendarium*. That state of fact is caused, among others, by the medieval setting that frames the vast majority of the post-LotR fantasy, leading to a strong association *à rebours* between the secondary world of Middle-earth and the European Middle Ages, an association that parallels, in a skewed way, the privileged relation between the English Middle Ages and the rest of Tolkienian literature through the scholarly and intellectual activity by Tolkien.

As medievalism works, there is no better device than the heraldic art with its multi-layered imagery and highly codified vocabulary and grammar. In fact, its visualness aside, the coat-of-arms motif provides, through its canonical description or *blazoning*, a sort of poor-man's High Speech, for the lazy (or too clever) author.

This fictional/literary heraldry is as old as the European literature, if one upholds the theory, dear to the late medieval and Renaissance heraldic writers, that the medieval heraldry has its roots in the figurative and non-figurative images borne on their shields by the Greek warriors of Antiquity (Pastoureau, *Figures de l'héraldique* 17), painted on the Attic pottery or described in the *Iliad*. Besides the theory of the Greek antiquity roots, another hypothesis is the one placing these roots in the insignia of the barbaric invaders of the Roman Empire, while a third one found the origin of the European medieval heraldry in the art of the Persian, Islamic and then Byzantine Near East, brought home by the European crusaders. Of course, such hypotheses on the origin of heraldry displaced more or less one another starting from the Late Renaissance, before being rendered obsolete when the Age of Enlightenment finally provided the scientific method based on logics and reasoning to the historical research.

The coats-of-arms of the fictional heroes, families or dynasties are not so different, in terms of imaginative effort, than the fictional coats-of-arms "granted" by the medieval authors to real historic figures like Alexander the Great, Julius Caesar, Constantine the Great or Charlemagne.

The fictional/literary heraldry of the Middle Ages is borne within few generations from the documented emergence of the "true" heraldry, somewhere in the second half of the 12th century, and there is no richer fictional armorial than the one dedicated to King Arthur and his Knights of the Round Table.

Around mid 15th century the number of fictional knights bearing fictional coat-of-arms reached 180 (Pastoureau, *Figures de l'héraldique* 88). The large amount of creative energy employed by such extensive fictional armorials testi-fies on the level of commitment the chivalric "way of life" required from the elites (and not exclusively the aristocracy) of the "twilight of the Middle Ages".

In fact, the chivalric literature has indirectly more bearing on the emergence and development of the medieval heraldry than the current theory on the heraldic phenomenon would accept, as the bearing of colours and images on one's armour and clothing is more appropriate and logic in the pageant and the *mêlée* of a tournament than in their real battlefield counterparts (Pastoureau, *Figures de l'héraldique* 19). This happens to such an extent that at the end of the Middle Ages a large number of non-human and even non-corporeal entities are granted with coats-of-arms by authors inebriated with symbols (the Holy Trinity, Jesus Christ, Death, the Innocence, Satan), in their desire to show the feudal order extended beyond the limits of mankind, in other words, its capacity to incorporate the incorporeal. The interlinked, highly regulated and encoded corpus of objects and rules that is the 14th- and 15th-century heraldry mirrors somehow the social ideal of the feudal world, aspired to but never reached.

This meta-society inhabited by visual signs and encrypted text snippets remains a sort of highly decorated robe-of-office that any Middle Age, historical, reconstructed or purely fictional, must wear. Such visual works like an unfolding map, revealing layers under layers of meaning, portraying the fictional bearer of the arms in vast complexity and richness, unfortunately are visible only to the heraldic literate.

In terms of semantic interpretation, the true heraldic device (coat-of-arms) is a mostly iconic sign (in the general frame of Peirce's formal semiotics icon-index-symbol) as is consubstantial with its object in authority, and to lesser extents index (as it belongs to the object) and symbol (its interpretation requires a certain extent of the frame of reference provided by the heraldic rules and language).

The iconic quality is the important one for the medieval frame of mind as the concept of authority permeates the pyramidal society and hierarchical culture of the medieval world, of various shades and flavours of feudality. The coat of arms *is consubstantial* with its grantee as any alteration of the bearers' power, authority or status is immediately reflected by its coat-of-arms, any offence or infringement upon the device is legally a crime against its bearer and any other object bound to the device becomes an extension of the bearer's body. This type of interpretation is in fact formalized in the late Renaissance, but the principles summarized above were already applied by the time Bartole de Sassoferrato wrote his *De Principiis et Armis* in 1350 (Van Malderghem iv).

The use of heraldic imagery in Tolkien's literary works can be split in four periods, both chronologically and technically, i.e. the precursory period including the earliest description of Tuor's armour, in the *Fall of Gondolin*, *The Hobbit*, *The Lord of the Rings* and the Elven heraldry of his own special design, referred to in *The Silmarillion*.

The first group consists in descriptions of heraldic devices of several heroes of the Second Age in texts elaborated in the earliest phase of his *legendarium*. The arms of Tuor, a swan's wing: "his helm was adorned with a device of metals and jewels like to two swan-wings, one on either side, and a swan's wing was wrought on his shield" (LT 2 152), (presumably "*purple*, a swan's wing *argent*"), are "medieval" and "heraldic" in their bestowing, description and meaning. The arms are granted by the sovereign (King Turgon), are borne on the shield and on the helm's crest, they follow the heraldic rule of tinctures (placing metals on top of colours) and depict a defining moment in the bearer's life (the episode of the three swans guiding him in his progression to the sea and to the mouths of Sirion). The text does not mention the colour of the field. We assume that it is purple, after the sails of the Swanwing, Tuor's ship in his final voyage, as depicted in an outline of the *Song of Eärendel*, (LT 2 196), dating from 1916-17, i.e. contemporary with the *Fall of Gondolin*, rather than black (*sable*), more in line with Tolkien's later heraldic compositions, but assigned here to the treacherous Meglin and to his followers: "the sign of Meglin was a sable Mole" (LT 2 153).

In fact, the Fall of Gondolin is the finest example of the way the coat-of-arms of the protagonists and their "high-speech" description is used to make the narrative even more heroic. The colours and devices of King Turgon, fit into the paradigm as royal arms: "their [the king's house] colours were white and gold and red, and their emblems the moon and the sun and the scarlet heart" (LT 2 241).

In a passage reminiscent of the Round Table declamatory pageantry, the eleven Elven houses of Gondolin (of which Tuor's is the twelfth) have their arms described, complete with the more ornate and complex shields and crests borne by the houses' chiefs. The heraldic display precedes the arraying of armies before the last battle in the Siege of Gondolin and the description of the colours and devices of both the champions and the rank-and-file conveys the visual sense of glorious doom of a commemorative roll-of-arms:

> ... the folk of the Swallow bore a fan of feathers on their helms, and they were arrayed in white and dark blue and in purple and black and showed an arrowhead on their shields.
> ...they of the Heavenly Arch being a folk of uncounted wealth were arrayed in a glory of colours, and their arms were set with jewels that flamed in the light now over the sky. Every shield of that battalion was of the blue of the heavens and its boss a jewel

built of seven gems, rubies and amethysts and sapphires, emeralds, chrysoprase, topaz, and amber, but an opal of great size was set in their helms. Egalmoth was their chieftain, and wore a blue mantle upon which the stars were broidered in crystal...
There too were the folk of the Pillar and of the Tower of Snow, and both these kindreds were marshalled by Penlod, tallest of Gnomes.
There were those of the Tree, and they were a great house, and their raiment was green...
There stood the house of the Golden Flower who bare a rayed sun upon their shield, and their chief Glorfindel bare a mantle so broidered in threads of gold that it was diapered with celandine as a field in spring; and his arms were damascened with cunning gold.
... the people of the Fountain, and Ecthelion was their lord, and silver and diamonds were their delight...
... the host of the Harp, ... and a harp of silver shone in their blazonry upon a field of black; but Salgant bore one of gold...
...the folk of the Hammer of Wrath, and of these came many of the best smiths and craftsmen, and all that kindred reverenced Aule the Smith more than all other Ainur ... The sign of this people was the Stricken Anvil, and a hammer that smiteth sparks about it was set on their shields...
This was the fashion and the array of the eleven houses of the Gondothlim with their signs and emblems, and the bodyguard of Tuor, the folk of the Wing, was accounted the twelfth.

(LT 2 243)

Christopher Tolkien's commentary outlines the fact that the "pageant" was part of the first version of the narration and was left untouched through the subsequent rewritings. As for the "pageant" as one of the main literary means to introduce a martial gathering and to pave the way for the violent/tragic climax of a story, one of the oldest and most popular examples comes from the *Old Testament*, as quoted by Fox-Davies, whose usage of it in his *Complete Guide to Heraldry* is poignant: "Every man of the Children of Israel shall pitch by his own standard, with the ensign of their father's house" (Num 2:2 quoted by Fox-Davies 6).

The only antagonist bearing heraldic devices during the Siege of Gondolin is the traitor, Meglin. Black is his colour and his device is a mole *sable*. The chromatic interpretation is layered, as Meglin and his people (mole-men, people of the Mole) are dark-skinned and accustomed to live in the dark underground, being miners (visual representation), Meglin is the son of Eol of the Mole-kin (gnomes that evolved later in the *legendarium* into Dwarves) (genealogical representation), while he is pledged to the Dark Lord, betraying his adoptive family, motivated by jealousy, lust and hatred, being therefore an evil character (symbolic representation). In a quite ironic twist, Meglin of the Mole-people in *The Fall of Gondolin* becomes Maëglin "The Sharp-Glance" in *The Silmarillion* (S 154), like an auctorial hindsight about the fact that one's keensightedness or darkness without tells nothing about the presence of one's darkness within.

The devices of the Gondolin combatants are both figurative (arrowhead, gemstone, harp, spark-striking hammer, sun-in splendour) and straightforward enough to bear finding their similes in Burke's *General Armoury* (the enlarged edition of 1884), Woodward & Burnett's *Treatise on Heraldry, British and Foreign* (1892), or Fox-Davies' *A Complete Guide to Heraldry* (1909), just three "more mainstream" titles from the plethora of books available on the subject of heraldry in the immediate pre-WW I period.

As a general commentary to the use of heraldic imagery within this first phase of Tolkien's creation, one cannot ignore the fact that all the above are conscribed to a "high-speech" storytelling, being used both to enhance the visuals of a heroic setting and to fine-tune the specifics of the characters, individual as well as collective.

The group of images from *The Hobbit* are fairly simple as structure of heraldic imagery, being, in fact, just colours. It is worth noting that the significance attached to these colours will not change from *The Hobbit* to *The Lord of the Rings*. The siege of the Lonely Mountain, precluding the Battle of the Five Armies, shows the flags of the Wood-Elves and of the Men of the Laketown: "They bore with them the green banner of the Elven king and the blue banner of the Lake" (H 222).

The green and the blue that will pass over as "good" colours from *The Hobbit* into LotR, on the banners of Rohan and Dol Amroth, respectively. On the other side of the Battle of the Five Armies, the goblins/orcs of the Misty Mountains are flagging black and red banners: "Their banners were countless, black and red" (H 238).

This meaning of "bad" that will also carry on into LotR, as during the Battle of the Pelennor Fields, the flags of the Mordor&Morgul armies are black, the same black as on the sails of the pirate fleet from Umbar and on the shields of the Haradrim expeditionary force. In the same respect, the banners and war paraphernalia of the Harad army ambushed by Faramir's men in Ithilien are red with gold trimmings: "And some have red paint on their cheeks, and red cloaks; and their flags are red, and the tips of their spears; and they have round shields, yellow and black with big spikes" (LotR 646). We see now that the "bad" meaning of red and black is consistent with their original showing in *The Hobbit* (for a more in-depth analysis of the colour-coding of evil and otherness, cf. Sinex 176, 183).

Since the target audience of *The Hobbit* is quite specific, its simplified representational imagery is understandable. The use of plain colours as markers and their association with the signified entities is not as random as it might seem. While the use of green and blue (*sinople* and *azure*) to identify the good factions is responding well to both medieval and modern sensibilities, as well as is the association of black with evilness, the red flags among the black ones above the forest of spears of the goblin armies is quite a puzzle. A medieval colours/virtues/vices correspondence table built by Pastoureau (*Figures et couleurs* 40) links colour red with courage and force and largesse as virtues, and with cruelty and rage and pride as vices. Although the modern heraldic science disregards this type of interpretation of heraldic tinctures (Fox Davies 5), the layered meanings of the colours within a heraldic composition is very popular in medieval Europe, and to such an extent that by mid 16th century an intellectual reaction was already expressing itself, condemning the "fantasies".

Bilbo Baggins, the unlikely hero, possesses the above virtues and before the end of the story he gets the opportunity to reveal them, to himself and to others. Bilbo's "red" virtues are though amended by his prudence and moderation, another pair of medieval virtues. We have to consider the fact that without moderation courage is brashness, largesse is wastefulness and force is ferocity. In fact, by themselves, "red" virtues are easily translated into vices by the lack of moderation. The large body of ethical and educational writings inherited in the 12th-14th centuries (Lachaud 105) emphasise the importance of moderation as a fulcrum for the rest of the virtues in building the self into a better, Christian, man. The idea is present as early as Martinus of Braga's *Formula Honestae Vitae* (6th cent.), as the pursuit of *mensura rectitudinis*, whose absence leaves the rest of virtues unaccomplished (Lachaud 107), a work that became fundamental for the moralists and ethical theorists and educators of the European Middle Ages.

In fact, the Baggins side of Bilbo's personality, the *bourgeois*-ness of a middle-class Edwardian Englishman (*Encyclopaedia* 65, *sub voce* Bilbo Baggins), with his common-sense and level-headedness (Shippey, *Noblesse* 287), is moderating his adventurous, Tookish side, enabling the small hero to perform amazing feats of useful heroism, like survival after a successful dragon-talk. The example of Bilbo Baggins as moderated hero serves to illustrate our theory on colour-coding the ethical choices and therefore categories of people within the story. However, our interpretation of the red colour going bad due to a lack of moderation is not so different (as it may seem) from the one of red going bad through the "dragon sickness". The association between the reddish gold and the red as the colour of the dragon is embodied in Smaug, the "vast golden-red dragon" (H 184), while the gold is as often as not "red" (LotR 982). The greed as a vice, Tolkien's "dragon sickness" is viewed by him as the major channel for the corruption of the good things in the world. The fact that Bilbo does not succumb to Smaug's temptation is another building block of his true heroism, which main virtue is lack of greed, as argued in one of Tolkien's earlier poems, the 1923 *Iumonna Gold Galdre Bewunden*, "the first version of what was to become in 1970 *The Hoard*" (Shippey, *Road* 80). The red-gold-dragon triune concept is illustrated by the author himself, in the drawing *Conversation with Smaug* (see Hammond/Scull 138, image 133). The golden-red dragon curled on his bed of riches radiates an alluring brilliance, while his golden nest is surrounded by the white bones of the fallen dwarves laying in pools of black shadow. The chromatic play of meanings in the image is rich, however, this direction of interpretation leads away from matter of the study.

We assume that the further along this line of interpretation goes, the more fractal the matter and its interpretation becomes. We have to point out, though, that the use of colours in *The Hobbit* is by no means exclusively (or mainly) heraldic. Their meanings and the messages conveyed by their use by Tolkien are general and non-formal and, consequently, above the formal strictures of the heraldic language. However, the few conclusions emerging from a cursory analysis indicate the formation of a visual language-within-language used for conveying moral choices, both within and without the story itself. The colours' visual "tongue" at the moment of *The Hobbit* might be however different from the light-dark imagery employed throughout the story and its moral significance. In this regard, Parker's commentary (Drout 142, *sub voce* Colors) is quite superficial, both in sourcing and in commentary, while the absence of interpretation can be explained by the reference character of the work. However, the direction of our research is not to make a comprehensive study of the colours in Tolkien's visual language, neither to reiterate the whole corpus of discussion on the light-dark, white-black, good-evil theme (two abundantly prolix themes that we tried to skirt as much as was feasibly possible), but to analyse the degree of inclusion of the heraldic paradigm in his literary work, and the usage of the heraldic elements and methods to his creative ends.

To conclude, although a measure of colour symbolism is present in the "insignia" illustrated in *The Hobbit*, and the core of the symbolic paradigm derives somehow from the scholastic system of virtues and vices, the use of coloured banners at this creative stage reveals only a moderate use of heraldic imagery, which corresponds with the employment of low-speech throughout the story and with its somewhat juvenile target audience.

The third group of heraldic descriptions includes the simple arms of Rohan (the silver horse galloping on a green field: *sinople*, a running horse *argent*) as well as the complex iconography associated with the King, and the devices and colours of their antagonists and allies, included in LotR.

In terms of chronology of both story and *legendarium*, the first depicted arms are those of the renewed House of Elendil, as they appear on the blade of Narsil: "The Sword of Elendil was forged anew by Elvish smiths, and on its blade was traced a device of seven stars set between the crescent Moon and the rayed Sun" (LotR 276).

The three motifs (they have not *heraldic charges* since they are not assembled in a coat-of-arms, within a shield) of stars, Crescent Moon and Sun, congregated onto the blade, together with the motif of "reforging" might point to the reunification of the Kingdom, by joining the Seven Stars of Elendil with the Sun of Anarion(?) and the Moon of Isildur(?) (Drout 248, *sub voce* Gondor).

It is important to notice that the usage of representational imagery in this third phase goes beyond the heraldic canon, being more than heraldic devices and charges, as the sun, harp, hammer and mole were shown to be in *The Fall of Gondolin*. This multilayered iconography can be perceived even since the first description of the "device", quoted above.

It is worth mentioning that, unlike the Elven arms described in the pageant of Gondolin armies, the coats-of-arms depicted throughout *The Lord of the Rings* show a quite visible tendency to deviate from the heraldic canon of colours. The description of various devices as white (and not the canonical silver) might reveal a tendency on Tolkien's part to set aside the canons and towards a personal system of representational imagery, only resembling to the medieval coat-of-arms.

The arms of Rohan, Dol Amroth and of the Stewards of Gondor are presented to the reader well in *The Two Towers* and then in *The Return of the King*, first the silver horse on a green field of Rohan on the weapons gifted by Théoden to Gimli: "a small shield he also took. It bore the running horse, white upon green, that was the emblem of the House of Eorl" (LotR 522).

And then, in the beginning of the fifth book, the arms of Imrahil, Lord of Dol Amroth by the sea, with Elven blood in his veins (LotR 872), during another "pageant", of the forces sent by the lieges of Gondor, although the Prince of Dol Amroth is the only one flying a banner: "Imrahil, Prince of Dol Amroth, kinsman of the Lord, with gilded banners bearing his token of the Ship and the Silver Swan" (LotR 771). The colour of the field is depicted later on, upon the sortie made by the Prince and his knights to rescue Faramir and his men during the retreat from Osgiliath: "the swan-knights of Dol Amroth with their Prince and his blue banner at their head" (LotR 820).

The arms of the Stewards of Gondor, by purpose unlike the Royal Arms, I believe, are plain silver, as seen first by Gandalf and Pippin arriving in view of Minas Tirith: "and white banners broke and fluttered from the battlements" (LotR 751). The field of plain *argent* is then depicted in almost heraldic language, verging on high-speech: "and upon the White Tower of the citadel the standard of the Stewards, bright argent like snow in the sun, bearing no charge nor device" (LotR 966).

The unlikeness between the Steward's banner and the Royal Arms is made explicit in the *Annexe A*, as the intention of the first kingless Stewards to have the *regalia* intact and free of usurpation during their caretaking:

> Nonetheless the Stewards never sat on the ancient throne; and they wore no crown, and held no sceptre. They bore a white rod only as the token of their office; and their banner was white without charge; but the royal banner had been sable, upon which was displayed a white tree in blossom beneath seven stars. (LotR A 1053)

The heraldic meaning of the Arms of Rohan is straightforward as the device identifies the ruling house of the Horse-People, their king and their land. The now established identification of the Rohirrim with the "what if" Mercian Anglo-Saxons (Shippey, *Tolkien* 54) and of their horse *argent* on a green field with the pervasive mental imprint of the White Horse of Uffington (also Drout 690, *sub voce* Vale of the White Horse) received sufficiently extensive analysis of both the heraldic and general symbolic meaning arms of the House of Eorl.

The arms of Dol Amroth deserve a bit of scrutiny, as the silver swan-ship is reminiscent of the imagery associated with Eärendil. The House of Dol Amroth supposedly received its share of Elven blood through Galador, the first lord of Dol Amroth, the son of Imrazór from Númenor and Mithrellas (UT note 39), one of the maidens of Nandorin princess Nimrodel. The *Lay of Nimrodel* tells how her lover Amroth lost her and of his hopeless search (LotR 339-340). The device of swan-prowed ship (or swan above ship) could be in fact a reference to a much older time, as Imrazor is said to be related to Elendil (UT note 39) (and consequently a descendant of Elros/Tar Minyatur, Eärendil the Mariner and Tuor of the Swan).

The arms of the antagonists are simple and straightforward and described without much *high-speech*. The All-Seeing Eye of Sauron is borne by the Mordor orcs on their shields, in the chase across Rohan as a red eye on a black field: "long-armed crook-legged Orcs. They had a red eye painted on their shields" (LotR 455).

The master of Minas Morgul, the lord of the Nazgûl, possesses his own coat of arms, although the device of death-faced moon identifies rather with the land, the former Tower of the Moon (Minas Ithil) overtaken by the servants of Sauron and transformed in a den of evil (S 357), than with the former Witch-King of Angmar, whose arms are unknown and whose relation with the Moon is also unknown: "Two liveries Sam noticed, one marked by the Red Eye, the other by a Moon disfigured with a ghastly face of death" (LotR 903).

The Moon of Minas Ithil (in its genuine, untainted form), as well as the White Hand, are figured, in Tolkien's hand, on the project for the dust jacket of *The Two Towers*, with the moon under the white tower and the hand under the black one (see Hammond/Scull, 181, image 180).

Another heraldic image used to individualize one of the antagonists appears during the battle of the Pelennor Fields, on the flag raised by the standard bearer of the chieftain of the Haradrim: "displaying his standard, black serpent upon scarlet, he came against the white horse and the green with great press of men" (LotR 839).

As opposed to the three coats-of-arms described above, the banner of the Chieftain is not on a field of black, but on red (*gules*) and, while the general heraldic rule of never apply colour upon colour or metal upon metal is respected throughout the story, the arms *gules, a serpent sable* of the Chieftain is the single example of "armes fausses" (Fox Davies 87) included by Tolkien in *The Lord of the Rings*. The explanation eludes the reader and it could be obscure even to the scholar. One can assume that the "armes fausses" of the Chieftain derive from the ignorance and disdain professed by the Southrons for the traditions and customs of their neighbours.

On the other hand, apart from a few occurrences of the noun "herald", there is no indication of the existence of formal, regulated heraldry, (rolls of arms, officers of arms etc.) in Middle-earth. We can forward the opinion that the violation of the rule-of-tinctures by the Chieftain's arms is a means to emphasize the chaotic nature of the Haradrim, not only through the colours (see above, the treatment of the use of banners in *The Hobbit*), but also by alluding to the highly formalized visual and verbal language of heraldry. As for the charge, the black serpent, the reference to Glaurung and its ilk aside, the serpent, together with the monkey, the dragon and the toad constitute a group of diabolic charges, used throughout the medieval and Early Renaissance literature for the imaginary coats-of-arms assigned to negative personages, Satan included (Pastoureau, *Figures d'Heraldique* 85).

The device of Saruman, the *de-facto* arms of Isengard displayed by the Uruk-hai is described as seen by Aragorn, investigating the aftermath of the battle of Parth Galen: "Upon their shields they bore a strange device: a small white hand in the centre of a black field" (LotR 415).

The chromatic scheme of the Isengard arms shows a strange similitude with the one later revealed by the Royal Banner, i.e. white on black (*argent* on *sable*, if one uses the canonical language, which might not be the intention of the author). Such apparent similitude, which puzzles the commentator, is linked to the use of black (the "bad" colour of choice) for the field of the royal coat-of-arms. The black standards of the orcish army in the Battle of the Five Armies and the blackness/darkness/swarthiness of the various antagonists throughout LotR should prove the clear choice of black as the colour of badness. Nevertheless, the black field of the Royal Banner is visually stressed in all the occurrences of the royal arms, from its first mention onwards.

The unveiling of the King, furthering Aragorn's challenge is marked by the depiction of the developed Royal coat-of-arms, on the standard sent from

Imladris. First, the royal standard is unfurled at the Summoning at the Stone of Erech, but, since the return of the King is not yet fully proclaimed, the insignia are still invisible, only the black field (*sable*) can be discerned: "And with that he bade Halbarad unfurl the great standard which he had brought; and behold! it was black, and if there was any device upon it, it was hidden in the darkness" (LotR 789).

The "darkness" hiding the royal devices could be the explanation of the black field of the Royal Banner. The black field is fought by the silver of the Tree and Stars and Crown, which were hidden through centuries beneath the darkness and, in the hour of their revealing, the Silver challenges the Sable, as the light of the West fights against the darkness of Mordor, as in the memorable scene at the Crossroad (LotR 702).

The Royal Standard and the return of the king are simultaneously proclaimed in full after the Battle of Pelargir, before the landing of the now royal army at Harlond, as narrated by Gimli: "we came in the third hour of the morning with a fair wind and the Sun unveiled, and we unfurled the great standard in battle" (LotR 877). The description proper of the Royal Standard is delivered as seen by Éomer in the dark hour of the Battle of the Pelennor Fields, by the auctorial voice, in high-speech: "upon the foremost ship a great standard broke, and the wind displayed it as she turned towards the Harlond. There flowered a White Tree, and that was for Gondor; but Seven Stars were about it, and a high crown above it, the signs of Elendil that no lord had borne for years beyond count" (LotR 847).

A variant of the Royal Arms is figured on the dust jacket intended by Tolkien for *The Return of the King*, with the Tree with the Seven Stars, surmounting the Winged Crown, above the royal throne of Gondor and on a dark, shadowy background (Hammond/Scull, 183, image 182).

There is an immediately visible difference between the "device" engraved onto the blade of the royal sword and the Royal Arms, as we shall momentarily understand them, depicted on the great standard borne by Halbarad, who is now officially the royal standard-bearer. The Sun and the Moon have been replaced by the Tree and the Crown. One might think that the Moon of Isildur was replaced by the Tree and the Sun of Anarion by the Crown. Actually such perception is contradicted by the fact that "the high crown above it" cannot be imagined as the "diadem" of the Northern Kingdom. The high crown in the Royal Arms is definitely the crown of Gondor, as described (and sketched) by Tolkien himself in a letter in 1958: "I think the crown of Gondor (the S. Kingdom) was very tall, like that of Egypt, but with wings attached, not set straight back but at an angle. The N. Kingdom had only a diadem (III 323). Cf. the difference between the N. and S. kingdoms of Egypt" (L 281).

The discrepancy is not in fact an evolution or transformation, but the two heraldic compositions are different by substance. The interpretation of the "device" on Narsil's blade could be that the image is a composite heraldic badge of the owner, the (still) Hidden King, made out of the insignia of Elendil, the faithful ruler of the restored kingdom, combined with the two Elven invocations of the Lords of the West, the sun and the moon as descendent images of the two Trees of Light, rather than the canting arms of Anarion and Isildur, respectively. As such, the engraved "device" is both owner's badge in the heraldic sense (Fox-Davies 454) and invocative blessing on a heroic weapon (Drout 703, *sub voce* Weapons, Named).

The Royal Standard combines four heraldic units (the black field and the three silver charges) with their multiple layers of meaning, into one composition both identifying and evocative of the past, the present and the future of the Kingdom. At the simplest level, the silver charges on the black field point to the victory of the light over the darkness and to the whole infinitely extended field of literary and symbolic interpretation of light-dark antagonism in Tolkien's literary creation, an interpretation which is not the scope of the present work. The blazoning of the Royal Arms, as depicted on the standard, could be: *sable*, a tree in blossom *argent* between seven stars, in chief a winged, crowned helmet, all of the same. The image of the standard in *The Return of the King*, quoted above, marks clearly the joining of the arms of Gondor (the silver tree) and the personal arms of Elendil, inherited by Aragorn (the seven stars beneath the tall crown), on a black field. On the other hand, the tree and the stars are mentioned as the royal arms of the Southern Kingdom: "the royal banner had been sable, upon which was displayed a white tree in blossom beneath seven stars" (LotR A 1053).

Taking into account that the "high crown" is also of Gondor, the Royal Arms are not anymore joined, but renewed, as all the charges are referring to the origins of the Kingdom as founded by Elendil the son of Amandil the Faithful (the seven stars) and his son Isildur (the silver tree in blossom), descendants of Elros/Tar-Minyatur the first king (the high crown). As such, the Royal Arms of King Elessar constitute a renewed coat-of-arms, directly connected to his person and his restoration of the kingdom. In this regard, the Royal Arms are consubstantial with the King and the Kingdom, as the man and the land are restored in both status and substance as close to grace as their blessed ancestor was at the beginning of the Second Age.

The fourth group of heraldic imagery includes the concept of Elven heraldic devices and the conceptual heraldry that appears as such alluded in the definitive text of *The Silmarillion*: "Shields also they made displaying the tokens of many houses and kindreds that vied one with another" (S 71).

In the *legendarium*, the role of "herald" and banner-bearer is as old as the creation of the Arda, although Eönwë the Maia, "whose might in arms is surpassed by none in Arda" (S 21) could hardly fulfil the role of King-of-Arms, as there are no coats-of-arms at the beginning of days. There is though a group of creations that are connected mainly to the Noldorim, which exists also as drawings, by Tolkien's hand. That this group is linked to the last decade of Tolkien's life is demonstrated by the "patterns" category of his paintings and drawings, dated by both Carpenter (233) and Hammond/Scull (191-196) in the first years of the 1960s, inheriting, at the same time, the idea of complex Elven heraldry from the early texts like *The Fall of Gondolin*.

Those "devices" are mainly coloured geometric drawings, both abstract and repetitive, drawn by rule and compass: "marvellously intricate patterns on the backs of old newspapers" (Carpenter 233; cf. Hammond/Scull 188, fig. 184). These drawings started as doodles and became the illustration of a personal system of representational-*cum*-genealogical imagery, whose rules and structure are delineated probably after several such devices were created and assigned:

> Women within a circle personal
> Men within a lozenge
> general (impersonal) designs or
> emblems of a family square
> (or [?] once, circular).
> The rank was usually held to be
> shown by number of 'points' which
> reached the outer rim
> four was prince, 6-8 kings
> the great ancestors
> sometimes had as many [as] 16 as in
> House of Finwë. (cf. Hammond/Scull 199, note 17)

Most of the important characters of the *Quenta Silmarillion* were granted such a "device", even several of them, as is the case of Idril (Hammond/Scull 192, images 188-189). A number of "later" creations, which could be dated after the laying out of the "heraldic" rules quoted above, go beyond the simple rule-and-compass drawings, being beautifully and carefully crafted graphics, such are the emblems of Fingolfin (Hammond/Scull 195, image 192) or Eärendil and Gil-galad (Hammond/Scull 193, image 190). A pity that the system was left on the drafting table and not included in his literary works in an extensive and integrate manner. However, its existence indicates an evolution of an attitude on the part of Tolkien towards heraldry, heraldic scholarship and representational imagery and iconography in general. From the use of the heraldic imagery as given, in the early phase, through various manifestations of dissatisfaction with its power of artistic and symbolic expressiveness, his creative effort produced a personal system of "heraldic" signs and rules, the final phase of devising a secondary heraldry, which could be used in illustrating his created lineages, heroes and mythic kingdoms.

To conclude, the research showed us that, in spite of its light use in Tolkien's creation, heraldry underwent the same process of appropriation and transformation into a mythographer's tool and artifice, like all the rest of primary-world cultural items that are woven into the Tolkienian *cosmos*. It is worth pointing out that, in line with Tolkien's creative thoroughness, the heraldic rules and visual canon are treated with the same philologist's care as the vocabulary and grammar rules of his created languages. One cannot refrain to think of what Tolkien's own heraldry could have been if it benefited from a similar intensity of endeavour at a comparable moment in time.

Bibliography

Carpenter, Humphrey. *J.R.R. Tolkien. A Biography*. Boston: Houghton Mifflin, 2000

---. Ed. (with the assistance of Christopher Tolkien). *The Letters of J.R.R. Tolkien*. Boston: Houghton Mifflin, 2000

Drout, Michael D. C. (Ed.). *J.R.R. Tolkien Encyclopaedia. Scholarship and Critical Assessment*. New York: Routledge, 2007

Fox-Davies, Arthur C. *Complete Guide to Heraldry*. Ware: Wordsworth, 1996

Hammond, Wayne G. & Christina Scull. *J.R.R. Tolkien, Artist and Illustrator*. Boston: Houghton Mifflin, 1995

Honegger, Thomas. "Tolkien through the Eyes of a Medievalist". *Reconsidering Tolkien*, Ed. Thomas Honegger. Zurich/Berne: Walking Tree Publishers, 2005, 45-66

Lachaud, Frédérique. *L'Ethique du pouvoir au Moyen Age. L'Office dans la culture politique (Angleterre, vers 1150 – vers 1330)*. Paris: Classiques Garnier, 2010

Van Malderghem, Jan. "Essai critique sur L'Art de Blasonner", introduction to the critical edition of *Le Blason des Armes, suivi de l'armorial de villes etc., par Corneille Gaillard, héraut d'armes de l'Empereur Charles-Quint* (1557). Bruxelles: Ch. & A. Vanderauwera, 1866, I-XX

Pastoureau, Michel. *Figures et couleurs. Etudes sur la symbolique et la sensibilité médiévale*. Paris: Leopard d'Or, 1986

Pastoureau, Michel. *Figures de l'héraldique*. Paris: Gallimard, 1996

Shippey, Tom. "Noblesse Oblige. Images of Class in Tolkien". *Roots and Branches*. Zurich/Jena: Walking Tree Publishers, 2007, 285-301

---. "Tolkien and the West Midlands: The Roots of Romance". *Roots and Branches*, 39-59

---. *The Road to Middle-earth. How J.R.R. Tolkien Created a New Mythology*. London: HarperCollins, 1992

Sinex, Margaret. "'Monsterized Saracens', Tolkien's Haradrim, and Other Medieval 'Fantasy Products'". *Tolkien Studies* VII (2010): 175-196

Tolkien, John Ronald Reuel. *The Lord of the Rings*. 50th Anniversary Edition. London: HarperCollins, 2004

---. *The Hobbit*. London: HarperCollins, 1996

---. *The Silmarillion*. London: HarperCollins, 1999

---. *The Book of Lost Tales*. 2 Vols. New York: Ballantine, 1992

---. *The Unfinished Tales of Númenor and Middle-earth*. Boston: Houghton Mifflin, 2001

The Dying Sun:
Wagner's *Ring* and Tolkien's *Legend*
Renée Vink (Hilversum)

At the end of the Foreword to his father's posthumously published *The Legend of Sigurd & Gudrún*, Christopher Tolkien brings up Richard Wagner's four part opera cycle *Der Ring des Nibelungen*, also known as the *Ring*. The reason behind this is not difficult to guess: the *Ring* and the first and longer of the two Legend poems *The New Lay of the Völsungs* (NLV) have mostly the same subject-matter. Maybe Christopher Tolkien wanted to draw attention to this before anyone could suggest he was trying to ignore it. Especially since Peter Jackson turned *The Lord of the Rings* into a cinematic epic, comparisons between the *Ring* and Tolkien's main work keep popping up, both in the printed media and on the internet. The *Legend* ran the risk of adding fuel to the fairly widespread idea that Tolkien is a Wagner epigone.

Tolkien's son concedes that his father and the German opera composer used the same sources for the NLV and the *Ring* cycle: the lays of the *Poetic Edda* and the *Völsunga saga*. He points out that Wagner's *Ring*, though 'raised indeed on old foundations, must be seen less as a continuation or development of the long-enduring heroic legend than as a new and independent work of art' (LSG 10). He concludes by emphasizing that his father's alliterative poems have little to do with it, as they are different in both spirit and purpose. This may be the case, but does it mean they have nothing in common at all? This paper will review some of the evidence.

That Wagner's libretti as such are a work of art is debatable. However, as it is the plot that is based on the medieval sources, not the music, we can assume Christopher Tolkien is referring to the texts. For the purpose of this paper, this will be sufficient as well.

One can only speculate what lies behind the decision to stress the difference between Tolkien's treatment of the old story and Wagner's. Was it the genuine conviction that the two have nothing in common, or was it rather the wish to steer readers away from undesirable associations? Wagner remains a controversial figure, because of his anti-Semitism and even more because the Nazis recruited his works into their service. Whatever is the case, though, Christopher Tolkien can hardly be naive enough to think such a statement will prevent readers familiar with the *Ring* cycle from making the comparison. After all, the connection between Wagner and Tolkien goes back to the moment people started to notice the similarities between their rings of power. Because of its subject-matter, the *Legend* is hardly going to undermine that notion.

Both the *Legend* and the *Ring* tell what is essentially the tale of the Dragon-slayer, Sigurd or Siegfried, but they embed it in Norse mythology as a whole. In the medieval Icelandic sources, the tale begins with a transgression by the gods. They rob a dwarf of his treasure to pay for a wrong committed against a third party. However, both Wagner and Tolkien use the creation of the world as their starting point. Tolkien follows the account of the *Völuspá* in the *Poetic Edda*, Wagner combines elements from both *Eddas*. He also throws in elements of his own, and most importantly, he adds the creation of the world from a single note of music.

Likewise, unlike the Icelandic poets, both end their stories with *ragnarök*, meaning judgement or fate of the Gods. Wagner used the term *Götterdämmerung*, 'Twilight of the Gods', a translation of 'ragna rök' going back on a misunderstanding caused by Snorri in the *Prose Edda*. Wagner knew this and at some point even considered changing the title of the fourth *Ring* opera (C. Wagner 122). His version of the doom of the Gods differs markedly from the version in his Eddaic sources, of which the *Völuspá* was the most important. This poem describes how Gods and monsters fight each other in a last battle, how the old Gods fall, the Sun turns black and the Earth sinks into the sea. But that is followed by a new beginning in a renewed world, in which the next generation of gods replaces the old ones. *Siegfried's Tod*, as *Götterdämmerung* was called at first, ended with the renewal of Wotan's reign. But Wagner struck out the renewed reign of the gods, possibly influenced by Ludwig Ettmüller, whose *Völuspá* translation was among his sources, and who believed the stanzas describing the reborn world were a late, Christian addition to a heathen poem (Ettmüller 53). In the final version of *Götterdämmerung* the abode of the gods, Walhall, burns with all its denizens. Left are human beings, free to make a fresh start.

One of Tolkien's purposes in writing the two *Legend* poems was to harmonize all the existing, contradicting versions of the tale into a coherent whole. For that reason, he generally follows the medieval Icelandic sources more closely than Wagner does, both in the alliterative NLV and in the rhyming *'Prophecy of the Sybil'* which constitutes Appendix B of the *Legend*. We have the Gods and the monsters — the legions from Hell — as well as the last battle and the renewed Earth in both poems. Yet Tolkien also introduces elements not found in the Eddaic sources, or not explicitly.

The question whether the *Völuspá* is the work of a Christian poet retelling the beliefs of his pagan ancestors, or a Christian work using the pagan images of previous generations, is still under debate today. The Norwegian philologist Bugge suggested that the myths in Old Icelandic literature, especially the *Edda*, derived from Christian and classical concepts. Bugge was the editor of the *Hauksbók*, one of the two surviving *Edda* manuscripts (the other being the *Codex Regius*). The

Völuspá version in this text contains some lines believed to be a foreshadowing of the coming of Christ: 'Then comes the mighty one / to the great judgment / the powerful from above / who rules o'er all' (*Hauksbók, Völuspá*, st. 57). Tolkien probably agreed with Bugge[1], an assumption on my part based on his personal beliefs, on his use of the figure of Sigurd in the *Legend* and on the fact that he translates 'ragnarök' as 'Day of Doom' (LSG 63, 179).

In the first *Legend* poem, Sigurd is the hero who, having tasted death dies no more but 'shall deathless stand' (179) to prevent the Earth from perishing. The poem does not explain how he will achieve this, but only says that his participation in the great battle on the Day of Doom is necessary to save the Earth. The Icelandic source texts know nothing of this; various combatants are mentioned, but Sigurd Fáfnisbane, the serpent slayer, is not among them. They do speak of a glorious figure which dies and returns to reign benevolently over the new Earth, but this is not Sigurd, nor does he take up arms at ragnarök or slay serpents. Tolkien mentions him in the final stanza of the Prophecy poem, which ends with the line: 'all ills be healed in Baldur's reign' (LSG 367).

In Norse mythology Baldr, or Balder, is a god associated with light, love and beauty. In *Gylfaginning*, the first part of the *Prose Edda*, Snorri describes him as follows:

> 'The second son of Óðinn is Baldr, and good things are to be said of him. He is best, and all praise him; he is so fair of feature, and so bright, that light shines from him... He is the wisest of the Æsir, and the fairest-spoken and most gracious... He dwells in the place called Breidablik, which is in heaven; in that place may nothing unclean be'   (*Prose Edda* 36).

Balder is mostly known for the manner of his death. One night, both he and his mother Frigg dreamed he would die. Frigg then decided to demand a vow from everything on earth not to harm her son, but omitted the mistletoe, considering it harmless. When the mischievous Loki found out about the secret from Frigg herself, he made a weapon of mistletoe. While the gods engaged in the game of throwing all sorts of objects at Balder to see if they would hurt him — which they didn't — Loki gave the mistletoe weapon to Balder's blind brother Höðr or Hother, whispering to him that he should throw it. Hother did so, according to some versions guided by Loki, and the mistletoe killed Balder and the gods mourned him deeply. With his death, light and beauty diminished in the world, and the onset of ragnarök drew near.

After his death, Balder had to remain in the underworld until after ragnarök. At that point, he would return, so the *Völuspá* suggests, to rule the new Earth

---

1   Tolkien knew Bugge; see Hostetter/Smith 183, and Agøy 39f.

together with other sons of the old gods and the surviving Hother, with whom he would be reconciled. The last stanza of the Prophecy refers to this reign, but Tolkien only mentions Balder by name.

The Norse god Balder has often been compared to the dying vegetation gods of many mythologies and religions and not surprisingly, also with Jesus Christ. The fact that he was the son of the chief god Odin, and his Christ-like perfection seem to support the idea that the Balder-myth was influenced by the Gospel. That Balder does not rise from the dead and only returns after ragnarök, however, suggests a pre-Christian origin for the myth. As is the case with *Völuspá*, the matter remains under debate, but it seems probable Tolkien considered the story a foreshadowing of the Gospel.

Because Snorri describes Balder as being 'so bright, that light shines from him', it has been claimed that he was a sun-god. The same applies to Sigurd. Among the scholars who viewed him as a sun-god or solar hero was the 19th-century philologist Max Mueller. He called Balder 'the divine prototype of Sigurd' (*Customs* 103), interpreting the stories about the dying god and the slain dragon-slayer both as solar myths. Just like sunset and winter are inevitable, the powers of darkness will in the end overcome these heroes, but they will rise again.

There are indeed some obvious parallels in the stories of Balder and Sigurd, apart from the fact that both the 'best god' and the 'purest of men' become victims of betrayal and are murdered. Tolkien adds something to this: he compares Sigurd to the sun in a way none of his sources do. The NLV contains a number of passages associating Sigurd with light in general and with the sun in particular. This begins with his birth:

> Sigurd golden
> as a sun shining,
> forth came he fair
> in a far country.   (LSG 97)

Brynhild addresses him as 'bright and fair' (122). When he rides to war with the Niflungs, 'flamed all before / the fire of Sigurd' (134). On his wedding day we see 'golden Sigurd / glorious shining' (143). At the wedding of Gunnar and Brynhild, 'in came Sigurd / as sun rising' (153). After Sigurd's death, Brynhild orders the Niflungs to prepare a pyre and

> in flames send forth
> that fairest lord
> now as sun setting
> who as sun did rise!   (LSG 178)

In the first stanza of *Guðrúnarkviða en nýja*, (*New Lay of Gudrún*), the passing of Sigurd is also compared with the setting of the sun. None of this is found in the *Eddas* or the *Völsunga saga*, Tolkien's main sources. This is all the more remarkable as Tolkien usually follows his sources quite closely, often even literally. Was he influenced by Müller's solar myth theory?

Probably not. In his lecture on fairy stories of 1939, he dismisses the theory according to which gods were mere personifications of natural phenomena and the stories about them, the myths or mythical allegories, were originally accounts of elemental changes and processes of nature. He points out that it is the personality of Man that lends significance to these stories about natural objects.[2] The Norse god Thórr, for instance, may have a name meaning Thunder and a hammer called Lightning (Miöllnir), but he has a marked personality:

> Which came first, nature-allegories about personalized thunder in the mountains, splitting rocks and trees; or stories about an irascible, not very clever, red-beard farmer of a strength beyond common measure? ... To a picture of such a man Thórr may be held to have 'dwindled', or from it the god may be held to have been enlarged. But I doubt whether either view is right — not by itself, not if you insist that one of these things must precede the other. It is more reasonable to suppose that the farmer popped up in the very moment when Thunder got a voice and face; that there was a distant growl of thunder in the hills every time a story-teller heard a farmer in a rage. (OFS 42f)

So, it is highly unlikely that Sigurd is a personification of the sun: he has sun-like qualities, but he is a person, not an allegory.

It is more likely that Tolkien intended Sigurd to be a Christ-like figure. He is more than just a warrior picked by Odin to add to the ranks of those fighting in the last battle: Sigurd is 'the World's chosen', the hero who shall rescue the world. In this first part of the poem this hero is not yet identified. It is only when the lines about the World's chosen are repeated later in the story, that it becomes clear that this hero is Sigurd. But those lines

> In the Day of Doom
> he shall deathless stand
> who death tasted
> and dies no more (LSG 179f)

---

2   Wagner would have concurred. In his 1852 treatise *Oper und Drama*, he suggested that in order to find explanations for the various phenomena in the world around them, humans had imagined beings not unlike themselves: the gods. People wanted to recognise themselves in an admired or beloved object of representation. (Wagner, O&D 161f)

have a strong Christian ring to them. Tolkien could not cast Balder in the part of the Chosen. He does not play a role on the Day of Doom, nor does he fit the profile of a great warrior. And having both Balder and Sigurd as light heroes would have been redundant. That Balder was present in Tolkien's thoughts concerning the ruin and renewal of the Earth is attested by the 'Prophecy of the Sybil', though.

As the NLV in Wagnerian fashion covered both the beginning and the end of the world, Tolkien was in need a saviour figure. He consistently calls Sigurd the 'serpent-slayer' in the stanzas about the Day of Doom, and this also suggests his hero is to fulfil the role of the god who slays the World Serpent at ragnarök. In the sources, predominantly the *Völuspá*, it is Thor who slays the serpent and in his turn is killed by it. Tolkien does not actually show his hero taking the place of the god, but his choice of words is suggestive enough.

If Bugge was right in assuming that the account of ragnarök is the Norse version of the Christian Last Battle, the Armageddon (including the victory over the ancient serpent, the devil) why not go all the way, and replace the victorious sons of the fallen gods mentioned in the *Völuspá* by a Christ-like hero of light? This hero could only be Sigurd. He has Odin, the chief god of the Norse pantheon, for an ancestor. Tolkien makes him almost flawless, putting the blame for his death on other things: on Andvari's curse, on women — Grímhild, Brynhild and Gudrún — and on Gunnar's weakness of character. He also points to Odin, who looks to 'ages after' (LSG 71) and for that reason wants his hero in Valhöll. Sigurd foresees his own death but seems resigned to it, instead of actively trying to prevent it. In short, he fits the Christ role, with Odin as God the Father.

The stag symbolism reinforces this. In Gudrún's dream in the *Völsunga saga*, Sigurd is represented by a stag. This is a traditional Christ symbol. If Tolkien intended Sigurd to be a Christ-like figure, this would explain why he retained the stag in the dream Gudrún has in the NLV. And it would explain why he got rid of the golden-feathered hawk which in the saga also plays a role in her dream.

Tolkien was by no means the first to turn the legendary dragonslayer Sigurd into a saviour figure. Wagner had done the same more than eighty years previously, giving him the German version of the name: Siegfried. In 1843 he had begun to read everything he could lay hands on about German history, mythology and medieval literature. One of these books may have been Mone's Introduction to the *Nibelungenlied*. That text suggests that Balder and Siegfried are really the same. It is possible that the composer, basing himself on Mone, consciously linked Siegfried and Balder. Writing the first draft of what later would become *Siegfried*, he inserted a reference to the death of Balder as the event that brought on the end of the Gods. However, he deleted this at a later stage, after he had decided it would be Siegfried's death that would mark the onset of the Gods' downfall (Hauer 61). The moment Siegfried became the dying solar hero of the *Ring*, references to Balder became redundant. Substituting the god with the human hero has been called a bold move on Wagner's part, but if he believed them to be one and the same it seems a logical step.

Before he wrote his *Ring* text, Wagner's foray into Germanic history and myth had already resulted in a rather muddled essay, called *Die Wibelungen*. In that essay he did not only describe Siegfried as a sun god, but also identified him with Jesus Christ. He is a son of God whom his kinsmen call Siegfried, but who is called Christ by the rest of humankind, thus Wagner.[3] He actually went as far as claiming that the Siegfried myth had already existed in the Germanic world before the coming of Christianity, making it easier for the pagans to believe in a god who died and rose again.

The initial version of *Götterdämmerung* bears out this idea: after their immolation Brünnhilde and Siegfried ascend to Walhall to live happily ever after, assuring the Gods that their wrongdoings have been expiated, since Siegfried has taken their fault upon himself. This is blatantly close to Christ expiating the sins of mankind. Furthermore, just like Balder in the *Völuspá*, Siegfried is destined to be Wotan's successor and the next ruler of the world, comparable to Christ reigning after the downfall of Satan.

Wagner repeatedly changed the ending of this last part of the *Ring* cycle and in the process he struck the passage as too optimistic. Yet not all traces of Siegfried-as-Christ have disappeared from the definitive version. Towards the end of act 2 of *Götterdämmerung* Brünnhilde declares that Siegfried's death alone will serve as payment for the treason of all, and in act 3 Siegfried sings *Mich dürstet*, 'I thirst' (G 91), one of the Words of Christ on the Cross.

Was Tolkien influenced by Wagner when he made his Sigurd a Christ-like figure? Not necessarily. Christ is compared to the sun without Northern solar heroes as intermediaries–in the *Bible* itself. In the *Old Testament*, the prophet Malachi refers to the coming Messiah as the Sun of Righteousness (4:2). In the New, Jesus is called the Light of the World in John 8:12 and 9:5, and the Light of the World is the sun. In Matthew 17:2, His face shines like the sun. Christ is a serpent-slayer as well, vanquishing the 'ancient serpent' that first reared its ugly head in Genesis 1. And while Tolkien gives us a Christ-like figure who will be victorious in the end — providing the story with a future eucatastrophe — Wagner removed the victory from the final version of his tetralogy, leaving his audience with a dead sun that will rise no more. Humankind will and must go on, but without gods or shining heroes: it is up to ordinary mortals to shape

---

3   In the essay, Siegfried is also the ancestor of Friedrich Barbarossa, King Arthur's once and future German counterpart, who sleeps under a mountain until the people of Germany will have need of him.

their own future. This is a fundamental difference, and Tolkien remains closer to the Icelandic sources here.

Yet it remains remarkable that both the *Ring* and the NLV are using so many light metaphors for the chief hero. References to the sun, fire, flames, light, radiance, et cetera abound in both works, but they tend to cluster around Sigurd/Siegfried. Examples from the NLV have been given above; here are a few from Wagner's *Ring*:[4] Brünnhilde calls Siegfried *siegendes Licht*, 'victorious light' two times in the awakening scene on the mountain (S 112,113), and also *leuchtender Spross*, 'radiant scion' (S 120). His star shines on her, she says, and at the end of act 2 of *Götterdämmerung* she speaks of Siegfried's flashing eye that gleamed at her (G 73). The Rhine-maidens ask *Frau Sonne*, 'Lady Sun' to send them the hero who will return the Rhine-gold to the waters (G 81). In the end Brünnhilde says that his light illuminates her *wie Sonne lauter*, 'clear like the sun'. Siegfried has already died at that point, but to her, he still radiates.

So, Sigurd's role as a solar hero with overtones of Christ, Tolkien's major addition to the source material, is a surprisingly Wagnerian addition. What he does not do, is connect Sigurd's death with ragnarök, the downfall of the gods. In the medieval texts it was Balder's death that brought it on and Tolkien's approach, though it allows for trimming, combining and harmonizing the different versions of the Dragonslayer story, excludes the conflation of characters from two separate tales. Still, the prophecy about ragnarök, given in NLV *Upphaf*, is repeated affirmatively right after the description of Sigurd's triumphant entry into Valhöll.

Related to this is the stress they put on the hero's eyes. The *Völsunga saga* mentions Sigurd's eyes the moment Brynhild realises she has been betrayed. As she tells him, when she saw the warrior resembling Gunnar enter her hall after having conquered her wall of flames, she was astonished, for she believed she recognized Sigurd's eyes. The idea behind this is that the eyes, the mirrors of the soul, remain the same when the rest of the body changes. However, Brynhild was unable to get a good look at these eyes, for 'her luck abandoned her'. Later on, the saga contains an indirect reference to Sigurd's eyes: when Gutthorm attempts to murder him, he is held back twice by the hero's piercing gaze. The third time Sigurd is asleep, and Gutthorm succeeds in killing him.

The *Prose Edda* does not mention Sigurd's eyes at all, nor do most of the Eddaic lays dealing with the subject. There are two exceptions. The first is the 'Shorter Lay of Sigurd', *Sigurdarkviða in scamma*. Here, Brynhild says that she wanted Sigurd for a husband because his eyes were unlike those of Gunnar and

---

[4] The examples will be limited to the libretti to keep Wagner and Tolkien on an equal footing, but Wagner's original stage directions prescribe a strong light on Siegfried whenever he appears; when he dies, the stage is darkened.

Högni (*Edda* 213). The second, more significant, is the fifth stanza of Fáfnismal, where Fáfnir calls Sigurd a *fráneygi sveinn* (*Edda* 181). *Sveinn* means boy; *fráneygr* is a poetic word meaning 'with flashing or glittering eyes'.

Tolkien and Wagner draw more attention to the hero's eyes than any of their sources do. Wagner takes over the dragon's assessment of Siegfried's eyes, calling him a *helläugiger Knabe*, a bright-eyed boy. In act 2 of *Götterdämmerung*, the betrayed Brünnhilde sings after realising that the Gunnar-lookalike who abducted her was Siegfried in disguise:

> *Ein einz'ger Blick seines blitzenden Auges,*
> *das selbst durch die Lügengestalt*
> *leuchtend strahlte zu mir,*
> *deinen besten Mut machte er bangen.* (G 73)
> (A single look of his flashing eye,
> which even through his false shape
> radiantly shone to me,
> and your highest courage would falter.)

Here, Wagner combines both eye-references from the *Völsunga saga*, the recognition as well as the fearsome gaze, into one, but he adds three words that stress their shining quality. The 'flashing eye' even sounds like a translation of *fráneygr*, although it is hard to say if Wagner was aware of this. He did not use the word in Fafner's speech in *Siegfried*. But he knew that glittering, piercing eyes were a special trait of the Völsungs. In act 1 of *Die Walküre* he attributes it to the Wälsungen twins, Siegmund and Sieglinde: their antagonist Hunding remarks that a 'glistening serpent shines out of [their] eyes' (DW 11), a striking image.

As for Sigurd's eyes, Tolkien's first *Legend* poem contains no less than five references to them. The last of these passages, in which Gotthorm, the assassin, is 'by fear blinded / of awful eyes' (LSG 172), comes straight out of the *Völsunga saga*. Everywhere else, Sigurd's eyes are said to be 'gleaming', almost certainly a reference to Norse *fráneygr*, though none of these passages have a direct equivalent in the saga. The second and third of them occur in Part VIII, 'Brynhild Betrayed':

> What shall I answer
> in hour o'ershadowed,
> Gunnar, Gunnar,
> with gleaming eyes? (LSG 150)

> Gunnar, Gunnar,
> with gleaming eyes
> on day appointed
> I shall drink with thee. (LSG 152)

That points ahead to the moment when Brynhild repeats the phrase to Sigurd, having realized it was not Gunnar who conquered the wall of flames encircling her:

> Gloom was round us.
> Thy gleaming eyes,
> thine eyes gleaming
> anguish gave me. (LSG 161)

Now she knows that the gleaming eyes in reality belonged to Sigurd. The NLV also retains the recognition scene from the *Völsunga saga*, but in contrast with the saga and Wagner's *Ring* the identification is achieved indirectly, through the use of the phrase 'gleaming eyes'. As this phrase was used earlier in the passage about Sigurd's birth, where 'grey steel glitters / in his gleaming eyes' (LSG 97), the attentive reader knows to whom these eyes belong. But though Tolkien repeatedly compares Sigurd to the sun, he does not lay a direct link between the sun and Sigurd's eyes in the NLV.

Here, Wagner is the one sticking somewhat more closely to the source, in this case the *Völsunga saga*, by bringing the hero's eyes into play only after he has been recognized by the woman he has forced to follow him. All he adds is their luminous quality, for which he uses three different words. Tolkien adds three extra references to the eyes in preparation for the recognition scene. Strictly speaking this wasn't necessary: at that moment Brynhild has already discovered the betrayal, while the audience has known about it all along. The extra references do not add any new information. Tolkien is really hammering it home here, so he must have attached a great deal of importance to these gleaming eyes. Is he suggesting that Brynhild could have realized sooner it was Sigurd who abducted her, as she had looked him in the eye when he woke her from her long sleep? It is possible: Tolkien is putting much of the blame for the tragedy on her.

Whether or not this was intentional, the effect is that Sigurd looks all the better for it. He is not flawless: instead of travelling on to Brynhild's hall after re-conquering his father's kingdom, as Odin admonishes him to do, he returns to Gjúki's court — with the well-known, fatal consequences. He goes along with Grímhild's deception, changing shape with Gunnar to help him woo Brynhild. But he does not knowingly betray any of his oaths, neither the ones made to her, nor those he has sworn to Gunnar and Högni.

Brynhild acknowledges as much in the end. Before his death, she calls Sigurd a 'cruel forswearer' twice (LSG 160, 162). But once he has been murdered, she says to Gunnar:

> Oaths swore Sigurd
> all fulfilled them...
> Bonds of brotherhood

> in blood mingled
> with murder kept ye;
> he remembered them.
> A sword lay naked
> set between us,
> Gram lay grimly
> gleaming sheathless. (LSG 175)

In this, Tolkien follows the *Völsunga saga* and the fragmentary *Lay of Sigurd*. Wagner, too, follows those texts. First, Brünnhilde charges Siegfried with perjury, but once she discovers he was duped, her judgement changes in the finale of *Götterdämmerung*:

> *Wie Sonne lauter strahlt mir sein Licht:*
> *der Reinste war er, der mich verriet!*
> *Die Gattin trügend, treu dem Freunde*
> *von der eignen Trauten, einzig ihm teuer,*
> *schied er sich durch sein Schwert.*
> *Echter als er schwur keiner Eide;*
> *treuer als er hielt keiner Verträge,*
> *lautrer als er liebte kein andrer.*
> (Clear like the sun his light shines on me:
> the purest was he, who betrayed me!
> Deceiving his spouse, faithful to his friend,
> from his own true love, alone dear to him,
> he separated himself with his sword.
> More truly than he none ever swore oaths;
> More faithfully than he none ever kept treaties;
> more purely than he none ever loved.) (G 105f)

Here, more than anywhere else in the *Ring*, Siegfried is a hero of light — as he is for Tolkien at the end of the NLV, where we find yet another sun image:

> On his head the Helm
> in his hand lightning,
> afire his spirit,
> in his face splendour. (LSG 180)

Finally, there is the expansion of Odin's role.[5] In the medieval texts this manipulative god disappears after the killing of the dragon. He begets a human

---

[5] Michael Papadopoulos of Leeds Trinity and All Saints College discussed the role of Odin in his paper for the 24th International Studies in Medievalism Conference 2010 in

dynasty, sticks a sword into the great tree in Völsungs hall for his descendant Sigmund to pull out, causes the latter's death and provides Sigurd with a heroic steed. Previously, in a different source text, Odin raised a wall of flames and lightning around a Valkyrie he had put to sleep because she had disobeyed his orders. Tolkien mentions all these scenes, except the one in which Odin provides Sigurd with advice regarding the slaying of Fáfnir. He considered this an intrusion modelled on other stories, diminishing Sigurd's achievement as a dragonslayer (LSG 208).

Once Sigurd has killed the dragon, the god vanishes from the saga, leaving the human characters to their own devices. In the NLV, though, Odin keeps showing up: He sends Sigurd back to Gjúki's court after the hero has defeated the enemies of his kin and he raises a new wall of fire around Brynhild's hall after she has returned home, to prevent the unworthy from approaching her. All this is part of Odin's plan to bring about Sigurd's death, thereby assuring himself of the hero's presence in Walhall at the onslaught of ragnarök.

A god manipulating events is familiar to the audience of Wagner's *Ring*. Wotan does some of the same things Odin does in the source texts and in Tolkien's poem. In *Die Walküre* he begets offspring with a human woman, leaves a sword in a tree trunk and causes Siegmund to be slain. He puts a disobedient Valkyrie to sleep and raises a wall of flames around her. But he also makes a number of appearances not mentioned in the source texts. In act 1 of *Siegfried*, Wotan, now in his role as Wanderer, challenges the dwarf smith Mime to a riddle contest. In act 2 he briefly shows up before Siegfried slays the dragon, but not to give advice, for Siegfried is a free hero who must determine his own actions. In act 3 the Wanderer vainly attempts to prevent Siegfried from approaching the rock with the sleeping Brünnhilde. In *Götterdämmerung*, finally, Wotan prepares the conflagration of Walhall, but this happens off-stage. None of this, though, influences the course of events: after Fafner's death Wotan is incapable of doing so anymore. In this respect Wagner also was more faithful to the sources than Tolkien, at least in a literal sense. The hero has asserted himself by slaying the dragon; the god withdraws.

Shippey suggests that Tolkien deviated from his original because the *Völsunga saga* is a combination of two radically different legends and he decided to present the whole story as part of a divine plan; his Odin echoes God the Father.[6] In the lays of the *Poetic Edda* the world of the gods was strictly separate from that of men. By the time the saga was written, around the middle of the

---

Groningen: Wagner's treatment of Óðinn in *Der Ring des Nibelungen* and his influence on Tolkien's *Sigurd and Gudrun*. An abstract is found here: http://www.medievalism.net/conferences/abstracts.pdf (but when the present paper was written, the full text was not available in print)

6 One of Odin's names in Icelandic poetry is Allfather, which Tolkien translated into Quenya as Ilúvatar.

13th century, this distinction was no longer felt to be of importance. Therefore the author felt free to combine the two worlds, but without entirely smoothing out the seams. Tolkien may have believed that Odin's sudden disappearance was a result of this and wanted to amend things (Shippey 206f).

Wagner wrote at a time when Germanic philology was still more or less in its infancy and had probably no idea about this. He had a different agenda for his expansion of Wotan's role. *Legend*-Odin mostly remains the remote and mysterious divinity he is in the *Völsunga saga*, but Wotan is one of the main characters of the *Ring* cycle — some argue he is *the* main character — and thoroughly 'human'. As Wagner wrote to his friend Röckel, Wotan resembles us in every way (Wapnewski 186). He could not simply vanish halfway the story and in fact he remains present, though he leaves the stage in the last act of *Siegfried*.

The way Wagner and Tolkien handle the scene in the *Völsunga saga* where the god sticks the sword in the tree is a good illustration of the differences between them. In the saga, a man enters the hall where the wedding feast of Siggeir and Signý takes place. No one knows him by appearance. The rim of his hat obscures his face, he is barefoot and clad in breeches of white linen. He appears to be old and grey and has only one eye. In his hand he has a sword which, to everyone's astonishment, he thrusts to the hilt into the bole of the big tree growing inside the hall! 'Whoever pulls this sword out, may keep it as a gift,' he announces, 'and he himself will prove that he has never wielded a better blade.' Having said so, he strides out of the hall.

Tolkien omits the hat, the absence of footwear, the missing eye and the white linen breeches. Instead a 'hoary-bearded', huge man enters the hall wearing a dark cloak, from which he pulls the sword he thrusts into the tree trunk. Tolkien turns this man's words into a challenging invitation to heroic doom, leaves out the claim to the weapon's quality and has the greybeard identify himself by applying one of the many names of Odin to himself: 'Who dares to draw / doom unfearing, / the gift of *Grimnir* / gleaming deadly?' By having him predict openly that the sword will bring doom, Tolkien removes the god's untrustworthiness, which in medieval Norse literature had been one of Odin's characteristics–which would be in keeping with the idea that his Odin is the story's version of God the Father.

Wagner describes the scene through Sieglinde, who replaces Signý in his version. He, too, does not mention that the man is barefoot and wearing white linen breeches, giving him the traditional blue robe of Odin instead. But as in the saga, he is described as a stranger, old and grey, and wearing a hat. This hat obscures 'one of his eyes'. The men in the hall are afraid of the 'ray of light' coming from the other, visible eye (a sun image added by Wagner, as the original held none). But Sieglinde is both teary-eyed and comforted when she sees it. The man swings a sword which he sticks into the tree to the hilt. He does not speak a single word.

Tolkien replaces the stranger's laconic and businesslike announcement, so typical of Icelandic saga literature, by a heroic challenge. He adds a trademark reference to doom and an equally trademark name. Wagner presents a light effect and various emotions. He makes the stranger even more mysterious by not giving him any text. Both lend the scene a characteristic flavour. One goes for the heroic tone of voice, showing his fondness for the concept of doom and, not surprisingly, for names. The other goes for theatrical effect, drawing attention to the symbolism and taking a psychological approach. It is in these details that the differences lie. Still, each in his own way accentuates the role of the chief god beyond what is found in the medieval Icelandic sources.

The conclusion is that Wagner's Siegfried and Tolkien's Sigurd have some elements in common they do not share with their Icelandic template: they are being compared to the sun and they are, each in his own way, Christ-like figures. Add to this the reintroduction of consistent alliteration, Odin's expanded role, the embedding of the tale in Norse mythology as a whole and, to a certain extent, the substitution of the god Balder with a (semi)-human hero; and it becomes clear that the similarities between Wagner's *Ring* and Tolkien's *Legend* are not limited to their elementary subject matter.

That Tolkien, consciously or unconsciously, had Wagner at the back of his mind when he wrote the New Lay of the Völsungs, seems likely. To say his work is 'different in spirit and purpose' from Wagner's begs the question in what way they differed. Establishing this in more detail than I have done here will be easier when it is first acknowledged what both works have in common. To that, I hope to have made my own contribution here.

Bibliography

Agøy, Nils Ivar, *Mytenes mann. J.RR. Tolkien og hans forfatterskap*, Oslo: Tiden Norsk forlag, 2003

The Bible, Authorized version of 1611

Bugge, Sophus, *Studier over de nordiske Gude- og Heltesagns Oprindelse*. Christiania [Oslo]: Alb. Cammermeyer, 1881

Dorson, Richard M. (Ed.) *Peasant Customs and Savage Myths, Selections from the British Folklorists*. Chicago: University of Chicago Press, 1968, 67-199

Edda. Die Lieder des Codex Regius nebst verwandten Denkmälern. Hg. Gustav Neckel. Vierte, umgearbeitete Auflage von Hans Kuhn. Heidelberg: Carl Winter Universitätsverlag, 1962

Ettmüller, Ludwig, *Vaulu-Spá*, Leipzig: Weidmannsche Buchhandlung, 1830

Germanic Mythology. Texts, Translations, Scholarship. *The Manuscript Texts of Völuspá.* II –Hauksbók: www.germanicmythology.com/works/hauksbokvoluspa.html

Hauer, Stanley R. "Wagner and the Völospá." *19th Century Music* XV/1 (1991): 52-63

Haymes, Edward R. *Wagner's Ring in 1848.* New Translations of The Nibelung Myth and Siegfried's Death, Rochester NY: Camden House, 2010

Hostetter, Carl F. & Arden R. Smith. "A Mythology for England". *Proceedings of the J.R.R. Tolkien Centenary Conference.* Eds. Patricia Reynolds & Glenn H. Goodknight, Milton Keynes: Mythopoeic Press, 1995, 281-290

Mone, Franz-Joseph, *Einleitung in das Nibelungenlied: zum Schul- und Selbstgebrauch.* Berlin: Georg Reimer, 1821

The Prose Edda of Snorri Sturluson. Transl. Arthur Gilchrist Brodeur. New York: The American-Scandinavian Foundation, 1916: www.sacred-texts.com/neu/pre/index.htm

The Saga of the Volsungs. The Norse Epic of Sigurd the Dragon Slayer. Transl. with and Introduction, Notes and Glossary by Jesse L. Byock. London: Penguin Books, 1999

Shippey, Tom. Review of LSG. *Tolkien Studies 7* (2010): 291-324

Sturluson, Snorri. *Edda. Gylfaginning og Prosafortellingene av Skáldskaparmál.* Hg. Anne Holtsmark og Jón Helgason. Oslo: Oscar Andersens Boktrykkeri, 1971

Tolkien, John Ronald Reuel. *On Fairy Stories.* Expanded edition, with commentary and notes. Eds. Verlyn Flieger & Douglas A. Anderson. London: HarperCollins, 2008

---. *The Lay of Sigurd and Gudrún.* London: HarperCollins, 2009

Wagner, Cosima. *Tagebücher.* Eine Auswahl von Marion Linhardt & Thomas Steiert. München/Zürich: Piper, 2005

Wagner, Richard. *Oper und Drama.* Stuttgart: Reclam, 1984 (Original edition Leipzig: J.J. Weber, 1852)

---. *Der Ring des Nibelungen. Ein Bühnenfestspiel für drei Tage und einen Vorabend. Das Rheingold (DR), Die Walküre (DW), Siegfried (S), Götterdämmerung (G).* Insel Bücherei 93-96. Leipzig: Insel Verlag, o.J.

---. *Die Wibelungen. Weltgeschichte aus der Sage.* Leipzig: Otto Wiegand, 1850

Wapnewski, Peter. *Der traurige Gott. Richard Wagner in seinen Helden.* München: DTV, 1982

The Middle Ages Tolkien Shunned.
Tolkien and Chivalry

Martin G. E. Sternberg (Bonn)

When thinking of Tolkien and the Middle Ages, we usually turn quickly to his project of creating a mythology which he could dedicate to England, a mythology drawing on many medieval sources which Tolkien used, expanded and clarified in a complex process. Tom Shippey has demonstrated this time and again, and we see it already at work in Tolkien's 1914 poem on Eärendel, who sprang from the Old English poem *Christ* by Cynewulf into the "Ocean's cup" of Tolkien's poem *The Voyage of Eärendel* (Garth 44f).

However, Tolkien's perception of a mythological lack in the English cultural framework and his impulse to fill it with a medievalising myth might have seemed strange to many of his compatriots up to World War I, for a core element of the Middle Ages had a deep influence on British society of Victorian and Edwardian times: chivalry. If we see myth with Mircea Eliade as a corpus of exemplary actions and models of behaviour (Eliade 87f) then such a mythology on medieval patterns had already been in existence for a long time.

Camelot in Tolkien's Time

To see how present chivalry was even at the beginning of the 20th century, let us turn to the year 1912, when Tolkien was already 20 years old. In this year in London, a tournament took place as part of the tercentenary celebrations of "Shakespeare's England". Not only the audience was drawn from the highest echelons of society — Queen Alexandra was present — but also many active participants: Vicountess Curzon gave the Queen of Beauty and Vita Sackville-West one of her attending ladies. The six jousting knights were all peers, the Duke of Marlborough among them, spurred on by the herald with the words: "fight on, brave Knights. Man dies but glory lives; fight on, Death is better than defeat, fight on, Brave Knights, for bright eyes behold your deeds" (Girouard 6f).

Nobody came to harm there, but people did actually die with recourse to chivalry in 1912, too. When the Titanic went down, the men on board applied the rule "women and children first" when it came to manning the lifeboats, and they did so with the express intention to act and die as gentlemen. Punch printed a full-page drawing of a mourning Britannia with the words:

> What courage yielded place to other's need,
> Patient of discipline's supreme decree,
> Well may we guess, who knew that gallant breed
> Schooled in the ancient chivalry of the sea.
>
> (quoted after Girouard 6)

How gentlemen lived and died depended largely upon how knights were thought to have lived and died (Girouard 7). Robert Falcon Scott's failed expedition to the South Pole in 1912, with its many examples of endurance and sacrifice, was seen in terms of knightly behaviour, for the heroes of the polar expeditions were "unequalled in all the deeds of knight errantry" (Girouard 4). Little wonder then that the monument erected for the pupils of Clifton College in Bristol who had fought and died in the Boer war showed a St George strongly resembling a public schoolboy in plate armour (Girouard 171).

However, people took recourse to chivalric models not only when dying. When somewhere in the year 1912 one of the first boy scouts practiced his daily good turn, he thought himself walking in the footsteps of knights: "In peace time, when there was no fighting to be done, the knight would daily ride about looking for a chance of doing a good turn to any wanting help," so Lord Baden-Powell in his *Scouting for Boys*, published in 1912 (Girouard 255).

Medieval chivalry thus was still drawn upon to provide models of behaviour in Tolkien's youth, and the process of adapting it creatively for current needs was far from over, as Baden-Powell shows. Its presence in British culture ranged from LARP-like events to influences on social conduct whose chivalric foundations had been partly forgotten, but could be successfully reactivated, as in the case of the boy scouts. At this point, the chivalric revival could look back on a tradition of roughly 120 years, starting from the building of the first new castles and the publication of collections and translations of medieval romances, ballads and chronicles and the building of new castles around 1800 (Girouard 42ff). Of fundamental importance was the publication in 1822 of Kenelm Digby's *The Broad Stone of Honour*, which defined the virtues of a knight as "belief and trust in God, high honour, independence, truthfulness, loyalty to friends and leaders, hardihood and contempt of luxury, courtesy, modesty, humanity, and respect for women" (Girouard 61f).

The ideal of chivalry had, via the conception of life as fighting, infiltrated other realms of life such as work, Thomas Carlyle coining the term "chivalry of work" (Girouard 131, 161), and had been adapted to its contemporary needs until even doing away with cribs in class could be seen as an example of chivalric conduct, such as was the case in *Tom Brown's Schooldays* (Girouard 168). Chivalric ways of conduct had influenced the introduction of sports and games into public school education and had considerably shaped the ideas of sportsmanship and *playing the game*. Giving such great weight to games in education had been a new idea. Games were thought to be excellent for character-building, and character and an intuitive recognition of what was right and wrong were deemed more desirable than intelligence and learning (Girouard 166-169). Sportsmanship in turn shaped the contemporary attitude to war and fighting. In Sir Henry Newbolt's famous poem *Vitai Lampadai*, a soldier spurs on his comrades in a desperate situation with the same words which his captain once used on the cricket field: "Play up! Play up! And play the game!" (Girouard 233f).

Tolkien on Chivalry

Tolkien was very well aware of the connections between the idea of the gentleman, current English morality, and chivalry. In his introduction to *Sir Gawain and the Green Knight* (written after 1950 and so well after the Great War), he wrote that the character of Sir Gawain allows us to "give serious thought to the movement of the English mind in the 14th century, which he represents, from which much of our sentiment and ideals of conduct have been derived" (SGG 5). In his essay on the poem, he explains the problems of chivalric honour which Gawain faces in the terms of *playing the game* and school education, comparing Gawain's self-reproach for not having handed to Sir Bertilak the belt which the lady had given him to "tearing off the school tie (as someone not worthy to wear it)" (MC 100).

This strong chivalric current still present in the English culture of Tolkien's times, and his awareness of it, pose a problem when dealing with Tolkien and the Middle Ages. We are used to comparing Tolkien's works with texts of the Early Middle Ages, with *Beowulf* and the northern sagas, and we elaborate on how Tolkien adapted concepts such as the northern theory of courage and its idea of heroism. By this, we run the risk of being unaware that this work had been done by others a long time before: by the transformation of the Germanic warrior into the Christian knight in the High Middle Ages and by the 19th century's adaptation of chivalry. In Mark Girouard's description of this *Return to Camelot* we meet many old companions of Tolkien scholarship. The modification of northern heroism through the incorporation of mercy, compassion and self sacrifice was nothing new, as were Tolkien's ideas on dragons and dragon sickness, which can be seen as a warning against capitalist greed (Shippey, *Road* 104): The play *Where the Rainbow Ends* from 1912 has a Dragon King who casts gold dust into the eyes of the English to tempt them away from their true destiny (Girouard 2), and an aversion against money and commerce was a mainstay of the concept of the chivalric gentleman (Girouard 65). We might be forced to side with Andrew Lynch and to admit that what we see as unique to Tolkien is in fact nothing more than trickles of broad streams of medievalising 19th-century culture which have fallen into oblivion (Lynch 78), and Tolkien's achievement (if we rate it as such) would be to have carried them through the catastrophe of World War I and to have made them flourish in a new guise.

There are reasons for caution however. Tolkien's mythopoetic impulse had already become apparent when the chivalric revival was spurred one last time by the start of World War I. His first poems on Eärendel, Kor and Kortirion evolved before 1916 and his entry into active service, and they are free of any chivalric elements. In the face of the still strong presence of chivalry, Tolkien's turning to pre-chivalric Germanic and Northern literature may well express dissent, a dissent from precisely those adaptations of the northern tradition which the Middle Ages and the 19th century had achieved.

Tolkien dealt explicitly with chivalry in two texts: *The Homecoming of Beorhtnoth Beorhthelm's Son* and in his Essay on *Sir Gawain and the Green Knight*. In the *Homecoming*, he calls Beorhtnoth's decision to give the Vikings passage from the islet on which they were trapped, and to engage in a pitched battle which he lost, an "act of misplaced chivalry". Beorhtnoth had risked and lost his life and those of his men to gain glory and the praise of minstrels: "The desire for honour, in life and after death, tends to grow, to become a chief motive, drawing a man beyond bleak heroic necessity to excess to chivalry" (TL 170). So Beorhtnoth did set the wrong priorities, and he was induced to do so by exactly the spirit of playing the game, a spirit so much extolled in the hymn of Tolkien's King Edward School:

> Oftentimes defeat is splendid
> Victory may still be shame
> Luck is good, the prize is pleasant,
> But the glory's in the game   (quoted after Shippey, *Author* 44)

When Shippey calls the use of the words *chivalry* and *knight* anachronistic when Tolkien deals with the Battle of Maldon (Shippey, *Homecoming* 332), this is true only with regard to the times of that battle. Tolkien's own times are the reason for his use of those words, which was deliberate and constant: in several letters, he described the subject of the *Homecoming* as "heroism and chivalry" (L 219, 350).

Tolkien finds a kind of chivalry that follows the right priorities in *Sir Gawain and the Green Knight*. Already in the *Homecoming*, Tolkien points to Sir Gawain as a positive contrasting example, for Sir Gawain accepts the challenge of the Green Knight only to protect King Arthur, and because he thinks of himself as the member of the Round Table who is the most expendable (TL 173f). In his essay on *Sir Gawain*, Tolkien sees Sir Gawain in a conflict of three sets, and planes, of values: Gawain's refusal of Sir Bertilak's wife is a breach of the rules of courtesy and the rules of courtly lovemaking, which require complete obedience to the wishes of the lady, but they are justified by the higher rules of morality, for adultery is sin. Below these two levels is the level of "jesting pastimes", of "playing the game", represented by the compact with Sir Bertilak to exchange what each one has gained during the day at its end (MC 95f). This games-pact is broken by Gawain when he keeps the belt that the lady gave him, and which should protect him from all harm, and he does so in obedience to the lady's wish to keep the gift of the belt secret from her husband. It is for this failure to play the game that Gawain accuses himself of cowardice and possessiveness, in Tolkien's translation:

> Through care for thy blow Cowardice brought me
> To consent to coveting, my true kind to forsake,
> Which is free hand and faithful word that are fitting to knights.
> (MC 98)

When returning to Arthur's court, Gawain proclaims to wear that belt as a sign of shame till the end of his life, which the court – in Tolkien's view justly – quits with laughter (MC 96, 98).

So the *Homecoming* and the *Battle of Maldon* on the one hand and *Sir Gawain and the Green Knight* on the other represent for Tolkien bad and good chivalry, and yet for all their differences, they share one thing as its foundation: excess. Tolkien sees Gawain affected by excess in other matters than a quest for glory. He is characterised by a warmth and generosity as "impulsive excess" (MC 80, 94), and his shame on breaching his games-pact with Sir Bertilak Tolkien calls "the reaction of a man truly 'gentle' but not deeply reflective", whose "words and behaviour are largely a matter of instinct and emotions" (MC 97). Such qualities Tolkien sees as expressions of the poet's description of Gawain's individuality, but they meet with general characteristics of Victorian and Edwardian chivalry. Kenelm Digby had put the "virtues of the heart" over "reason and understanding" (Girouard 61): "he who is possessed of simple faith and of high honour is, beyond all comparison, the more proper object of our affection and reverence" (Girouard 64). Gawain's excessive generosity not with his goods but with his life was mirrored by many in the years before the Great War:

> Mon ame a Dieu
> Mon vie au Roi
> Mon coeur aux Dames
> Et honneur pour moi.

These were the words on a piece of paper which John Manners, a descendant of Lord Manners of the Young England Movement, gave to his mother before going to war, and being killed a few weeks later (Girouard 283). This is excessive generosity indeed where everything is given away and only honour remains, because it is the only thing that *can* remain. It is an inflationary preparedness for sacrifice in which sacrificing oneself for an ideal provides the seal of chivalry, something exemplified in paintings like George Frederic Watts *The Happy Warrior*.

Looking for Knights in Middle-earth

Tolkien's academic papers on chivalry thus show a certain reprehension of chivalry, and they do so in the clear knowledge of its continuing relevance for British, even English, culture. Turning to the relation between Tolkien's narrations, his mythology, and the mythology of chivalry, I want to proceed from the outside in: I want to search for clear and explicit references to chivalry and to see whether they provide clues for a deeper understanding of this relation, rather than for compliance with abstract ideas on chivalry. This approach seems to me justified both from the perspective of mythology in general and the myth of chivalry in the 19th and 20th century because myth works by means of core symbols with a strong appellative effect which point to more complex and abstract meanings, and which effect certain dispositions in the beholder (so far as he belongs to the group for which the symbol is relevant) which shape his actions and emotions (Geertz 55). For the myth of chivalry, these core symbols are, as Mark Girouard demonstrates throughout his *Return to Camelot*, the castle, the knight on horseback *in plate armour* (nearly all the many representations of knights in Girouard's book wear plate armour), courtly love as service to a lady and women in general – and the dragon as the archetypal foe of the order of society that the knight is to protect.

Looking for castles in Middle-earth means to find them largely absent. It is awash with fortifications, but they are either cities with citadels like Gondolin, Minas Tirith, Osgiliath as "Fortress of the Stars" among others, or caves like Menegroth, Nargothrond and the dwarven cities. When they are of a lesser scale, the word castle is nearly always avoided: Maedhros builds his "chief citadel" on the hill Himring (S 118), and there is the "fastness Eithel Sirion" (S 112) whose Sindarin name Barad Sirion (= Tower of the Sirion) points to Tolkien's metonymic practice of naming cities and fortresses as towers. This could be seen as a reflection of the fact that the keep is the core element of the castle on the British Isles, and that castles usually started as a motte and bailey structure, growing into compounds such as the Tower of London. Another effect of the metonym *tower* is to obscure everything else that makes up a castle, and it opens up the architectural timeframe considerably backwards as there are Iron Age towers in Scotland called *brochs*. The image of the castle and medieval fortifications is further avoided by having fortresses made, or rather "happened" out of natural or inexplicably formed rock, like Orthanc and the first ring of Minas Tirith. With the Hornburg, Tolkien has to go to great length not to trigger castle associations, for here we have a proper castle with tower, gate and wall, which is furthermore the residence of a feudal lord, Erkenbrand, "master of Westfold" (LotR II 163f, 167; Hammond/Scull 165). The Hornburg is referred to as *fastness* and *burg* (LotR II 164, 167), and the latter expression was used, according to the OED, in Tolkien's time only as a colloquial expression for a town. The cases in which the word castle is used are few and have either a negative connotation – "castles with an evil look" in *The Hobbit* (H 40) and "the old castle of Durthang" (LotR III 245) in the Mountains of Shadow, or they reflect popular misunderstandings such as Butterbur's image of the king "sitting in his big chair up in his great castle" (LotR III 331). There is one positive exception only: "Prince Imrahil in his castle of Dol Amroth by the sea" (LotR III 20).

Only with the entry of this Prince of Dol Amroth into Minas Tirith do knights enter Tolkien's Middle-earth in word and image. The word *knight* is used for the first time, and these knights come "in full harness" (LotR III 46) in the sense of plate armour, so that Imrahil can notice Éowyn's faint breath on his "bright-burnished vambrace" (LotR III 142): after thousands of years, the evolution of armour in Middle-earth finally meets the requirements of the chivalric imagery of the 19th century. Before Imrahil, there was only mail to be found. After Imrahil's entry Théoden too has knights about him (LotR III 133, 136), who can prove themselves in battle in the same way as Imrahil's. We even find the idea of conferring a knighthood when Éowyn tells Éomer about Merry: "And what about the king's esquire, the Halfling? Éomer, you shall make him a knight of the Riddermark, for he is valiant!" (LotR III 171) This however does not happen: Merry remains "Holdwine of the Mark" (LotR III 315). That being a knight is a double-edged honour shows up when Aragorn calls Pippin a knight: "But the Palantir of Orthanc the King will keep, to see what his servants are doing. For do not forget, Peregrin Took, that you are a knight of Gondor, and I do not release you from your service" (LotR III 315).

Already in *The Silmarillion*, there would have been ample opportunity to call a group of warriors close to the king his knights, but it is not done: we only read of *guard, people of his household* or the *warriors of the king* (S 250, 252). Avoiding the knight and his plate armour is complemented by avoiding to speak of his chief weapon as a horseman: his lance. The word *lance* is used, but only in an elvish context, the lance of Gil-galad (LotR I 249) or the eyes of Galadriel and Celeborn, "keen as lances in the starlight" (LotR I 460). With the Rohirrim, we only ever read of spears despite the fact that they are handled as lances (thrust, not thrown) and the proper term for this weapon is lance, which cannot be lost on someone like Tolkien who served for a time with the cavalry unit King Edward's Horse (Garth 24f).

The nearly complete absence of traces of chivalry in word and image is not compensated by chivalric behaviour, values, or role models. Beregond says about Faramir that "in these days men are slow to believe that a captain can be wise and learned in the rolls of lore and song, as he is, and yet a man of hardihood and swift judgement in the field" (LotR III 40). The full weight of this sentence can only be understood in the light of the preference for character qualities gained of the playing fields over learning and erudition that was part of the idea of the chivalric gentleman. In Digby's words:

> The scholar may instruct the world with his learning, the philosopher may astonish and benefit it by his researches, the man of letters may give polish and a charm to society, but he who is possessed of simple faith and of high honour is, beyond all comparison, the more worthy object of our affection and reverence.
>
> (quoted after Girouard 64)

In protecting the Shire, the Dunedain are protecting the weak, yet their depiction as rangers prevents all associations of chivalry from arising. This is true even of Aragorn. His skills as a fighter are beyond doubt, and he would make a perfect knight errant for all his wanderings, but his most important achievements in the War of the Ring are either those of a ranger — bringing the hobbits to Rivendell — or those of a king — raising the Shadow host as Isildurs heir, and challenging Sauron by means of a palantir that he can use effectively only because of his royal descent. Aragorn's special quality is not his fighting prowess, but his ability to know the land, to live in it, and to gain from it what he needs by knowing it, be it healing herbs or hosts of the dead. Overall, those perform exceptional feats of fighting who are clearly separated from the image of a knight by being hobbits (Frodo and Sam against Shelob) or Gothic-Anglo-Saxon Rohirrim.

The absence of chivalry could have various reasons, be it resentment or just a lack of interest. Clear reference to chivalry could have been avoided either to modify its content or to present its contents to a public that had grown wary (and perhaps weary) of chivalry. From the aspect of creating a mythology, avoiding the knight could be due to chronological reasons because chivalry is so tied up with the historic Middle Ages that its appearance in Middle-earth would be an anachronism. Furthermore, chivalry, as a concept of the High Middle Ages and therefore something Norman (and French), would have clashed with Tolkien Anglo-Saxon predilections. However if this were the case, any reference to chivalry would have had to be avoided. And if the references to chivalry that we find were just due to the fact that knights are the company of great princes, Théoden should have had knights well before the advent of Prince Imrahil, as should the Elven kings of *The Silmarillion*.

Another chivalric concept that has a weak position in Tolkien's narrations is courtly love and service to a lady. It is true that many of Tolkien's characters strive for high women who are very difficult to gain, Beren and Lúthien being the prime example. But these ladies are won in the end, and the aim of the hero's endeavours is never the service to a lady per se, but marriage and procreation, serving dynastic purposes which may even be part of the salvation history of Middle-earth. This fits in well with the Victorian interpretation of courtly love in which women were seen as higher beings to be revered and protected by men, a love whose aim, in contrast to its medieval predecessor, was faithful marriage. The image of the knight kneeling before his lady was appropriate only during courtship but not in marriage, in which the man had the leading role (Girouard 198f). With Tolkien, the greatest contrast to the idea of a knight performing deeds in honour of his lady is the fact that the ladies in question play a part of their own in fulfilling the task: Lúthien helps Beren to win the Silmaril, and in fact carries the greater share, and Elwing brings the Silmaril to Eärendil. Aragorn and Arwen come nearest to the Victorian model of courtly love, but apart from pure love, Aragorn follows his destiny as Isildur's heir and

Beren's remote descendant. Moreover, this love is tucked away mostly into the *Appendices*, as if not to distract from Aragorn's struggle to regain his kingdom (Flieger 132f).

There is only one example of pure courtly love: Gimli's reverence for Galadriel. It shows itself in such typical ways as being prepared to fight with Éomer on the question of her beauty, and she is indeed a high lady Gimli can never hope to win. For good reason, Marco Prost at the seminar called Gimli "the courteous dwarf", but Gimli scarcely resembles a knight, and it is telling that the most exact rendering of knightly and courtly love takes place between non-humans.

The circumstances in which the few references to chivalry are allowed to appear point to a competing relation between the British myth of chivalry and Tolkien's elf-centred mythology which is also a competition between the chivalric mythology of the deed and the Tolkienian mythology of place. The appearance of castles and knights with the Prince of Dol Amroth and the appearance of courtly love with Gimli and Galadriel are both set within an elvish context: Legolas's recognition of the Prince's Elven ancestry is shared by the author's voice, and Gimli's reverence is directed at an Elven lady of royal descent. All this is bound together in a manner both very low-key and very consistent with what could be called the Amroth complex. It begins when the fellowship reaches the Nimrodel, and it ends when Legolas sets sail into the West with Gimli who follows Galadriel in the same way that Amroth left his kingdom for Nimrodel. This Amroth complex deals, on many levels and with great intricacy, with just one question: the question *where,* the question of the right place.

This question is dominant at its very beginning: Where do the Galadrim live now, where has Nimrodel gone, and where did Amroth follow her? Gimli in the end will follow Amroth's example when, despite being a dwarf and by nature unwilling lo leave Middle-earth, he will accompany Legolas to Valinor because of this friendship with an elf and to see Galadriel again. Both his friendship with Legolas and his love of Galadriel however have their root in the love of places: in Galadriel's sympathy with Gimli's wish to visit Moria, which the elves would likewise feel for Lórien even it had become an abode of dragons, and in her naming the places of Gimli's desire in his own ancient tongue. It is fitting that Gimli and Legolas make a pact to visit the place that the other one holds dear, the Glittering Caves and Fangorn. Prince Imrahil is connected to the theme of 'staying in place' by his part of Elven blood, which is due to the fact that one elf at least beside Lúthien and later Arwen did not pass into the west, and by his residence of Dol Amroth, which is Cerin Amroth by a slightly different name (Amroth's hill and Amroth's mound). These places share a similar structure too, for Cerin Amroth, with its great central tree amid two circles of trees, echoes a castle with keep and encircling walls. It is fitting that it is Gimli and Legolas who meet the prince when his Elven descent is established.

Both of them resemble knights-errant so far as they do not return home, and thus it could seem that not winning but losing the proper place is their theme. But through their wanderings, they become the founders or restorers of places, the Glittering Caves and a restored Ithilien. The tension between wandering and "knight-errantry" and the desire to settle in one's proper place is solved in favour of the latter, for Legolas' voyage to Valinor is in fact a journey home to the dwelling place ultimately intended for the elves.

Farmer Giles' Goodbye to Chivalry

The clash between the mythology of the knight and Tolkien's mythology comes to the fore in *Farmer Giles of Ham*. Patrick Brückner has shown that this story contains a conflict between chivalric and heroic violence. Chivalric violence is exercised by the knights of the king and is integrated into a high-medieval courtly order for which the knights gain their victories (Brückner 88f). In contrast, *Farmer Giles* represents heroic violence, which stands on its own, and which breaks the courtly structure of society and rule. The heroic hero partly assimilates the foe he has overcome. He gains his strength and qualities, which makes his reintegration into society difficult if not impossible. In Giles' case, this assimilation takes place through gaining a part of the dragon's treasure, and through gaining the dragon's allegiance by which Giles can fight off the king and his knights in the battle at the bridge (Brückner 94f). In *Farmer Giles*, the hero defeats the knight with the help of the dragon, the knight's archetypal enemy.

It is strange that among Tolkien's works, *Farmer Giles* is the one that best achieves Tolkien's aim of creating a mythology for England by means of philology, for this story is presented as an explanation for the place names *Thame* and *Worminghall* (FGH 65f). *Farmer Giles* tells the origin myth of the Little Kingdom as a story of sedition and secession, and it is a myth indeed because the existence of the Little Kingdom ultimately depends on the incursion of the supernatural into the human sphere: without dragon and dragon hoard no King Giles, who stresses time and again that he is no knight and that chivalric codes of behaviour do not apply to him (FGH 95, 113). Giles refusal to being called a knight has another point: "I am a farmer, and proud of it" (FGH 95). A free farmer and a king have one thing in common: they define themselves by tilling or ruling a certain piece of land, whereas a knight defines himself by service to other people, lord or lady. This makes him so dependent on his renown among people, and prone to an excessive quest for glory.

The triumph of hero and dragon over the knights of the realm is a triumph over chivalry, which takes place through an alliance with evil — unique in Tolkien's work. This makes it a rather subversive text, the impact of which has to be diminished by being written as a satire. Nonetheless, it is through this satiric exaggeration that *Farmer Giles* brings to the fore Tolkien's conflict with and dislike of the myth of chivalry that became apparent in his essay on *Sir Gawain* and in the *Homecoming*, and through the absence of chivalry in *The Silmarillion* and *The Lord of the Rings*. Chivalry, which was the medieval tradition most prominent and most alive in Tolkien's lifetime, is exactly the part of the Middle Ages that Tolkien shunned. It is where Tolkien must be read not in harmony with medieval or medievalising source material, but in contrast with it. And in the same way as in *Farmer Giles*, the stand against chivalry serves to gain and secure a sense of place through a mythology centred on places.

A strong argument against all this could be that serving the land was at the core of the myth of chivalry in Britain, but on a closer look, this chivalric service is again stained by the chivalric vice of excess:

> If I should die, think only this of me:
> That there's some corner of a foreign field
> That is forever England. There shall be
> In that rich earth a richer dust concealed;
> A dust whom England bore, shaped, made aware,
> Gave, once, her flowers to love, her ways to roam,
> A body of England's, breathing English air,
> Washed by the rivers, blest by suns of home.
>
> (Brooke 302)

Rupert Brooke's famous lines again focus on self-sacrifice, (imperialist) expansionism and the uprooting effect of knight-errantry. This kind of love of England is that of service to a high lady, for which the knight performs great deeds in foreign lands–and loses himself. At the core of Tolkien's mythology however lies, as John Garth has stressed, from the beginning "the spirit of place" (Garth 110), and a strong "sense of place" for Middle-earth is a widespread reaction among Tolkien's readers (Curry 60) and a fundamental influence on writers of fantasy (Martin 3). Already for this reason alone, the knight-errant is no suitable mythological model.

The sense of place also sheds light on Tolkien's contrasting of heroic necessity with chivalric excess through the lens of philology: both necessity and excess have in them the Latin verb *cedere*, to go. So heroic necessity means to *ne cedere*: not to leave one's place, and to defend it; while chivalric excess refers to *ex-cedere*: to leave one's place to seek renown in foreign lands as a knight-errant.

And to be rooted in one place and to live by its spirit requires one thing above all: staying alive. Those who criticise Tolkien for being too soft to his characters when it comes to loss of life (see Shippey, *Road* 363) have to consider the alternative: the inflationary preparedness for sacrifice and loss which was a hallmark of Victorian and Edwardian chivalry. Given the centrality of the spirit of place in his works, it may even be said that Tolkien let Frodo die in the adequate manner: not by losing his bodily life, but by losing "the spirit of place" that bound him to the Shire which he is no longer able to enjoy after his return.

For all his great indebtedness to medieval and medievalising sources and traditions, Tolkien did without, and even rejected, that medieval tradition which was most alive during his lifetime, and of whose continuing influence he was well aware. Tolkien's attitude to chivalry gives weight to the question of which medieval material Tolkien did *not* take up into his mythology, and why. We cannot take a positive attitude to the Middle Ages for granted. Chivalry, far more than heroes of northern literature, provided the dominant model for heroic behaviour before and in World War I. Unlike the war poet Robert Graves, Tolkien did not say *Goodbye to all that*, but *Goodbye to quite a lot of it* when he refused to let chivalry enter Middle-earth on a significant scale.

Bibliography

Brooke, Rupert. *The Collected Poems*. 3rd edition. London: Sidgwick & Jackson, 1942

Brückner, Patrick. »Von kühner Recken Streiten. Höfische Akteure und heroische Gewalt in Tolkiens *Farmer Giles of Ham*«. *Hither Shore* 6 (2009): 86-100

Curry, Patrick. *Defending Middle-earth*. London: HarperCollins, 1997

Eliade, Mircea. *Das Heilige und das Profane. Vom Wesen des Religiösen*. Frankfurt am Main: Insel Verlag, 1984

Flieger, Verlyn. "Frodo and Aragorn: The Concept of the Hero." *Understanding The Lord of the Rings. The Best of Tolkien Criticism*. Eds. Neil D. Isaacs & Rose A. Zimbardo. Boston/New York: Houghton Mifflin Company, 2004, 122-145

Garth, John. *Tolkien and the Great War*. London: HarperCollins, 2003

Geertz, Clifford. *Dichte Beschreibung*. Frankfurt am Main: Suhrkamp 1987

Girouard, Mark. *The Return to Camelot. Chivalry and the English Gentleman*. New Haven/London: Yale University Press, 1981

Hammond, Wayne, & Christina Scull. *J.R.R. Tolkien, Artist & Illustrator*. London: HarperCollins 2004

Lynch, Andrew. "Archaism, Nostalgia, and Tennysonian War in *The Lord of the Rings*". *Tolkien's Modern Middle Ages*. Eds. Jane Chance & Alfred K. Siewers. New York: Palgrave Macmillan, 2009, 77-92

Martin, George R.R. "Introduction". *Meditations on Middle-earth*. Ed. Karen Haber. New York: St. Martin's Press, 2001, 1-5

Shippey, Tom. *The Road to Middle-earth*. Revised and expanded edition. London: HarperCollins, 2005

---. "Tolkien and 'The Homecoming of Beorhtnoth'". *Roots and Branches. Selected papers by Tom Shippey.* Zurich/Jena: Walking Tree Publishers, 2007. 323-339

Tolkien, John Ronald Reuel. *Sir Gawain & the Green Knight, Pearl, and Sir Orfeo.* London: Unwin Hyman Limited, 1988

---. *The Hobbit.* London: Unwin Paperbacks, 1984

---. *The Letters of J.R.R. Tolkien.* Ed. Humphrey Carpenter. London: George Allen & Unwin, 1981

---. *Smith of Wootton Major & Farmer Giles of Ham.* New York: Ballantyne Books Inc., 1970

---. *The Lord of the Rings.* 4th ed. London: Unwin Hyman, 1988

---. *The Monsters and the Critics and Other Essays. Ed.* Christopher Tolkien. London: HarperCollins, 1997

---. *The Silmarillion.* Ed. Christopher Tolkien. Boston/New York: Houghton Mifflin, 2004

---. *Tree and Leaf, Smith of Wootton Major, The Homecoming of Beorhtnoth Beorhthelm's Son.* London: Unwin Paperbacks 1982

Romantische Sehnsucht im Werk J.R.R. Tolkiens

Julian Tim Morton Eilmann (Aachen)

Der Bezug zwischen Tolkien und der Romantik war das Thema des Tolkien Seminars 2010. Es wurde damals viel darüber gestritten, ob bzw. inwiefern sich Romantikbezüge in Tolkiens Werk finden lassen und Tolkien somit möglicherweise sogar in Tradition der Romantik zu sehen ist. Mit meinem Seminarvortrag zur romantischen Nostalgie in Tolkiens Schriften und einem anderen Beitrag zur Romantik (Eilmann, *Sleeps*) befand ich mich auf der Seite der Romantikbefürworter, war es doch mein Anliegen nachzuweisen, dass Tolkiens vielschichtiger Umgang mit dem Topos des Heimwehs große Ähnlichkeiten zu zentralen Positionen der deutschen Romantik aufweist. Aus Zeitgründen war es mir damals nicht möglich, zwei Nebenaspekte meiner Romantikforschungen näher vorzustellen.

Das soll hier nachgeholt werden, um die Grundlagen für ein vertieftes Verständnis der geistesgeschichtlichen Verbindungen zwischen Tolkien und der romantischen Weltanschauung zu legen. Dementsprechend werden vor dem Hintergrund der romantischen Nostalgie und Sehnsucht zwei Aspekte des Romantischen in Tolkiens Werk thematisiert: Einerseits soll der Blick auf Eriol im *Buch der Verschollenen Geschichten* gelenkt werden, einen Charakter, den wir, wie deutlich werden wird, aufgrund seiner Erlebnisse auf der Elbeninsel Tol Eressea als einen Romantiker im Feenland verstehen können. Andererseits wird aufgezeigt, wie die existentielle Nostalgie des Subjekts in Tolkiens Werk (vgl. Eilmann, *Nostalgie* 106ff) entscheidend mit der Meeressehnsucht verbunden ist und das Meer somit ein zentrales Sehnsuchtssymbol in Tolkiens Werk darstellt.

Eriol oder der Romantiker im Feenland

Die Überschrift dieses Kapitels muss auf den ersten Blick irritieren: Beim Seefahrer Eriol aus Tolkiens Mythologie soll es sich um einen Romantiker handeln? Noch dazu um einen Romantiker im Feenland? Wodurch ist eine solche Bezeichnung gerechtfertigt? Eine Antwort darauf wird ersichtlich, wenn wir uns die Bedeutung der romantischen Sehnsucht in der Geschichte Eriols vergegenwärtigen. Werfen wir zunächst einen Blick in das *Buch der Verschollenen Geschichten*, das uns von Eriols Schicksal berichtet. So wie die Geschichte dort erzählt wird, handelt es sich bei Eriol um einen jener glücklichen Sterblichen, der aus Mittelerde auf die Elbeninsel Tol Eressea gelangt, wo er eine zeitlang bei den Elben wohnt und von ihnen in die historische und mythologische

Überlieferung ihres Volkes eingeweiht wird. Für Eriol wird es eine wundersame poetische Erfahrung im Reich der »fairies« (LT I 19) werden.

Im Hinblick auf den Topos der romantischen Nostalgie und Sehnsucht findet sich im Text der *Verschollenen Geschichten* eine höchst bedeutsame Szene: eine ausführliche Beschreibung von Eriols Erlebnis, als er sich an seinem ersten Abend in der elbischen Zuflucht zum Schlafen niederlegen möchte, zuvor jedoch noch ans Fenster herantritt und den nächtlichen Garten betrachtet. Die Art und Weise, wie Tolkien den Ausblick und die Wirkung des malerischen Landschaftsbildes auf Eriol beschreibt, könnte in dieser Form direkt aus einem romantischen Roman stammen:

> Ere he laid him down however Eriol opened the window and scent of flowers gusted in therethrough, and a glimpse he caught of a shadow-filled garden that was full of trees, but its spaces were barred with silver lights and black shadows by reason of the moon; yet his window seems very high above those lawns below, and a nightingale sang suddenly in a tree nearby. Then slept Eriol, and through his dreams there came a music thinner and more pure than any he heard before, and it was full of longing. Indeed it was as if pipes of silver or flute of shapes most slender-delicate uttered crystal notes and threadlike harmonies beneath the moon upon the lawns; and Eriol longed in his sleep for he knew not what.
>
> (LT I 46)

Die Situation des an einem nächtlichen Fenster lauschenden Individuums, das den Blick über eine nächtliche verwunschene Landschaft schweifen lässt, ist ein zentrales Motiv, das in epischen und lyrischen Texten der deutschen Romantik immer wieder verwendet wird. Auch in der romantischen Malerei begegnet man häufig einer Fensterfigur, die den Blick auf eine weite Landschaft oder einen verwunschenen Garten richtet.[1] Joseph von Eichendorffs bekanntes Gedicht *Sehnsucht* bietet sich hier zum Vergleich an, da er darin ein lyrisches Ich zu Wort kommen lässt, das ähnlich wie Eriol in einer »prächtigen Sommernacht« (Eichendorff 35) am Fenster lauscht, die nächtliche Landschaft auf sich wirken lässt und dessen Herz von den bezaubernden Eindrücken derart tief bewegt wird, dass die für die Romantik so entscheidende Sehnsucht entflammt:

---

[1] Der bekannteste Maler der deutschen Romantik, Caspar David Friedrich, inszeniert in seinen Gemälden immer wieder imposante Szenen mit Rückenfiguren, die in eine verwunschene oder erhabene Landschaft blicken. Ziel eines solchen Bildaufbaus ist es, dass sich der Bildbetrachter mit den Bildfiguren identifiziert und seinen Blick in ähnlich sehnsuchtsvoller Weise in die Ferne schweifen lässt. Bekannte Beispiele für dieses Prinzip des Bildaufbaus sind Friedrichs *Der Wanderer über dem Nebelmeer* (1818) und *Mann und Frau in Betrachtung des Mondes* (um 1824).

Es schienen so golden die Sterne,
Am Fenster ich einsam stand
Und hörte aus weiter Ferne
Ein Posthorn im stillen Land.
Das Herz mir im Leib entbrennte,
Da hab ich mir heimlich gedacht:
Ach, wer da mitreisen könnte
In der prächtigen Sommernacht!

Zwei junge Gesellen gingen
Vorüber am Bergeshang,
Ich hörte im Wandern sie singen
Die stille Gegend entlang:
Von schwindelnden Felsenschlüften,
Wo die Wälder rauschen so sacht,
Von Quellen, die von den Klüften
Sich stürzen in die Waldesnacht.

Sie sangen von Marmorbildern,
Von Gärten, die überm Gestein
In dämmernden Lauben verwildern,
Palästen im Mondenschein,
Wo die Mädchen am Fenster lauschen,
Wann der Lauten Klang erwacht
Und die Brunnen verschlafen rauschen
In der prächtigen Sommernacht. (ebd.)

Bemerkenswert an Eichendorffs Gedicht ist, dass er das Fenstermotiv gleich auf zwei verschiedenen narrativen Ebenen verwendet: Einerseits das lyrische Ich und andererseits die Mädchen, von denen die »junge[n] Gesellen« (ebd.) singen, lauschen am Fenster in die Nacht hinein. Dabei erinnert insbesondere Eichendorffs märchenhaftes Gartenbild in der dritten Strophe an Tolkiens Schilderung des verzauberten Elbengartens in den *Verschollenen Geschichten* (s.o.). Die Fenstersituation eines romantischen Individuums bringt dabei zentrale Wirkungsintentionen der Romantik zum Ausdruck: Die Begegnung von Drinnen und Draußen, von einsamem Träumer und weiter Landschaft, von Beschränkung (Zimmer) und Entgrenzung (Natur) ist eine Zusammenführung von Gegensätzen und soll jene Romantisierung bzw. Verzauberung der alltäglichen Wirklichkeit herbeiführen, die im Zentrum der romantischen Dichtung steht.[2]

---

2 »Die Welt muß romantisirt werden. So findet man den urspr[ünglichen] Sinn wieder... Indem ich dem Gemeinen einen hohen Sinn, dem Gewöhnlichen ein geheimnißvolles Ansehn, dem Bekannten die Würde des Unbekannten, dem Endlichen einen unendlichen Schein gebe, so romantisire ich es« (Novalis II 545). Vgl. Eilmann, *Sleeps* 178-182.

Der Platz am nächtlichen Fenster wird auf diese Weise ein Ort des Fernwehs und der transzendenten Sehnsucht.

Erweckt bereits Tolkiens Naturschilderung eines im Mondenschein friedlich vor sich hin träumenden Gartens den Eindruck, als stamme ein solch märchenhaftes Landschaftsbild direkt aus einem Gedicht Eichendorffs oder Brentanos, so ist insbesondere die singende Nachtigall, die Tolkien hier — wie es scheint — beiläufig erwähnt (»and a nightingale sang suddenly in a tree nearby« LT I 46), ein schon fast stereotypisches Motiv aus Erzählungen und Gedichten der deutschen Romantik. Man denke beispielsweise nur an Eichendorffs Gedicht *Nachtzauber*, in dem er wie auch in zahlreichen anderen Gedichten eine schwärmerische Nachtstimmung schildert, die Eriols Blick in den elbischen Garten stark ähnelt. Dass im Falle von Eichendorffs Gedicht die Nachtigall eine prominente Rolle spielt und der Liebessehnsucht des lyrischen Ichs Ausdruck verleiht, ist im Kontext der Romantik schon fast zu erwarten:

> Hörst du nicht die Quellen gehen
> Zwischen Stein und Blumen weit
> Nach den stillen Waldesseen,
> Wo die Marmorbilder stehen
> In der schönen Einsamkeit?
> Von den Bergen sacht hernieder,
> Weckend die uralten Lieder,
> Steigt die wunderbare Nacht,
> Und die Gründe glänzen wieder,
> Wie du's oft im Traum gedacht
>
> Kennst die Blume du, entsprossen
> In dem mondbeglänzten Grund?
> Aus der Knospe, halb erschlossen,
> Weiße Arme, roter Mund,
> Und die Nachtigallen schlagen,
> Und rings hebt es an zu klagen,
> Ach, vor Liebe todeswund,
> Von versunknen schönen Tagen —
> Komm, o komm zum stillen Grund! (Eichendorff 228)

Der Ruf der Nachtigall ist in der Romantik ein Ruf, der die Sehnsucht weckt, ein Ruf, der den lauschenden Träumer wachrüttelt und das Herz öffnet für die Poesie, die nach romantischer Vorstellung in allen Dingen schlummert (vgl. Eilmann, *Sleeps* 167f). Wichtig für unser Verständnis von Eriols Sehnsuchtserlebnis im Kontext der Romantik ist, dass Eriol das Ziel seiner Sehnsucht nicht genau bestimmen kann (»and Eriol longed in his sleep for he knew not what« LT I 46). Die romantische Sehnsucht ist grundsätzlich unbestimmt, rührt sie

doch an etwas im Herzen, das letztlich auf eine existentielle Disposition des Subjekts und eine jenseitige Heimat verweist (vgl. Eilmann, *Nostalgie* 106f).
Betrachtet man Eriols Sehnsuchtserlebnis vor dem Hintergrund von Tolkiens Gedicht *Kortirion among the trees* (vgl. ebd. 104f), dann wird ersichtlich, dass Tolkien in seiner Schilderung von Eriols Erfahrung ähnliche Formulierungen verwendet, um das Gefühl eines latenten Verlusts und einer verzehrenden Sehnsucht zu beschreiben: So heißt es in den *Verschollenen Geschichten*, Eriol vernehme im Schlaf den Klang silberner Pfeifen und Flöten sowie Kristallklänge mit Harmonien voller Sehnsucht (vgl. LT I 46). Solche Metaphern lassen sich nicht nur im Romantikkontext verorten (s.o.), sondern sind auch in *Kortirion among the trees* in ähnlichen Formulierungen zu finden (vgl. ebd. 33-36). Können wir aber darüber hinaus die Sehnsucht, die Eriol im Schlaf empfindet, genauer erfassen?

Da es sich bei Eriol um einen im Elbenland gestrandeten Menschen handelt und wir in den *Verschollenen Geschichten* erfahren, dass Eriol die Sehnsucht nach dem Feenland von seinen Vorfahren geerbt hat, wäre es nahe liegend, dass sich die Sehnsucht, die Eriol empfindet, auch auf die Elben und die mit ihnen assoziierte Poesie und Schönheit richtet. Ein solches Sehnen nach der Poesie des Feenlands ist es ja gerade, das Eriols Vorfahren gequält hat. So soll einer von Eriols Vorvätern den Weg ins Elbenland gefunden und dort als Kind eine poetische Schönheit kennengelernt haben, die ihn in ihren Bann geschlagen hat:

> Then Eriol said: 'I remember me of certain words that my father spake in my early boyhood. It had long, said he, been a tradition in our kindred that one of our father's fathers would speak of a fair house and magic gardens, of a wondrous town, and of a music full of all beauty and longing — and these things he said he had seen and heard as a child, though how and where was not told.'
> (ebd. 20)

Wir erfahren also, dass Eriols Vorfahr, ebenfalls ein Seefahrer, die Begegnung mit solch feenhafter Schönheit zeitlebens nicht vergessen konnte und dass ihn diese Erfahrung bis an sein Lebensende mit einer unstillbaren rastlosen Sehnsucht erfüllte: »Now all his life was he restless as if a longing half-expressed for unknown things dwelt within him« (ebd.). Die Sehnsucht richtet sich demnach darauf, die einmal gemachte Erfahrung zu erneuern, wieder nach Tol Eressea zu gelangen und dort für immer zu bleiben.

Da das Sehnen von Eriols Vorfahr auf eine endgültige Rückkehr ins Feenland abzielte, können wir in diesem Zusammenhang berechtigterweise für den Begriff der Sehnsucht auch den Begriff des Heimwehs verwenden. Es ist die nostalgische Sehnsucht eines Sterblichen, der nach seiner Rückkehr aus dem Feenland die Welt der Menschen als prosaisch, ja sogar als Exil empfinden muss, als einen Ort, an dem er nicht mehr heimisch ist. Dass solche Individuen, die unfreiwillig aus dem Elbenland den Weg zurück in die Menschenwelt finden, zu den großen Dichtern ihres Volkes werden (ebd. 19), ist vor dem Hintergrund der Romantiktradition naheliegend. Die Betätigung als Dichter stellt für diejenigen, die einmal die elbische Poesie erfahren durften, die einzige Möglichkeit dar, die Erfahrung von Magie, Schönheit und Poesie mit den Fähigkeiten eines Sterblichen erneut in Poesie auszurücken. Im Falle von Eriols Ahnherrn ist es demnach nachvollziehbar, dass dieser nach seiner Rückkehr in die Menschenwelt eine nostalgische Sehnsucht nach Tol Eressea empfindet. Warum aber sollte Eriol selbst, nachdem er das Elbenland betreten hat und sich somit gewissermaßen im Zentrum der Poesie befindet, eine solche Sehnsucht empfinden?

Was es mit dieser nächtlichen Sehnsucht auf sich hat, die er nach seinem Blick in den nächtlichen Garten empfand, versucht auch Eriol zu ergründen. In Gesprächen mit den Elben Kortirions wird ihm eine Erklärung angeboten: Die Sehnsuchtsmusik, in der ein wundersamer Zauber lebendig sei (»a marvel of wizardry liveth in that fluting« ebd. 94), werde von einem Wesen namens Timpinen, in der deutschen Fassung Zwitschervogel, angestimmt. Dieses Wesen, halb Naturgeist halb Elb, ist ein wahrer Sehnsuchtswecker. Seine Musik wird als »heart-breaking« (ebd.) bezeichnet und ruft beim Zuhörer ein Gefühl tiefer Sehnsucht hervor, das diesen zeitlebens heimsucht, wie die Elbin Vaire gegenüber Eriol verkündet:

> Now, however, for such is the eeriness of that sprite, you will ever love the evenings of summer and the nights of stars, and their magic will cause your heart to ache unquenchably. (ebd. 95)

Ein solcher Musiker, der eine wundersame Zaubermusik erklingen lässt, und damit eine unbestimmte ziellose Sehnsucht bei den Zuhörern weckt, ist — ähnlich der Nachtigal — eine Figur, die in der Tradition der romantischen Dichtung steht und die wir uns auch passend in einer romantischen Erzählung Eichendorffs oder Tiecks vorstellen können. Auch die Anlässe, in denen Timpinens Sehnsucht erweckende Musik erklingt, bilden charakteristische romantische Situationen, ertönt seine Musik doch gerade in Momenten romantischer Abend- oder Nachtstimmungen: »But on a sudden will his flute be heard again at an hour of gentle gloaming, or will he play beneath a goodly moon and the stars go bright and blue« (ebd. 94f). Dass durch Timpinen ein Sehnsuchtsruf an ein romantisches Individuum erklungen ist, macht Eriols Reaktion auf die nächtliche Musik explizit deutlich:

> 'Aye,' said Eriol, 'and the hearts of those that hear him go beating with a quickened longing. Meseemed 'twas my desire to open the window and leap forth, so sweet was the air that came to me

from without, nor might I drink deep enough, but as I listened I wished to follow I know not whom, I know not whither, out into the magic of the world beneath the stars.' (ebd. 95)

Vergegenwärtigen wir uns abschließend die Ergebnisse dieses Kapitels und die deutlichen Bezüge zu zentralen Motiven der Romantik, insbesondere zum Motiv der nostalgischen Sehnsucht, dann scheint es nicht unangemessen, Eriol als einen Romantiker im Feenland zu bezeichnen. Sein weiterer Aufenthalt in Tol Eressea, so wie er uns in den *Verschollenen Geschichten* geschildert wird, ist ein Versuch, sich von der unstillbaren Sehnsucht, die ihn peinigt, zu befreien.

Die existentielle Sehnsucht und das Meer

Bei meiner Untersuchung der romantischen Nostalgie in Tolkiens Werk habe ich auf eine spezifische Form der Nostalgie in Tolkiens Werk hingewiesen, die ich als existentielles Heimweh des Menschen bezeichnet habe (vgl. Eilmann, *Nostalgie* 106-108). So finden wir in Tolkiens Mythologie die Vorstellung einer existentiellen Heimatlosigkeit des Menschen in Arda. Der Mensch verhält sich aus Sicht der Elben in Arda wie ein Fremder und Heimatloser, der sich letztlich nach einer jenseitigen Heimat außerhalb der Welt sehnt, was zur Folge hat, dass die Sinnenwelt ihren Wert für den Sterblichen durch ihre Zeichenhaftigkeit gewinnt und immer wieder auf die jenseitige Heimat verweist (vgl. ebd. 107). Entscheidend ist nun, dass in Tolkiens Werk die existentielle Sehnsucht des Subjekts fundamental mit der Meeresmetaphorik verbunden ist. Der Gedanke, dass der nostalgische Gestus von Tolkiens Figuren häufig in einer Hinwendung zum Meer Ausdruck findet, wurde von mir bereits unter einer anderen Fragestellung diskutiert (vgl. Eilmann, *Lied* 122-133) und soll nun im Kontext der Romantikdiskussion aufgegriffen und vertieft werden, insbesondere unter Bezug auf eine bisher kaum beachtete Textstelle.

Was bedeutet Meeressehnsucht bei Tolkien? Und warum ist dieser Aspekt für unsere Fragestellung von solcher Bedeutung? In Tolkiens Kosmologie manifestiert die Welt jene göttliche Melodie, die durch das göttliche Schöpfungswort »Ea! Es sei!« (S 19) ins Dasein gerufen wurde. In Abwandlung des Bibelwortes steht am Anfang von Tolkiens Schöpfung nicht das Wort, sondern die Musik (vgl. Eilmann, *Lied* 123). Die göttliche Schöpfungsmusik, aus der alle Dinge entstanden sind, klingt im Rauschen des Wassers nach und kann von empfindsamen Personen intuitiv erahnt oder sogar kurzzeitig erfahren werden:

[B]ut of all these [elements] water they most greatly praised. And it is said by the Eldar that in water there lives yet the echo of the Music of the Ainur more than in any substance else that is in this

Earth; and many of the Children of Ilúvatar hearken still unsated
to the voices of the Sea, and yet know not for what they listen.
(S 8)

Relevant für unser Verständnis der existentiellen Nostalgie und Sehnsucht wird dieser Gedankengang, da die Sehnsucht des Subjekts gerade in der Hinwendung zum Meer Ausdruck findet. Das Bild des im Herzen tief bewegten Tuor, der mit weit ausgebreiteten Armen auf das unermessliche Meer hinausblickt, stellt sicherlich eines der schönsten Bilder Tolkiens für die Meeressehnsucht des Menschen dar:

[A]nd at last at unawares… he came suddenly to the black brink of Middle-earth, and saw the Great Sea, Belegaer the Shoreless. And at that hour the sun went down beyond the rim of the world, as a mighty fire; and Tuor stood alone upon the cliff with outspread arms, and a great yearning filled his heart. It is said, that he was the first Man to reach the Great Sea, and that none, save the Eldar, have ever felt more deeply the longing that it brings. (UT 24f)

Vor dem Hintergrund der romantischen Weltanschauung und der existentiellen Nostalgie, wie Tolkien sie in der *Athrabeth Finrod ah Andreth* darstellt (vgl. Eilmann, *Nostalgie* 106-108), wird ersichtlich, dass Tuors ekstatisches Meereserlebnis als Ausdruck eines existentiellen Heimwehs des Menschen verstanden werden kann. Denn in Übereinstimmung mit Finrods Einschätzung des menschlichen Daseinszustands in der *Athrabeth* nimmt Tuor das Naturschauspiel nicht als ein lediglich schönes Erlebnis wahr, sondern als »tokens or reminders« (MR 318), als Symbol oder Zeichen. Der Blick auf das rauschende Meer stellt somit eine ergreifende Erfahrung dar, die Tuor letztlich auf etwas Jenseitiges verweist, was er jedoch nicht explizit benennen kann. Dass in diesem Moment ein großes Verlangen sein Herz erfüllt (»and a great yearning filled his heart« UT 24f), ist eine Formulierung, die im Sinne der *Athrabeth* das existentielle Sehnen des Menschen ausdrückt.

Vergegenwärtigt man sich nun die enge Verbindung zwischen dem Meer und der Schöpfungsmusik, dann wird deutlich, dass Tuors Sehnsucht als ein existentielles Streben des Subjekts zu verstehen ist. Der Begriff des existentiellen Heimwehs bietet sich gleichzeitig im Sinne der Romantik an, da Tuor nach dieser ersten Begegnung mit dem Großen Meer zu einem Meeresbegeisterten wird, der von einer unerfüllbaren Sehnsucht getrieben wird und immer wieder die Begegnung — ja sogar die Vereinigung — mit dem Meer sucht. Da bei Tolkien im Rauschen des Meeres das Echo der Schöpfungsmusik nachklingt, kann die Vereinigung mit dem Meer als die finale Heimkehr eines an existentiellem Heimweh krankenden Individuums verstanden werden.

Meeressehnsucht im verworfenen Epilog des *Herrn der Ringe*

Für die Untersuchung der existentiellen Sehnsucht in Tolkiens Werk erweist sich eine entlegene, bisher kaum beachtete Textstelle als aufschlussreich: In der *History of Middle-earth* findet sich eine frühe Version eines Epilogs zum *Herrn der Ringe*.[3] In dieser Fassung schließt sich an das finale Kapitel *Die Grauen Anfurten* und das allseits bekannte Ende mit Sams Ausruf »Well, I'm back« (LotR 1008) ein kurzer Epilog an, in dem wir Sam im Dialog mit seiner Familie erleben und einen Einblick in deren glückliches Familienleben erhalten.

Wichtig ist nun, wie Tolkien beabsichtigte, diesen Epilog — und damit den *Herrn der Ringe* — enden zu lassen. Nachdem sich das Ehepaar Sam und Rosie vor dem Eingangsportal zu Beutelsend noch einmal seine Liebe gestanden hat, kehren beide ins Innere zurück. Der Text schließt daraufhin mit den Worten:

> They went in, and Sam shut the door. But even as he did so, he heard suddenly, deep and unstilled, the sigh and murmer of the Sea upon the shores of Middle-earth. (SD 128)

Weshalb ist dieser letzte Satz einer frühen Fassung des *Herrn der Ringe* für unsere Fragestellung von Bedeutung? Auf den ersten Blick könnte man zu der Ansicht gelangen, dass es sich bei dem Meeresrauschen, das Sam hier zu vernehmen meint, lediglich um ein literarisches Stimmungsbild handelt, das als atmosphärisches Detail die Geschichte abschließen sollte. So einfach ist es jedoch nicht. Dass Tolkien mit der von ihm gewählten Formulierung auf etwas ganz Bestimmtes hinweisen wollte, ist an verschiedenen inhaltlichen und sprachlichen Merkmalen des Satzes ablesbar. Ruft man sich die Geographie Mittelerdes vor Augen, wird sofort klar, dass Sam in Hobbingen gar nicht den Klang des Meeres hören kann. Das Auenland liegt von der nächsten Küste mehr als 150 Meilen entfernt. Bei dem vernommenen Meeresrauschen kann es sich demnach nicht um ein rein alltägliches Phänomen der akustischen Wahrnehmung handeln. Vielmehr muss es sich um einen Klang handeln, den Sam tief in seinem Inneren als eine rein subjektive Wahrnehmung vernimmt. Wie durch die bisherigen Ausführungen deutlich wurde, müssen wir diesen speziellen Verweis auf ein Rauschen der See als Ausdruck der existentiellen Meeressehnsucht ansehen, die für Tolkiens Werk von so symbolhafter Bedeutung ist.

---

3   Zur Textgeschichte des Epilogs vgl. Christopher Tolkiens Ausführungen in SD 129-132. Offensichtlich gelangte Tolkien zu dem Schluss, dass der Epilog der Geschichte letztlich nicht dienlich war: »An epilogue giving further glimpse (though of a rather exceptional family) has been so universally condemned that I shall not insert it. One must stop somewhere« (SD 132).

Dass diese Deutung zutreffend ist, wird bereits daran ersichtlich, dass das Wort »Sea« (ebd.) von Tolkien in dieser Textpassage großgeschrieben wird. Dadurch wird deutlich, dass es sich beim erwähnten Meer explizit um das Trennende Meer Belegaer handelt. Belegaer jedoch ist in Tolkiens Mittelerde-Mythologie auf engste mit dem entrückten Valinor, dem irdischen Sehnsuchtsort der Elben und auf diese Weise mit Paradieses- und Jenseitsvorstellungen verbunden.

Weiterhin ist an Tolkiens Formulierung bemerkenswert, dass Sam in dieser Textstelle das Meeresrauschen an den Küsten Mittelerdes zu vernehmen meint (»upon the shores of Middle-earth« ebd.). Tolkien spricht von Küsten im Plural, sodass die Vorstellung eines ganz Mittelerde umfassenden Erlebnisses noch unterstrichen wird. Es ist demnach nicht nur das singuläre Meeresrauschen an einer einzigen Küste, dem Sam hier lauscht, sondern es ist das Meeresrauschen an allen Küsten, das hier das Subjekt berührt und seelisch bewegt.

Auch die weitere Charakterisierung dieses Meeresrauschens ist aufschlussreich. Der Klang der Wellen wird als ein Seufzen und Murmeln (s.o.) beschrieben und mit den Adjektiven »deep and unstilled« (ebd.) weiter gekennzeichnet. Das Meer wird durch diese Schilderung personifiziert und als aktive Kraft präsentiert, die anscheinend selbst einen tiefen unstillbaren Verlust beklagt. Eine solche Personifizierung der See und die Beschreibung des Meeresrauschens als Seufzen sind in der Literatur nicht ungewöhnlich. Im Kontext von Tolkiens Werk jedoch ist eine solche Wortwahl mehr als ein sprachliches Klischee, sondern Ausdruck des beschriebenen Zusammenhangs zwischen Meeresrauschen und Schöpfungsmusik. Ist man sich bewusst, dass das Meeresrauschen in Tolkiens Werk auf die kosmologische Struktur seiner Mythologie, insbesondere auf den Schöpfungsakt, verweist, dann wird die Tragweite dieses Epilogs zum *Herrn der Ringe* ersichtlich.

Das zentrale Bild der romantischen und existentiellen Sehnsucht in Tolkiens Werk stand in dieser Textfassung am Ende der Geschichte. Das zeigt: Tolkien war es in dieser Phase der Arbeit am *Herrn der Ringe* wichtig, den Leser mit dem Klang des Meeresrauschens und der damit verbundenen Sehnsucht aus seiner großen Erzählung zu entlassen.

Bibliographie

Eichendorff, Joseph v. *Ausgewählte Werke*. Erster Band. Hg. Paul Stapf. Wiesbaden: Emil Vollmer Verlag. o. J.

Eilmann, Julian. »Das Lied bin ich. Lieder, Poesie und Musik in J.R.R. Tolkiens Mittelerde-Mythologie«. *Hither Shore* 2 (2005): 105-135

---. "Sleeps a song in things abounding. J.R.R. Tolkien and the German Romantic Tradition". *Music in Middle-earth*. Hg. Heidi Steimel & Friedhelm Schneidewind. Zürich/Jena: Walking Tree, 2010, 167-184

---. »J.R.R. Tolkien und die romantische Nostalgie«. *Hither Shore* 7 (2010): 94-109

Novalis. *Schriften. Die Werke Friedrich von Hardenbergs*. Hg. Paul Kluckhohn & Richard Samuel. 5 Bde. Stuttgart: Kohlhammer, 1960ff

Tolkien, John Ronald Reuel. *The Book of Lost Tales*. Hg. Christopher Tolkien. (The History of Middle-earth I + II) London: HarperCollins, 2002

---. *The Lord of the Rings*. London: HarperCollins, 1995

---. *Morgoth's Ring*. Hg. Christopher Tolkien (The History of Middle-earth X). London: HarperCollins, 2002

---. *Sauron Defeated*. Hg. Christopher Tolkien (The History of Middle-earth IX). London: HarperCollins, 2002

---. *The Silmarillion*. Hg. Christopher Tolkien. London: HarperCollins 1999

---. *Unfinished Tales of Númenor and Middle-earth*. Hg. Christopher Tolkien. London: Allen & Unwin, 1980

Simple Pleasures in Tolkien's Poetry
Eating and Drinking and the Depth of Things
Guglielmo Spirito (Assisi) & Emanuele Rimoli (Roma)

Would it have been really unexpected or even implausible if Christopher Tolkien would have said he had found out a new piece from the — rather messy — mound of drafts of his outstanding, creative father, so as to introduce us to an unheard-of dialogue between a king of old and his attendant?

'That's it, my lord, the carter told him, you'll see. We'll have a nice rest here, and maybe even a bite to eat.' He thought he should sow that seed early, since he had had nothing himself since close on dawn. 'We've got shade from the heat and plenty of cover. No one will spy us here.'
He led the king down through soft sand to the water's edge. He indicated to the man that he should sit, then sat very contentedly himself, letting the goodness of the cool clean water extend its reviving benefit from his feet to his whole being.
His spirits, which till now had been clouded by uncertainty and a fear of so much that was still unknown, cleared and lightened.
'It might be as well if you took a bite to eat, my lord. Just a mouthful. To keep your strength up.'
There were olives, plump black ones. Pumpkin seeds. A stack of little griddlecakes of a golden yellow colour and about the size of a medallion.
'Ummm, you can taste the lightness! I've eaten twenty of these little fellows at a single setting. Not out of greed, sir, but for the joy they bring to the heart. The flavour comes from the buttermilk, but owes something as well, I dare say, to the good humour of the cook, and the skill, you know, of her fingers in the flipping. That too you can taste.'
So it was that the king allowed himself to be persuaded and took one of the little cakes in his fingers, broke of a morsel, and tested.
It was very good. What the driver had said of its lightness was true, and of its effect on the spirit.
It was bewildering but not unpleasurable. On the whole he felt easy with himself, both in body and spirit; comfortably restored.
It had never occurred to him that the food that came to his table so promptly, and in such abundance, might have ingredients. That a griddlecake or pikelet might have some previous form as

batter. That batter might consist of good buckwheat flour and buttermilk, and that what you experienced as goodness might depend on the thickness of the batter or the lightness of a wrist. Or that ingenious arrangements might need to be made before a thing as simple as a pikelet could make its entry into the world. Or that one of the activities a man might give his attention to, and puzzle his wits over, was the managing of these arrangements, the putting together, in an experimental way, of this or that bit of an already existing world to make something new.
All that had been none of his concern. It had had no interest for him. Now it did. And he looked at the old fellow who had revealed these things to him with growing respect.
The good colour of the buttermilk as it poured out of the crock: he liked what came to his senses when he pictured that. It had done him good, all that, body and spirit both. He wanted more...

The king, led by his driver, was starting to perceive and recognise that

> The brilliant smell of water,
> The brave smell of a stone,
> The smell of dew and thunder
> They haven't got no noses,
> And goodness only knowses
> The Noselessness of Man. (Chesterton 25f)

Is this a forgotten draft of a dialogue between, say, king Théoden and Merry, speaking about cake-lore, as they have had an unfinished talk about herb-lore? No indeed.

This comes from *Ransom*, by David Malouf, the Australian writer who brilliantly recast the journey of an old man who sets off for the enemy's camp: Priam king of Troy off to ransom the body of his son (Malouf 114-129).

But Idaeus, the carter, has a seemingly hobbit-like way of enjoying simple things, and Priam learns from him an unexpected thing: tasting anew, for one.

The Most of Savour Possible

Following Fernando Pessoa (Alberto Caeiro): "I try to undress myself of what I have learned. I try to forget the mode of remembering they taught me, and scrape off the paint with which they painted my senses, to unpack my true emotions in order to be me" (quote in Alves 18).

This is indeed a strange theory of learning. I am ready to accept this strangeness and make mine Lichtenberg's words:

> I would like to become unfamiliar with everything
> in order to see again,
> to hear again,
> to feel again. (ibid.)

But it is Roland Barthes who gives me the proper words:

> The experience of unlearning has, I believe, an illustrious and old fashioned name, which I dare taking here without shame, at the very intersection of its etymology: Sapientia:
> no power,
> a bit of knowledge,
> a bit of wisdom,
> and the most of savour possible... (ibid.)

So we arrive at the topic of our inquiry: simple pleasures as eating and drinking in Tolkien's poetry. At a first glance, it might sound difficult to put together 'eating and drinking' with 'poetry'; not, at least, at the same 'level', if one would follow Bilbo's statement: "Not that hobbits would ever acquire quite the elvish appetite for music and poetry and tales. They seem to like them as much as food, or more" (LotR 254).

> 'I feel like singing myself,' laughed Frodo. 'Though at the moment I feel more like eating and drinking!'
> 'That will soon be cured,' said Pippin. 'You have shown your usual cunning in getting up just in time for a meal.' (LotR 242)

Eventually hobbits *do* put things together, nevertheless keeping the proper (hobbits') order:

> After eating with Gildor and the Elves, Pippin afterwards recalled little of either food or drink, for his mind was filled with the light upon elf-faces, and the sound of voices so various and so beautiful that he felt in a waking dream. But he remembered that there was bread, surpassing the savour of a fair white loaf to one who is starving; and fruits sweet as wild berries and richer than the tended fruits of gardens; he drained a cup that was filled with a fragrant draught, cool as a clear mountain, golden as a summer afternoon. Sam could never describe in words, nor picture clearly to himself, what he felt or thought that night, though it remained in his memory as one of the chief events in his life. The nearest he ever got was to say: 'Well, sir, if I could grow apples like that,

I would call myself a gardener. But it was the singing that went to my heart, if you know what I mean.'
Frodo sat, eating, drinking, and talking with delight; but his mind was chiefly on the words spoken. (LotR 95f)
Health and hope grew strong in them, and they were content with each good day as it came, taking pleasure in every meal, and in every word and song. (LotR 291)

A View on Food

But why, one may ask, should we follow a hobbit's view on the matter? There could be a simple reason: that it seems rather closer to our own experience. But there is a second one: for we find an ample amount of simple pleasures related with food and drink described in the few poems/songs of *The Lord of the Rings*, which are mostly 'hobbits' stuff', as one should expect: as in the *A Drinking Song*, *The Bath Song*, *The Man in the Moon*, *The Rhyme of the Troll*, and even in *Gollum's Song*...

We may find "several meals at which it snowed food and rained drink, as hobbits say" (LotR 55), and we may share Gimli's reaction at Isengard after meeting Merry and Pippin, finding them "feasting and idling — and smoking!" and wonder about their alleged "few well-earned comforts" (580f). Or share Aragorn's smile in realizing that they eat peacefully crumbs of *lembas* in the Uruk-hai camp (cf. 510).

Our concern will be to try to answer what the place of eating and drinking is in Tolkien's sub creation — with its mingling *poetry* and *prose* —, and in the primary world. Why and how is Tolkien so brave in depicting simple pleasures of normal, earthly 'hobbit-like' life? Food — and drink — matters, as pleasure and joy matters: "There lives the dearest freshness deep down things", as Gerard Manley Hopkins would have said (84).

First we shall speak of *food*, and then of *words* (or poetry). For eating precedes speaking. The mouth is the place of eating long before it is the place of speaking. When Ludwig Feuerbach, an expert of words, said that 'we are what we eat' (*man ist, was man ißt*) he pointed to the place where Word and flesh make love. 'I eat, therefore I am'. Eating comes before speaking. And speaking, throughout our whole lives, is a form of eating. Mallarmé, who had the dream of writing a book with a single word, would envy the child who silently sucks the mother's breast. It dwells in a wordless poem. An interpreter of dreams could have told him that what he desired was to return to the condition of a child, in order to witness the birth of the first word.

Even before having ever touched the mother's breast, the mouth sucks the void, confident that it exists.

Hunger and food,
void and fullness,
desire and satisfaction...
And Augustine would add: the restless heart and the Three...
The sucking mouth knows that life is not its possession. It must come from outside. It is a gift. It is grace.
The mouth learns then, the second lesson: life and pleasure are joined in the same object. As the child sucks the breast, it enjoys blessedness...
Eating is living;
Eating is pleasure.

We are what we eat. Alexander Schmemann, the Russian-orthodox theologian, comments:

> Long before Feuerbach the same definition of man is given by the Bible. In the biblical story of creation man is presented as a hungry being and whole world as his food. Man must eat in order to live; he must take the whole world into his body and transform it into himself, into flesh and blood. He is, indeed, what he eats, and the whole world is presented as one all embracing banquet table for man. And this image of the banquet remains the central image of life. It is the image of life at its creation and also at its end and fulfilment: 'that you eat and drink at my table in my kingdom'.
> (Quote in Alves 76-78)

But paradise was lost. We are no longer the child... and we learn another lesson: the world outside is not a breast. The world is hard, raw, bitter and sour...

But the body has not forgotten, and slowly, we have found a way out: we have mixed the fire of desire with reality, and cooking was invented. Cooking is an alchemic operation whereby the raw, by the magic of fire, is transformed in food... Wootton Major

> was a remarkable village in its way, being well known in the country round about for the skill of its workers in various crafts, but most of all for its cooking. It had a large Kitchen which belonged to the Village Council, and the Master Cook was an important person. (SWM 5)

So began J.R.R. Tolkien's last work to be published in his own lifetime. In the tale, The Great Cake and Faery — and simple pleasures — are blended, kneading together in such an amazing way that hobbits would have been delighted with it.

On Cooking

Nothing is allowed to remain the same. Fire and its allies are at work... the hard must be softened. Smells and tastes which were dormant inside are forced to come out: cooking is to give the magic kiss which wakes up sleeping pleasures. Alchemy metamorphoses: cooking joins what nature has separated.

Was not this what Sam experienced in Ithilien? "...he had begun to long for a good hot meal, 'something hot out of the pot'", in contrast with Gollum's taste (the chapter's significant title: *Of Herbs and Stewed Rabbit,* LotR 675).

Space is abolished. Salt, garlic, pepper, sugar, thyme, clove. Parsley, oregano, cinnamon, chilli, paprika and cumin are all invited from the distant lands where they grow. The sweet, the sour, the bitter and the salty are forced to enter into non-existent combinations. Everything is made anew.

Leaven, this silent ally of fire, does its work without noise. Beverages of all kinds, unknown to nature: beer, wine, brandy and whisky, each in its own way, are liquids in which 'spirits' lie bottled.[1]

New tastes and smells appear with new colours and shapes. The eyes gain a new potency. Linked to the mouth and to the nose, they are given the power to taste. Reds, greens, yellows, browns and whites are set in rare combinations. And water, milk and oil celebrate alliances with the fire. Even those things which seem to be served raw — tomatoes, lettuce, radishes — they are all transformed by the taste, smell and touch of dressings.

> 'Not make the nasty red tongues', hissed Gollum — 'I'm going to stew these coneys', said Sam. 'Stew the rabbits!' squealed Gollum in dismay. 'Spoil beautiful meat Sméagol saved for you, poor hungry Sméagol! What for?' (680)

For him, only raw meat is desirable:

> So sleek, so fair!
> What a joy to meet!
> We only wish
> to catch a fish,
> so juicy-sweet! (646)

---

1 'Spirits' hardly suffer mingle themselves with other liquids: that was the care of Merry and Pippin, saving (also) wine and beer from the flood at Isengard — "I would sooner learn how they came by the wine", laughed Legolas — with typical wooden-elvish taste (581), and surely the three of them would have shared Noah's opinion — in Chesterton's words: "I don't care where the water goes if it doesn't get into the wine" (12).

Which seems quite similar to the Troll's taste for raw fresh meat (though the original three large trolls turned into stone, "where caught by Gandalf quarrelling over the right way to cook thirteen dwarves and one hobbit", as Frodo — laughing — recalled, and "felt his spirits reviving" (222):

> 'But how would this suit?" said Sam. 'It ain't what I call proper poetry, if you understand me: just a bit of nonsense. But these old images here brought it to my mind.' Standing up, with his hands behind his back, as if he was at school, he began to sing to an old tune.
> Troll sat alone on his seat of stone,
> And munched and mumbled a bare old bone;
> For many a year he had gnawed it near,
> For meat was hard to come by.
> Done by! Gum by!
> In a cave in the hills he dwelt alone,
> And meat was hard to come by.
> [then up came Tom and asked him to hand the old bone over]
> 'For a couple o'pins,' says Troll, and grins,
> 'I'll eat thee too, and gnaw thy shins.
> A bit o'fresh meat will go down sweet!
> I'll try my teeth on thee now.
> Hee now! See now!
> I'm tired o'gnowing old bones and skins;
> I've a mind to dine on thee now.' (223)

Not so for Sam and his cooking gear — even in fair Ithilien, "a supper, or a breakfast, by the fire in the old kitchen at Bagshot Row was what he really wanted" (678).

Gollum, after taking a corner of the *lembas* handed over to him by Frodo, nibbled it, spat, and a fit of coughing shook him (cf. 647). The latter was horrified to see Sam ready to stew the rabbits, but Sam answered him: "Each to his own fashion. Our bread chokes you, and raw coney chokes me." (680)

The pans, frying pans, knives, forks, spoons, ovens and stoves are all mediators — the kitchen knows Augustinian theology: in it, the order of *uti* never forgets that it exists only for the sake of the *frui*.

The cook also lives from words. Recipes. He names what he wants to eat. He names what he believes the others would like to eat. Pleasurable food.

> Sam busied himself with his pans. 'What a hobbit needs with coney', he said to himself, 'is some herbs and roots, especially taters – not to mention bread. Herbs we can manage, seemingly.' (680)

And, by the power of those words he calls, joins, mixes, adds, subtracts, roasts, boils, bakes, and fries. The objects we long for are not ready, in nature. Cooking is the art of making real what is unreal; of making present what is absent. The food is pleasurable, indeed. But the cook eats even more the joy that he sees in the other's face, as they eat.

The Latin languages preserve an intuition which seems to be absent from English. Their words for 'knowledge' and 'taste' come from the same root. 'Sapere', in Latin means both 'to know, to understand' and 'to taste, to have flavour'. In Italian, *sapere* = to know, and *sapore* = to taste. To know something is to feel its taste. "All hobbits, of course, can cook, for they begin to learn the art before the letters (which many never reach); but Sam was a good cook, even by hobbit reckoning" (679).

There is a link between *sapore* and *sapere* (savouring and knowing). Perhaps the kitchen and the library are in fact united by one and the same splendid desire: the desire to both savour and know.

Tita, the heroine of Laura Esquivel's novel *Like Water for Chocolate*, has a unique gift: knowledge and wisdom in matters of food. The lovers in this narrative grow in knowledge of each other's love by seeing, smelling, touching, and savouring the culinary pleasures that Tita prepares: "Tita knew through her own flesh how fire transforms the elements, how a lump of cornflour is changed into a tortilla, how a soul that hasn't been warmed up by the fire of love is lifeless, like a useless ball of cornflour" (quote in Mendez Montoya 45f).

Growing, cooking, and eating food are intense somatic or bodily experiences that bring about knowledge. We are never totally divorced from the reality of embodiment, as George Lakoff and Mark Johnson rightly argue (cf. Mendez Montoya 35). If this is so, one could also argue that knowledge displays a dimension of participation in the known via the senses — most particularly by touch and taste at the moment of eating and drinking, a knowledge which involves a communal practice of delight and sharing.

Fellowship of Bread and Word

Food points to the root of being ultimately relational, says Sergei Bulgakov, hinting to the Trinitarian superabundance communion and sharing, and the Eucharistic meal as well (cf. Mendez Montoya 89-198). Alimentation is the gift that heals hunger, a gift that nourishes our basic hunger for another. At the heart of the cosmos there is an intimate metabolic exchange of nourishing and being nourished: a *cosmic banquet*, to recall Bulgakov's notion. From a Trinitarian and Eucharistic perspective, the gift, hunger or appetite is a mark of excess, plenitude and sharing. And, like Babette's feast (and more), is transformative.

Andrei Roublev's icon on the *Hospitality of Abraham* both foreshadows and offers a taste of it. That all our eating, drinking and sharing is — a sort of — splendid *"aperitif"*, might open a reflexion on *lembas*, but we shall not follow this (tempting) path, which is far above hobbits' simple pleasures.²

Nevertheless, we are involved in this *Fellowship (of the Ring): fellowship* in Italian is *compagnia*, from the Latin *cum-panis*, literally: 'those who share bread'. We should recall that *The Hobbit* opens up with 'An Unexpected Party', in which the dwarves almost 'plunder' Bilbo's kitchen and storerooms and its epic continuation, *The Lord of the Rings*, opens with 'A Long-Expected Party', in which the whole Shire does almost the same.

Constance Classen explains that taste is a form of touch, only more intense. In fact, as Classen points out, the origin of the English word 'taste' is "the Middle English *tasten*, to feel, derived from the Latin *taxare*, to feel, touch sharply, judge." Classen explains that it was around the 14th century that taste became associated with savouring. Accordingly, the sense of taste gives an account of knowledge as something "savourable", so that to know something means, to some extent, to have a taste of it, to feel and touch and enter into a relationship with it (cf. Montoya 62).

The Greek word *geusis* was later Latinised as *gustus*, which in Italian and Spanish was then transformed into *gusto* (savouring, flavour, or tasting).

Cuisine, like language, contains a vocabulary, (the products and the ingredients), that is organised according to grammatical rules (recipes that give meaning to the ingredients and transform them in dishes), a syntax (the menus, that is, the order of dishes), and rhetoric (social protocols): "After such long journeying and camping, and days spent in the lonely wild, the evening meal [at Henneth Annun] seemed a feast to the hobbits: to drink pale yellow wine, cool and fragrant, and eat bread and butter, and salted meats, and dried fruits, and good red cheese, with clean hands and clean knives and plates" (LotR 703).

But to make others 'taste' using words, it seems that poetry is more helpful. "Poetry is metamorphosis, transformation, alchemic operation", says Octavio Paz; as cooking somehow is, we might say?

To Isak Dinesen's *Babette's Feast*, we would say of what might happen during a meal that "nothing definite can here be stated" (quote in Mendez Montoya 16).

Poetry is the language of what is not possible to say. What the poem says is not present in its words. Indeed, the poet does not know what he is (not) saying.

---

[2] The short but deep analysis by Thomas Honegger includes the hints at the relation of waybread and the Eucharistic *viaticum* (cf. Letters 288). Turin and the Fellowship seem to have been the only ones we know about sharing *lembas*, beside the Eldar. Nor shall we develop other themes closely connected, such as fasting: I refer to the dynamic awareness that fasting gives value to food, just as heroism to the point of death is affirmative of life. (Cf. Ramfos 76; Milhaven 375).

Like the empty hands in a shell: they can hold water in their void, but they know nothing about water. Poetry says without saying. It evokes — with few words —, awakes, recreates, reverberates something impalpable, that prose with its many words hardly, if ever, might do. Besides, among hobbits we have *modest* poetry blended with song and humour: a sprinkling radiance of simple merriment.

> I am only a hobbit, and gardening's my job at home, sir, if you understand me, and I'm not much good at poetry — not at making it: a bit of a comic rhyme, perhaps, now and again, you know, but not real poetry — so I can't tell you what I mean. It ought to be sung.
> (LotR 706)

> 'Can you sing?' 'Yes', said Pippin. 'Well, yes, well enough for my own people. But we have no songs fit for great halls and evil times, lord. We seldom sing of anything more terrible than wind or rain. And most of my songs are about things that make us laugh; or about food and drink, of course.' (838)

A hobbit poem — or a song — involving eating and drinking will evoke an experience of inner joy which refreshes both the spirit and the body, and renews the perception that, in spite of everything, all's well. "The wine cores in their veins and tired limbs, and they felt glad and easy of heart as they had not done since they left the land of Lórien" (703).

Eating and drinking trigger particular moods, kindle various degrees of emotion, and awaken memories. Food matters. There is a relationship between people's "foodways" and people's understanding of self and other.

Good cooking is good in part because of the emotional attachment you have to the people for whom you are cooking, to the tools you are using and to the foods you are making.

Chesterton asked:

> But who will write us a riding song
> Or a hunting song or a drinking song,
> Fit for them that arose and rode
> When day and the wine were red?
> But bring me a quart of claret out,
> And I will write you a clinking song,
> A song of war and a song of wine
> And a song to wake the dead. (43)

Frodo propped his back against the tree-trunk, and closed his eyes. Sam and Pippin sat near, and they began to hum, and then to sing softly:

> Ho! Ho! Ho! To the bottle I go
> To heal my heart and drown my woe.
> Rain may fall and wind may blow,
> And many miles be still to go,
> But under a tall tree I will lie,
> And let the clouds go sailing by.
>
> Ho! Ho! Ho! They began again louder. They stopped short suddenly. Frodo sprang to his feet. A long-drawn wail came down the wind, like the cry of some evil and lonely creature. (LotR 103)

Finally they crossed the ferry and got to Crickhollow:

> Snatches of competing songs came from the bathroom mixed with the sound of splashing and wallowing. The voice of Pippin was suddenly lifted up above the others in one of Bilbo's favourite bath-songs.
>
> O! Water cold we may pour at need
> down a thirsty throat and be glad indeed;
> but better is Beer, if drink we lack,
> and Water Hot poured down the back.
>
> There was a terrific splash, and a shout of Whoa, from Frodo. It appeared that a lot of Pippin's bath had imitated a mountain and leaped on high.
> Merry went to the door: 'What about supper and beer in the throat?' he called. Frodo came out drying his hair. (115f)

The late supper at Crickhollow, we know, followed an early supper at Maggot's farm, where "[t]he kitchen was lit with candles and the fire was mended… There was beer in plenty, and a mighty dish of mushrooms and bacon, besides much other solid farmhouse fare. The dogs lay by the fire and gnawed rinds and cracked bones" (109).

And much later — in the middle of Flotsam and Jetsam, at the ruined arched doors of Isengard, Merry offered to their companions "man-food, as Treebeard calls it. Will you have wine or beer? There is a barrel inside there — very passable. And this is first-rate salted pork. Or I can cut you some rashers of bacon and broil them, if you like. I am sorry there is no green stuff: the deliveries have been rather interrupted in the last few days! I cannot offer you anything to follow but butter and honey for your bread. Are you content?" (584).

A Little Beer would Suit me Better

"Drink is not enough for content, Treebeard's draughts may be nourishing, but one feels the need of something solid. And even lembas is none the worse for a change", as Merry said (585). Nevertheless it seems that *beer* has a special place in hobbits' (and dwarves') preferences:

> 'Come along in, and have some tea!' [Bilbo] managed to say [to Balin] after taking a deep breath.
> 'A little beer would suit me better, if it is all the same to you, my good sir,' said Balin with the white beard. 'But I don't mind some cake — seed-cake, if you have any.' 'Lots!' Bilbo found himself answering, to his surprise; and he found himself scuttling off, too, to the cellar to fill a pint beer-mug, and then to a pantry to fetch two beautiful round seed-cakes which he had baked that afternoon for his after-supper morsel. (H 19)

Let us turn now from thoughts about drinking to one drink itself: beer. It seems fit to focus our attention on one drink which is part of the Anglo-Saxon heritage so much that the word used to describe it simply means 'drink'. *'Beer'* was adapted from a Latin word *biber*, 'a drink', itself a late development of *bibere* 'to drink'. As an English word, 'beer' dates from the 6th or 7th century; German 'Bier' is from the same period. The earlier English word was 'ale', derived from Old Norse (cf. Dunkling 79).

'Ale' is still used as a manly, vigorous way of saying beer. If a man can 'hold his ale', there can be little wrong with him. Go into a country pub at midday and hear a group of friends tell each other, 'We shifted some ale last night. Hey, didn't we shift some ale last night?' It is not a bad boast, for it claims no more than companionship and good cheer in a manner that is as old as England herself.

Peter Haydon says that in AD 361, the Emperor Julian described the Teutonic northern European races as 'sons of malt', but that none are so as much as the British. Then he continues affirming that he himself wrote "a history of England as seen through the bottom of a pint glass." Or perhaps, as Bishop Brougham, "see Truth dawn…over the glass's edge" (Haydon 1 † 274).

Indeed, throughout its entire history, "the British love affair with the beer has endured" (Brown 3). William Hogarth's († 1794) painting called *Beer Street* came with an inscription:

> Beer! happy produce of our isle,
> Can sinewy strength impart,

And wearied with fatigue and toil,
Can cheer each manly heart.

Cesar de Saussure wrote home in 1726: "Would you believe it, although water is to be had in abundance in London and on fairly good quality, absolutely none is drunk? The lower classes, even the paupers, do not know what is to quench their thirst with water. In this country nothing but beer is drunk... it is said more grain is consumed in England for making beer than making bread" (quote in Brown 53).

Benjamin Franklin spent some of his early days in London working in a printing house. He made the enormous social faux pas of drinking water, which earned him the nickname 'Water-American' at work. Franklin wrote that his companion at the printing press drank: "A pint before breakfast, a pint at breakfast with his bread and cheese, a pint between breakfast and dinner, a pint at dinner, a pint in the afternoon about six o'clock, and another when he had done his day's work" (quote in Brown 54).

The quantity of beer seems too large. That was what Ishmael thought, reading the list of the outfits for the larders and cellars of a ship for whale fishery: 10,800 barrels. "But this was very far North, be it remembered, where beer agrees well with the constitution" (Melville 642). Or, with Edgar Allan Poe († 1849):

Fill with mingled cream and amber,
I will drain that glass again.
Such hilarious visions clamber
Through the chamber of my brain —
Quaintest thoughts — queerest fancies
Come to life and fade away;
What care I how time advances?
I am drinking ale today.[3]

On Inns (and more Beer)

'A little beer would suit me better', and though it is always true, it is never more true than in an *Inn*.The *Eagle and Child* (or *Bird and Baby*) was the Inkling's pub *par excellence* as we see in J.R.R. Tolkien's *Letters* (*Lamb and Flag* was Second Best choice, usually when the first run short of beer).

---

3 Quoted by Tidy 35. This poem was attributed to Poe by Thomas Ollive Mabbott in 1939, and again in 1969. The original manuscript supposedly hung on the wall of the Washington Tavern in Lowell MA for many years. It was apparently last seen around 1892. It was recalled from memory by a former bartender there about 1939. Although of questionable origin, the attribution has some merit and has not been seriously opposed.

This is a typical English trait, as the biography — for instance — of C.S. Lewis, J.R.R. Tolkien and the other *Inklings* shows quite well: "The Daily Telegraph wrote a peculiarly misrepresentative and asinine paragraph of Tuesday last. It began 'Ascetic Mr Lewis' — !!! I ask you! He put away three pints in a very short session we had this morning, and said he was 'going short for Lent'" (L 56). Not to mention Hilaire Belloc († 1953):

> When you have lost your inns
> then drown you sorry selves,
> For you will have lost the last of England.
> (Quote in Haydon 306; cf. Carpenter; Duriez)

It is such an English attribute, that in Chesterton's poem *The Englishman* even Saint George is involved:

> St. George he was for England,
> And before he killed the dragon
> He drank a pint of English ale
> Out of an English flagon.
> For though he fast right readily
> In hair-shirt or in mail,
> It isn't safe to give him cakes
> Unless you give him ale. (9)

We have a few *worthy* inns mentioned in *The Lord of the Rings*:

> No one had a more attentive audience than old Ham Gamgee, commonly known as the Gaffer. He held forth at *The Ivy Bush*, a small inn on the (Bywater) read... 'There's some not far away that wouldn't offer a pint of beer to a friend, if they lived in a hole with golden walls. But they do things proper at Bag End.' (34.36)

> Sam Gamgee was sitting in one corner near the fire in *The Green Dragon* at Bywater, and opposite him was Ted Sandyman, the miller's son; and there were various other rustic hobbits listening to their talk... 'Well, friends, I'm off home. Your good health!' He drained his mug and went out noisily. Sam sat silent and said no more. (57f)

Note: there is also *The Floating Lod* at Frogmorton (1038), closed by Sharkey's men: "'No welcome, no beer, no smoke, and a lot of rules and orc-talk instead', said Sam" (1037).

The inn has a particular ambience, with the magic combination of hospitality, friendship, conversation, food and beer — that form together a sort of alchemy of a very enjoyable piece of existence:

> 'All right!' said Pippin. 'I will follow you into every bog and ditch. But it is hard! I had counted on passing the *Golden Perch* at Stock before sundown. The best beer in the Eastfarthing, or used to be: it is long time since I tasted it.'
> 'That settles it!' said Frodo. 'Short cuts make delays, but inns make longer ones. At all costs we must keep you away from the *Golden Perch*. We want to get to Bucklebury before dark. What do you say, Sam?'
> 'I will go along with you, Mr. Frodo,' said Sam (in spite of private misgiving and a deep regret for the best beer in the Eastfarthing).
> (101)

Of course, *The Prancing Pony* in Bree is the most relevant inn in the tale:

> They were washed and in the middle of good deep mugs of beer when Mr. Butterbur and Nob came in again. In a twinkling the table was laid. There was hot soup, cold meats, a blackberry tart, new loaves, slabs of butter, and half a ripe cheese: good plain food, as good as the Shire could show, and homelike enough to dispel the last of Sam's misgivings already much relieved by the excellence of the beer. (170)

There they met "a strange-looking weather-beaten man sitting in the shadows near the wall. He had a tall tankard in front of him, and was smoking a long-stemmed pipe curiously carved." And there Frodo "began a ridiculous song that Bilbo had been rather fond of (and indeed rather proud of, for he had made up the words himself). It was about an inn; and that is probably why it came into Frodo's mind just then

> There is an inn, a merry old inn
> beneath an old grey hill,
> And there they brew a beer so brown
> That the Man in the Moon himself came down
> one night to drink his fill.
> ...
> The Man in the Moon took another mug,
> and then rolled beneath his chair;
> And there he dozed and dreamed of ale,

> Till in the sky the stars were pale,
> and dawn was in the air.
> ...
> They called for more ale, and began to shout: 'Let's have it again, master! Come on now! Once more!' They made Frodo have another drink, and then begin his song again..." (172-176)

They might have used the words of John Milton († 1674):

> when the merry bells ring round,
> And the jocund rebecks sound
> To many a youth and many a maid
> Dancing in the chequered shade;
> And young and old come forth to play
> On a sunshine holiday
> Till the livelong daylight fail:
> Then to spicy nut-brown ale. (in Tidy 38)

After all that happened that night, the landlord was afraid of Gandalf's wrath: "turn all my ale sour, I shouldn't wonder. He's a bit hasty" (183). But it turned good at last for him (and his ale): "May your beer be laid under an enchantment of surpassing excellence for seven years!", said Gandalf, overjoyed by the news that Strider went away with the hobbits (281).

Especially in war-like times, the beer remains a potent symbol of everyday (English) life. Air Vice-Marshal Sir Cecil Bouchier recalled how important beer was to RAF aircrew during World War II:

> This was their one great relaxation, the beer they had dreamt about all day. No-one drank anything but draught beer and mighty good stuff it was, food and drink to the tired and thirsty. Often a leader bringing his squadron home, fearful of being late, would radio from halfway across the Channel — 'Keep the bar open. We'll be down in twenty minutes.' (Quote in Brown 200f)

This was not Pippin's experience as well, when he arrived at Minas Tirith:

> 'What would you know, Master Peregrin?', asked Beregond.
> 'Er well', said Pippin, 'if I venture to say so, rather a burning question in my mind at present is, well, what about breakfast and all that? I mean, what are the meal-times, if you understand me, and where is the dining-room, if there is one? And the inns? I

> looked, but never a one could I see as we rode up, though I had been borne up by the hope of a draught of ale as soon as we came to the homes of wise and courtly men.' (LotR 791)

As William Shenstone († 1763) said:

> Whoe'er has travelled life's dull round,
> Where're his stages may have been,
> May sigh to think he still has found,
> The warmest welcome at an inn. (Quote in Haydon 126)

> 'The fire is very cosy here [at Elrond's house], and the food's very good, and there are Elves when you want them. What more could one want?
> The Road goes ever on and on
> Out from the door where it began.
> Now far ahead the Road has gone,
> Let others follow it who can!
> Let them a journey new begin,
> But I at last with weary feet
> Will turn towards the lighted inn,
> My evening-rest and sleep to meet.'
> And as Bilbo murmured the last words his head dropped on his chest and he slept soundly. (LotR 1024)

Or, in the words of Jerome K. Jerome: "Let your boat of life be light, pace with only what you need — a hotel home and simple pleasures, one or two friends, worth the name, someone to love and someone to love you, and a pipe or two, enough to eat and enough to wear, and a little more than enough to drink; for thirst is a dangerous thing" (Jerome 27).

> The Northfarthing barley was so fine that the beer of 1420 malt was long remembered and became a byword. Indeed a generation later one might hear an old gaffer in an inn, after a good pint of well-earned ale, put down his mug with a sigh: 'Ah! That was proper fourteen-twenty, that was!' (LotR 1062)

This — one fruit of the blessings of Galadriel's gift to Sam — is the last entrance of 'inn' and 'beer' in *The Lord of the Rings*...

Conclusion

Two Franciscan friars have wrote down these reflections, 'drinking' in a long tradition of monastic (and especially Franciscan) *sapientia*, which was not dualistic nor avoided to enjoy the goodness of created things, that *unquenchable cheerfulness* which we see clearly in Pippin (810). As a well known rhyme said:

> 'To drink like a Capuchin
> is to drink poorly,
> To drink like a Benedictin
> is to drink deeply,
> To drink like a Dominican
> is pot after pot,
> But to drink like a Franciscan
> is to drink the cellar dry.'
>
> (Dunkling 87; Moulin 93f)

When Arda will be mended and reshaped again, unmarred, at the End of Time — like and unlike the fallen forms that we know —, shall come a-calling to restore all beauty and all pleasure in fellowship, "as brewery-men go round collecting old beer barrels, to fill'em up again" — as the carpenter in *Moby Dick* said (Melville 679; cf. Wood 156-165): a *sacrum convivium* in which physical and spiritual hunger — and thirst — will be no more.

> Before they ate, Faramir and all his men turned and faced west in a moment of silence. Faramir signed to Frodo and Sam that they should do likewise. 'So we always do, 'he said, as he sat down: 'we look toward Númenor that was, and beyond to Elvenhome that is, and to that which is beyond Elvenhome and will ever be.'
>
> (LotR 702f)

The Italian term for *convivium* is *convivere*, which is a twofold notion: to *live*, and *with*. It means to create a communal space, which is inaugurated by a gesture of hospitality that offers nourishment to the other. This gives a glimpse of the *freshness deep down things*, the pleasurable simple things of life. A far-off gleam of everlasting joy. An *aperitif*, tasteful as it is...

But for now, we shall go on, for is time:

'Sam!' he called. 'Sam! Time!'
'Coming, sir!' came the answer from far within, followed soon by Sam himself, wiping his mouth. He had been saying farewell to the beer-barrel in the cellar. (83)

At last Sam turned to Bywater, and so came back up the Hill, as day was ending once more. And he went on, and there was yellow light, and fire within; and the evening meal was ready, and he was expected. (1069)

And so are we...

Bibliography

Alves, Rubem A. *The Poet, The Warrior, The Prophet*. London: SCM Press, 2002
Carpenter, Humphrey. *The Inklings*. London: HarperCollins, 1997
---. Ed. *The Letters of J.R.R. Tolkien*. Boston: Houghton Mifflin, 2000
Chesterton, Gilbert Keith. *Wine, Water and Song*. London: Methuen & Co., 1919
Honegger, Thomas. "Lembas". *J.R.R. Tolkien Encyclopedia. Scholarship and Critical Assessment*. Ed. Michael D.C. Drout. New York/London: Routledge, 2007, 353-354
Dunkling, Leslie. *The Guinness Drinking Companion*. New York: Lyons & Burford, 1995
Duriez, Colin. *Tolkien and C.S. Lewis. The Gift of Friendship*. Mahwah: Hidden Spring, 2003
Haydon, Peter. *Beer and Britannia. An Inebriated History of Britain*. Stroud: Sutton, 2001
Manley Hopkins, Gerald. *La freschezza più cara. Poesie scelte. Testo inglese a fronte, a cura di Antonio Spadaro*. Milano: Biblioteca Universale Rizzoli, 2008
Melville, Herman. *Moby Dick or The Whale*. New York: The Modern Library, 2000
Maluf, David. *Ransom*. London: Chatto & Windus, 2009
Mendez Montoya, Angel F. *The Theology of Food: Eating and the Eucharist*. Chichester: Wiley/Blackwell, 2009
Milhaven, Giles. "Asceticism and the Moral Good: A Tale of Two Pleasures". *Ascetism*. Ed. Vincent Wimbush & Richard Valantasis. Oxford: Oxford University Press, 1998, 375-394
Moulin, Leo. *La vita quotidiana dei monaci nel medioevo*. Milano: Mondadori, 1988
Ramfos, Stelios. *Like a Pelican in the Wilderness. Reflections on the Sayings of the Desert Fathers*. Brookline: Holy Cross Orthodox Press, 2000
Tolkien, J.R.R. *Tree and Leaf*. London: HarperCollins, 1988
---. *The Hobbit*. London: HarperCollins, 1993
---. *The Lord of the Rings*. London: HarperCollins, 1993
---. *Smith of Wootton Major. Extended Edition*. Ed. Verlyn Flieger. London: HarperCollins, 2005
Wood, Ralph C. *The Gospel According to Tolkien. Visions of the Kingdom in Middle-earth*. Westminster: John Knox Press, 2003

Zusammenfassungen der englischen Beiträge

Augustinische und Boethianische Einsichten in Tolkiens Gestaltung von Mittelerde
Annie Birks

Zu den Denkern, die am meisten zum intellektuellen Charakter des Mittelalters beitrugen, gehörten Augustinus von Hippo (354-430) und Boethius (ca. 480-524 od. 525). Einige Tolkienforscher haben bereits den möglichen Einfluss dieser beiden Philosophen und Theologen auf die Schriften des Mediävisten und christlichen Professors J.R.R. Tolkien reflektiert. Dieser Beitrag folgt ihren Überlegungen und versucht, weitere mittelalterliche Untertöne in der Geschichte Mittelerdes zu finden, indem er einen besonderen Akzent auf die vieldiskutierten Fragestellungen der Prädestination, des Vorwissens und freien Willens legt. Zu den möglichen in Betracht gezogenen Hinweisen zählen Visionen, Träume, Prophezeiungen und sogar etymologische Bezüge. Sie werden untersucht mit der Absicht, Licht zu werfen auf diese wesentlichen Fragen, mit denen sich schon Generationen von Gelehrten auseinandergesetzt haben und dies — wenig überraschend — immer noch tun.

Paganismus in Mittelerde
Cécile Cristofari

Viele Forschungen haben sich dem christlichen Element des Werkes Tolkiens gewidmet. Jedoch war Tolkien auch ein Gelehrter, der von altenglischer Literatur und der angelsächsischen Zeit fasziniert war; einer Epoche, von der er in *The Monster and the Critics* schrieb, sie durchlaufe wegen des Übergangs zwischen Heidentum und Christenheit eine Krise. Tatsächlich gibt es vieles in der Geschichte Mittelerdes, wie sie in *The Silmarillion* und *The Lord of the Rings* erzählt wird, das die existentielle Krise einer Welt re-inszeniert (re-enact), die zwischen zwei Religionen, zwei Gesellschaften und zwei Weltsichten gefangen ist.

Es muss festgestellt werden, dass in Mittelerde nicht von einem religiösen System gesprochen werden kann: Der Konflikt zwischen Heidentum und

Christentum muss in den Ereignissen selbst gelesen werden. *The Silmarillion* (es schildert die Hoch-Zeit der Elben und Númenorer) repräsentiert ein mythisches Zeitalter der Helden, das antiken europäischen Mythen wie der *Ilias* vergleichbar ist. In *The Lord of the Rings* jedoch beleben nur noch wenige der Helden der antiken Mythen Mittelerde. Ihr Blut, Garant der Nobilität, ist auf bestimmte Menschen, vor allem Aragorn, übergegangen, die den Glanz der alten Welt in die neue tragen werden. Die Zerstörung des Rings in den passend bezeichneten Schicksalsklüfte zeichnet eine Apokalypse, die eine neue Welt gebiert, in der die Helden gegangen sind, aber ihr Vermächtnis dem neuen König Legitimation verleiht — einem König, der zugleich der Erbe von Mythen und eine Erlösergestalt ist, indem er die Welt vor der Zerstörung bewahrt und Ordnung in der Welt wiederherstellt, während er ein neues Königreich errichtet.

In dieser Welt in der Krise repräsentieren Hobbits die letzten Heiden oder Paganen (etymologisch »Landleute« auf Latein): Sie leben in einer abgeschlossenen Welt, abgeschnitten von den Veränderungen außerhalb, sie verkörpern die Bauern und einfachen Menschen mit engeren Beziehungen zu ihrem Land als zu irgendeiner Religion oder Weltanschauung, das nichtsdestoweniger diesen Veränderungen nicht entgehen kann, und spielen trotz ihrer selbst darin sogar eine Rolle. Die Integration des Auenlandes in die Welt der Menschen und die fortschreitende Assimilierung der Hobbits ist das letzte Stadium des Übergangs vom Paganismus zum Christentum.

Dieser Beirag konzentriert sich auf die religiöse Metaphorik in Tolkiens Werken und wie sie auf seine eigene Analyse des *Beowulf* im angelsächsischen Kontext bezogen werden kann.

Zeit und Tide — Mittelalterliche Interpretationsmuster für das Vergehen der Zeit in Tolkiens Werk

Thomas Honegger

Tolkiens Darstellung von Zeit im *Hobbit* und im *Herrn der Ringe* zeugt von einer grundsätzlich prä-technologischen und vormodernen Sichtweise. Diese wird ergänzt durch die Konzepte der *translatio imperii* und der typologischen Interpretation in ihren jeweils spezifisch mittelalterlichen Ausrichtungen. Es sind diese beiden Elemente, die wesentlich zur Einbindung der Sekundärwelt in einen übergreifenden und strukturierten Gesamtzusammenhang beitragen und damit auch dem modernen Leser ein wenig ›mittelalterliches Lebensgefühl‹ vermitteln.

Das Auge und der Baum.
Die Semantik der Heraldik in Mittelerde
Catalin Hriban

Eine gründliche Studie der literarischen Werke Tolkiens zeigt viele Fälle, in denen das Wappenmotiv oder andere heraldische Elemente verwendet werden, um eine moralische Botschaft zu transportieren, die Charakterisierungen zu verstärken oder bestimmte Momente der Geschichte besser zu illustrieren. Die vorliegende Analyse ist keinesfalls erschöpfend, will aber die Grundlage einer anderen Interpretation der visuellen Sprache Tolkiens legen.

Die Beziehung zwischen der hochformalen Sprache der heraldischen Kunst und Wissenschaft und die nicht weniger hoch imaginative und strukturierte Schöpfung von Tolkiens *legendarium* ist verwickelt. Es können vier Hauptstadien dieser Beziehung ausgemacht werden, die formal durch die Weise bestimmt werden, in der Tolkien heraldische Symbolik und ›Sprache‹ einsetzt.

Die erste zeigt sich in *The Fall of Gondolin*, wo die Embleme der Personen die Hochsprache verstärken und somit den Helden und Antagonisten einen Hauch formalen und geordneten kriegerischen Gepränges verleihen. Die zweite Stufe ist in *The Hobbit* zu finden, wo die formale heraldische Sprache zugunsten eines einfacheren und direkteren Zugangs aufgegeben wird und die Farben der Banner als Mittel dienen, moralische Kategorien auszudrücken und einige ethische Entscheidungen des Autoren (im Einklang mit mittelalterlichen christlichen Werten) zu unterstreichen. Drittens ist die Phase der Aneignung zu nennen, die sich im Dritten Zeitalter des *legendarium* und *The Lord of the Rings* zeigt. Die heraldischen Elemente und Banner werden gemäß des vollen Potentials ihres mittelalterlichen Gebrauchs eingesetzt als vielschichtige Bedeutungspakete, die Charakterisierungen, Atmosphäre, und Geschichte ausdrücken und somit die Geschichte hinter der Narrative verstärken. Das königliche Banner von Aragorn/Elessar ist ein Fenster in die heroische Vergangenheit, eine moralische Erklärung, ein verstärkender Anspruch und eine Herausforderung. Auf einer etwas anderen Ebene identifizieren die zu dieser Phase gehörenden Elemente die Träger in einem Ausmaß, aus dem gefolgert werden kann, die in der Jurisprudenz des Mittelalters und der frühen Renaissance ausgedrückte Konsubstantialität der Wappen mit ihrem Eigentümer sei eine der Bedeutungsebenen, die Tolkien in seiner Geschichte aufgenommen hat. Das vierte Stadium ist schließlich das kreative, in dem die Begrenzung des Vokabulars und der Grammatik der formalen Heraldik sich als unzureichend für Tolkiens mythopoetische Ziele erweist. Wie in seiner kreativen Jugend mit den Elbensprachen, wird eine visuelle und strukturelle Schöpfung unternommen, um schließlich ein eigenständiges heraldisches System als eine visuelle, repräsentationale und genealogische Komponente der Sekundärwelt zu erschaffen.

Tolkiens mythopoetische Transformation der Landschaft: Gruften, Grabhügel und Hügelgräber
Judith Klinger

Gräber sind bedeutsame Schwellen- und Übergangsorte, die im vormodernen Weltbild unterschiedliche Zonen der Realität miteinander verbinden und jenseits der profanen Alltagswelt Andersräume eröffnen, die als ›übernatürliche‹ Orte zugleich dem innersten Kern der Natur entspringen. Der Beitrag befasst sich mit Konstellationen von Grabhügeln, Gräbern und natürlicher Landschaft in Tolkiens Werken, um Bezüge zu mittelalterlichen Denkmustern aufzudecken, die weniger die Rituale des Todes als spezifische Raumkonzepte und -erfahrungen betreffen. Erstens geht es dabei um Herrschafts- und Gedächtnisfunktionen, die königlichen Gräbern zukommen. Zweitens wird die grundsätzliche Opposition von Grabhügel und Gruft in den Blick genommen, deren ganz unterschiedliche Bedeutung sich aus einem gegensätzlichen Verhältnis der Grabstätte zu Natur bzw. Zivilisation erklärt. Im Grabhügel stellt sich idealtypisch eine Konvergenz von Natur und Kultur her, die auf eine der Landschaft eingeschriebene, höhere Ordnung verweist und diese erfahrbar macht. Den eigentlichen Schwerpunkt bilden daher heilige und ›übernatür-liche‹ Orte sowie Tolkiens poetische Strategien, solche dem modernen Denken fremde Räume zu erschließen.

Vor dem Hintergrund mittelalterlicher Texte und Kulturpraktiken hebt sich Tolkiens mythopoetisches Verfahren ab, das Grabstätte, lebendige Natur, Gedächtnis und Stimme zu einem Resonanzraum verbindet, der grenzüberschreitende Erfahrungen ermöglicht. Indem Tolkien solche Andersräume poetisch evoziert, unternimmt er vor dem Horizont postindustrieller Entzauberung eine erneute ›Verzauberung‹ der natürlichen Welt, die an magisch-religiöse Erlebnisweisen der Vormoderne anschließt, diese jedoch aus moderner Perspektive transformiert.

Ist der Tisch bei Elronds Rat rund?
Marguerite Mouton

Es gibt keinen Hinweis, dass es bei Elronds Rat tatsächlich einen Tisch gab. Der Autor nennt nur Sitze und sogar diese können unregelmäßig verteilt gewesen sein: Aragorn sitzt in einer Ecke (233), Sam in einer Ecke auf dem Boden (264) und Boromir etwas abseits (234). Aber der Mangel an Präzision in der allgemeinen Beschreibung regt die Vorstellungskraft des Lesers an, wie bei den Dramatisierungen dieser Szene in Filmen gesehen werden kann. Ralph Bakshis Cartoon bietet 1978 das Bild eines langen, hölzernen und rechteckigen

Tisches an, während Peter Jacksons Film von 2001 einen kleinen, steinernen und oktogonalen Tisch in der Mitte eines Kreises regelmäßig angeordneter Sitze mit einem besonderen Thron für Elrond zeigt.

Leser sind frei, sich die Anordnung des Rates so vorzustellen, wie sie wünschen. Indes gibt es eine große mittelalterliche Tradition von Räten, die um eine runde Tafel herum gehalten werden, und wir kennen Tolkiens (nicht nur) berufliches Interesse an der Literatur dieser Zeit. Warum wurde der Rat dann nicht um eine runde Tafel herum gezeigt? Und sollte er? Um zu bestimmen, ob es aus symbolischer Sicht richtig wäre, die Tafel an Elronds Rat als einen runden Tisch oder nicht zu repräsentieren, ist es interessant zu untersuchen, wie Tolkiens Werk sich zu dieser Tradition verhält, wie die Vorstellung des Autors Aspekte von ihr aufnimmt und teilweise aufspaltet und sie in ein originelles Muster einfügt.

Tolkiens *The Lay of Aotrou and Itroun* — Mittelalterliche englische Literatur und die frühen Stadien der Zweitschöpfung

Rafael J. Pascual/Eduardo Segura

The Lay of Aotrou and Itroun ist ein narratives Gedicht Tolkiens, das bislang relativ wenig Aufmerksamkeit erfahren hat. Es stammt aus einer frühen Zeit seiner Karriere und erzählt die Geschichte eines Ehepaars mit Kinderwunsch, der Zuflucht des Mannes zur Hilfe einer Hexe, damit seine Frau schwanger werde, und des tragischen Endes, das aus der Begegnung mit Magie und Verzweiflung folgt. Die von Tolkien gewählte Form, um eine solche Geschichte zu erzählen, war das mittelalterliche Genre franko-keltischen Ursprungs: die bretonische *Lai*.

Das Ziel dieses Beitrags ist es, das Gedicht im Kontext der mittelalterlichen Literatur zu untersuchen, um zu zeigen, dass *The Lay of Aotrou and Itroun* das englische Äquivalent einer bretonischen *Lai* ist. Wir zeigen ferner, dass Tolkien die bryhtonische Tradition erzeugte, in die er mehr Englisches einarbeitete — vergleichbar dem *Gawain*-Dichter. Als Folge wird dieses Gedicht im Kontext Tolkiens früher Jahre als Autor betrachtet, was es erlaubt, es als einen von seinen ersten Versuchen anzusehen, die verlorene Literatur seines Landes zu rekonstruieren, als die Komposition des *Book of Lost Tales* schon begonnen war. Darüber hinaus wird deutlich, zu welchem Ausmaß solch eine frühe Geschichte dem Tolkien'schen Verständnis einer *fairy tale* entspricht, das er in seinen späteren, reiferen Texten ausformuliert hat.

Beleg und Túrin im Licht der mittelalterlichen Tradition von Freundschaft unter Kriegern

Guglielmo Spirito/Emanuele Rimoli

Die Beziehung zwischen Beleg Cuthalion und Túrin Turambar in *The Children of Húrin* ist ein hervorragendes Beispiel für Freundschaft unter Kriegern. Zusammen mit den gut bekannten Paaren kämpfender Freunde in *The Lord of the Rings*, Legolas & Gimli und Aragorn & Éomer, haben wir in ihnen ein paradigmatisches Beispiel der Freundschaft im Kontext militärischer Exzellenz, wie sie in der mittelalterlichen Tradition gesucht wurde.

Das mittelalterliche Byzanz behielt teilweise wegen des anhaltenden Einflusses der griechischen Kirchenväter wie Gregor von Nazianz eine Wertschätzung der Kriegerfreundschaft, wie sie in der *Ilias* dargestellt ist. Dagegen wurden im lateinischen Westen nicht-homerische Modelle der Freundschaft eingeführt. Durch den Zisterzienser Aelred von Rievaulx und sein Werk *De spiritali amicitia* mit Roland & Oliver und Amis & Amile haben wir perfekte Paare von Kriegerfreunden in Leben und Tod. Es gibt sogar geteilte Grabsteine — graviert mit beiden Schilden und beiden Helmen —, um die Einheit dieser Schwertfreunde auch über den Tod hinaus zu bezeugen.

Mit der Hilfe dieser mittelalterlichen Texte können wir in der Lage sein, in einem tieferen Sinn die Schönheit der Freundschaft unter Kriegern — episch, tragisch oder mit einem glücklichen Ende — zu empfinden, wie sie in Tolkiens Werken präsentiert wird.

Einfache Genüsse in Tolkiens Lyrik: Essen und Trinken und die Tiefe der Dinge

Guglielmo Spirito/Emanuele Rimoli

In *The Lord of the Rings* werden zahlreiche einfache Genüsse beschrieben, die sich auf Essen und Trinken beziehen. Wie zu erwarten, ist dies vor allem ›Hobbitkram‹, wie in *A Drinking Song, The Bath Song, The Man in the Moon, The Rhyme of the Troll* oder *Gollum's Song*.

Wir mögen Gimilis Reaktion in Isengard teilen, nachdem er Merry und Pippin getroffen und sie »feasting and idling — and smoking« aufgefunden hat und sich nach ihren angeblichen »few well-earned comforts« fragt, oder Aragorns Lächeln, als ihm bewusst wird, dass die beiden friedlich im Lager der Uruk-hai Lembas aßen. Wie dem auch sei, wir werden von der Einfachheit und der Tiefe, dem Einblick in die durch die Erzählung evozierte ›inner consistency of reality‹ bewegt.

Zumindest zwei Fragen stellen sich: Warum und wie ist Tolkien so mutig, einfache Freuden eines normalen, weltlichen ›hobbitähnlichen‹ Lebens zu beschreiben? Welchen Ort haben Essen und Trinken in Tolkiens Wahrnehmung von Beziehung, Freundschaft, Abenteuer etc. und somit in der Zweitschöpfung, mit ihrer Verbindung von Poesie und Prosa, und in der Wirklichkeit? Essen ist wichtig, wie Genuss und Freude: »There lives the dearest freshness deep down things« (Gerard Manley Hopkins).

Tolkiens vermiedenes Mittelalter: Tolkien und das Rittertum
Martin G.E. Sternberg

Tolkien wird so oft als ›Wiederentdecker‹ mittelalterlicher Traditionen gepriesen, dass darüber häufig vergessen wird, dass jedenfalls in seiner Jugend das Mittelalter in Großbritannien sehr präsent war. Zentriert war diese Mittelalterrezeption um den Begriff des Rittertums, und sie äußerte sich in unterschiedlichen Formen, von Turnieren bis zum Einfluss auf Verhaltensnormen des täglichen Lebens, vor allem auf den Begriff des Gentleman, so dass man von einer britischen Mythologie des Rittertums sprechen könnte. Tolkien war sich dieses Einflusses auch sehr bewusst, aber seine Haltung zum Rittertum war eher negativ: Im *Homecoming of Beorhtnoth* setzt er Beorhtnoths fatale Ruhmsucht mit Ritterlichkeit gleich, und in seinem Essay über *Sir Gawain and the Green Knight* sieht er in Gawain zwar ein positives Rittertum des Dienstes und der Demut verwirklicht, erkennt aber auch hier eine gefährliche Neigung des Rittertums zum Exzess. Dieser Exzess, gerade im Sinne einer persönlichen Opferbereitschaft, hatte viele Entsprechungen im viktorianischen und edwardianischen Großbritannien.

Im *Silmarillion* und im *Lord of the Rings* scheinen Hinweise auf Ritter und Rittertum bewusst vermieden zu werden, und dies und die Umstände der wenigen Nennungen von Rittern deuten auf einen Konflikt zwischen einer ritterlichen Mythologie der Tat und einer entgegengesetzten Tolkien'schen Mythologie des Ortes hin. Dies zeigt sich etwa im Prinzen von Dol Amroth und in der Figur Aragorns, der weniger als ein Idealbild ritterlicher Tugenden und Fähigkeiten denn als jemand zu sehen ist, der sich als Ranger wie als König durch die Fähigkeit auszeichnet, im und aus dem Lande zu leben. Dieser Konflikt prägt auch *Farmer Giles of Ham*, der Tolkiens Projekt einer »Mythologie für England« auf philologischer Grundlage zudem am besten verwirklicht. *Farmer Giles* erzählt den Ursprungsmythos des Kleinen Königreiches als Rebellion, in der die Ritter des Königs von Farmer Giles im Bündnis mit ihrem archetypischen Feind, dem Drachen, besiegt werden.

Bei der Bewertung von Tolkiens Umgang mit dem Mittelalter sollte also berücksichtigt werden, dass er mit der Zurückweisung des Rittertums ausgerechnet das mittelalterliche Element nicht übernahm, das zu seiner Lebenszeit noch am vitalsten war. Tolkien setzte somit mittelalterliche und mediävalisierende Traditionen des 19. Jh. nicht einfach fort, sondern setzte sich von der dominanten Tradition sogar deutlich ab

Summaries of the German Essays

From Middle-earth to the Middle Ages — There and Back Again
Patrick A. Brückner

On even the most superficial reading of Tolkien's texts, it is easy to imagine Tolkien and the Middle Ages as somehow conjoined. The fact that Tolkien was a philologist makes it even easier. However, when reflecting on systems of periodisation as constructed by literary scholarship, i.e. literary epochs, it becomes evident rather quickly that there is no base for postulating a causal nexus between mediaevalist methods of interpretation and Tolkien's texts. After all, all literary texts by Tolkien are texts of the 20th century. This essay postulates that it is indeed useful to use mediaevalist methods to explore his œuvre. Starting with identifying traces the Middle Ages might have left in his texts, the questioning turns to asking which kind of "Middle Age" one can discover in his writings and how we are to characterise its claim to reality. Another aspect touched upon is where a "Middle Age" as imagined by Tolkien could be found in the various constructions of that epoch by the diverse disciplines of medievalist literary and historical studies. Most important of all, however, this essay probes how his literary œuvre might indeed resist any attempt at such categorisation.

Romantic Longing in the Works of J.R.R. Tolkien
Julian T.M. Eilmann

In this paper, which is based on his study of romantic nostalgia in Tolkien's Middle-earth mythology, Julian Eilmann focuses on another romantic topos in Tolkien's work: romantic longing. On the one hand he takes a close look at Eriol in *The Book of Lost Tales* and makes clear that in context of the romantic tradition this Tolkien protagonist can be understood as a romantic wanderer in Fairy-land. On the other hand he exemplifies that the existential desire and nostalgia of Tolkien's characters (cf. Eilmann, HS 7, *Nostalgie* 106ff) is associated with the sea longing. The sea thus is a central symbol for transcendental longing and nostalgia in Tolkien's cosmos.

Against the backdrop of Romanticism one important scene in *The Book of Lost Tales* is Tolkien's depiction of Eriol looking out of his window on his first evening in the realm of "fairies" (LT I 19). Tolkien's description of the picturesque scenery, the enchanting impression it has on Eriol and especially the dream "full of longing" (ibid.) he has after watching the fairy-like garden are reminiscent of many stereotype situations in novels and poems of the romantic age (cf. ibid. 46). A comparison to Joseph v. Eichendorff's famous poem *Sehnsucht*, which tells of an individual making a marvellous experience looking out his window and hearkening to post horns and songs from far away, illustrates the romantic context of the heart-rending longing that awakes in Eriol. It is interesting that Tolkien in this passage refers to a nightingale, a prominent figure in romantic texts that personifies longing. Tolkien furthermore introduces us to the character of Timpinen, half an elf and half a spirit of nature, whose music "will cause [the listener's] heart to ache unquenchably" (ibid. 95).

The topic of romantic longing, which is in fact an existential longing and homesickness of Men, is in line with Romantic philosophy. In *Athrabeth Finrod ah Andreth* Tolkien presents the idea that Men in Arda suffer from an existential homelessness, so that to them all things in Middle-earth function as "tokens or reminders" (MR 318) of an eternal home. Considering that, the sight of the endless sea is a symbol for the transcendent longing of the mortal. Interestingly, in a discarded epilogue for LotR Tolkien intended the novel to close with the phrase that Sam "heard suddenly, deep and unstilled, the sigh and murmer of the Sea upon the shores of Middle-earth" (SD 128). Remarkably, the topos of romantic longing symbolised in the see would in this version of the book have been present in the very last sentence.

Summaries

Mythology versus History or from Mythology to History?
Thomas Fornet-Ponse

This article deals with the relationship of mythology and history in Tolkien's work since on the one hand he claimed to write a mythology and on the other hand he included many elements which are characteristic for historiography but not for a mythology. The text begins with some remarks on the history of the terms "myth/mythology" and "history" and with pointing out the differences between them — especially the oral character and the remoteness of a myth versus the written character and the nearness of history. This provides the basis for a discussion of Tolkien as historian (especially his use of "Annals" and the intimate relation he sees between myth and history) and of his understanding and use of myths. This shows a clear resemblance to Plato both in their theoretical understanding of myth and their method — both use myths for referring to a primarily historical tradition. Furthermore, both create the background and a culture for their myths and this feigned tradition authenticates the mythology. This explains why Tolkien claimed to reconstruct and not to invent the myths since this is necessary for such an authenticating system. His stress on the tradition of his diverse tales, their historicity, and their carefully constructed authorship also supports this system and is not to be understood as trying to write historiography. Without the mythological elements, Tolkien's tales would rather have been historical novels and would not have satisfied the criteria for Fantasy mentioned in *On Fairy-Stories* — and without the historicising elements they would have been a "written mythology" which is a *contradictio in adiecto*. Thus, it is necessary to combine them and perhaps, Tolkien's art was his skill in finding a balance which contributes to the "inner consistency" of his secondary world.

Reviews/Rezensionen

John Perlich & David Whitt (Eds.): Millenial Mythmaking. Essays on the Power of Science Fiction and Fantasy Literature, Films and Games
Jefferson NC/London: McFarland, 2010, 202 pp.

Katherine A. Fowkes: The Fantasy Film
Chichester: Wiley-Blackwell, 2010, 201 pp.

Axel Melzener: Weltenbauer. Fantastische Szenarien in Literatur, Games und Film
Boizenburg: Verlag Werner Hülsbusch, 2010, 391 S.

Angeführt von Franchise-Unternehmen um Kino-Blockbuster wie *The Lord of the Rings* (2001-2003), *Harry Potter* (2001-2011) und *Pirates of the Caribbean* (2003-2011) haben Fantasy-Formate in der ersten Dekade des neuen Jahrtausends einen selbst schon sagenhaft anmutenden Aufschwung genommen. Auf verschiedenen medialen Plattformen von belletristischer und Comic-Literatur über den Film bis zu TV-Serien und Videospielen erlebt das Genre eine Konjunktur, die es bis ins Zentrum der Unterhaltungsindustrie geführt hat. Ob es sich nun um Kino-Blockbuster, TV-Serien, Computerspiele oder virtuelle Netzwelten handelt: Nahezu ausnahmslos enthalten die weltweit kommerziell erfolgreichsten Produkte der internationalen Medienwirtschaft immer auch fantastische Elemente und lassen sich unter einen weit gefassten Begriff der Fantasy bringen. Umso dringlicher stellt sich die Aufgabe, Ursachen, Verlauf und Folgen dieser Renaissance der medialen Fantasy im Auge zu behalten, nicht zuletzt im Hinblick auf die unkontrollierte Dynamik, mit der der Genrebegriff im medialen Wechsel und den dazugehörigen Rhetoriken von Vermarktung und Rezeption inflationär oszilliert. Unter jeweils ganz unterschiedlichen Vorzeichen stellen sich die drei vorliegenden Bücher dieser Aufgabe.

Die Beiträge zum Sammelband *Millenial Mythmaking* von Perlich und Whitt halten sich dabei kaum einmal bei der Definitionsproblematik des Genrebegriffs auf. Wie der Haupttitel bereits suggeriert, steht im Zentrum des Interesses an neueren Werken der zeitgenössischen Fantasy weniger deren Genreästhetik oder gar -identität als vielmehr der Begriff »Mythos« und die spezifische Verwendung »mythischer« Erzählmuster bzw. die Ausprägung einer »modernen Mythologie« im Rahmen populärer Unterhaltung. Entsprechend weit ist das Spektrum der betrachteten Gegenstände und Themenstellungen gesteckt.

Die erste Sektion »Contrasting Colors« umfasst Untersuchungen zur Farbsymbolik in Joanne K. Rowlings *Harry-Potter*-Romanen (Kirstin Cronn-Mills und Jessica Samens) und zur veränderten Darstellung der Rassenproblematik in *Planet of the Apes* (1968) und dessen Neuverfilmung, die Tim Burton 2001 unternommen hat (Jason Edwards und Brian Klosa). Richard Besel und Renée Smith Besel gehen Aktualisierungen und Umdeutungen der »Wicked Witch of the West« aus L. Frank Baums *The Wonderful Wizard of Oz* (1900) in Victor Flemings Verfilmung aus dem Jahre 1939, vor allem aber in Geoffrey Maguires Roman *Wicked* (1995) und dem aus diesem hervorgegangenen Musical nach, in denen der Mythos von der bösen Hexe gebrochen und psychologisch hinterfragt bzw. performativ aufgelöst wird. Die »New Champions« überschriebene zweite Sektion versammelt Beiträge von Dee Geortz und den beiden Herausgebern, die auf der Folie von Campbells Monomythos neue »Heldenfiguren« auf ihre archetypischen Züge hin überprüfen: Dass es sich hierbei mit der jungen Protagonistin des japanischen Zeichentrickfilms *Chihiros Reise ins Zauberland* (2001), der Großmutter Madame Souza aus der französischen Zeichentrickproduktion *Das große Rennen von Belleville* (2003) und dem Mädchen Ofelia aus *Pans Labyrinth* (2006) um drei weibliche Figuren handelt, mag den Vorlieben der Autoren geschuldet und sicher nicht repräsentativ sein, stellt aber dennoch eine zumindest erwähnenswerte Akzentuierung dar. Die dritte Sektion »No Boundaries« öffnet die bis dahin vornehmlich an Büchern und Filmen entwickelten Perspektiven auf TV- und Webproduktionen hin: Die Wechselwirkungen zwischen Schauspieleridentität, Starimage und Rollenprofil bei der Konstitution neuer »mythischer Helden« diskutiert Djoymi Baker am Beispiel von William Shatner als Captain Kirk und Christopher Ecclestone als Doctor Who. Im Ergebnis ihrer kritischen Analyse der innerhalb der virtuellen Welt zur Anwendung kommenden rhetorischen Muster widerspricht der Beitrag von Ellen Gorsevski der weit verbreiteten Vorstellung von einer vermeintlich befreienden Rolle, die *Second Life* mit Blick auf die Geschlechteridentitäten ihrer Nutzer und deren Avataren spielen soll. Dagegen entwirft Jay Scott Chipman am Beispiel der beiden japanischen Animes *Ghost in the Shell* (1995) und *Ghost in the Shell 2: Man-Machine Interface* (2005) die Konturen einer zukünftigen »cyborg mythology«, deren Norm der hybriden Identität allerdings nur zum Preis eines prinzipiell posthuman orientierten Denkens zu haben ist.

Insgesamt machen die von Perlich und Whitt versammelten Fallstudien eindrücklich auf die thematische Breite und mediale Vielfalt aufmerksam, in denen Fantasy-Stoffe aktuell aufbereitet werden und in der Öffentlichkeit präsent sind. Wie schon im Falle des vom selben Herausgebertandem verantworteten Vorgängerbandes *Sith, Slayers, and Cyborgs: Modern Mythology in* the *New Millenium* (2008) entfernen sich die Studien zu einer »komparativen Mythologieforschung«, in deren Mittelpunkt die Frage nach der aktuellen gesellschaftlichen Funktion mythologischer Formen steht, dabei unweigerlich von der spezifischen Diskussion moderner Fantasy als Genreform und kultureller Tradition. Eine Divergenz, die umso mehr ins Auge springt, als das Tolkien entlehnte Motto »There and Back Again«, das den einleitenden Bemerkungen der Herausgeber ihren Titel gibt, nicht inhaltlich motiviert ist, sondern lediglich noch metaphorisch auf den Umstand zu verweisen hat, dass der mit ihm eingeleitete Band die Fortsetzung eines früheren darstellt.

Weitaus präziser wird der Genrebegriff der Fantasy von Katherine A. Fowkes mit Blick auf seine stilbildenden filmischen Ausprägungen gefasst. In drei Eingangskapiteln diskutiert sie in ihrem Buch, das sich als Einführung in das Filmgenre versteht, zunächst die Definitionsproblematik (Kap. 1: »What's in a Name: Defining the Elusive Fantasy Genre«), liefert einen Abriss der Entwicklung der Fantasy in der Filmgeschichte (Kap. 2: »Once Upon a Time: A Brief Historical Overview«) und trifft in Form eines Forschungsüberblicks zentrale Unterscheidungen zwischen literarischer und filmischer Fantasy auf der einen, Science Fiction und Horror auf der anderen Seite (Kap. 3: »A Brief Critical Overview: Literary and Film Fantasy, Science Fiction and Horror«). Zum zentralen Kennzeichen des Genres erhebt sie das Moment eines »ontologischen Bruchs«, der vom Zuschauer bewusst als integraler Bestandteil des fiktionalen Universums wahrgenommen wird. Ihm nachgeordnet werden weitere Charakteristika wie die Verwendung von Magie anstelle von physikalischer Kausalität, körperliche Transformationen und Elemente des Fliegens. Generell dient Fowkes die — nicht zuletzt im Anschluss an poetologische Überlegungen Tolkiens entwickelte — Triade von »recovery, escape and consolation«, d.h. die hoffnungsstiftende Funktion des Genres und dessen unhintergehbare Mehrdeutigkeit, als wirkungsästhetisches Bestimmungsmerkmale des Fantasy-Films gegenüber der Science Fiction und dem Horrorgenre.

Das in den ersten drei Kapiteln konzise und kenntnisreich ausgearbeitete Genremodell wird anschließend an einem (wie die Autorin selbst zugibt) eher eklektisch zusammengestellten Korpus von insgesamt zehn Fallstudien exemplifiziert, denen je ein eigenes Kapitel gewidmet ist. Das Spektrum reicht von *The Wizard of Oz* (1939), über *Harvey* (1950), *Always* (1989), *Groundhog Day* (1993), *Big* (1988), *Shrek* (2001) und *Spider-Man* (2002) bis zu Peter Jacksons *The Lord of the Rings*, Disneys *The Chronicles of Narnia* (2005) und den *Harry-Potter*-Filmen 1-6 (2001-2009). Während es Fowkes in den meisten Fällen mitunter auf bestechend überraschende Weise gelingt, die Fantasy-Elemente mithilfe ihres Analyseinstrumentariums an Filmbeispielen herauszupräparieren, in denen sie auf den ersten Blick eher marginal oder sekundär anmuten, fällt die abschließende, weitgehend auf Produktionsdetails, Rekapitulationen der Erzählverläufe und einzelne Szenenbeschreibungen beschränkte Diskussion der drei modernen Klassiker des Genres doch eher enttäuschend aus. Der interpretative Ansatz reduziert sich hier auf eine eher pauschal angebrachte Ideologiekritik, die sich im gleichen Maße vom eigenen theoretischen Zugang zum Genre entfernt wie sie sich an sattsam bekannte filmkritische Topoi aus dem breiten Presseecho anlehnt.

Dies wirft die Frage auf, warum der Autorin ausgerechnet zu den wichtigsten jüngeren Beiträgen zur filmischen High Fantasy so wenig eingefallen ist. Ein Grund mag darin bestehen, dass sie zumindest Tolkien und C.S. Lewis, die ihrer theoretischen Fassung des Genres so deutlich Pate gestanden haben, vor der kommerziellen Medienverwertung und gesellschaftspolitischen Indienstnahme ihrer Werke und Ideen vor dem Hintergrund von 9/11, Irakkrieg und dem »War against Terror« in Schutz nehmen zu müssen glaubt. Das ist an sich legitim, es lässt sich aber nur im Modus jener konsequenten Allegorisierung der dargestellten fantastischen Welten betreiben, die nicht nur einer Grundüberzeugung Tolkiens zuwiderläuft, sondern auch quer steht zu dem eingangs von Fowkes so schlüssig hergeleiteten ästhetischen Bedingungsgefüge des Genres.

Auf gewisse Weise lässt sich in der Wendung, die Fowkes' Buch in seinen letzten drei Kapiteln nimmt, nicht zuletzt jene Spannung zwischen »Fluch und Segen« von Tolkiens überragender Hinterlassenschaft erkennen, die Axel Melzener zum Angelpunkt seiner Darstellung fantastischer Szenarien in Literatur, Games und Film macht. Ein Segen sei Tolkiens Erbe in seinem enzyklopädischen Reichtum und seiner nahezu unerschöpflichen Inspirationskraft. Sein Fluch bestehe allerdings darin, dass sich die nachfolgenden Autoren, Filmemacher und Game-Designer bis heute nicht von den Tolkien'schen Fantasy-Konventionen hätten emanzipieren können. Dies sei, so Melzener, jedoch notwendig, um das Genre immer wieder zeitgemäß erneuern und seine Zukunft sichern zu können (S. 135). Melzeners Buch, das lediglich populärwissenschaftliche Ansprüche erhebt, gliedert sich um den Angelpunkt Tolkien grob in zwei Teile: Die erste Hälfte bietet einen ausführlichen historischen Abriss der Fantasy von ihren Ursprüngen in Legenden, Mythen und Märchen bis in die unmittelbare Gegenwart. Lesenswert ist die Darstellung vor allem dort, wo sie von der intimen Kenntnis des Autors auf dem Gebiet der historischen Entwicklung von Rollen- und Computerspielen profitiert, die sich bisher (zumindest im deutschsprachigen Raum) für das Fantasy-Genre wohl nirgends sonst derart detailliert nachvollziehen lässt. Zahlreiche Einzelporträts von wichtigen Repräsentanten der modernen Fantasy (vor allem Tolkien, aber auch C.S. Lewis, Marion Zimmer Bradley, George Lucas, Richard Garriot) sind in den Verlauf der Darstellung der »Geschichte des Genres« und seiner »Konventionen und Motive« eingestreut.

Ziel des zweiten Teils des Buches sollte es eigentlich sein, entlang unterschiedlich gelagerter Konstruktionsebenen von fantastischen Welten (Tonalität; materielle, soziale, geistige Welt; Magie) Wege aufzuzeigen, auf denen die angesprochene Emanzipation von Tolkien zu geschehen hätte. Dies gelingt Melzener nicht zuletzt deshalb nur sehr bedingt, weil er seine durchaus originelle und in sich schlüssige Typologie und Topologie des Genres eher als letztlich deckungsgleichen Parallelentwurf zu existierenden Konzepten (etwa denen Tolkiens) entwickelt und weniger als Anleitung zur konsequenten Überwindung etablierter Konventionen. Dennoch ist Melzeners Versuch einer integralen, medienübergreifenden Darstellung des Fantasy-Genres von allen hier rezensierten derjenige, der sich der eingangs angesprochenen Aufgabe so entschlossen wie kein anderer stellt. Michael Wedel

Fastitocalon.
Studies in Fantasticism Ancient to Modern. Vol I-2 (2010). Immortals and the Undead.
Trier: WVT, 2010, 110 pp.

Mit dieser Ausgabe liegt der zweite Teil des ersten Jahrgangs der in 2010 von Thomas Honegger und Fanfan Chen gegründeten Zeitschrift für Phantastik *Fastitocalon* vor, der dem Thema »Unsterbliche und Untote« gewidmet ist. Wie der erste Teil, so zeichnet sich auch dieser durch eine große Bandbreite — synchron wie diachron — berücksichtigter Texte aus, reichen diese doch vom Mittelalter bis in die Gegenwart und von Conan Doyle zu Pratchett. Die Herausgeber verweisen in ihrem Vorwort völlig berechtigt darauf, dass die hier vorliegenden Beiträge diejenigen des ersten Teils fortführen (in einem Fall ist es eine tatsächliche Fortsetzung) und ergänzen, insofern ähnliche Fragestellungen aufgegriffen werden.

So behandelt der erste Artikel von Bruce Wyse anhand von Bulwer-Lyttons *A Strange Story* die Frage einer unmoralischen Unsterblichkeit, da die Seele des Protagonisten dessen Versuch einer Erneuerung seines Lebens nicht begleitet, und berührt dabei vor allem die metaphysische Frage, wie ein solches Leben des Körpers ohne die Seele aussähe. Einer ähnlichen Frage, allerdings in breiterem Kontext, wenden sich Roger Bozzetto und Fanfan Chen zu, nämlich der Entwicklung der Suche nach Unsterblichkeit in Science Fiction und Fantasy. Hierzu stellen sie auf der Grundlage kulturanthropologischer Ausführungen die Neuartigkeit der Unsterblichkeit in der Science Fiction heraus und führen dies anhand der über Transplantation und Klonen angestrebten organischen Unsterblichkeit sowie der posthumanen Unsterblichkeit (Cyborgs) aus.

Einem gänzlich anderen Thema widmet sich Anna Caiozzo: den Darstellungen von Unsterblichen in mittelalterlichen orientalischen Manuskripten, d.h. schlafenden Helden, dem Propheten und dem Messias, Khadir und Ilyas. Sie betont dabei den eschatologischen Charakter und weist auf die symbolische

Geographie und Topographie hin sowie auf den Zusammenhang von Geographie und Heiligung. Mit den Untoten bei Terry Pratchett setzt sich Thomas Scholz mit einem noch lebenden Autor auseinander, wobei er das von Koestler vorgeschlagene Konzept der Bisoziation heranzieht, um deren humoristischen Effekt zu erklären. Daher führt er zahlreiche Beispiele an, in denen zwei mögliche, aber miteinander inkompatible Referenzrahmen aufeinanderstoßen, von denen meistens einer allgemeinen Charakters ist, während der andere von Pratchett etabliert wurde. Es schließt sich die Fortsetzung des Beitrags von Eugenio M. Olivares Merino über Wiedergänger und Vampire in der englischen Literatur des 12. Jahrhunderts an. Diesmal bespricht er die *Historia rerum anglicarum* und *De Nugis Curialium*. In der Zusammenfassung seines gesamten Artikels kann er einige allgemeine Aspekte nennen wie den definitionsgemäß bösen Charakter der Wiedergänger, die hohe Bedeutung nordischer paganer Glaubensüberzeugungen oder den Unterschied zwischen der kultivierten Ebene des kirchlichen Erzählers und der populären der Zeugen bzw. Opfer. Im letzten Beitrag behandelt Robert Eighteen-Bisang ausgehend von der Bekanntschaft zwischen Arthur Conan Doyle und Bram Stoker die Parallelen und Ähnlichkeiten zwischen *Dracula* und *The Adventure of the Illustrious Client* und sieht Conan Doyles Text als eine Transformation der makabren »fairy tale into a rationalized detective story« (185) an.

Neben den Artikeln enthält die Ausgabe zwei Notes von Douglas Anderson: zum einen wiederum eine über vernachlässigte phantastische Autoren, zum anderen kritisch über die These von M.R. James über eine Vorlage für Bram Stokers *Dracula*.

Der positive Eindruck der ersten Ausgabe von *Fastitocalon* wird in diesem zweiten Teil bestätigt. Gerade die Berücksichtigung so unterschiedlicher Texte und Fragestellungen aus verschiedenen Epochen trägt sehr zum überzeugenden Konzept bei — es dürfte wohl niemanden geben, der nicht irgendetwas Neues bei der Lektüre (kennen) lernt.

Thomas Fornet-Ponse

Tolkien Studies. An Annual Scholarly Review. Vol VII. 2010
Morgantown: West Virginia University Press, 401 pp.

The seventh volume of *Tolkien Studies*, the most substantial to date, offers no less than ten articles plus one shorter note, and a significant piece of Tolkien's early creative writing, *The Story of Kullervo* together with his two essays on the *Kalevala*.

The first article, by Vladimir Brljak, investigates the relationship between the main stories and their extensive paratext. Whereas Shippey and Flieger see the

Prologue and Appendices of *The Lord of the Rings* as a means of gaining depth and verisimilitude, Brljak argues that, since it cannot be definitively established where in the fictional chain of transmission the journal of Bilbo and Frodo was turned into novelistic form, the paratext can be seen as a postmodern distancing mechanism which undermines the authenticity at the same time as it creates it. With reference to Borges, he attempts to invert the accepted reading by regarding the main story as a comment on its narrative frame. This ingenious reasoning undoubtedly works on the level of critical theory, although a comparison with the *Letters* forces the reader to conclude that according to this interpretation Tolkien must have been a very poor reader of his own work!

Péter Kristóf Makai and Michael Milburn both interrogate Tolkien's conception of fantasy. Makai argues that if Tolkien's impact on fantasy is so fundamental, then the theorisation of virtual reality should reflect his ideas as formulated in *On Fairy-Stories*, while computer games should constitute a realisation of "Faërian Drama" which will in turn feed back into more expressive and immersive kinds of stories. The case is hard to make decisively, since a number of variables are involved in the comparison, and the set of variables is not necessarily the same in both media. He also relies on an interpretation of *imagination* and *fantasy* which owes more to dictionary definitions than to the historical debate in literary studies. Milburn addresses specifically this problem of definition, how Tolkien differs from Coleridge, and what exactly he meant by Faërie. To throw new light on the question he considers the drafts of FS edited by Flieger and Anderson, reaching the conclusion that the differences are more real than apparent because Tolkien may have confused varying definitions of *imagination*. Milburn's argument is more focused and cogent than Makai's but both run into difficulties because they fail to take into account the highly allusive and metaphorical mode of expression that Tolkien used in FS, sometimes disingenuously presenting fairies or elves as real, and sometime treating them in a more symbolic manner. This is an aspect of the essay which is all too often glossed over and therefore deserves further study.

In an in-depth review of Tolkien's writings on the subject, Thomas Fornet-Ponse rebuts Verlyn Flieger's claim that only Men and not Elves have free will. Although his argument is convincing, it raises the methodological question of whether all Tolkien's posthumously published writings can be considered to be equally authoritative or whether they represent a progression in his ideas, with some concepts being left behind in favour of others. I would have welcomed a dating of the documents as far as that is possible, and a more explicit critical evaluation of any differences or even contradictions. The quality of argumentation is high, but the text contains a small number of Germanisms which slightly held up this reader's comprehension on occasions and which should have been emended by some sympathetic editing.

There follow three articles concerned with medieval sources and analogues. Mary R. Bowman, in a comparison of Tolkien's depictions of heroic behaviour with those of Old English poetry, once again rehearses Byrhtnoth's conduct at the Battle of Maldon, but also goes on to examine the motives of the subordinate warriors left behind after their leader's death. The most convincing of her comparisons with bravery in LotR is the example of Sam at Cirith Ungol, who rejects his immediate emotions of despair and defiance in favour of a choice that will be of most benefit to the rest of humanity.

Thomas Honegger attempts to correct the inaccurate suggestion that Tolkienian fantasy is derived from medieval romance in general. With a conciseness which might be recommended to other writers he suggests that Tolkien had a specific Middle English romance in mind: he proposes *Sir Orfeo* not just as a source of the scenes involving the Wood Elves in *The Hobbit*, but also as an exemplar of the characteristics of fantasy suggested by Tolkien in FS. It offers "escape" for Orfeo from his familiar world and "recovery" of his long-lost wife, while in a final eucatastrophe he is returned to his throne and full happiness.

The following two articles leave more questions open. Sherrylyn Branchaw, following up the still relatively unexplored Classical influences on Tolkien's writing, suggests that the sons of Elrond reflect Indo-European heavenly twin myths, in particular the Greek Castor and Polydeuces. Her argument is attractive on the surface, although on closer examination the resemblances are more apparent than real, which is not surprising considering that the pair were introduced at a fairly late stage of the composition (TI 274) and seem to have been written in retrospectively as little more than shadowy presences on the margins. The argument that Tolkien intended them to represent sons of a sky god will not hold water, since Tolkien's interpretation of the name Elrond varies too much to be relied on. The definition in S as a kenning for "sky" which Branchaw relies on comes from the Etymologies of c. 1936-8 (LR 345) and is followed over the next 30 years by two contradictory interpretations (L 282 and PM 371). The most likely explanation is that the name was coined for its similarity to Elwing, Elboron, Elbereth, etc., and continued as a given for which interpretations were invented on an *ad hoc* basis.

Yoko Hemmi's exploration of Tolkien's concept of "native language" attempts to elucidate this unusual aspect of his linguistic thought incorporated in the lecture "English and Welsh", and in particular to trace whether what is introduced as a Primary World phenomenon can also be identified in the literary Secondary World. Unfortunately, she becomes bogged down in trying to prove the unprovable, such as whether Sam's spontaneous verse in Sindarin in Cirith Ungol represents a subconscious "native language" of Middle-earth, or if there can be such a thing as an "indigenous" language of Middle-earth based upon Tolkien's many disparate accounts of Elvish languages, while unaccountably failing to mention what Treebeard says on the origins and transmission of language. It is also unfortunate that much of the first section, on Tolkien's debt to Welsh, has been largely superseded by the considerably more detailed book-length treatment by Carl Phelpstead, which was published not long after the article appeared.[1]

Margaret Sinex compares elements in Tolkien's descriptions of the Haradrim with a process of "othering" to be found in Classical and medieval texts. Ptolemy of Alexandria, for example, suggests that not only the physical appearance but even the savage customs of so-called barbarians is determined by the climate in which they live. Such ideas were carried over into the medieval period to create stereotypical images of Jews and Muslims. Sinex points out that Tolkien's depiction is much more differentiated and therefore does not deserve the simplistic charges of racism that have sometimes been levelled against his writing.

Finally, Kristine Larsen attempts to identify some untranslated names of stars and constellations from their characteristics in Tolkien's astronomical myths. Based on the appearance of the night sky from where Tolkien lived, she argues convincingly that Telumendil and Anarríma represent Boötes and Sagittarius respectively, and corroborates Christopher Tolkien's opinion that, in spite of an unresolved ambiguity in the drafts concerning the star's apparent movement, Morwinyon is to be understood as Arcturus.

In the section "Notes and Documents" there is a short biographical note by John Garth conclusively identifying the little boy who poured scorn on the young Tolkien's suggestion of flower fairies as Hugh Cary Gilson, the step-brother of his friend Robert Quilter Gilson, son of the headmaster of King Edward's School. However, the greatest part of this section is taken up with the first publication of Tolkien's *The Story of Kullervo* and his two essays on the *Kalevala*, edited by Verlyn Flieger. The former is a significant addition to the Tolkien canon, in spite of its brief and fragmentary nature, since it reveals some of his thought processes at the very beginnings of his creative writing, and really deserves a complete review devoted to this alone. In the three and a half pages of introduction Flieger limits herself to explaining the background against which the pieces were written, together with her clear and straightforward principles for editing, although she offers a small amount of interpretation, particularly of names, in the notes which follow the texts.

The Story of Kullervo shows the young Tolkien attempting to make one coherent story out of what were clearly two different versions in Lönnrot's compilation, one in which the hero's family are killed and one in which they are still alive. The choices that he makes already foreshadow some of the incidents in the later tales of Túrin, such as the destruction of Brodda's hall

---

1   Phelpstead, Carl. *Tolkien and Wales: Language, Literature and Identity*. Cardiff: University of Wales Press, 2011. Cf. the review by Thomas Honegger in this volume.

partly as an act of revenge, but also partly as a result of his own embittered and guilt-ridden personality. The dog Musti, who is only briefly mentioned in the *Kalevala*, here plays a more significant part and can be seen as foreshadowing the role of Huan in the Beren and Lúthien story. A striking development is the tendency to experiment with names, changing them from their original Finnish forms to completely new ones that seem to belong more to the earliest forms of Q(u)enya, so that gradually something like an independent story begins to emerge. A detailed analysis of what Tolkien did with his source is clearly a research priority. As regards form, it would be interesting to plot where the wording closely follows Kirby's formulations and where it departs markedly from them. Tolkien played down his knowledge of Finnish, but his remarks in the essays on the difference in the feel of the metre between source text and target text, together with several derogatory remarks about Kirby's translation, makes one wonder whether he was already using translation as a form of text criticism, as he would do later with his translations from Middle English.

The essays are well worth reading for Tolkien's views on the "primitive undergrowth" (248) of mythology at this stage in his career, as well as for his brash dismissal of Longfellow, a significant contributor to 19th-century medievalism, as "a mild and rather dull American don" (272).

The volume concludes with 107 pages of the usual book reviews, "Year's Work in Tolkien Studies 2007" and a bibliography for 2008. There is no space here to review reviews, but Tom Shippey's 24-page review of Tolkien's *The Legend of Sigurd and Gudrún* makes a significant contribution to scholarship on this unusual and compelling work which is neither a translation nor an original composition — like *The Story of Kullervo* only so much more so. Allan Turner

Liam Campbell: The Ecological Augury in the Works of J.R.R. Tolkien
Zurich/Jena: Walking Tree Publishers, 2011, 305 pp.

Liam Campbell's study is the latest contribution to the same emerging tradition of eco-critical inquiry into Tolkien's works that has already brought forth seminal texts like Patrick Curry's *Defending Middle-earth* or, more recently, *Ents, Elves and Eriador* by Matthew Dickerson and Jonathan Evans. As its title suggests, Campbell's book considers a variety of different works by Tolkien, though admittedly there is a particular focus on *The Lord of the Rings*, and it aims at showing up a systematic and consistent undercurrent of ecological themes and motifs within these works, thus exposing them as a form of ecological augury.

Reasonably, Campbell relies on the results of his eco-critical predecessors and does not start from scratch, but he also dares to explore new territory and addresses difficult issues that have puzzled generations of Tolkien critics. Some of the results of these explorations must surely be considered controversial, but that does not make Campbell's book less interesting.

Having outlined the objectives of his study in a short introduction, the author sets out to examine Tolkien's personal views on nature and technology, referring both to Tolkien's letters and personal details of his life, but sometimes also to recurring motifs from his literary works. Campbell's theoretical underpinnings, which are not stated explicitly but seem to be a combination of biographical, new historical and text-centred approaches, must be considered typical of eco-critical studies and require a little getting used to.

The next two chapters are devoted to showing how Tolkien's views on nature are mirrored in *The Lord of the Rings* and focus on what Campbell calls "cultures of opposition", i.e. pairs of contrasting characters who serve as (positive or negative) moral templates for the reader. Though Campbell's choice of character pairs seems debatable, his analysis leads to interesting results and, by the way, offers some quite remarkable propositions concerning the literary function of Tom Bombadil — a topic which has haunted Tolkien Criticism for ages.

Chapter four explores the importance of the non-human in Tolkien's writings, approaching the matter from a variety of different perspectives and relating Tolkien's works, among other things, to the theology of St. Francis, to Celtic mythology and to the eco-critical theories by Joseph Meeker and Don Elgin.

The final chapter places Tolkien within an eco-critical context, offering a comparison between *The Lord of the Rings* and Rachel Carson's *A Fable for Tomorrow*, examining the hobbits as manifestations of the English pastoral tradition and finally referring to Tolkien's ideas on fantasy and the writing process, laid out in his famous essay *On Fairy-Stories*.

In spite of its easily comprehensible language, Campbell's book is clearly not intended as an introduction to Tolkien Studies, nor, for that matter, does it qualify as an introduction to eco-critical Tolkien Studies, owing to its focus on detail. Rather, it should be considered an exciting read for experts, providing them — in addition to a multitude of well-established ideas — with some new and inspiring insights into Tolkien's works.

Though generally very reasonable and meticulously researched, there are certain aspects of Campbell's analysis that some readers will presumably find hard to agree with. For example, it seems fairly self-evident that Frodo's hiking song in which he mentions that "all woods there be must end at last" does not, as Campbell suggests, anticipate the dying of the woods, but rather expresses

Frodo's hope of finally reaching the edge of the scary Old Forest. Similarly, and in spite of all the evidence provided by Campbell, one might argue that the most obvious contrast character for Saruman is not Tom Bombadil, but rather Gandalf who takes Saruman's place as the leader of the White Council and who later claims: "Indeed I am Saruman... Saruman as he should have been."

All in all, Campbell's book remains an entertaining and informative study with a number of new and inspiring ideas, some of which might be considered controversial and in need of refinement. However, isn't that what many Tolkien scholars have been longing for?   Eike Kehr

Paul Kerry (Ed.): The Ring and the Cross. Christianity and *The Lord of the Rings*
Madison/Teaneck: Fairleigh Dickinson University Press, 2011, 310 pp.

Das Anliegen des vorliegenden Bandes ist es, einen differenzierten Beitrag zur Frage des christliches Einflusses auf Tolkiens Werk zu leisten, indem zum einen ein chronologischer und thematischer Überblick über die Hauptargumente gegeben wird und zum anderen die verschiedenen Standpunkte deutlich werden.

Dementsprechend beginnt das Buch mit der ausführlichen Einleitung Paul Kerrys, die dem genannten Überblick dient und in einer beeindruckenden Materialfülle die unterschiedlichen Forschungsmeinungen zu Themen wie den Fragen, woher die Moralität in *The Lord of the Rings* stammt oder wie sich Tolkiens Verständnis als Christ und der oft behauptete moderne Charakter des Werkes zueinander verhalten, dem Guten und Bösen und der Willensfreiheit, dem Vergleich mit dem *Beowulf*-Autor, christlichen Verweisen, Zweitschöpfung und Eukatastrophe, aber auch spezifisch römisch-katholische Interpretationen vorstellt.

Die anschließenden Beiträge sind in zwei Teilen angeordnet: Der erste Teil »The Ring« verhält sich eher kritisch gegenüber dem behaupteten christlichen Charakter des Werkes Tolkiens und stellt vor allem die Bezüge zur nordischen Mythologie heraus; im zweiten Teil »The Cross« werden die christlichen Bezüge betont.

Den Anfang macht ein Wiederabdruck eines Beitrages von Ronald Hutton, der für einen »paganen Tolkien« plädiert, insofern dessen Mythologie in beträchtlichem Umfang nichtchristliche Elemente enthalte, die zum Wesen seines Werkes und daher auch zu seinem gehören, ohne damit dessen Selbstverständnis als gläubiger Christ infrage stellen zu wollen. Gegen diese These argumentiert Nils Ivar Agøy in seiner Replik, die auf methodische Mängel der Argumentation Huttons abhebt, aber auch einige Aspekte der inhaltlichen Kritik aufzunehmen sucht und letztlich zu einem vernichtenden Urteil der Plausibilität der These Huttons gelangt. Wie die sich anschließende Antwort Huttons auf Agøys Kritik zeigt, kann dieser zwar einigen Argumenten zustimmen, sieht aber seine Kritik nicht im Kern getroffen und bleibt bei seiner Grundüberzeugung: »that the mythology that Tolkien composed and reworked between the 1910s and the 1930s was based on a creation myth that is drawn principally from Christian sources. I also think that, once the products of that creation hit the earth, we are in what is in most respects a pagan world, based on clear ancient pagan antecedents, in which the remaining action — the vast majority of the cycle of stories — is set« (104).

In eine ähnliche Kerbe schlägt Stephen Morillo, der sich auf die Spiritualität in LotR und *Silmarillion* konzentriert und wegen der Betonung des Niedergangs, des Verlusts und des Schicksals diese als nicht spezifisch christlich auszuweisen sucht. Vielmehr plädiert er dafür »that a combination of the Norse paganism that he studied and the peculiar medievalism of Tolkien's own imagination produced a spiritual sensibility in his works that is not notably Christian, a sensibility focused on loss, pervaded by sadness, and haunted by the inevitability of fate, and in which redemption plays little role« (106).

Sehr stark etymologisch orientiert ist der Beitrag von John R. Holmes, der sich, ausgehend von dem Vergleich Denethors, sie würden wie die heidnischen Könige brennen, anhand des verwendeten Vokabulars der Frage nach dem christlichen oder heidnischen Charakter des Werkes widmet, insofern Wörter als Palimpseste — als wiederverwendete Pergamente, bei denen neue Texte über ältere geschrieben werden — verstanden werden können. Als Ergebnis hält er eine Pattsituation zwischen der christlichen und der säkularen Sicht fest.

In einem kurzen Artikel wirft Ralph C. Wood einen Blick auf *The Children of Húrin*, worin er die Verbindung von Zufall und Notwendigkeit herausstellt und gegen eine göttliche Monokausalität genauso argumentiert wie gegen eine völlige Ablehnung einer Teleologie.

Anschließend wendet sich Catherine Madsen auf der Basis ihrer früheren Argumentation für eine »natürliche Religion« bei Tolkien der Frage nach der minimalistischen Kosmologie in LotR hin, insofern dort Eru im Unterschied zu *The Silmarillion* keine Erwähnung findet und die Abwesenheit religiöser Verweise als großen Vorteil betont, da diese Lesern erlaubt, »some of whom would ordinarily be at odds, common imaginative access to a serious tale of danger and wonder and sacrifice« (167).

Im sehr knappen letzten Beitrag des ersten Teils leitet Chris Mooney zum zweiten Teil über, indem er auf einige Äußerungen über die Christlichkeit des Tolkien'schen Werkes eingeht und diesen säkulare Positionen gegenüberstellt.

Der zweite Teil beginnt mit einem Artikel von Carson L. Holloway zu Tolkiens Verständnis der Zweitschöpfung, ihrer Beziehung zur menschlichen Natur, ihren Gefahren sowie ihrem Verhältnis zur Kontemplation und Erlösung. Wenngleich Tolkiens Überlegungen möglicherweise nicht unmittelbar als katholisch zu erkennen seien, seien sie nichtsdestoweniger kompatibel mit katholischen Glaubensüberzeugungen, wie der Autor mit einem Verweis auf eine Enzyklika Johannes Pauls II. deutlich macht.

Es folgt ein Beitrag von Jason Boffetti, der sich nicht nur auf die Mythologie, sondern auch auf die theoretischen Schriften Tolkiens bezieht und einen starken Einfluss seines Glaubens ausmacht, ohne seiner Zweitschöpfung durch explizit christliche Bezüge Gewalt anzutun, womit er Mittelerde als »the fruit of his Catholic vocation to know and live the ›Truth,‹ one that permeated every aspect of his life« (204) verstehen kann.

Michael Tomko untersucht Tolkiens Geschichtsverständnis — mit den Aspekten der langen Niederlage, der starken Präsenz von Ruinen und Verlust, aber auch der Wiederbelebung — und sieht dabei deutliche Parallelen zu Frederick Faber und Newman oder anderen englischen Katholiken. Die das Werk durchziehende »›blessed sadness‹ of this countersecular art does not conform to the age's temporal seductions of triumph, empire, or acquisition, but its cultural engagement still looks persistently to transform the age through acts of faith, hope, and love« (222).

Ebenfalls den katholischen Charakter Tolkiens betont Pearce, wenn er sich dem Platz und der Rolle des Individuums innerhalb einer Gemeinschaft im LotR zuwendet und dabei klare Einflüsse durch die katholische Soziallehre ausmacht.

Nachdem er in der Einleitung die verschiedenen christlichen Deutungen Tolkiens vorgestellt hat, konzentriert sich Kerry in dem nun folgenden Beitrag auf den katholischen Einfluss, wobei er auch die methodologische Frage nach der Nachweisbarkeit eines Einflusses berücksichtigt.

Marjorie Burns widmet sich in ihrem Aufsatz Frauen in einer eher religiösen Funktion, nämlich in ihrer Rolle als heiligmäßige und entfernte Mütter, die idealtypisch in der Alten Prinzessin in zwei Büchern MacDonalds behandelt werden. Diese wird mit verschiedenen der in Tolkiens Werk präsenten Frauen — besonders Varda, Galadriel und Éowyn — verglichen, wobei Burns deutlich macht, dass die Rolle der Kriegerin bei Tolkien nicht vollständig verschwindet.

Schließlich verbindet Bradley J. Birzer in seinem Beitrag die beiden Grundperspektiven des vorliegenden Buches, also die nordische Mythologie und das Christentum. Er plädiert u.a. anhand der als johanninisches Ragnarök gedeuteten letzten Schlacht dafür, dass Tolkien sich im Laufe seines Lebens vom Nationalisten zum Universalisten entwickelt habe, da seine »love of Catholic Christendom and a Johannine understanding of the divine economy incorporated and sanctified Tolkien's idyllic attachment toward Anglo-Saxon England« (259).

Zwischen den verschiedenen Beiträgen des Bandes können neben den intendierten und sehr willkommenen Unterschieden in der Deutung auch Unterschiede im Argumentationsniveau — was teilweise lediglich durch die Länge bedingt sein mag — oder im Umfang der konsultierten Sekundärliteratur ausgemacht werden, ohne dass ein Beitrag »durchfällt«. Nichtsdestoweniger ist dies ein lesenswertes Buch, da die Leserin ein sehr vielschichtiges Bild hinsichtlich der Frage nach dem paganen oder dem christlichen Charakter des Tolkien'schen Werkes erhält, das gut als Sowohl-als-auch charakterisiert werden kann. Es ist somit gut geeignet, Instrumentalisierungen — seien es christliche oder säkulare — als dem Werk nicht gerecht werdend auszuweisen.

Thomas Fornet-Ponse

Jason Fisher, Ed.: Tolkien and the Study of his Sources
Jefferson NC/London: McFarland, 2011, 228 pp.

This is a collection of articles on Tolkien's literary sources which nails its colours to the mast. Numerous writers in the past have claimed to know where he found, borrowed, or even purloined motifs and words in his tales; others have been content to suggest a more indirect influence. This publication, under the competent conceptual guidance of Jason Fisher, attempts not only to collect together a well-matched set of studies, but above all to place them within a reasoned model of source criticism.

One problem that any study of this kind has to tackle is Tolkien's well-documented antipathy towards research based upon the person of the author. The first two articles, by E.L. Risden and Jason Fisher respectively, present the theoretical kernel of the collection. They form a complementary pair giving a justification for source criticism, the first on a general level and the second with reference specifically to Tolkien.

Risden cites Harold Bloom's *The Anxiety of Influence* to show how writers cannot avoid the influence of what has been done by their predecessors, but must react either by incorporating and transforming it or by reacting against it, which is a good enough starting point. Unaccountably, though, his argument strays into the similarities between source criticism and textual criticism, becoming preoccupied in the second half of the article with uncovering the world-beliefs latent behind *Old Testament* texts before finally moving on to the plays of Shakespeare. Therefore it is not easy to see what benefits these methods might bring when applied to a near-contemporary author.

Fisher takes this interesting but nebulous background and applies it very cogently to the specific case of Tolkien criticism. He points out that Tolkien himself was willing to inquire into what the *Gawain*-poet did with motifs that he had inherited; moreover, in his letters he also acknowledged certain debts to writers of the past. Therefore it is legitimate to investigate which motifs Tolkien himself derived from others and what he did with them. However, certain criteria must be met: there must be a reasonable degree of probability that Tolkien knew the source that he was allegedly appropriating, and it must be shown how this contributes significantly to our appreciation of his works. In my opinion, every Tolkienian source-hunter should have these principles framed on his or her writing desk. It remains to be seen how thoroughly they have been applied in the rest of the volume.

Nicholas Birns attempts to trace the influence of the more mythical parts of the *Old Testament* on Tolkien's mythology. He seems to be on fairly safe ground here, since there is little doubt that Tolkien knew the *Bible* well, and actually referred to Elendil as a "Noachian" figure. Indeed, in so far as Birns concentrates on structural similarities between Biblical and Tolkienian myths, he is able to demonstrate meaningful similarities. The argument falters somewhat when he discusses points of linguistic detail such as the similarity between *Uruk* and *Erech* and their use in Tolkien's nomenclature, since he is unable to demonstrate any significance in a possible allusion to the real Middle East, without which the phenomenon must be seen as no more than a chance resemblance (for which see my remarks on Shippey below).

Kristine Larsen, a professional astronomer, is known in Tolkien circles for her identification of the Elvish names for stars and constellations and their place in Tolkien's early fragments of cosmic myths (see the review of *Tolkien Studies VII* in this volume). Here she takes a two-pronged approach to the story of Eärendil and Elwing, on the one hand showing how Elwing, who in one version is said to "f[a]ll back" in her attempts to reach her stellified husband, can be identified with the planet Mercury, and on the other pointing out similarities to the Classical myth of Ceyx and Alcyone, best known from the version by Ovid, which Tolkien is highly likely to have known.

The article by Miryam Librán-Moreno suggests a number of close parallels between the history of Gondor, mostly to be found in *Appendix A* of *The Lord of the Rings*, and that of the late Roman and Byzantine Empires. Tom Shippey has already suggested this as a possible direction of research by his identification of the similarity between the Battle of the Pelennor Fields and that of the Catalaunian Fields; Librán-Moreno has filled in many of the gaps in a much longer history. It is up to the reader to decide whether these constitute a consistent calque or whether the events would be a logical development in the decline of any powerful empire into a long middle age, but there is little doubt that Tolkien as a medievalist was well aware of these particular sources, so that they could well have been at least unconsciously in his mind when compiling *Appendix A*.

The source examined by Thomas Honegger is not a text, or even a compendium of texts, but a whole people. Were the Rohirrim really based on the Anglo-Saxons (only with horses), as most critics claim but Tolkien denied, or were they Goths, or none of those? Honegger concludes that to all intents and purposes they were Anglo-Saxons, although Tolkien may well have conceived them as more an abstraction of supposed Germanic virtues. Although it does not state it explicitly, the article at least implies that just as for Tolkien a text was not an allegory unless there was a precise one-to-one correspondence, so the Rohirrim were not Anglo-Saxons unless they could be accurately identified in all details.

Judy Ann Ford suggests Caxton's *Golden Legend* as a possible source for LotR. It is pleasing to have saints' legends finally recognised as a medieval contribution to the fantasy genre, although they tended to be every bit as formulaic as their modern counterparts. Ford offers for consideration a number of similarities, but does not convince this reader either that Tolkien clearly had them in mind, or that their recognition contributes to our understanding of the work.

The next two contributions can again be viewed as a pair, since they both trace the influence on Tolkien's writing of British adventure stories of the period roughly 1885 to 1930. Tolkien himself stated that he knew *She* by Sir Henry Rider Haggard, and his appropriation of the name *Kôr* for "a city lost and dead" is striking. John Rateliff demonstrates that Tolkien was a keen reader of other Rider Haggard novels, and points out a whole series of convincing parallels which involve not just individual motifs but fundamental approaches to the creation of fantasy. It is clearly time for a re-appraisal of Rider Haggard's achievement, allowing for the apparent carelessness of the actual writing which has damned him in the eyes of many critics.

Mark Hooker has a reputation for his erudition in the details of text and the breadth of his (largely Anglophile) reading. In his article on the influence of John Buchan, though, his compendious memory allows him to produce such a plethora of apparent similarities that the reader is forced to ask how significant they can possibly be. Is there a conscious connection or are both writers unconsciously drawing on the common coinage of adventure stories, of which there were a vast number published in the early twentieth century? This question arises particularly in the case of linguistic details. Hooker suggests that the use by both writers of the phrase "high and puissant" is unlikely to be a coincidence. But for Tolkien to have taken these words straight from Buchan would mean either that he had the text in front of him, or that a chance collocation had stuck in his memory, probably for many years. It is far more likely that this is the kind of medievalising expression from the Edwardian adventure story that would occur spontaneously to both writers, and no doubt to a good many others if we only had the time to look through their output.

The last article is different in its approach. Diana Pavlac Glyer and Josh B. Long take the events of Tolkien's life as the basis of his inspiration. Many of the examples have been adduced before, such as his frustration with the long gestation of LotR in *Leaf by Niggle*, or the identification of characters in *The Notion Club Papers* with various Inklings. However, here it is presented as a consistent model for further investigation. It is certainly one that Tolkien would not have approved of for himself, but there is no denying its legitimacy as a recognised form of literary research.

To end at the beginning, the Introduction by Tom Shippey may be allowed the last word. As someone who pointed out as long ago as 1982 a number of possible lines for source studies of Tolkien, Shippey is an appropriate person to ask "Why source criticism?" (note the deliberate ambiguity of syntax!). His answer recognises its validity as he perceives it in the articles presented in this volume, but also adds some caveats which are no less present for being sounded *pianissimo*. His own exegesis is an attempt to show the influence not of a particular text source but of a whole mode of thinking, namely the recreation of a lost, or partially lost, past attempted by the discipline of comparative philology; the implication is that to concern oneself with specific details may be misguided. Furthermore, linguistic similarities have to fit into a significant pattern or they are of no value. Here the implication, strongly echoed in Fisher's article discussed above, is that other details have to be shown to be significant too. A raven may bear some similarity to a writing desk (not least the alliteration), but if it were meaningful there would be no point in Lewis Carrol's joke. This book deserves to be read for the wealth of interesting insights that it contains, but ultimately each reader will have to decide individually how far each one adds anything to our understanding of Tolkien and his works.

Allan Turner

Tolkien Studies. An Annual Scholarly Review. Volume VIII. 2011
Morgantown: West Virginia University Press, 311 pp.

Douglas Anderson, Verlyn Flieger, Michael Drout and their collaborators have delivered the eighth volume of *Tolkien Studies* in good time for the summer break reading. One thing struck me immediately: out of 311 pages, only 106 contained essays and notes and documents. This means that about two thirds of the volume consist of reviews and publication notes — which vividly illustrates the rapid growth in this field. I am not going to review the reviews, though, but limit my comments to the six papers and 'documents'. Although all contributions differ in their thematic orientation or investigate different aspects of a shared topic, they all focus on 'marginal' figures or events, starting their explorations of Tolkien's work from the periphery rather than the centre.

The essay section opens with a substantial and important essay by Philip Irving Mitchell. He investigates in detail and with great erudition the place of Tolkien's *On Fairy-Stories* within the contemporary discussion about evolution, religion and history. Mitchell skilfully outlines the positions of G.K. Chesterton, Owen Barfield and Christopher Dawson on those topics and is thus able to contextualise many of Tolkien's (to a modern reader often rather enigmatic) arguments. This paper is to some extent a sequel to Verlyn Flieger's "'There would always be a fairy-tale': J.R.R. Tolkien and the Folklore Controversy", which appeared in *Tolkien the Medievalist* (2003 edited by Jane Chance), and a welcome and necessary contribution to the ongoing examination of what has become a key-theoretical text for the understanding of Tolkien's mythopoeic work.

John M. Bowers, a medievalist by training, explores the parallels between the figure of Goldberry and the well-known medieval English lyric *The Maid of the Moor*. Bowers is well qualified to provide the reader with a competent discussion of this rather enigmatic lyric and the relevant scholarship — and his paper lives up to expectations. It is a nicely executed piece of 'traditional' sources-and-analogues hunting that helps to shed some light on Goldberry, an otherwise rather neglected figure in Tolkien's *legendarium*.

The next essay takes us into the realm of 'asterisk Gothic'. Lucas Annear undertakes a close analysis and discussion of the linguistic qualities and contextual meaning of Tolkien's neo-Gothic poem *Bagme Bloma* (published in 1936 in the now rare *Songs for the Philologists*). The discussion of the individual grammatical forms is something for the specialist in that field and I could spot only one obvious typo: on page 39 Annear writes: "Tolkien's use of *fl* instead of *pl* may not have been *that* bold", which should read "*fl* instead of [thorn]l". Also, I wondered whether some in-depth research among Tolkien's academic papers (deposited and accessible at the Department of Western Manuscripts in the Bodleian Library, Oxford) would have provided some additional information on his ideas on Gothic word-formation and related topics. I do remember having read various comments on the Gothic language in some of his lecture notes while doing research at the Bodleian. Furthermore, the discussion of the metre (pp. 42-43) would have profited from a contextualisation within the larger medieval tradition. There exists, for example, one Old English 10th-century poem that uses alliteration, internal rhyme and end rhyme: the aptly called 'Rhyming Poem' surviving in the *Exeter Book* manuscript. A comparison of Tolkien's use of metre in his neo-Gothic poem might have proved illuminating.

The remaining three contributions all explore different aspects of Tolkien's biography. José Manuel Ferrández Bru gives a well-researched account of the life and background of Tolkien's guardian Father Francis Morgan and a reassessment of the importance of this man for Tolkien's intellectual development — together with some much-welcomed information about Tolkien's ill-fated journey to France in 1913. Tolkien's friend and TCBS member Robert Quilter Gilson, who was killed in action during the Somme offensive on 1 July 1916, stands at the centre of John Garth's 'A Brief Life in Letters'. Once again we are indebted to Garth for his endeavours to expand and deepen our knowledge of this crucial era in Tolkien's life by providing authentic and sometimes rather moving historical documents. Janet Brennan Croft, finally, investigates the relevance of Tolkien's participation in the Officers Training Corps while at King Edward's School for his depiction of military life in his literary works. Merry's experience in the camp of the Rohirrim, for example, mirrors Tolkien's 'cadet' experience of the 1914 OTC summer camp.

The extensive book review (with a noteworthy review essay on the two volumes of *The Ring Goes Ever On* by Deidre Dawson), 'Year's Work' and 'Bibliography for 2009' sections round off this carefully produced tome.

Thomas Honegger

Paul Kerry & Sandra Miesel (Eds.): Light Beyond all Shadow. Religious Experience in Tolkien's Work

Madison/Teaneck: Fairleigh Dickinson University Press, 2011, 220 pp.

Der vorliegende Band sollte ursprünglich gemeinsam mit *The Ring and the Cross* einen einzigen bilden, wurde aber aus Platzgründen als eigener Band mit einer etwas unterschiedlichen Zielsetzung publiziert. Während sich jener den christlichen Einflüssen in Tolkiens Werk widmet, indem sein Katholizismus und seine Studien der nordischen Mythologie betrachtet wurden, weitet dieser das Spektrum auf Religion, religiöse Erfahrungen und Transzendenz aus. Einige Beiträge wurden ganz oder teilweise an anderen Orten schon einmal publiziert; einige wurden eigens für diesen Band übersetzt.

In der Einleitung führt Sandra Miesel zunächst in Tolkiens Zweitschöpfung ein, indem sie einen kurzen Überblick über wesentliche Inhalte seiner Mythologie gibt (mit einem Akzent auf den theologisch-philosophischen Inhalten), bevor sie kurz die einzelnen Beiträge vorstellt und in einen größeren Rahmen einordnet.

Der erste Beitrag (von Matthew Dickerson) widmet sich dem Zusammenhang von Wasser, Ökologie und Spiritualität — ein auf den ersten Blick vielleicht etwas unübliches Thema. Es gelingt Dickerson aber, die große symbolische Bedeutung von Wasser in Tolkiens Werk unter dieser besonderen Perspektive deutlich herauszustellen, da es »perhaps the greatest connection between creatures and their creator« (27) ist und reinigende/erlösende Wirkung besitzen kann.

Roger Ladd widmet sich in seinem Artikel dem Wesen der Macht in *The Silmarillion* und *The Lord of the Rings*, wobei er große Ähnlichkeiten zu Foucaults Ansatz sieht. Diese bestehen darin, verschiedene Formen von Macht anzunehmen, von denen eine dezentral, interaktiv und über Machtbeziehungen ist und eine andere den Opfergedanken enthält und das Individuum betrifft. Den Unterschied zwischen Tolkien und Foucault sieht Ladd in Tolkiens Theismus und der damit verbundenen Favorisierung des zweiten Modells.

Anschließend untersucht Anne C. Petty die mythopoetische Ikonographie in Mittelerde mit Blick auf christliche Bezüge, näherhin geflügelte Boten (vor allem die Adler), Feuer, Schatten und gefallene Engel, Licht und den Vater der Lügen (hier behandelt sie vor allem Túrin und Glaurung). Sie betont, man dürfe die Ikonographie nicht allein auf biblische oder christliche Einflüsse zurückführen: »Through imagery, Tolkien the scholar and wordsmith is discovered to be equally pagan mythmaker and devout Catholic« (66).

Ein ähnliches Thema behandelt Glen Robert Gill mit biblischen Archetypen, wobei er weniger überzeugend ist als Petty, da er einige Bezüge vielleicht überbetont, wenn er beispielsweise in der Durchquerung der Furt des Bruinen Anklänge an den Exodus sieht und Gandalfs Begegnung mit Théoden mit dem Propheten Jesaja vergleicht.

Wiederum plausibler sind die Ausführungen Lobdells über die Beziehung von Imagination und Tolkiens Katholizismus sowie von katholischer Theologie und Religion im *The Lord of the Rings*. Wenngleich Tolkien auch unorthodox scheinende Positionen vertrete, sieht er letztlich keinen Widerspruch: »Unquestionable — to my mind — he has rebaptized in Roman fonts our English sensibility and imagination grown up long ago in Celtic and Saxon realms, with their concentration on that fair elusive beauty — that some call celtic« (94).

Einer deutlich anderen Thematik, und nicht auf das Christentum eingeschränkt, widmet sich Julian T.M. Eilmann in seinem *Hither-Shore*-Lesern bekannten Beitrag über Musik, Poesie und das Transzendente in Tolkiens Werk: Er untersucht u.a. die Bedeutung von Liedern und Gedichten für die kulturelle Kommunikation, die Macht der Poesie, die sich auch im engen Zusammenhang zur Magie zeigt, oder die Beziehung von Musik, Wasser und dem Transzendenten.

Der anschließende kurze Beitrag von John Warwick Montgomery fragt nach den Gründen der großen Resonanz, die Tolkien in okkulten Kreisen genießt.

Er sieht keine inhaltlichen Gründe dafür, sondern meint, Tolkiens Popularität führe dazu, von diversen Seiten vereinnahmt zu werden.

Robert Lazu nimmt wieder einen katholischen Blickwinkel ein, indem er Tolkiens Ausführungen über die menschliche Kreativität als Ausdruck der Gottebenbildlichkeit mit den geistlichen Übungen des Ignatius von Loyola in Beziehung setzt und Literatur als eine geistliche Übung bestimmt, deren wichtigste Wirkung in einer Neuorientierung unseres Leben besteht.

Im folgenden Beitrag setzt sich Sandra Miesel mit Frauen in Tolkiens Werk auseinander, wobei sie angesichts der positiven und negativen Beispiele (wie plausibel es ist, den Ring als feminin anzusehen, sei dahingestellt) vor allem ihre Bedeutung als Lebensspenderinnen herausstellt; ferner seien sie in der Regel weitsichtiger, mutiger, loyaler und geduldiger als die Männer. Bei diesem Beitrag hätte der Bezug zur religiösen Dimension noch stärker herausgestellt werden können.

Stärker biographisch orientiert sind die Ausführungen von Colin Duriez über Tolkien und die Inklings, worin er ausführlich auf die Eigenschaften dieser Gruppe eingeht und den literarischen Charakter hervorhebt sowie ihre gemeinsame Vision der Beziehung von Imagination und Mythen zur Realität.

Die letzten beiden Beiträge von Russell W. Dalton und Christopher Garbowski weiten den Blick über die Bücher hinaus auf die Verfilmung von Peter Jackson. Dabei stellt Dalton heraus, wie die von Jackson ursprünglich geplanten Änderungen des Schlusses (mit einem Duell zwischen Aragorn und Sauron) als Ausdruck einer eher manichäischen Sicht des Bösen sich den Charakteristika des Mediums Film (als zeitbegrenztes, visuelles, charaktergetriebenes und affektives Medium) verdanken. Garbowski hingegen fragt anhand der dargestellten spirituellen Werte danach, was von Tolkiens »katholischer« Erzählung in der Verfilmung übrig geblieben sei, wobei er auch ausführlich auf Fantasy im Film eingeht. Er attestiert Jackson, bei den Protagonisten trotz einiger Unterschiede Tolkiens Emphase auf Gemeinschaft und den Sinn für den eigenen Ort sowie auf die Bedeutung der Unschuld gerecht geworden zu sein.

Angesichts der Bandbreite der behandelten Themen ist dieser Band sicherlich thematisch nicht so geschlossen wie *The Ring and the Cross*, womit er aber andererseits die Vielfalt der untersuchungswerten Aspekte deutlich herausstellt. Auch dem Thema geschuldet sein dürfte der Umstand, dass nicht alle Artikel als weiterführende Forschungsbeiträge konzipiert sind, sondern eher Überblicks- und Informationscharakter tragen. Alles in allem ist die Lektüre des Bandes durchaus lohnend, wenn man sich mit vielfältigen Aspekten des Religiösen in Tolkiens Werk auseinandersetzen will, auch wenn ein Beitrag wie derjenige Gills deutlich abfällt.

Thomas Fornet-Ponse

Carl Phelpstead:
Tolkien and Wales: Language, Literature and Identity
Cardiff: University of Wales Press 2011, 184 pp.

Tolkien's passion for languages is a well-known fact. English (and its historical forms) was certainly the one of greatest importance for his academic studies, but there was a series of other languages, such as Welsh, Finnish, Gothic or Hebrew, that influenced both his academic and creative work. Of those it is certainly Welsh that takes precedence — both bio-chronologically and impact-wise. We know about the importance of Welsh from Tolkien's published *Letters*, his public lectures (notably *Celts and Teutons* [unpublished], *English and Welsh* and *A Secret Vice*) and Carpenter's *Biography*. And yet there existed to date no in-depth study of this aspect.

It is therefore all the more laudable that Carl Phelpstead, Reader in English Literature at Cardiff University, undertook the task of systematically viewing and assessing the evidence. The product of this labour is a very readable, informative and carefully edited volume,[1] which proved salutary reading after Zettersten's mistake-riddled text (see the review in this volume).

Phelpstead divides his study into three parts of varying length (parts I & II with three chapters each, part III with one short chapter only).

The first part 'Language' focuses on Tolkien's first contact with Welsh words, his (academic) publications on the language, his involvement with establishing courses in medieval Welsh at Leeds (where he also taught it) and later on Oxford, and his private studies of the Celtic languages themselves. For the latter Phelpstead looked at and analysed the contents of Tolkien's 'Celtic Library' and discusses the evidence we can glean from Tolkien's (sometimes extensive) annotations in numerous texts. What is even more, the author also consulted Tolkien's academic papers (deposited at the Department of Western Manuscripts at the Bodleian), discusses the development of Tolkien's main concepts within that field and puts them not only into the context of (for Tolkien) contemporary research, but also gives a brief assessment of their place within the current discourse. Phelpstead is often cautious not to judge quickly and thus, for example, treads very softly when discussing Tolkien's 'heretical' (or at least controversial) yet for him central concept of 'native (hereditary) language'. He also provides a

---

[1] I spotted only one single typo (p. 90: 'Tolkien and Jones had became friends') and one factual mistake (p. 73: 'giant king Thingoll').

competent while for the general reader comprehensible overview of the development of the Elvish languages Quenya and Sindarin, and the influence of Welsh on the latter, and comes to the conclusion that Sindarin's "widespread appeal to speakers of English would, for Tolkien, confirm his assertion in 'English and Welsh' that for many English speakers Welsh may come closer than their own mother tongue to their personal 'native' language" (50).

The second part focuses on Tolkien's knowledge of Celtic (and especially Welsh) literature and its discernible influence on his work. The author illustrates how the comparative method developed in philology was also applied to mythology, and by means of a discussion of Tolkien's notes and drafts shows how he successfully uses that method for his paper on 'Nodens'. A close study of the annotations, glosses and working papers that go with the books in Tolkien's 'Celtic Library' illustrates his extended work on the *Mabinogion* in the original language and puts Tolkien's use of and allusions to motifs from Celtic prose literature — especially those from the Arthurian tradition — into a wider context. All in all, Phelpstead's assessment of these influences is much more level-headed and informative than many a previous scholar's.[2]

The discussion of Tolkien's Breton *Lay of Aotrou and Itroun*, published in 1945 in *The Welsh Review*, within the framework of 'Welsh literature' proves highly illuminating and Phelpstead's chapter is an important and welcome contribution to the study of this neglected text (see also the essay by Rafael Pascual and Eduardo Segura in this volume).

The third and final part, entitled 'Identity', comprises one chapter of only ten pages. I'd see it as a 'coda' rather than as a full-blown third part. Phelpstead briefly sketches the process of 'devolution' on the British Isles and relates them to Tolkien's much earlier views on cultural, linguistic and literary 'regional' identity — stressing the Professor's Mercian (or rather 'Hwicca') roots and his identification of 'home' with the area in the Welsh Marches. An 'Appendix' listing the books of Tolkien's Welsh books at the Bodleian Library and the English Faculty Library and an 'Index' round off this nicely produced volume.

Tolkien and Wales is a good read — in more than one way. Firstly, Phelpstead presents his clearly structured account of Tolkien's involvement with Wales and Welsh in elegant and accessible language. Secondly, he bases his account on a solid knowledge of primary and secondary sources. And thirdly, his research into Tolkien's academic notes, drafts and manuscripts as well as the contents of his 'Celtic library' give us new insights into the degree and extent of the Professor's study of Welsh. I can therefore recommend Phelpstead's book without reservation to all and sundry. Thomas Honegger

---

2 Most notably Alex Lewis and Elizabeth Currie who, in their *The Epic Realm of Tolkien* (2009), "risk[ed] undermining their case by overstating it" (Phelpstead 74).

Arne Zettersten: J.R.R. Tolkien's Double Worlds and Creative Process. Language and Life.
New York: Palgrave Macmillan 2011, 243 pp.

Prof. Zettersten is one of the few academics still alive who did, in their early career, work with or, more correctly, in the same field as Prof. Tolkien. In the case of Zettersten it was his edition of the 'Vernon' text of the Ancrene Riwle and his interest in the AB language which brought him into personal contact with Tolkien from the late 1950s onwards. Readers may therefore expect an informed account of Tolkien the scholar as well as Tolkien the person, expectations raised by the programmatic subtitle: Language and Life. And that is more or less what they get.

I add the qualifying 'more or less' because the book's structure left me more than a bit dissatisfied. On the one hand, there are vivid passages describing Zettersten's personal encounters with Tolkien and a competent and knowledgeable evaluation of his scholarly work and interests — though chapter 14 on 'Interplay between Research and Fiction', focussing on *Sir Gawain and the Green Knight*, is unfortunately not very convincing. On the other hand we have a re-telling of (basically) Carpenter's biography along chronological lines and a rather general assessment of Tolkien's fictional work riddled with typos and factual mistakes (see list below).

The basic problem for me is that this book is (implicitly) aimed at a mass-audience of undergraduates or non-academics (which would explain the — to me — out-of-place summary of Tolkien's background in the Appendix). For them it will do (most of the time) a wonderful job, summarising Carpenter, Garth, Shippey etc. while adding a vivid personal touch in places. For me, as an academic and old hand in matters Tolkien, it stops short exactly when it gets interesting: in Zettersten's own personal experiences with Tolkien, his own view of matters and the in-depth discussion of scholarly problems and questions. This is all the more deplorable since Zettersten 'knows his Tolkien' in every meaning of the expression. He collaborated with the Professor, met him personally on various occasions and also studied Tolkien's academic and literary manuscripts at the Bodleian Library and Marquette University. But all those strengths have not been put to the best of uses and the result is a book that fails to meet my expectations. The final two chapters 19 and 20 hint at what new ideas Zettersten may have wanted to contribute to Tolkien studies, yet they remain rather 'isolated' in their attempt at a philosophical assessment of the truth-value of myths and their discussion of the relationship between fact and fiction.

My irritation with the book grew also due to the fact that the text has still too many factual mistakes and layout-problems. I know from my experience as series editor and editor that getting the texts into a decent shape is a lot of work, and wonder whether a publisher such as Palgrave Macmillan cannot afford the manpower to secure a 'clean' text — obviously not, even though the price of 63,99 € is rather on the expensive side.

I cannot, therefore, join the eminent scholars quoted on the back-cover in their enthusiastic praise of the book. It is a highly readable 'biography' for 'newcomers' interested in Tolkien (though its many typos and factual mistakes greatly diminish its value in that field) and provides some new glimpses of Tolkien's personal and professional life for experienced scholars, but it does not make a reading of Carpenter, Garth and Shippey (to name only the most eminent ones) redundant — on the contrary.

Thomas Honegger

Addendum:

A selection of the numerous typos and mistakes. The list has been compiled with the generous help of Dr. Allan Turner.

p. 13: burielmounds of Old Uppsala — burialmounds
p. 27: typo: the Christopher Tolkien interview is 1992, not 1962. The poet should be S.T. Coleridge, not C.T.
There is some misrepresentation on this page; "a sudden glimpse of the underlying reality…" is not a specific gift from God to Tolkien but is a general characteristic of successful fantasy (M&C 155). "Literary belief" is not peculiar to children in Tolkien's argument. Some more precise references to Tolkien's essay would be useful. Where he gives page numbers at the bottom of the page, those do not correspond to the edition given in the bibliography.
p. 28: *Children of Huron* should be *Children of Húrin*
p. 35: HoME since 1983, not 1984.
Joy Hill has become Joe Hill!
Niemor should be Nienor.
p. 37: Carpenter died 2005, so 2003 is not the year before his death.
p. 37, 39: wrong kind of apostrophe-signs
p. 46: typo: Lord of the Kings
"I always got a clear impression from our discussions … holistic view" — So is it still a part of his personal impressions on the next page when he says "Tolkien tended to regard himself as a kind of recorder"? Z. does not differentiate

sufficiently between his own reminiscences and his conclusions based on what he has read. This is partly a result of not identifying his sources in sufficient detail.

p. 47: "he constructed all his fictional languages first" — not accurate enough. From what has been written it seems clear that the languages and the stories were pursued in parallel and influenced one another.

p. 52: 'discontinued around the middle of the 1980s' — should be 1880s (in connection with John Suffield, Tolkien's maternal grandfather).

p. 63: 'The mill was inaugurated in 1069 and is now open to the community as a museum.' — suppose the mill at Sarehole was inaugurated in 1969.

p. 68/69: King Edward's twice becomes St. Edward's, which is a school in Oxford.

p. 78: It seems unlikely that Tolkien's copy of Vergil was published in 1997.

p. 79: Brewerton was not the "head master".

p. 89: 'not to get in touch with Edith before her twenty-first birthday' — almost; Tolkien had to wait until his 21st birthday (i.e. his coming of age), not Edith's.

p. 96: *Artist and Illuminator* — almost; the title of the book is *Artist and Illustrator*.

p. 101: Since when has Warwick been in Somerset??

p. 107: typo: Prof. L.W. Forster, not I.W.

p. 174: och (instead of 'and')

p. 176: *Roverandum* — the book is called *Roverandom*.

p. 194: There is no University College, Cambridge!!

p. 199: James Branch Cabell (1979-1958) — Cabell did not live backwards, but was born in 1879.

p. 200: 'England and Wales' (1955) — should be 'English and Welsh'.

Unsere Autoren und Autorinnen

Annie Birks lehrt Englische Sprache und Literatur an der Katholischen Universität des Westens in Angers (Frankreich). Sie promovierte an der Sorbonne über *Vergeltung in den Werken J.R.R. Tolkiens*. Ihre gegenwärtigen Forschungsinteressen fokussieren im Wesentlichen die theologischen Perspektiven der Schriften Tolkiens.
annie.birks@neuf.fr

Patrick Brückner studierte Germanistische Mediävistik und Soziologie mit dem Schwerpunkt Soziologie der Geschlechterverhältnisse sowie Volkswirtschaftslehre an der Universität Potsdam. Er arbeitet über Genderfragen in den Werken Tolkiens und hat mit Judith Klinger Seminare über »Tolkien und das Mittelalter« an der Universität Potsdam gehalten. Seine Veröffentlichungen beinhalten Beiträge zu *Hither Shore* sowie zu *Tolkien and Modernity 2* (Walking Tree Publishers, Hg. T. Honegger & F. Weinreich).
patricbrueckner@aol.com

Cécile Cristofari lehrt Englisch an der Universität der Provence in Aix-en-Provence (Frankreich). Gegenwärtig schreibt sie ihre Dissertation über imaginäre Universen in Science Fiction und Fantasy. Andere wissenschaftliche Interessen umfassen die Geschichte der Popkultur und ihrer Mentalitäten, mittelalterliche Kultur und kreatives Schreiben.
cecile.cristofari@gmail.com

Julian Tim Morton Eilmann studierte in Aachen und Nottingham Geschichte, Germanistik und Kunstgeschichte und ist gegenwärtig Gymnasiallehrer. Neben seinen akademischen Arbeiten ist er seit mehreren Jahren bei einer Film- und TV-Produktion als Autor von Reportagen und historischen Dokumentation tätig und darüber hinaus Inhaber einer Kunstgalerie und Kurator einer Künstlerstiftung. Schwerpunkte seiner Tolkien-Forschungen sind Tolkiens Lieder und Gedichte sowie die Filmadaption von Peter Jackson.
julianeilmann@aol.com

Thomas Fornet-Ponse, Dr. theol., studierte Katholische Theologie, Philosophie und Alte Geschichte in Bonn und Jerusalem und promovierte in Fundamentaltheologie und Ökumene. Er veröffentlichte zahlreiche Aufsätze zu Tolkien, Pratchett und Lewis, war bis 2009 Beisitzer im Vorstand der Deutschen Tolkien Gesellschaft und ist inhaltlicher Koordinator des Tolkien Seminars wie von *Hither Shore*.
thomas.fornet-ponse@tolkiengesellschaft.de

Authors/Autoren

Thomas Honegger, Prof. Dr. phil, hat in Zürich promoviert und zahlreiche Bände zu Tolkien, mittelalterlicher Sprache und Literatur herausgegeben und verschiedene Beiträge zu Chaucer, Shakespeare und mittelalterlichen Romanzen publiziert. Seit 2002 lehrt er als Professor für Mediävistik an der Friedrich-Schiller-Universität Jena.
www. anglistik.uni-jena.de/personen/thomas-honegger/

Catalin Hriban, PhD, arbeitet im Archäologischen Institut der Rumänischen Akademie der Wissenschaften in Iași, besonders zu Heraldik, mittelalterlicher Topographie, aber auch zu Waffen, vor allem Schwertern. Er ist u.a. seit 1997 Mitglied der Kommission für Heraldik, Genealogie und Siegelkunde der Rumänischen Akademie und hat verschiedentlich dieses Fachwissen auf die Interpretation literarischer Werke angewandt.

Eike Kehr, Dr. phil., studierte Anglistik und Mathematik an der Justus-Liebig-Universität Gießen und der Royal Holloway, University of London. Von 2003 bis 2005 war er Referendar am Studienseminar Gießen. Seitdem arbeitet er als Gymnasiallehrer in Weilburg. Im Frühjahr 2011 promovierte er mit einer Arbeit über Natur und Kultur in Tolkiens *The Lord of the Rings*.
eikekehr@aol.com

Judith Klinger, Dr. Phil., studierte Germanistik und Anglistik an der Universität Hamburg sowie Dokumentarfilm und Fernsehpublizistik an der Hochschule für Fernsehen und Film, München. Sie promovierte über Identitätskonzeptionen im Prosa-*Lancelot*. Nach einer Lehrtätigkeit an der Universität Bayreuth ist sie seit 1995 am Lehrstuhl für Germanistische Mediävistik der Universität Potsdam beschäftigt. Sie verfolgt ein Habilitationsprojekt im Bereich der Gender Studies.
jklinger@uni-potsdam.de

Marguerite Mouton erwarb ihre *Agrégation* in Moderner Literatur und einen Magister in Politikwissenschaften in Paris und verfolgt gegenwärtig ein Promotionsstudium in Vergleichender Literaturwissenschaft an der Université Paris 13.
marguerite.mouton@laposte.net

Rafael J. Pascual studierte Englische Literatur und Sprache an der Universität Granada und promoviert über die rhythmische Prosa des Ælfric von Einsham. Seine Hauptinteressen liegen bei der altenglischen Sprache und Literatur, der Entstehung der metrischen Tradition des frühmittelalterlichen Englisch und bei historischer Linguistik. Er ist Mitglied in der Spanischen Gesellschaft für Mittelalterliche Englische Sprache und Literatur und in der Spanischen Tolkiengesellschaft.
rjpascual@ugr.es

Emanuele Rimoli OFM Conv. ist Franziskaner-Konventuale aus Kalabrien und promoviert in Rom in anthropologischer Theologie. Er ist Gastdozent am Theologischen Institut von Assisi sowie Koautor dreier Bücher über Literatur und Spiritualität und hat schon mehrfach zu Tolkien publiziert.
emanuelerimoli@yahoo.it

Eduardo Segura, Dr. phil., hat verschiedene Bücher und Artikel über Tolkien und die Inklings geschrieben und herausgegeben, u.a. *El Viaje des Anillo* (2004), was auf seiner Doktorarbeit über einige Elemente der Narrative in LotR aus einer narratologischen und ästhetischen Perspektive basiert. Ferner übersetzte er Tolkiens *The Monsters and the Critics and Other Essays* (1998) und Shippeys *The Road to Middle-earth* (1999) ins Spanische. Gegenwärtig unterrichtet er Englische Literatur an der Universität Granada.
www.inklinga.es

Rudolf Simek, Prof. Dr. phil., promovierte und habilitierte in Wien und ist seit 1995 Professor für Ältere Germanistik unter Einfluss des Nordischen an der Rheinischen Friedrich-Wilhelms-Universität Bonn. Neben zahlreichen Veröffentlichungen zur Skandinavistik publizierte er besonders zur germanischen Mythologie und Religion, u.a. *Mittelerde. Tolkien und die germanische Mythologie.*
simek@uni-bonn.de

Guglielmo Spirito OFM Conv., Prof. Dr. theol., studierte u.a. Philosophie und Ägyptologie, erwarb in Rom sein Doktorat (mit der Spezialisierung in Spiritualität) am Antonianum. Seit 1994 ist er Professor am Theologischen Institut Assisi. Über Tolkien hat er nicht nur u.a. in Italien, England, Deutschland und Frankreich doziert, sondern auch verschiedene Essays, Aufsätze und Bücher publiziert; er ist auch Mitglied der Italienischen Tolkiengesellschaft.
fraguspi@gmail.com

Martin G.E. Sternberg hat 1990-1996 in Münster Alte Geschichte, Mittlere Geschichte, Kunstgeschichte und Rechtswissenschaften studiert. Er arbeitet als Referent bei einer Bundesbehörde. Ein Schwerpunkt seines Geschichts- und Philosophiestudiums lag in der Spätantike und im frühen Christentum.
lasgalen@web.de

Allan Turner, PhD, studierte Deutsche Philosophie, Mediävistik und Allgemeine Linguistik. Seine Dissertation in Übersetzungswissenschaften untersucht die inhärenten Probleme bei der Übersetzung philologischer Elemente in *The Lord of the Rings*. Gegenwärtig liegt sein Interessenschwerpunkt auf dem Stil der Werke Tolkiens. Er unterrichtet Englische Sprachpraxis und British Cultural Studies an der Friedrich-Schiller-Universität Jena.
allangturner@aol.com

Renée Vink hat skandinavische Sprachen (u.a. Altnordisch) studiert und arbeitet(e) als Übersetzerin aus dem Schwedischen, Norwegischen, Dänische, Deutschen und Englischen. U.a. ist sie die Niederländisch-Übersetzerin der Dichtung in *The Legend of Sigurd and Gudrún*.

Antje vom Lehn erhielt 2009 ihren B.A. in Skandinavistik und Internationalen Literaturen. Derzeit macht sie ihren M.A. in Skandinavistik an der Universität Tübingen. Ihre Schwerpunkte liegen auf mittelalterlicher und Fantasy-Literatur.
antjevomlehn@gmail.com

Michael Wedel, Prof. Dr. phil., lehrt Mediengeschichte im Digitalen Zeitalter an der Hochschule für Film und Fernsehen »Konrad Wolf« in Potsdam-Babelsberg. Er veröffentlichte u.a. *Die »Herr der Ringe«-Trilogie. Attraktion und Faszination eines populärkulturellen Phänomens* (zusammen mit L. Mikos, S. Eichner, E. Prommer).

Dirk Wiemann, Prof. Dr. phil., hat in Oldenburg Anglistik, Germanistik und Politikwissenschaften studiert, über Exilliteratur in Großbritannien 1933-1945 promoviert und über englischsprachige indische Romane der Gegenwart habilitiert. Er arbeitete als DAAD-Lektor in Hyderabad und Delhi sowie als Assistent in Magdeburg und als Akademischer Rat in Tübingen, bevor er 2008 Professor für Englische Literatur an der Universität Potsdam wurde.
dwiemann@uni-potsdam.de

Silke Winst, Dr. phil., hat im Bereich der Germanistischen Mediävistik zum Thema »Amicus und Amelius: Kriegerfreundschaft und Gewalt in mittelalterlicher Erzähltradition« an der Freien Universität Berlin promoviert. Derzeit ist sie Wissenschaftliche Mitarbeiterin in einem DFG-Projekt zur Edition des *Loher und Maller* an der Universität Potsdam. Ihr Habilitationsvorhaben trägt den Titel »Minnekrankheit in mittelalterlicher Literatur: Zur Pathologisierung und Kultivierung von Begehren«.
silke.winst@uni-potsdam.de

Our Authors

Annie Birks teaches English Language and Literature at the Université Catholique de l'Ouest in Angers (France). She has received a doctorate from the Sorbonne on *Reward and Punishment in the Works of J.R.R. Tolkien*. Her current research interests focus essentially on the theological perspectives of Tolkien's writings.
annie.birks@neuf.fr

Patrick Brückner studied German Medieval Literature, Women's Studies and Sociology at the University of Potsdam (Germany). He is working on aspects of gender in the works of J.R.R. Tolkien and held joint seminars with Judith Klinger on *Tolkien and the Middle Ages* at the University of Potsdam. His publications include contributions to *Hither Shore* and *Tolkien and Modernity 2* (Walking Tree Publishers, edited by T. Honegger & F. Weinreich).
patricbrueckner@aol.com

Cécile Cristofari teaches English at the University of Provence, Aix en Provence (France). She is currently writing a PhD dissertation on imaginary universes in science fiction and fantasy. Other academic interests include the history of popular culture and mentalities, mediaeval culture and creative writing.
cecile.cristofari@gmail.com

Julian Tim Morton Eilmann studied History, German Philology, and History of Arts at Aachen (Germany) and Nottingham (UK) and is currently working as a teacher. Furthermore, since several years he is working as a journalist and author of films and TV productions, and as a developer of historical TV documentations. In addition, he is fulfilling the functions of gallery owner and conservator for an artists' foundation. His works on Tolkien focus an Tolkien's songs and poems and the movie adaptation by Peter Jackson.
julianeilmann@aol.com

Thomas Fornet-Ponse, Dr. theol., studied Catholic Theology, Philosophy and Ancient History at Bonn and Jerusalem. He received his doctorate in Fundamental Theology and Ecumenism from the University of Salzburg (Austria). He was a committee member of the German Tolkien Society and has been charged with conceptually coordinating the Tolkien Seminars as well as *Hither Shore*.
thomas.fornet-ponse@tolkiengesellschaft.de

Thomas Honegger holds a PhD from the University of Zurich. He edited several volumes on Tolkien, medieval language and literature and published papers on Chaucer, Shakespeare,and medieval romance. He teaches, since 2002, as Professor for Mediaeval Studies at the Friedrich Schiller University Jena (Germany).
www. anglistik.uni-jena.de/personen/thomas-honegger/

Catalin Hriban, PhD, is a historian working at the Institute of Archaeology of the Romanian Academy, Iași Branch. His fields of expertise are heraldry and medieval topography; he also shows a special interest in the study of weapons, especially swords. He is inter alia a member (since 1997) of the Commission of Heraldry, Genealogy and Sigillography of the Romanian Academy — Iași Branch and has repeatedly applied his knowledge of heraldic science to the interpretation of literary works.

Judith Klinger, Dr. phil., studied German Philology and English Philology at the University of Hamburg, then Documentary Filming and TV Media Studies at the University of TV and film at Munich. Her PhD thesis deals with concepts of identity in the prose *Lancelot*. She taught at Bayreuth University and has been employed at the chair of German Medieval Studies at Potsdam University since 1995. She is currently working on a post-doctoral thesis in the field of gender studies.
jklinger@rz.uni-potsdam.de

Marguerite Mouton has the *Agrégation* of Modern Literature, an MA in Political Sciences (Sciences-Po Paris), and is currently a PhD student in Comparative Literature (Université Paris 13).
marguerite.mouton@laposte.net

Rafael J. Pascual holds a BA and an MA in English Literature and Linguistics from the University of Granada (Spain) and works there as a teacher student at the Department of English and German Studies. He is currently working on a PhD on Ælfric of Eynsham's rhythmical prose. His main interests are Old English language and literature, the evolution of the metrical tradition of early medieval English and historical linguistics. He is an active member of SELIM (Spanish Society for Mediaeval English Language and Literature) and of the Spanish Tolkien Society.
rjpascual@ugr.es

Emanuele Rimoli is a Conventual Franciscan Friar (= Minorit) and works and lives in Rome. He occasionally is a guest professor at the Theological Institute of Assisi. He is writing his PhD in Anthropological Theology on Dostoevskij at

the Pontifical Faculty of Saint Bonaventure in Rome. He gave papers on Tolkien in Italy and Germany, some of them published in *Hither Shore*.
emanuelerimoli@yahoo.it

Eduardo Segura holds a BA in Modern History (1990), a PhD in Philology (2001), and an MA in Philosophy (2010). He is the author and editor of some books and essays on Tolkien and the Inklings, including *El viaje del Anillo* (2004), based on his doctoral dissertation on some elements of the narrative in *The Lord of the Rings* in a narratological and aesthetical perspective. He translated Tolkien's *The Monsters and the Critics and Other Essays* (1998) and Shippey's *The Road to Middle-earth* (1999) into Spanish. He is currently a teacher of English Literature at the Department of English, University of Granada (Spain).
www.inklinga.es

Rudolf Simek holds a PhD from the University of Vienna and teaches, since 1995, as Professor for Old German under influence of Norse at Rheinische Friedrich Wilhelms University Bonn (Germany). His research interests include Germanic mythology and religions, but he has also written a book on Tolkien and Germanic mythology.
simek@uni-bonn.de

Guglielmo Spirito is a Conventual Franciscan Friar (= Minorit) and works and lives in Assisi. In Rome he got his PhD in Theology with specialitation in Spirituality at the Antonianum. He is professor at the Theological Institute of Assisi. He gave lectures on Tolkien in Italy, England, Germany, France and Canada. On J.R.R. Tolkien he had published essays, books and several papers with Walking Tree Publishers and *Hither Shore*.
fraguspi@gmail.com

Martin Sternberg studied Ancient History, Mediaeval History, History of Arts, and Law at Münster (Germany) from 1990 to 1996. He is currently working in a federal authority. During his studies, he specialised in Late Antiquity and Early Christianity.
lasgalen@web.de

Allan Turner, PhD, studied German Philology, Mediaeval Studies, and General Linguistics. His PhD thesis in translation studies examines the problems inherent in translating the philological elements in *The Lord of the Rings*. His main focus of interest is currently on the stylistics of Tolkien's works. He teaches English Language Skills and British Cultural Studies at Friedrich Schiller University of Jena (Germany).
allangturner@aol.com

Renée Vink has a university degree in Scandinavian languages, including Old Norse, and worked as a translator from Swedish, Norwegian, Danish, German and English. Among other things, she is the Dutch translator of the poetry in *The Legend of Sigurd and Gudrún*.

Antje vom Lehn received her B.A. in Scandinavian Studies and International Literature in 2009. She is currently working on her M.A. in Scandinavian Studies at the University of Tübingen (Germany). Her main fields of interest are mediaeval and fantasy literature.
antjevomlehn@gmail.com

Michael Wedel, Dr. phil., is professor for media history in the digital age at the University of Film and Television "Konrad Wolf" in Potsdam-Babelsberg (Germany) and has edited inter alia *Die Herr-der-Ringe-Trilogie. Attraktion und Faszination eines populärkulturellen Phänomens* (with L. Mikos, S. Eichner, E. Prommer).

Dirk Wiemann, Prof. Dr. phil., received his PhD from the University of Oldenburg with a dissertation thesis on exile literature in Great Britain 1933-45 and wrote his habilitation thesis on anglophone Indian novels. He worked as lecturer in Hyderabad and Delhi and as assistant professor in Magdeburg and Tübingen. Since 2008, he is professor for English Literature at Potsdam University.
dwiemann@uni-potsdam.de

Siglenverzeichnis

Die Schriften von J.R.R. Tolkien werden im Text jeweils ohne Angabe des Verfassernamens mit den folgenden Siglen zitiert. Die jeweils benutzte Ausgabe findet sich im Literaturverzeichnis.

AI:	The Lay of Aotrou and Itroun
ATB:	The Adventures of Tom Bombadil and other Verses from the Red Book / Die Abenteuer des Tom Bombadil und andere Gedichte aus dem Roten Buch
AW:	Ancrene Wisse and Hali Meiðhad
B:	Die Briefe von J.R.R. Tolkien
BA:	Bilbos Abschiedslied
BB:	Baum und Blatt
BGH:	Bauer Giles von Ham
BLS:	Bilbo's Last Song
BMC:	Beowulf: The Monster and the Critics
BT:	Blatt von Tüftler
BUK:	Beowulf: Die Ungeheuer und ihre Kritiker
BW:	Die Briefe vom Weihnachtsmann
CH:	The Children of Húrin
CP:	Chaucer as a Philologist
EA:	The End of the Third Age (History of Middle-earth 9). Auszug
EW:	English and Welsh / Englisch und Walisisch
FC:	Letters from Father Christmas
FGH:	Farmer Giles of Ham
FH:	Finn and Hengest
FS:	On Fairy-Stories
GD:	Gute Drachen sind rar
GN:	Guide to the Names in the Lord of the Rings
GPO:	Sir Gawain and the Green Knight, Pearl, and Sir Orfeo
H:	The Hobbit / Der Hobbit / Der kleine Hobbit
HB:	The Homecoming of Beorhtnoth Beorhthelm's Son
HdR:	Der Herr der Ringe
HdR I:	Der Herr der Ringe. Bd. 1. Die Gefährten
HdR II:	Der Herr der Ringe. Bd. 2. Die Zwei Türme
HdR III:	Der Herr der Ringe. Bd. 3. Die Rückkehr des Königs / Die Wiederkehr des Königs
HdR A:	Der Herr der Ringe. Anhänge
HG:	Herr Glück
HH I/II:	The History of the Hobbit
HL:	Ein heimliches Laster
KH:	Die Kinder Húrins
L:	The Letters of J.R.R. Tolkien
LB:	The Lays of Beleriand (History of Middle-earth 3)
LN:	Leaf by Niggle

Siglenverzeichnis

LotR:	The Lord of the Rings
LotR I:	The Fellowship of the Ring. Being the first part of The Lord of the Rings
LotR II:	The Two Towers. Being the second part of The Lord of the Rings
LotR III:	The Return of the King. Being the third part of The Lord of the Rings
LotR A:	The Lord of the Rings. Appendices
LR:	The Lost Road and other Writings (History of Middle-earth 5)
LSG:	The Legend of Sigurd and Gudrún
LT 1:	The Book of Lost Tales 1 (History of Middle-earth 1)
LT 2:	The Book of Lost Tales 2 (History of Middle-earth 2)
MB:	Mr. Bliss
MC:	The Monsters and the Critics and Other Essays
ME:	A Middle English Vocabulary
MR:	Morgoth's Ring (History of Middle-earth 10)
My:	Mythopoeia
NM:	Nachrichten aus Mittelerde
OE:	The Old English Exodus
OK:	Ósanwe-Kenta
P:	Pictures by J.R.R. Tolkien
PM:	The Peoples of Middle-earth (History of Middle-earth 12)
R:	Roverandom
RBG:	The Rivers and Beacon-hills of Gondor
RGEO:	The Road Goes Ever On (with Donald Swann)
RS:	The Return of the Shadow (History of Middle-earth 6)
S:	Silmarillion
SD:	The Sauron Defeated (History of Middle-earth 9)
SG:	Der Schmied von Großholzingen
SGG:	Sir Gawain and the Green Knight / Sir Gawain und der Grüne Ritter (Essay)
SM:	The Shaping of Middle-earth (History of Middle-earth 4)
SP:	Songs for the Philologists
SV:	A Secret Vice
SWM:	Smith of Wootton Major
SWME:	Smith of Wootton Major Essay
TB:	On Translating Beowulf
TI:	The Treason of Isengard (History of Middle-earth 7)
TL:	Tree and Leaf
ÜB:	Zur Übersetzung des Beowulf
ÜM:	Über Märchen
UK:	Die Ungeheuer und ihre Kritiker. Gesammelte Aufsätze
UT:	Unfinished Tales
VA:	Valedictory Address
VG 1:	Das Buch der Verschollenen Geschichten 1
VG 2:	Das Buch der Verschollenen Geschichten 2
WJ:	The War of the Jewels (History of Middle-earth 11)
WR:	The War of the Ring (History of Middle-earth 8)

Index

Ainulindalë	67, 132, 134, 138
Aragorn	26, 29, 90-96, 115, 125ff, 140, 144, 148, 154-158, 160, 173, 177, 207, 209, 234ff, 257
Arthur	77, 102f, 106f, 161f, 164, 167, 198, 218, 231f
Arwen	94, 156, 235f
Augustinus, Augustine	25, 59, 132-139, 145, 258, 260
Beleg	11, 20, 41-46, 50, 52, 114f, 123f, 126-130, 180ff
Beowulf	40, 49, 52, 73, 77, 80-83, 106, 115, 148, 156, 158, 170-173, 179f, 184, 194, 230
Bertilak	107, 230ff
Bilbo	12, 64, 81, 86f, 135, 146, 152f, 162, 203f, 256, 262, 264f, 268
Boethius	132ff, 138f, 145f
Boromir	122, 126, 139f, 148, 160, 162
Camelot	228, 230, 233
Charlemagne	76, 92, 95, 176, 198
Chaucer	35, 123, 125, 132f
Christ, Christus	89, 94f, 121, 148, 153, 156, 165, 199, 214-219, 225, 228
Christianity, Christentum	10, 95, 98, 103, 106, 111, 148f, 152, 155, 158, 218
Christian, Christlich	25, 49, 60, 63, 92, 94f, 98,103f, 111, 132, 134f, 148-157, 176, 186, 203, 213, 215, 218, 230
Dol Amroth	202, 205f, 233f, 236
Doriath	31, 43, 62, 126f, 195
Dreams	105, 133-137, 257
Edda	11ff, 15, 17f, 72, 149, 151, 153, 190, 194, 212ff, 216, 219f, 224
Eichendorff, Joseph von	243ff, 247, 282
Elendil	91, 177f, 180f, 205f, 208f, 299
Elrond	26, 63, 87, 97, 123, 140, 145, 151, 155f, 160-168, 291f
Éomer	115f, 125f, 208, 234, 236
Eriol	15, 27, 64, 66, 242f, 245-248
Eucatastrophe, Eukatastrophe	136, 145, 151, 218, 290, 294

Index

Faramir	126, 139f, 175, 202, 205, 234f
Flieger, Verlyn	56, 66ff, 86, 110, 141, 143, 236, 289f, 292, 300, 302
Free Will	42, 132f, 134ff, 139-143, 145f, 290
Frodo	28, 33-36, 115, 134-137, 139ff, 145f, 148, 152, 154-157, 161, 164-167, 177, 183ff, 235, 239, 260, 263, 268, 290, 294f
Galadriel	28, 30ff, 97, 111, 130, 134, 137, 145, 155f, 177, 234, 236, 270, 297
Gandalf	12ff, 16, 18, 24, 29, 73, 80, 93, 97f, 116, 135-140, 143, 146, 154f, 161-164, 167, 173, 177, 205, 260, 269, 295, 304
Gawain	102-111, 230ff, 238, 299, 308
Geschichte	12, 56-68, 72f, 75, 77, 80, 83, 242
Gil-galad	91, 210, 234
Gimli	24, 115f, 124, 205, 208, 236, 257
God	92, 95, 106, 119, 122, 124, 133-138, 145f, 148, 151-155, 158, 163, 165f, 218, 224, 229, 309
Gollum	86, 139, 145, 257, 259f
Gondolin	31, 62, 66, 112, 151, 200ff, 205, 210, 233
Gondor	24, 30, 91, 94, 144f, 156f, 177f, 205, 208f, 234, 299
Gott (christl.)	58, 64, 305
History	26, 40, 61, 63, 76, 88, 91-97, 107, 111f, 120, 132, 136, 138f, 143, 145f, 173f, 177, 179, 185, 190f, 196, 217, 235, 265, 299, 302
Homer	57f, 116ff, 120
Honegger, Thomas	64, 72f, 75, 78f, 84, 108, 262, 288, 291f, 300
Ilúvatar	31, 62, 67, 134, 138f, 143, 146, 150, 155, 224, 249
Imrahil	98, 156, 205, 233-236
Isildur	140, 150f, 178, 180, 205, 208f, 235
Jackson, Peter	20f, 78, 87, 160, 168, 212, 286, 305
Kôr, Kortirion	27ff, 32, 230, 246f, 300
Laketown	202
LeGoff, Jacques	25, 75, 78, 84
Legolas	91, 115f, 124, 150, 156, 236f, 259
Lewis, C.S.	10, 109, 122, 126, 148, 267, 287
Lórien/Lothlórien	30-33, 36, 73, 87, 137, 156f, 179, 236, 262
Lúthien	26, 156, 190-197, 235f, 293

Maëglin	202
Melkor/Morgoth	15, 25, 31, 41f, 45, 49-52, 97, 134, 139f, 143, 145, 149ff, 193ff
Messiah, Messias	94f, 218, 288f
Merry	115, 139, 157, 172, 183, 234f, 257, 264f, 303
Minas Morgul	184, 206
Minas Tirith	26, 156, 162, 175ff, 205, 233f, 269
Morgoth	→ Melkor
Moria	24, 175, 191, 236
Mythos	13, 56-59, 61, 63ff, 68
Mythology, Mythologie	10f, 17, 20f, 56f, 63-68, 149f, 242, 248, 251, 285f, 295, 297, 303
Nargothrond	31, 45f, 50f, 62, 233
Narsil	205, 208
Númenor	94, 150, 206, 271, 275
Odin	10-16, 195, 216f, 221, 223ff
Paganism	49, 148, 152f, 155, 158, 296
Pippin	115, 136, 139, 157, 167, 183, 205, 234, 257, 259, 263f, 269
Predestination	49f, 132-137, 140, 145f
Prescience	132f, 137, 139f, 145f
Providence	97, 132, 136, 138f, 146, 163, 166
Rohan	157, 170f, 177f, 185, 202, 204ff
Rohirrim	92, 173, 178, 206, 234f, 300, 303
Sam(wise Gamgee)	31, 73, 88, 98, 115f, 134, 137, 153f, 156f, 160, 164-167, 183, 235, 250f, 259ff, 263, 267, 270, 291
Saruman	12, 14ff, 88, 117, 139f, 143, 145f, 157, 161, 163, 207, 295
Sauron	14ff, 30, 91, 93, 98, 136, 138, 143, 145, 149ff, 154ff, 191f, 194, 196, 206, 235, 305
Shippey, Tom	56, 74, 80, 86, 100, 108, 112, 132, 148f, 196, 224, 228, 231, 289, 293, 299ff, 308f
Sigurd/Siegfried	11, 40, 212-225, 293
Smaug	203f
Snorri Sturluson	12f, 15
Théoden	115, 122, 139, 170, 172f, 175, 180, 205, 234f, 255, 304
Time	30-36, 86-98, 173, 179ff, 186f, 228, 254

Index

Túrin	40-53, 110, 114f, 123f, 126-129, 166, 180, 292, 304
Tol Eressea	242, 246ff
Tolkien, Christopher	40, 94, 126, 140, 179, 201, 212, 250, 254, 292, 309
Tom Bombadil	134, 139, 154f, 157, 162, 177, 183ff, 294f
Tuor	151, 200, 206, 249
Turgon	200
Valar	15, 31, 63, 66f, 111, 137f, 140, 143, 154f, 178, 195
Valinor	27, 31, 61f, 66, 145, 148-151, 156, 177, 236f, 251
Vision	16, 43, 97, 111, 115, 123, 133f, 136ff, 180, 186, 305
Völsunga saga	10, 12, 17, 48, 190-197, 212 216f, 219-223
Wagner, Richard	10, 212-225
Wappen	276
Zeit	73f, 275

www.ingramcontent.com/pod-product-compliance
Lightning Source LLC
Chambersburg PA
CBHW050335230426
43663CB00010B/1863